DRUCK u. VERLAG v. PHILIPP & KRAMER, WIEN. WIENER KÜNSTLER-POSTKARTE SERIE IV/6.

ART NOUVEAU POSTCARDS

Giovanni Fanelli

and

Ezio Godoli

Phaidon · Christie's

Oxford

Frontispiece: Anonymous (K. Moser?) 'Wiener Künstler-Postkarte', series IV n. 6 published by Philipp & Kramer, Vienna, 1898, chromolithograph.

Phaidon · Christie's Limited,
Littlegate House,
St Ebbe's Street,
Oxford OX1 1SQ

First published in English 1987

English language edition © 1987 Patrick Hawkey & Company Ltd, London

Original Italian edition © 1985 Giunti Barbera, Florence, Italy

Translated from the Italian by Linda Fairbairn
Design production of this edition by Robert Mathias, Publishing Workshop

British Library Cataloguing in Publication Data

Fanelli, Giovanni
 Art nouveau postcards.
 1. Postal cards 2. Art nouveau
 I. Title II. Godoli, Ezio III. La
 Cartolina art nouveau. *English*
 769′.5   NC1872

ISBN   0 7148 8048 5

Printed and bound in Hong Kong by South China Printing Co.

Contents

Preface

"When archaeologists of the thirtieth century begin to excavate the ruins of London, they will focus their attention on the picture postcard as the best means of penetrating the spirit of the Edwardian era. They will collect and collate thousands of these cards and they will reconstruct our epoque from the strange hieroglyphics and images they reveal, spared by the passage of time. For the picture postcard is a candid camera recording our amusements and pastimes, our habits and customs, our moral attitudes and behaviour."

THUS WROTE THE JOURNALIST James Douglas in 1907, to underline the documentary value of postcards in the story of human civilization. But there are other reasons that prompt us to study this invaluable mine of information about the art and taste of the modern world, and about the visual culture of which it is a particular expression.

In the history of twentieth-century graphic art, and in particular of Art Nouveau, postcards are doubly interesting: first, they are a form of expression in which some artists specialized completely, while other important late nineteenth-century artists turned to it only occasionally; secondly they are sometimes an important iconographic source, in that they reproduce graphic works of art intended for other ends.

This book considers only one type of picture postcard, the so-called 'artistic' type and it attempts to clarify the special features that define it as a particular form of applied graphic art.

Postcards are also important documents that reveal the international spread of the Art Nouveau idiom, even down to the popular level. It is in them that one can see the clearest evidence of the effort to combine the style of an international movement with long-lived national traditions – an effort which is a recurring theme throughout Art Nouveau from architecture to the decorative arts. Postcards are a good example of the use of a means of mass communication by modern artists as a vehicle for aesthetic statements. Taking it for granted that a study of postcards can be a start to useful contributions to our knowledge of the history of the graphic arts, we have limited our area of study to postcards by artists, excluding reproductions of their paintings but covering instead reproductions of their graphic art (posters, calendars, book illustrations, etc.),

which are sometimes extremely valuable as artistic records. This is the case with postcards illustrating graphic projects which were not realized in their originally intended form.

Many difficulties confront those who want to undertake research in this field, from the scarcity of bibliographical sources to the lack of well-organized public collections. Most publications on postcards are books that follow particular themes (women, sport, war, politics etc.), and are poorly written, or catalogues devised for commercial purposes. Few countries have made catalogues of their national production of postcards and those which do exist contain only very approximate information, omitting chronologies of the illustrators' work. (The Italians are exceptional in this, their catalogues being more precise than those of other countries.)

Collections of postcards in public museums are nearly always very small. Among them must be mentioned those in the libraries of the Musée des Arts Décoratifs, the Fondation Fournay, the Bibliothèque Nationale in Paris, the Biblioteca Bertarelli in Milan, and especially the Altonaer Museum in Hamburg. There are also small collections in some provincial libraries, but they are not easy to find.

In these circumstances it is almost impossible to make an exhaustive survey, without some possibly serious omissions, of postcards produced in the Art Nouveau period, and to catalogue them in a systematic way. The account attempted here is certainly more complete in its breadth and geographical scope than any produced until now, but it should be considered as a first attempt, which we hope will encourage others to work in the same field.

One methodological problem immediately faces all

students of Art Nouveau: whether to define it in terms of rigid stylistic formulae, or to regard it as an episode in the evolution of taste deriving from many sources, and hence to delimit it chronologically.

We have taken the latter approach. In the graphic art of the early twentieth century the same stylistic elements – from Pre-Raphaelitism to Japonism – in which Art Nouveau was rooted can also be found in graphic work unconnected with it. In picture postcards the mixture of styles with obvious different national traditions is even more prominent, and a pedantic analysis of stylistic components would probably lead to classifications being made that conflict with generally accepted interpretations.

The authors are grateful to all those who have allowed them to see and photograph their postcards. Those to whom we owe particular thanks are the directors and staff of the Library of the Musée des Arts Décoratifs and of the Fondation Fournay in Paris, the Royal Library in Stock-holm, the Finnish Postal Museum in Helsinki, the Centre Municipal de l'Affiche de la Carte Postale et de la Graphique in Toulouse, the Biblioteca Bertarelli in Milan, and the Biblioteca Comunale in Forlí; to Professor Gerhard Kaufmann, the director of the Altonaer Museum in Hamburg: to Franco Bertoni, for pointing out the postcards by Nonni; to Päivi Hovi, for help with the research into postcards in Finland; to Antonio and Pia Dell'Aquila, for information on Kirchner; to Carlo Ambrogi for information on Enrico Sacchetti; to Paolo Vannini, Leandre Villarogna and Paolo Riario, for information and help in the selection of postcards for reproduction.

For their contribution to the production of this book our thanks are also due to Franco Bevilacqua, Bill Carr, Yolanda Di Leone, Catherine Dobai, Laura Graziano, Karole Guggenheim, Mario Lupano, Donata Macelli and Sara Fanelli.

The Art Nouveau Postcard

The origin of postcards

THE PUBLICATION ON 1 OCTOBER 1869 of the *Correspondenz-Karte* by the Post Office of the Austro-Hungarian monarchy marks the official beginning of the postcard. Intended as a letter-telegram, this first postal note was made of thin cream card measuring 85 × 122mm. On the front it bore the imprint of the two-Kreuzer stamp with the portrait of the Emperor Franz Joseph in the upper right-hand corner, the inscription 'Correspondenz-Karte' above the imperial Habsburg eagle (or the National emblem of Hungary) and three dotted lines for the address of the recipient. On the back was a white space for the message and a short note releasing the postal services from all responsibility for the contents of the message. The novelty was immediately successful: it is believed that more than nine million cards were sold in the first year. It was hailed as a triumph of democracy, because it would extend the use of the postal services to many levels of society by making a considerable reduction in the cost of postage (the price of the stamp was in fact determined by the distance of the journey and by the number of sheets of paper in the letter).

The *Correspondenz-Karte* had been keenly promoted in Austria by Emmanuel Herrmann, a professor of political economics at the military academy in Vienna, who, on 26 January 1869, published in the influential *Neue Freie Presse*[1] a documented study of the great economic advantages which would accrue to the Treasury from the introduction of the *Postkarte*. Some years earlier, on the occasion of the Austro-German postal conference in Karlsruhe in 1865, Heinrich von Stephan, a high official of the postal services of the North German Confederation, had published a report, *Vorschlag zur Einführung der Postkarte*, in which he put forward his own proposal for an *offenes Postblatt*, but his arguments were not well received. The fear that the introduction of this means of communication would bring about a notable reduction in the income of the postal administration made them reject Von Stephan's project. Similarly, the requests of two Leipzig booksellers, Friedlein and Pardubitz, for the rights to circulate a 'Universal-Correspondenz-Karte' were rejected.

Even though officially the idea was unwelcome, it is known that postcards were produced privately, and therefore without the printed stamp, and some were used in the North German Confederation (as

1 E. Hermann, 'Über eine neue Art der Correspondenz mittelst der Post', *Neue Freie Presse*, 26.1.1869.

well as in other countries, such as France). These were usually made for companies to announce their representatives' visits etc.[2]

Outside Europe some kinds of postcards were already in circulation from the beginning of the 1860s, put on the market by private businesses. Among them was 'Lipman's Postal Card' patented in Philadelphia in the United States in 1861.

The Austrian example was quickly followed by other European countries. On 1 July 1870, on the eve of the Franco-Prussian war, Bismarck signed the decree for the issue of German *Correspondenz-Karten*, which, unlike the Austrian ones, did not bear a printed stamp. The postcard was then introduced in October of the same year in England and Switzerland; in 1871 in Belgium, the Netherlands, Denmark, Sweden, Norway and Canada; in 1872 in Russia, Chile, France and Algeria; in 1873 in the United States (where, in the first six months of issue, 60 million were sold), Spain (where, their issue had already been approved in 1871 by royal decree), Serbia and Rumania; and in 1874 in Italy.

The spread of this new means of postal communication throughout the world needed to be regulated. In 1878 the World Congress of the Universal Postal Union looked at the problem of setting a standard for postcard dimensions and decided to fix the largest format at 90 × 140mm[3]. In 1886 the Congress of the Universal Postal Union meeting in Lisbon sanctioned the circulation of postcards internationally; previously it had been confined within national borders.

The origin of picture postcards

THE ORIGIN OF PICTURE POSTCARDS is a controversial subject that is often embellished by unsubstantiated anecdotes, complicated by the circulation of forgeries, and confused by uncertainty about the real meaning of the term 'picture' postcard. Added to this, some authors in their search for 'incunabola' tend to put back the date of origin by equating them with visiting cards or with eighteenth- or nineteenth-century greetings cards, which often had fairly elaborate ornamental friezes and were often designed by well-known artists like Fragonard, Bartolozzi and Henry Cole, or with decorated note-paper, which Goethe is known to have enthusiastically collected, or with ornate envelopes (the kind used by the English in the 1830s).[4] It should be noted, however, that the first official *Correspondenz-Karten* had a particular graphic style. Most of them followed the 1869 Austrian model with minimal variation – this was usually confined to the position of the stamp. The *Carte-correspondance* issued in Belgium on 1 January 1871 moved away from this design and had a more elaborate composition, with figurative elements which introduced, albeit still in academic form, symbolic themes relating to modern civilization. Designed by M. H. Hendricks and engraved by A. Doms, this postcard is decorated at the top by a frieze with two female figures, symbolizing

I. Anonymous, postcard by the publisher Vogel of Leipzig. 'Do not wonder about the meaning of this picture; this card tells you clearly what it is I expect of you'.

2 F. Staff, *The Picture postcard and its origins*, London 1966, p. 46.

3 The format 105 × 148mm (DIN format) was adopted in the Thirties.

4 In 1840 when the famous stamp 'the Penny Black', was issued, a 'penny pre-paid envelope' also appeared. 'These postal notes were excellently designed by the well known Royal Academician William Mulready. The design symbolized an economic and efficient postal service, and showed Brittania with a lion at her feet sending messages all over the world, while tradesmen of all nationalities and people in their own homes received their letters. It was a very refined artistic endeavour but it did not please the public, and Mulready's note became the target of jokes from its first appearance. Immediately enterprising publishers printed caricatures of Mulready's sense of humour' (F. Staff, *op. cit.*, pp. 22-23).

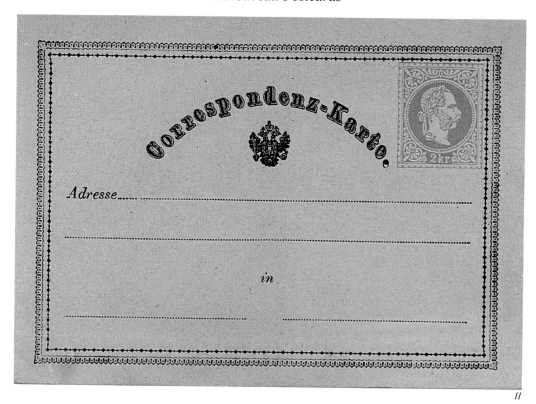

II

III

V

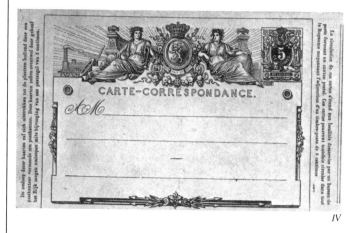

IV

VI

industry (on the left) and commerce (on the right), leaning on an escutcheon bearing the Belgian lion and the royal crown. In the background, the hatched lines are an allusion to the dawning of a new era, while on the far left the idea of modernity is restated by the image of the smoking locomotive, which balances the 5-centimes stamp on the opposite side.

Leaving aside the special category of pre-paid letter-cards, there were a number of postcards that pioneered the introduction of figurative elements in their design after the outbreak of the Franco-Prussian war in 1870. In 1870 a German bookseller, A. Schwartz, who did business with the Oldenburg Printing Works, had a vignette showing an artilleryman loading a cannon printed in the upper left-hand corner of a *Correspondenz-Karte*, with which he gave his brother-in-law the news of the declaration of war with France. In the same year the Frenchman Léon Bésnardeau, a bookseller from Sillé-le-Guillaume (Sarthe district), produced a series of postcards (66 × 98mm) for the soldiers of the Breton army with lithographs of military emblems, patriotic allegories and the arms of Brittany. Also in 1870 an English postcard appeared which can be seen as the forerunner of the publicity type of card: the postcard for the Royal Polytechnic in London. For Christmas the same year, the lithographer John S. Day, also in Great Britain, printed a coloured decorative frame of holly and mistletoe enclosing the words 'good wishes' on the back of an official half-penny postcard. This was the first coloured picture postcard, and it belongs to the typically Anglo-Saxon tradition of Christmas cards, a greetings card bearing a message combined with decorative or figurative motifs. This card can be seen as the transition from the Christmas card to the Christmas postcard, which in the following years became particularly successful and was exported to the rest of Europe and to the United States.

Some experts, however, identify a postcard printed in Vienna in 1871 by R. von Waldheim and designed by the Serbian lieutenant Petar Manöjlovic as the first picture postcard, arguing that in this card the illustration is not marginal but occupies one whole side of the card. It represents a dragon[5] holding a scroll in its claws, and below it the skylines of Istanbul and Moscow; modern means of transport are also shown, in the form of a steamship and a train emerging from a tunnel.

Another postcard with a particularly interesting subject was published in 1872 by the English publishing house of Grant & Co, to advertise their book on London illustrated by Gustave Doré, in which a drawing frames a white rectangle to be used for the address. This postcard, too, is an important precedent for a type which would be common during the years of Art Nouveau: the publicity postcard for illustrated books.

In the following years the use of the postcard as a means of publicity increased. It was used particularly to advertise department stores (in 1873 the first card was printed for 'La Belle Jardinière', the firm which later would have cards with graphic designs by Grasset and Mucha); great exhibitions (Chicago 1873, Cincinnati 1874, Halle 1881, Nurem-

5 In Serbian, dragon is *Zmaj*, which was the title of a Serbian newspaper then published in Vienna. Manojlovic was a friend of the paper's editor, who published the postcard for Serbian residents in Vienna.

VII

berg 1882, etc.); and holiday resorts and hotels (in this group German hoteliers were particularly active in the first half of the 1870s).[6]

The pioneering phase of the history of the picture postcard started in the early 1870s and continued to the middle of the 1890s, when the introduction of new printing techniques and the extension of licences to publish postcards to private industry created a vast increase in production[7]. This came about because of the growth of collotype printing on an industrial scale, which led to a proliferation of photographic postcards and colour lithography using photographic colour separation.

The social and cultural factors which encouraged this form of communication should not be forgotten. Robert Burnaud has concisely summarized some of the reasons for its widespread use: 'Postcard, later sister, poor sister of the letter, providential refuge of narrow imaginations, of hesitant syntax, of shaky spelling, resource of people in a hurry, normal means of expression of a world which never moves fast enough, picturesque documentation at a low price, popularizer; postcard, friend of the traveller, of the lover of folklore, of the local historian [. . .]'[9].

The brevity of the verbal message, determined by the space provided, and the presence of the illustration matter, which augments the written word, amplifying its meaning or charging it with allusions, are the reasons for the extraordinary popularity of postcards. 'Like many great inventions' – observed the English journalist James Douglas in 1907 – 'the postcard has brought a silent revolution in our habits. It has freed us unexpectedly from the fatigue of writing letters. There are still those alive who can remember the days when it was

VII. The picture postcard by P. Manojlovic for the newspaper Zmaj, printed by R. von Waldheim, Vienna, 1871.

considered necessary and even pleasant to write letters to friends. In those years there was plenty of time available. In fact our ancestors sat down and spent several hours on their long letters which would still supply the primary material for an industrious compiler of books. They say in London that there are even now tons of unpublished letters by Ruskin and indeed several pounds of letters by Robert Louis Stevenson which have not yet seen the light of day. It makes one sad to think of the books that these dead authors could have written had they saved the hours they squandered in private correspondence. Fortunately postcards have freed the modern writer from this drudgery [. . .]. In times gone by, when one went abroad, one had to leave the landscape and write laborious descriptions to one's friends at home. Now one can simply buy a picture postcard at every stop, write a few words in pencil and post it. The pleasure of the journey is increased [. . .]. The postcard is really a very short and unceremonious missive. It contains neither affectionate preambles nor reassuring conclusions. It begins without a prelude and finishes without a conclusion. The picture postcard takes coarseness to the extreme. There is no space for courtesy. Often one writes on a blue sky or a white road, but usually there is space only for a short breathless sigh'.[10]

The appearance of the postcard brought about a change in letter-writing habits. A letter's contents were concealed inside the envelope, and this was considered an improper means of communication for young lovers. A postcard, on the other hand, made it possible to inspect what was written and was therefore more acceptable. But the loss of secrecy implicit in using a postcard was offset by the relationship between the written word and the illustration, which could be charged with hidden meaning, the key to unravel it belonging to the private world of the couple.

In a period which had few means of mass communications at its disposal except for book and magazine illustration and photography, the postcard played an important part in the development of visual culture. It could satisfy all sorts of curiosity and interests, sometimes even perverse fetishes, from its revelation of exotic worlds to its voyeuristic glimpses of exceptional events (sometimes macabre ones, like executions, train or car accidents or great natural catastrophes), which are registered as 'direct impressions'.

There are those who see the postcard as a didactic instrument which can be used to educate taste and broaden a knowledge of different peoples and countries. 'The postcard', writes Matilde Serao 'will inevitably [. . .] develop that aesthetic sense which, in most people, is rather dull. [. . .]. Secondly [. . .], it makes one acquainted with countries which one has never seen [. . .]. Oh, picture postcard, you will increase the income of the railways!'.[11]

In the evolution of visual culture, according to some experts, series of postcards made up of photographs or drawings linked by a narrative, anticipate the *roman-photo* or *bandes dessinées*.

There is no complete statistical study of the production of postcards between the end of the nineteenth century and the First World War.

6 In the early years it was not permitted to send postcards outside of the country of issue [. . .] In the United States postcards could be sent to certain listed European countries by paying a tariff of 2 cents. In some countries, in particular Germany, Austria and Switzerland, there were minor restrictions, and not long after their introduction postcards were sold in Germany with little views of health resorts or places of interest printd on them: often a hotel or restaurant appeared on them. These images were usually printed very simply in black or brown, as a heading or sometimes along the edges, of the 5 pfenning postcards. In Austria too, similar postcards with New Year's greetings printed on them were used by the end of the Eighties (F. Staff, *op. cit.*, p. 49).

7 The acts giving private individuals the authority to print postcards came at different times in different countries: in Germany the right was granted already in July 1872 (cfr F. Staff, *op cit.*, p. 49); in France in January 1873 (Neudin, *L'Officiel International des Cartes Postales*, Paris 1893.[9], p. 52); in Great Britain 1st September 1894 (according to *Stanley Gibbons Catalogue*, Colchester-London 1983[3], p. xiv); in the United States in 1898 (the inscription 'Private Mailing Card. Authorised by Act of Congress, May 19, 1898' was on the postcards.

8 It is not easy to establish the date of the 'invention' of these new technical procedures, in part because in certain respects we are dealing with the successive perfecting of techniques rather than with inventions. However, it is certain that a consistent production in collotype was achieved only in c. 1895 and a few years later in chromolithography. A very rapid development followed, the example of Nancy is typical, according to Zeyons (S. Zeyons, *Les Cartes Postales*, Paris 1979, pp. 40-41): A. Bergeret installed a collotype press in his workshop in 1898: in 1901 the factory employed about 65 workmen and production reached 30 million postcards; in 1905 they merged with Bergeret, Humblot, and Helminger to become 'Imprimeries réunies', and brought the annual production in Nancy up to 90 million postcards, with a daily rate of 500,000 postcards, in 1909 the production rose to a global number of 100 million postcards.

9 cit. in L. Vollaire, *La carte postale n'est pas un gadget,*.in *Le carte postale illustrée, Actes du colloque 6-7-8 mai* 1977, Musée Nicéphore Niépce, Chalon-sur-Saône 1977, p. 34.

10 cit. in F. Staff, *op. cit.*, p.76, 81. It should be noted that the shortness of the message even inspired a literary genre; Peter Altenberg was a master in writing down brief thoughts or sketches called 'postcards'. In 1907 Clément Richie wrote an anthology of verse *Fantaisie pour Cartes Postales*. Even the theatre reflected the spread of interest in postcards; Louis Boulard's comedy *Cartes Postales* is dated 1903.

11 M. Serao, 'Cartoline illustrate' in *Il Raccoglitore di cartoline illustrate*, I (n. 20.9.1899), pp. 53-55.

The fragmentary facts allow only an approximate assessment to be made of the total increase in production from the last five years of the nineteenth century. It is calculated that in the member countries of the Universal Postal Union 1750 million were sent in 1894,[12] and 140 billion worldwide in the period 1894-1919 (1901: 2.5 billion; 1905: 7 billion).[13] The period around 1898 is important in the history of picture postcards because of the increase in production and the improved quality, and the abandonment of standard nineteenth-century designs. About this time important publishing houses started to publish postcards, commissioning artists already distinguished in other areas of graphic design and who were also pioneers of Art Nouveau. In Vienna in 1897, Philipp & Kramer began to publish their series of 'Kunstler-Postkarten', using artists like Koloman Moser, Josef Hoffmann, Leo Kainradl, Max Kurzweil and Walter Hampel. In Milan in 1898 and 1899 Casa Ricordi, which was already engaged in limited production in 1897, began to avail themselves of the most notable commercial artists already working for them (Giovanni Maria Mataloni, Adolfo Hohenstein, Leopoldo Metlicovitz, Achille Beltrame and Aleardo Villa). In Brussels in 1898, Dietrich & Co launched their series designed by Gisbert Combaz, Henri Cassiers and Henri Meunier with a publicity poster prepared by Meunier. In London in 1899, Raphael Tuck, who from the first years of the twentieth century circulated series designed by Raphael Kirchner and Eva Daniell, entered the postcard market.

During these years, magazines which were to play a crucial role in the spread of Art Nouveau graphics began publishing series of postcards: in Munich *Meggendorfer Blätter* in 1897 and 1899, followed by *Jugend* (1898) and *Simplicissimus* (1899); in Vienna *Ver Sacrum* (1898) on the occasion of the first Secession exhibition; and in France *Cocorico* (c. 1898) and *Le Rire* (1898).

Almost at the same time the first specialist magazines began to appear in various countries. Most had a short life and were more like information bulletins, in which the latest novelties were announced, and contributions from publishers and collectors were welcomed. In 1898 *Die Illustrierte Postkarte* appeared in Germany, and in Milan *La Cartolina Postale illustrata* began publication, edited by Edmondo De Amicis and Matilde Serao, followed the next year by *Il Raccoglitore di Cartoline Illustrate*, directed by Italo Vittorio Brusa, which appeared once a fortnight, and in 1900 by *Indicateur du philocartisme. Nouveau Journal de Kartophilie et variété pour collectionneurs*. The fact that the latter magazine was published in French is indicative of the interest of foreign markets in Lombard postcard publishing. To promote the improvement in the quality of postcards in his own country, the writer, essayist and art critic Emile Strauss launched *La Carte postale illustrée* in Paris in 1899, and in the same year the 'Compagnie française des cartes postales artistiques' published the monthly *L'Amateur de la carte postale illustrée*, of which only four issues appeared. The *Revue Illustrée de la Carte Postale*, the voice of the 'Association philatélique' of Nancy, was to survive longer; first published on 15 February 1900, it continued until 1921, possibly because it had the consistent financial

VIII

VIII. The cover of the magazine published by the postcard society of Nancy, 1900.

IX. 'The use of postcards in Germany: the postman as salesman and walking post-box', an illustration which appeared in the October issue of The Illustrated London News *1909.*

12 J. Philippen, *Histoire et charme de la carte postale illustrée*, Diest 1977, p. 25.

13 W. Till, *Alte Postkarten*, Munich 1983, p. 33

IX

support of its director, the publisher A. Bergeret, who was one of the first and most important producers of French collotype postcard views. In London *The Poster Collector* appeared in 1899, followed in 1900 by *The Picture Postcard* and *Postal Cards & Covers*. In Barcelona *España Cartófila*, the organ of the 'Sociedad Cartófila Española' came out in 1901.

The proliferation of these magazines indicates that there was a widespread interest in collecting. Paul Eluard wrote in 1933: 'Trésors de rien du tout, [. . .] les cartes postales plurent rapidement aux grandes personnes par leur naïveté et plus encore, hélas! par l'espèce d'égalité par en bas qu'elles établissaient entre l'envoyeur et le destinataire. Parmi les milliards de cartes postales (l'Allemagne seule en fabriqua jusqu'à neuf millions par mois) qui circulèrent en Europe de 1891 à 1914, il en est peu qui soient belles, touchantes ou curieuses. Nous les avons recherchées avec acharnement, en essayant de réduire autant que possible la part énorme que le découragement pouvait faire à l'excès d'imbécillité, au plus bas comique, à l'horreur, en sublimisant les raisons d'un pessimisme profond, inévitable'.

Furthermore, the postcard served as a substitute for those who could not afford first-hand experience of the places and subjects represented in them. And Eluard added: 'Commandées par les exploiteurs pour distraire les exploités, les cartes postales ne constituent pas un art populaire. Tout au plus la petite monnaie de l'art tout court et de la poésie. Mais cette petite monnaie de l'art tout court et de la poésie. Mais cette petite monnaie donne parfois idée de l'or'.[14]

For collectors there were sometimes special editions printed on luxury papers, such as *papier Chine* or *papier Japon*.

As with most kinds of collecting, postcard collecting was accompanied by eccentric behaviour: the 'Compagnie International des cartes postales illustrées' made its employees travel, solely for the purpose of sending postcards of views from every corner of the globe[15]. In European cities at the turn of the century, postcard stalls or kiosks were a common sight in public gardens and exhibition parks, as were salesmen passing along trains or from table to table in cafés and restaurants. A plate in the *Illustrated London News* of October 1909 shows one of these walking salesman at work in a café and carries the caption: 'A Postcard Habit in Germany: the Postman as a walking Stationer and letter-box'[16].

The rapid success of the picture postcard is amply shown by the increase in production in some countries[17] and by the sales figures in 1900 in others[18].

As collectors were mainly interested in postcards of views, these occupied almost 90% of the market, as against 10% taken up by so-called 'fantasy' postcards, a category also including 'artistic' postcards.

In the printing industry, postcards were an important export. For a long time Germany maintained a dominant role that was undermined only from the years immediately before the First World War by Great Britain, the United States and finally Italy[19].

14 P. Eluard, 'Les Plus Belles Cartes Postales', in *Minotaure*, nos 3-4, December 1933, p. 86.

15 L. Wiener, 'La Carte illustrée, in *Le Musée du Livre*, I (1922-23 n. 1., December 1922), p. 7.

16 See F. Staff *op. cit.*, p. 59.

17 The statistics for the production of picture postcards in 1899 are as follows: Germany: 88 million to 50 million inhabitants; Great Britain: 14 million to 38.5 million inhabitants; Belgium: 12 million to 6 million inhabitants; France: 8 million to 38 million inhabitants. Cfr S. Zeyons, *op. cit.*, p. 40.

18 The following data shows sales of postcards in 1900: France: 52 million, Germany: 1013 million; the United States: 670 million; Great Britain: 550 million. Cfr S. Zeyons, *op. cit.*, p. 48.

19 L. Wiener, *op. cit.*, I (1922-23, no. 2, January 1923), p. 16.

Postcards as graphic designs

THE PERIOD GENERALLY ACCEPTED as the golden age of the picture postcard ran from 1898 to 1918. During these twenty years, which close with the end of the First World War, the most representative artists of Art Nouveau in Europe and the United States were deeply preoccupied with this form of graphic art. Art Nouveau poetics, summed up in the famous slogans 'L'Art dans Tout' and 'L'Art pour Tous', are expressions of an ideal aesthetic which challenged the traditional academic boundaries between the fine and applied arts, and the artists who rose to the challenge of spreading the 'socialism of beauty' favoured the use of this means.

Serge Zeyons observed: 'It is obvious that the postcard has brought art within the range of everyone, even though it is often treated as the 'petite monnaie de l'art' as Paul Eluard called it'[20].

For some artists the postcard was an important source of income. One of them was Emil Hansen (better known under the pseudonym Nolde), who paid for his studies in Munich with the proceeds of his anthropomorphic views of mountains. For these artists it became a favourite field of activity. Amongst the most prolific postcard designers were Raphael Kirchner, Xavier Sager, Henri Boutet, Albert Guillaume, Theophile Alexandre Steinlen, Hansi, Orens, Luciano Achille Mauzan, Basilio Cascella, Leopoldo Metlicovitz, Marcello Dudovich, Aldo Mazza, Plinio Codognato, Edmondo Fontana, Ramón Casas, Manuel Wielandt, Paul Hey, Pauli Ebner, Bruno Wennerberg, Ferdinand von Reznicek, Raimund Wichera, Alphonse Mucha, Dana Gibson, Philip Boileau, Clarence Underwood, Harrison Fisher and Jenny Nystrom.

It was soon recognized that they were often exhibited and sometimes formed whole sections of art exhibitions. The first of these were held in Germany, in Leipzig in May 1898, and in Munich in July 1899. The 'Prima Espoiszione Internazionale di Cartoline Postali Illustrate', organized in August 1899 at the Terza Esposizione Internazionale D'Arte in Venice was much more important. It included items signed by artists like Cassiers, Combaz, Martini, Moser, Kirchner, Nolde, Wielandt, Mucha, Metlicovitz, Raffaele and Tafuri.[21] Three postcards influenced by Liberty, two designed by Tafuri and one by E. Paggiaro, were issued to mark the occasion.[22] In September of the same year another postcard exhibition opened in Ostend, in which prizes were awarded to the participants. James Ensor was a member of the jury. Also in 1899 there was a world exhibition of postcards in Nice; others took place in 1900 in Budapest and Warsaw. Following these major exhibitions, there was a flood of them in every country. Some were organized by publishers. The London publisher F. E. Southwood put on similar shows for at least four years from 1901 in his shop in Regent Street (the first including works by Mucha, Cassiers, and Boutet).

As was already the practice in the field of poster design public postcard competitions were promoted by companies and industries which recognized the publicity potential of the genre, as well as by

20 S. Zeyons, *op. cit.*, p. 133.

21 See A. Maggioni 'La Prima Esposizione Internazionale di cartoline postali illustrate a Venezia. Note e appunti', in *Emporium*, vol. x (1899), pp. 310-324.

22 Some publishers, like Ricordi, superimpose on their postcards the inscription, 'Prima Esposizione Internazionale di cartoline illustrate, Venezia 1899'. See F. Arrasich 'Le cartoline in cartolina', in *La cartolina*, II (1982, no. 7), pp. 17-20.

publishers who wanted to improve the quality of production. Sometimes the lead was taken by artistic associations (there was a competition in 1898 by 'Famiglia Artistica' in Milan) or by newspapers (in Italy by *Il Mattino* in Naples and by *Falstaff* in 1899). Likewise postcards became a means of publicizing sketches for work sent in to competitions and awarded a prize, but never carried out. Two famous examples are sketches for the 'Anís del Mono – Vicente Bosch – Badalona' series (shown at the 1898 competition) and the 'Byrrh' series (shown at the 1906 competition).

The artistic standing of postcards has readily been acknowledged, from the outset, but no-one has yet defined their specific graphic character as works of art. Eliseo Trenc Ballester, for example, declared: 'A study of the formal structure of artistic postcards is really of little interest, since it cannot be shown that a specific art form comprising postcards in fact exists. Most artistic postcards are reproductions of drawings of the period, magazine illustrations, or works designed for other purposes. . . It can be noted that the artistic genre which seems best adapted to the postcard, and which can be considered most representative of the period, is the small two- or three-colour drawing done as an illustration or small vignette, which is similar to the postcard in its size, simple, direct approach, composition and *espiritu* (its simple reflection of the spirit of the times). If, therefore, an analysis of the compositional aspects of postcards is of secondary interest, one cannot say the same for a study of their subject matter. This means establishing what postcards were used for and what were current practices during the *belle epoque*, since postcards, like other lesser art forms grouped together under the general heading of minor graphic arts are undervalued in their social importance'[23].

Similar prejudices clearly exist in the literature on picture postcards, which has undervalued their significance as separate works of art and has therefore concentrated mainly on their content. They have consequently been used as useful documents for the study of an era and seen only from the viewpoint of sociology and changing cultural taste.

It is undeniable that most picture postcards (except those which are simply photographic reproductions of works of art, and so do not concern us here) are reproductions of original works devised for other purposes, from decorative panels to book and magazine illustrations, from calendars to musical scores, and so on. But the need to reduce the design to a small, standard size for reproduction often suggest changes and adaptations of the image and its colour values in order to emphasize its immediacy and reinforce its meaning. Instead of reproducing a whole design, so possibly losing detail, which plays a fundamental role in Art Nouveau graphics, artists often concentrated on particular sections of the composition, using a technique similar to that of the zoom lens. Similar ideas influenced their decisions concerning colour which, in reducing the range of shading or sacrificing the intermediate tones, strove to capture the essence of the image with greater incisiveness by highlighting the relationships between the

23 E. Trenc Ballester, *Las Artes Graficas a la Epoca Modernista en Barcelona*, Barcelona 1977, p. 208.

X. E. Paggiaro, postcard for the 'Prima Esposizione Internazionale di Cartoline Postali Illustrate' held in August 1899 at the 'Terza Esposizione d'Arte' in Venice.
XI. Front of the postcard published by Philipp & Kramer, Vienna, to advertise their series of artistic postcards at the 1900 Exposition Universelle, Paris.

different areas of the composition. Another device was to dispense with the outline around a figure so that it stood directly on a flat background.

Leaving aside the factors involved in adapting an image to the smaller postcard format, those elements which really determine the design of a postcard derive from the need to provide a space for a handwritten message on the same side as the image. Until 1906 almost the whole of one side was reserved for the address of the recipient and

XII

XIII

the stamp, hence the need to organize the other side to contain both the image and the message[24].

The postcard designer found himself facing problems similar to that confronting commercial artists and book illustrators, but his working parameters were even more restrictive because of the small fixed dimensions of the card (90×140mm), which demanded great economy in the use of space. Artists produced a wide range of responses to this restrictive set of conditions, many of them showing considerable ingenuity.

Basically there are two ways of organizing the design area: 1. the space for the message is clearly separated from the image; 2. the space for the message is incorporated into the design without a clear frame.

The first basic design permits a wide range of variations:
a. A white strip along one edge, with a horizontal or vertical image without a margin (fig. XVI: 1).
b. A strip all round the image for the message. In some versions the

XII, XIII. A. Terzi, postcards without a publisher's name, from two successive series (nos. 187 and 186), which reproduce variants of the same design.

24 There are no studies on the introduction in various countries of the practice still in use today of dividing one side into two halves, one for the address and the stamp and the other for the written message. It is probable that the first country to use the 'divided recto' was Great Britain, in August 1902 (cfr. A. Byatt, *picture Postcards and their Publishers*, Malvern 1978, p. 20). France followed in 1903, Austria and Germany in 1905, Spain in 1906, Italy probably in 1906, the United States in 1907. It came into general use after the 'VI Congresso dell' Unione Postale Universale' held in Rome in 1906. However it seems that the decision to divide the recto was not uniformly and immediately applied; some publishers adopted it more quickly than others.

XIV

XV

XIV, XV. A. De Riquer, 'Inverno', decorative panel, 1897, painted in tempera on canvas (176 × 114cm) and a chromolithographic postcard c. 1900, with a variant on the same design.

width of the strip is not the same on all sides but is greater on one side (usually the bottom) or on two adjacent sides, thus forming an L (fig. XVI: 2-5). This sometimes occupies far more space than the image (fig. XVI: 6); in some versions the image is divided into sections (fig. XVI:7).

c. The space reserved for the message occupies half or more of the area, with the illustration enclosed in a square, circular or rectangular frame (fig. XVI: 8, 9); an interesting variant on the rectangular design, often found in the work of Italian designers (e.g. designs for Mascagni's 'Iris' by Mataloni and Hohenstein), is the division of the rectangle (a reference to Japanese models) into several smaller rectangles containing a unified image (fig. XVI: 10).

d. A decorative frame surrounding the area for the message (fig. XVI: 11).

e. Design with an unframed figure on a white or plain-coloured ground. Here the boundary between the areas for the message and the image is determined by the relationship between figure and background (fig. XVI: 12). Sometimes the boundary is accentuated by the use of

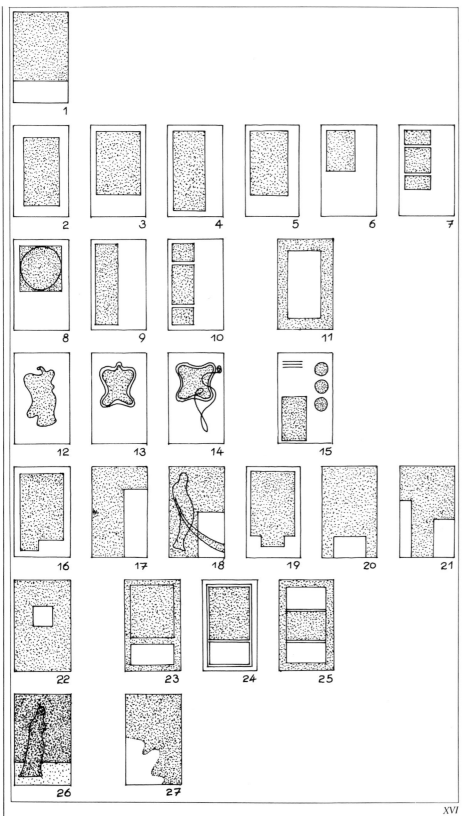

XVI. Basic ways of organizing the graphic field in artistic postcards during the Art Noveau period: Nos. 1-25 show the space for the message clearly separated from the image, Nos. 26-7 incorporate it in the design, without distinct separation.

XVI

borders in the Art Nouveau style (fig. XVI: 13), beyond which decorative elements or parts of the figure sometimes emerge (fig. XVI: 14).

f. Compositions of various figurative or decorative elements (often with geometric outlines) carefully placed on an even ground (fig. XVI: 15).

g. A space for the message consisting of one or more rectangular areas near the edge of the card and which break the frame of the image (fig. XVI: 16-21).

h. A space for the message clearly outlined and inserted in the centre of an overall design, with borders separating the image from the message (fig. XVI: 22).

The second basic postcard design comprises two types:

a. In a design covering a whole side of the postcard, certain areas (a pavement, wall, dress, beach, sky, mountain etc.) are treated with paler colours and used for the message (fig. XVI: 26); where the design technique employs flat areas of plain colours without outlines (as by Laskoff, Beggarstaff, etc.), the white surfaces or pale tones can be used for the message.

b. The area for the message occupies a sort of space left over at the edge of the design (fig. XVI: 27).

It should be noted that in some kinds of artistic postcards, especially in greetings cards, the space for the message is occupied by a printed inscription.

Sometimes graphic design elements can appear on the side reserved for the address, usually in the form of decorative frames, trade-marks or symbols (e.g. in the Wiener Werkstätte series, and on various commemorative cards, German *Feldpostkarten* for Bahlsen, etc.).

In the early years of the twentieth century postcard series were usually collected in a folder ('*pochette*') which had a different design from those on the cards themselves. Conceived as a means of attracting buyers, the '*pochettes*' often had designs of high quality.

Postcards as documents of the Art Nouveau style

POSTCARDS AND POSTERS are the most telling evidence of the attention paid by *fin de siècle* art to the use of means of mass communication as vehicles for aesthetic ideas. This is surely one of the most important, though undervalued, legacies of the period to the later avant-garde movements. It is significant that after the Art Nouveau artists, the futurists (from Balla to Prampolini and Depero), the expressionists, the dadaists and the surrealists (from Eluard to Breton), all reassessed the medium of postcards and posters and used it as a means of propaganda.

The *fin de siècle* artists already seemed to sense that combination of art and publicity that would later be categorically exploited by the futurists and by Depero when they used.the advertising potential of postcards not only to earn money in the market-place, but also to promote their art. It was no accident that commercial artists and book

XVII

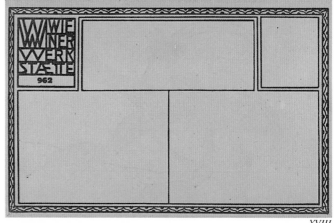

XVIII

XIX

XX

and magazine illustrators were in the majority among postcard designers and that postcards were often used to publicise works of graphic art, from illustrated books to 'ex-libris' slips, or the production of workshops, groups or artists' colonies working in different countries in Europe. The earliest picture postcards marking their revival included those which publicised the periodicals that were most influential in determining the direction of the graphic art of the period, such as *Meggendorfer Blätter, Jugend, Die Lüstigen Blätter, Cocorico, Simplicissimus, Pél & Ploma*, and *Italia Ride*. Alongside these, significantly, there were also those single-copy postcards designed for the Viennese 'Siebener Club' (1895) and those printed for the Künstlerkolonie Worpswede (c. 1897), the Karlsruhe Künstlerbund (c. 1897), the Vienna Secession (the *Ver Sacrum* series, c. 1898), the Berlin 'Steglitzer Werkstatt (c. 1900), the Künstlerkolonie in Darm-stadt (1901-1904), the Salon des Cent in Paris (1901) and the Círculo artístico in Barcelona (c. 1901).

Postcard reproductions of posters and book illustrations are a way of publicising the work of an artist as well as the product. There are whole series which reproduce the plates from an illustrated volume. Among the earliest are those of Henri Rivière and A. Vignola (possibly datable c. 1899), which reproduce the illustrations, executed in *ombres*

XVII-XX. Some treatments of the side of post-cards containing the address: XVII. K. Moser, postcard for the Jubilee of emperor Franz Josef, 1908 (cf. fig. 244); XVIII. Postcard for the Wiener Werkstätte series (cf. fig. 260); XIX. Postcard for the Werkbund exhibition in Cologne 1914 (cf. fig. 421); XX. C. O. Czeschka, military postcard advertising H. Bahlsen's Keks-Fabrik, Hannover, 1915 (cf. fig. 428).

chinoises, for Georges Fragerolle's musical poems, *La marche à 'Etoile* and *Le Sphynx*, and the illustrations by Caran d'Ache for *L'Epopée*. In France, Alexandre Théophile Steinlen (with *Dans la rue* by Aristide Bruant) and Albert Guillaume also regularly reproduced book illustrations as postcards. This was also customary in Great Britain; suffice it to mention Walter Crane and his *Flora's Feast* series.

At the end of the period under review the series for the 'Librairie de l'Estampe' by Raphael Kirchner, who often used the mischievous model Riquette in erotic poses, reproduced in colour the line drawings which had appeared in the book *Le Bandeau* written by Felicien Champsaur in 1914 but published in 1916 to raise the morale of French soldiers and Parisians.

Even some of the cabarets, which were important centres of artistic life in the Art Nouveau 'capitals', used postcards for publicity purposes, among them the *Le Chat Noir* in Paris, the *Quatre Gats* in Barcelona and the *Fledermaus* in Vienna.

Among the Art Nouveau personalities who used postcards to advertise their own work was the architect Hector Guimard, who circulated his series 'Le Style Guimard' in 1903. This contained collotype reproductions of his architecture: his Métro stations in Paris, the Castel Béranger, his chalets in the Paris area and his fashionable bathing establishments.

Like magazines, postcards were used as satirical and polemical weapons in artistic debates. The Künstlerkolonie in Darmstadt was the target of some postcards which grotesquely caricature the posters of P. Behrens or M. Olbrich. This kind of satire was still used in Germany in the 1920s: the photomontages which transform the Weissenhof Siedlung in Stuttgart into casbahs populated by Arabs and camels are well known.

Because they lend themselves to so many uses, postcards provide an invaluable repertory of Art Nouveau imagery around the world. Leaving aside designs conceived and executed exclusively for the genre, they often take on special importance as the only record of works of art intended for another form. Examples of this are series reproducing sketches for posters which won competitions but were never printed, fashion designs by the Wiener Werkstätte and book and story illustrations which were only produced as postcards.

The subjects of Art Nouveau postcards

WOMEN

WOMEN ASSUMED A CENTRAL ROLE in Art Nouveau iconography. The many types of models and symbolic interpretations of the female form were popularized by artists like Alphonse Mucha, Koloman Moser, Walter Hampel, Raphael Kirchner, Henri Meunier, Privat

XXI   *XXII*   *XXIII*

Livemont, Eugène Grasset, Paul Berton, Hans Christiansen, Fritz Rehm, Fidus, Charles Dana Gibson, Jessie Marion King and Aleardo Terzi. The Art Nouveau woman, observed Giovanna Massobrio and Paolo Portoghesi, does not represent modernity stripped of historical references, but a profoundly reworked rediscovery of historical precedents. 'What else can a woman be but a mixture of Greek virgin, medieval courtly lady, witch, geisha, Lucretia Borgia, Ophelia and Nefertiti? The Liberty lady is both pastiche and creative expression, because the girl dressed in a flimsy Greek tunic with her hair piled up in the style of a geisha is, for the high priests of the new taste, not a casual montage of elements but a journey through memory; she is a means of discovering deep analogies between Greek and Japanese elegance, between the common delight in line and two-dimensional forms that is found in two traditions so distant from each other in time and space.'[25]

The abandonment by artists of everyday reality and their escape into fantasy were expressed symbolically in their sublime elevation of womankind. Here reality and fantasy intermingled in a synthesis of ideal beauty derived from Japanese, Greek or medieval models, or inspired by the pagan Mediterranean mythologies, Nordic sagas, or various exotic sources. Female models close to the origins of Art Nouveau, such as the Pre-Raphaelite woman celebrated by artists all over the Continent, from France to Germany (Robert Engels) and Italy (Francesco Nonni) were internationally successful. So were the heroines of historical novels and nineteenth-century melodramas, who were deeply rooted in the popular imagination, from Brunhilde to Salammbo and from Herodias to Thais.

Woman in all sorts of guises was also a popular subject for postcards – a theme that can be seen to represent the expectation of a new aesthetic order, a socialism of beauty. 'Femmes-enfants, femmes-

XXI-XXIII. Examples of pochettes for series of postcards: XXI. W. Hampel, series LX of 'Wiener Künstler-Postkarten', Philipp & Kramer, c. 1900; XXII. F. Spiegel, series 'Aus goldener Zeit', printed by Kunst-Anstalt Hubert Köhler, Munich; XXIII. Anonymous artist, one of the series 'Künstler-Stein-Zeichnungen' depicting the town of Goslar, pub. R. Lederbogen, Halberstadt.

25 G. Massobrio, P. Portoghesi, La donna Liberty, Rome-Bari 1983, p. 12.

XXIV

XXV

XXIV, XXV. Examples of pochettes *for series of postcards: XXIV. H. Eliott, series 'La vie sportive', pub. S. Paris XXV. E. Bernard, series 'L'entôlage'.*

fleurs, femmes-étoiles, femmes-flammes, flots de la mer, grandes vagues de l'amour et du rêve, chair des poètes, statues solaires, masques nocturnes, rosiers blancs dans la neige, servantes, dominatrices, chimères, vierges illuminées, courtisanes parfaites, princesses de légende, passantes, elles construisent la force, les visages et la raison d'être de l'homme, béatifient sa faiblesse, font faillir la joie et croupir le chagrin. Une fille altière coiffée d'un paon, un chat à tête de femme, une beauté noiraude à la porte d'un cimetière, une jeunesse nue

XXVI   *XXVII*

renversée sur un rocking chair, une autre au fond de la mer, assise sur une table dans une pose indécente, fume une cigarette et se verse un verre de vin, une autre vole sur les fleurs, une autre flirte avec un papillon, une autre parle comme dans un rêve, une autre enfile ses bas, celle-ci, toute verte, faisant, à coup de fouet, tourner un coeur comme une toupie, c'est l'Hiver, celle-ci, dans une pensée, symbolise la Libellule, celle-ci s'épouvante d'un crabe qui monte vers son ventre, celle-ci compare ses seins à ceux d'une Venus de marbre, celle-ci surgit de la fumée d'une cigarette, celle-ci l'indomptable, est pourtant enchaînée, celle-ci balaie la rue, celle-ci lutte avec un singe'[26].

Paul Eluard here lists some of the most frequently recurring themes in the representation of women on postcards. He also points to the dream-like flight from everyday life, the triumph of the banal, the stimulation of the collective subconscious, aesthetic reveries, the desecration of style through irony and kitsch – all those elements that attracted the attention of the surrealists to the art of the early twentieth century. The representation of women in fact swung between opposing extremes – between, on the one hand, symbolism that conveyed

XXVI, XXVII. Postcards as documents for the history of modern art and its diffusion: postcard reproducing the painting 'Am Morgen' by G. Klimt, Lobmeyr collection, Vienna, in collotype (?), pub. Hof-Kunstanstalt J. Löwy, Vienna 1906; postcard by A. Mucha for the Barcelona exhibition 'Documents Décoratifs', 1903, phototypography.

26 P. Eluard. *op. cit.*, p. 86.

aesthetic messages and, on the other, double-entendres which are often commonplace and vulgar; between the elevation of the female form on to an ideal plane as a symbol of a new kind of beauty and in contrast, its reduction to the level of an object of pleasure and desire.

'La terre est en travail d'où doit surgir la Fleur; mais nos yeux ne verront rien se lever avant que l'anéantissement de l'actuel soit total!': wrote Henry Van de Velde in *Déblaiement d'art*, (1895) clarifying the symbolic value of that messenger of the new beauty: the 'Flower' in Art Nouveau iconography. Certainly the woman-flower is one of the images most overworked by postcard illustrators. But their symbolism did not only involve using typical elements of Art Nouveau iconography to celebrate the *Urmutter*, the source of creativity, the identification of the feminine principle with aesthetic invention, and the woman-nature combination as an expression of the neopagan spirit permeating the dawning consumer society. It also pervaded their commonplaces about the vices of Pandora, using irony and easily intelligible symbols for the benefit of the general public. There are many such allusions in the metamorphoses of women into animals which populate the world of postcards: inconstancy and fickleness are represented by the peacock-woman: seduction by the siren, and so on. When it is not a metamorphosis, the combination of animal and woman is usually a *double-entendre*, almost always with erotic and sometimes pornographic overtones.

Lust is often represented in the work of B. Patella and R. Wichera by young girls with doves, a reference to Semiramis, while other animals in the background or held by a woman represent slang or foreign words for phallic symbols. More important, at least in terms of the number produced, than postcards bearing stylized or symbolic images of women, were those that employed a greater degree of realism that is often overlain with disturbing provocative eroticism, and has the attributes of being modern and dynamic. The woman presented in postcards is the androgynous type, who smokes (Kirchner, 'Job' series, etc), who engages in sports (Mignot), from those more appropriate for women to those more suitable for men, ranging from car driving (Ramón Casas) to cycling (W. Hampel, R. Kirchner, F. Schon, H. Eichrodt, A. Barrère, etc), the type who walks with masculine strides (like the elegant ladies in the 'Eureka' and 'Zenit' series by Marcello Dudovich). The great success of these postcards can be mainly attributed to the ambiguity of their message. The female public could read into them the supreme achievement of women's emancipation, a recognition of coming equality, if not role reversal. But despite the apparent acceptance of new habits and new relationships between the sexes, the exploitation of women's image for erotic ends continued. Sport was the pretext for removing prudish layers of clothing from them, and for dressing them in clothes which clung to the body or aroused sexual fantasies, like the soft furs wrapped around the women drivers of Casas. Similarly, in the large number of postcards showing women on bicycles, the woman is no longer a passive object but is actively mounted on top. This was a response to what was apparently

XXVIII *XXIX* *XXX*

the need of the time: the desire for the woman to be sexually dominant.

Among the tremendous number of postcards devoted to the female image, there is a separate group consisting of the so-called 'donnine', or little women, series, which was very popular in Italy. At the beginning of the First World War it became a major field of activity for illustrators like Alberto Bianchi, Luigi Bompard, Aurelio Bertiglia, Adolfo Busi, C. Calderara, Plinio Codognato, E. Colombo, Tito Corbella, Aurelio Craffonara, Marcello Dudovich, Roberto Franzoni, Eugenio Golia, Luciano Achille Mauzan, Aldo Mazza, Leopoldo Metlicovitz, Rodolfo Paoletti, Enrico Sacchetti, Scattina, Aleardo Terzi and Adelina Zandrino. The historical, though not the stylistic precedent for this type, is the work of American artists like Philip Boileau, Clarence Underwood and Harrison Fisher. Here, woman is removed from the world of heroic legend, from her role as protagonist in woman's liberation and from her function as aesthetic symbol. Instead, she is portrayed immersed in the reality of everyday middle-class life. The wicked sorceress of the Art Nouveau era has had her claws trimmed, and has given way to stereotypes more akin to the ideal fiancée, whose seductive powers bear no mystery but consist in a combination of innocence and malice, in provoking without ever violating the bounds of modesty. In a world at war, the 'little woman' brought consoling messages to the generation which lived in the trenches. It was not by chance that the production of these postcards was greatly increased between 1915 and 1918; it continued for some years after the war, and remained popular with lovers all over Europe.

FASHION

The Art Nouveau postcard was both a means of promoting new fashions (the most obvious examples being those of the Wiener

XXXI

XXXII

XXXIII

XXVIII-XXXIII. P. Diffloth, drawings (La Beauté s'en va. Des méthodes propres à la rénovation de la beauté féminine, Paris s.d (1905), which show Parisian ladies of the twentieth century taken from some of the most important French satirical illustrators, (XXVIII) 'Bac type', (XXIX) 'Cardona type', (XXX) 'Gerbault type', (XXXI) 'Guillaume type', (XXXII) 'Iribe type', (XXXIII) 'Gosé type'.

Werkstätte), and a means of reflecting trends in current fashion. Of course, in most examples, the artist *interpreted* contemporary styles, and so in postcards womens' dress is neither that depicted in magazines nor couturier fashion, even though it was inspired by one or the other, or both. Such postcards are therefore special but nevertheless valuable records. The dress and female types invented by caricaturists are of no less documentary value than those designed by major artists: 'The satirical draughtsman can see better and further than the painter preoccupied with satisfying his model while remaining faithful to a style, and further than a photographer who seeks a pleasing expression and youthfulness. The drawings of Bac, Guillaume, Cardona, Guydo de Prejelan, Gosé, Iribe . . . are attractive and accurate in just this way. Through the individual style of each designer emerges the fine, elegant and delicate silhouette of the well-bred Frenchwoman of the beginning of the twentieth century'[27].

'Women's fashion' – wrote Adolf Loos in 1898 – 'is an appalling chapter in the history of civilization! [. . .]. But now even this period is over'[28].

The fact that the two main trends of the period opposed by Loos, although based on different philosophies, often produced the same results is clearly revealed in Art Nouveau postcards: these were the 'aesthetic' (ie inspired by the English 'Aesthetic Movement') and 'rational' trends. Aesthetic clothes in Great Britain, from those designed by Walter Crane to those by Edward William Godwin, derived from classical and medieval costumes and from works of art ('Primavera' by Botticelli); 'rational' clothing was an attempt to free women's bodies from restrictive corsets and to give them freedom of movement. The 'freedom' movement in clothes coincided with an increasing interest in women's sports (tennis, canoeing, bicycling) and

27 P. Diffloth, *La Beauté s'en va. Des méthodes propres à la rénovation de la beauté féminine*, Paris s.d. (1905), p. 94.

28 A. Loos, *ins Leere gesprochen*, 1921.

with women working outside the home (such as factory workers, nurses and shop assistants). Postcards which display these activities include those by Mignot, Eichrodt and Barrère, while the neo-Hellenic fashion promoted by the architect and designer E. W. Godwin at the beginning of the 1880s (he became manager of the dress department at Liberty's store in 1884) was promoted around 1900 in postcards by Crane and Henry Ryland.

Jessie Marion King projected her feminine artistry through her 'decorative' personal style of dress, a graphic style reflected in her illustrations and postcards. The Aesthetic Movement required that clothing and interior design should be in harmony; for this reason some of William Morris's designs for furnishing fabrics were also printed on muslin or silk for dresses. The same thing happened in Vienna with fabric designs for the Wiener Werkstätte, by Joseph Hoffmann, Carl Witzman and others, which also appeared on postcards.

Alongside 'artistic' dress for ladies, postcards record similar clothing for children, inspired by the book illustrations of Kate Greenaway, which were also popular outside Great Britain. The English Liberty fashions, which were shown in Wertheim department stores in 1904, were enthusiastically received in Germany and in Italy, where the fabrics produced by Liberty gave Italy the name for the national Art Nouveau style.

Some suggestion of the principles formulated by Henry Van de Velde for the German versions of 'aesthetic' fashions can be seen in the ladies' clothes on postcards by Fritz Rehm and Hans Christiansen.

Postcards by designers like Kirchner and Xavier Sager were very popular because they remained faithful to the illustrations in fashion magazines while adding personal, witty touches.

In the series of postcards published by Philipp & Kramer, Walter Hampel, Leo Kainradl, Rudolf Konopa and, above all, Kirchner interpreted the Viennese version of the emancipated Parisian woman's fashion, while the postcards by Maria Likarz, Mela Kohler, Edward Wimmer and Otto Lendecke in the series produced by the Wiener Werkstätte are a valuable record of the work of the Viennese workshop which tried to create a specifically Viennese fashion, even though it had links with Parisian trends through Paul Poiret.

Italian postcards show that fashion there followed the Parisian style imported by the magazines. But traces of the 'aesthetic' style were not totally absent as, for instance, in the art of the great Mariano Fortuny and the postcards of Francesco Nonni. As for the United States, many American women were at the time working outside the home as factory girls, telephonists or nurses, and this revolutionary fact had consequences for their clothing; they wore a more functional two-piece outfit consisting of blouse and skirt. With this informal, sporty type of clothing, the shirt was called a 'Gibson-girl blouse'.

The Italian 'donnine', or 'little women', type of postcard also illustrates the relationship between the war and fashion. In 1915 there was a clear need for practical, comfortable clothes: skirts were shorter and wider 'crinolines of war' were worn with ankle boots. The 'military style', in olive, khaki, grey, brown and black, was often brightened up by embroidered shawls, and was amply documented in postcards from countries which tried to create a 'national' dress as, for example, in Italy in the postcards by Mauzan, Sacchetti, Calderara and Bianchi, or in Austria in the postcards by Wimmer and the Wiener Werkstätte.

CHILDREN

Children figured prominently in picture postcards, especially in Britain and northern Europe, where the cult and respect for childhood is most deeply rooted. Here various artists, mostly female, were almost exclusively preoccupied with the subject. In Great Britain, childhood was a major theme for Kate Greenaway and Walter Crane; Ethel Parkinson, Florence Hardy and Millicent Sowerby also devoted much of their work to the subject. In America Jessie Willcox Smith was particularly distinguished in this field; in Holland, Rie Cramer and Henriette Willebeek Le Mair; in Belgium, Suzanne Cocq; and in Germany, the prolific Pauli Ebner. In Sweden, the world of childhood dominates the work of Carl Larsson, Jenny Nystrom, Signe Aspelin, Aina Stenberg, Helsa Hammar and Maj Lindmann. The subject was not, however absent in the work of illustrators in Latin countries. In France, Hansi's patriotic propaganda used children in Alsatian costume and tricolour cockades, while in Italy, A. Bertiglia put children alongside his *donnine*.

Scenes depicting Dutch children were internationally successful. This may have been due to the quaintness of their costumes, which almost seemed exotic in the European context, and also to the great success of Dutch stories.

The vogue for representing children in costume was not, however, restricted to Holland: in Germany Ebner liked clothing in the Biedermeier style, while in Great Britain, Hardy and Sowerby opted for Elizabethan dress.

In most cases, the image of childhood, with its uninhibited joy in living, its implicit message of hope for the future, and its innocence and openness, was bound up with the message of greeting on the postcard: Happy Christmas, Happy Easter, Happy New Year, and so on.

It was customary to issue cards designed by famous artists like Max Klinger and Carl Larsson for charity events held to collect money for poor children. Those with greetings or children's scenes were designed almost exclusively for postcards.

Childhood, however, was not always used for expressions of charity or greetings: children were sometimes depicted on erotic postcards.

PUBLICITY AND POSTERS

While publicity was one of the original purposes of picture postcards, the reproduction of posters in this small format resulted also from the widespread collecting of these products of graphic art, a habit which greatly increased during the last decade of the nineteenth century. Leopold Wiener, when analyzing this phenomenon, observed that while poster collecting was comparatively inexpensive, it needed a lot of space. The postcard makes it possible to collect posters in a smaller format. The reduced size also had other advantages: 'the postcard has the best size for our eyes to see it at the distance that we normally look at an image. You take all of it in at once, something that does not occur with other images. Therefore the postcard and only the postcard can be perceived perfectly'[29].

The first specialist magazines to contain small lithographic reproductions of posters were *The Modern Poster*, 1895; *The Illustrated Poster*, 1895; *Posters in Miniature*, 1896; *Les Affiches illustrées*, 1896; *Les Maîtres de l'Affiche*, 1896-1900; *Les Affiches étrangères*, 1897; *L'Estampe et l'Affiche*, 1897-1899; *L'Affiche Belge*, 1897; and *The Poster*, 1898-1901. They were soon followed by the first series of postcards devoted entirely to posters: the 'Cinos' series of 1898 contained posters by Jules Chéret, Eugène Grasset, Alphonse Mucha, Henri de Toulouse-Lautrec, Abel Truchet, Lucien Métivet, Pal, Albert Guillaume, Maurice Réalier-Dumas, Gaston Noury and others. Then came the 'Affiches de Chemins de Fer' series (Paul Berthon, Jules Grün, René Péan, Pal, etc), the 'Affiches Gerin' (Steinlen, Georges Meunier, etc) and the 'Collection Job', which reproduced posters and plates from publicity calendars for cigarette papers, designed by Jeanne Atché, Firmin Buisset, Jules Chéret, Alphonse Mucha, Charles Léandre, Ramón Casas, Armand Rassenfosse, Leonette Cappiello, Aleardo Villa and others.

In Italy, the Officine Grafiche Ricordi reproduced as postcards most of their own posters, designed by Adolfo Hohenstein, Leopoldo Metlicovitz, Aleardo Villa and others. In Great Britain, Raphael Tuck published various series entitled 'Celebrated Posters', which offered international coverage, but in which British artists predominated, such as Cecil Aldin, the Beggarstaff Brothers, John Hassal, Dudley Hardy and Phil May.

It would be rash to accept Wiener's[30] conclusion that the vogue for postcards put posters in the shade. Rather the reverse was true, because the immensely popular publicity postcard had already assumed the character of a poster in miniature by the end of the nineteenth century. The Milanese publisher Gabriele Chiattone, who produced a series of postcards in 1898 for the Lariana shipping companies operating on lakes Como, Garda and Maggiore, was one of the first to spread this type of card. It soon rejected nineteenth-century stereotypes in favour of the Liberty style overlain with a strong Japanese flavour.

In Belgium, also from 1898, the 'Red Star Line' series designed by Henri Cassiers were in the graphic style of the poster, but only a few of them were in fact reproductions of posters.

The practice of reproducing posters as postcards was not exclusively concerned with commercial publicity: it was often adopted for the

29 L. Wiener, *op. cit.*, I (1922-23 no. 1, December 1922), p. 8.

30 ibidem.

production of commemorative cards, which celebrated important national events, political demonstrations (such as 1st May celebrations), congresses, commercial and artistic exhibitions, centenaries of famous people, and so on.

THE WORLD OF THE STAGE

A sensitive barometer of the tastes and habits of ordinary people, the postcard promptly recorded new phenomena of popular culture, such as melodrama and its stars. Music publishers contributed to the launch of new operas by issuing series of postcards summarising the story in pictures; Casa Ricordi, especially, exploited this form of publicity, with its series for *La Bohème* by Puccini (designed by Metlicovitz in 1897), *Iris* by Mascagni (Mataloni and Hohenstein, 1898-99), *Colonia libera* by Illica and Floridia (A. Beltrame, 1899), *Tosca* by Puccini (Metlicovitz, 1900), *Germania* by Franchetti (Metlicovitz, 1902) and *Madame Butterfly* by Puccini (Metlicovitz, 1904). There were numerous series in Italy devoted to the operas of G. Verdi and to the composer himself; among them should be mentioned those published by Casa Ricordi and designed by Metlicovitz ('Verdi a Sant'Agata', 1900; 'Aida', 1901; 'Falstaff', 1901). The range of subjects used in postcards was greatly enriched by Wagnerian myths, which were given novel treatment in the heroic Teutonic manner by Franz Stassen and in a symbolist manner by Gaston Bussière. Like the melodrama, the straight theatre, variety and cabaret all beat their drum through postcards, which made their own contribution to the creation of stars. Whereas photographic postcards circulated thousands of pictures of the stars of the *belle époque* from Bella Otero to Lina Cavalieri, from Loïe Fuller to Yvette Guilbert, from Sarah Bernhardt to Eleonora Duse, comprising a vast portfolio of portraits, the work done by artists often destroyed their mystique through caricature loaded with propaganda intent. Outstanding in this type of work were French caricaturists such as Sem, Sacha, Guitry and Louise Abbema.

The work of famous Parisian song writers also became widely known through postcards, which often reproduced the cover of the score with the text and music. The postcards of the songs of Aristide Bruant carry the signatures of such famous artists as Steinlen and Toulouse-Lautrec, the latter's concealed beneath the anagram Treclau. The custom of reproducing scores on postcards was also very popular in Germany, Spain and Italy (Neapolitan songs).

SPORT

Sport, one of the major themes of Art Nouveau was given full treatment on picture postcards. It emerged as a new phenomenon during the *belle époque* and with its mass appeal, it became synonymous with modernism. Many ideas were woven into it: new ideas about health and hygiene, aspirations for an emancipated morality which would lead to the equality of the sexes, the notion of competition, which was also a product of the development of modern technology. Sports illustrators revealed different attitudes to all this. Some saw an involvement in sport and physical culture as a positive victory in the struggle for equality between the sexes (significantly, woman is the principal subject in their work even when there is a man at her side).

Others took a philistine attitude, which apparently accepted the new ideas, but contained a veiled warning against the danger of moral corruption. The association of sport with sex, to which the best draughtsmen delicately alluded (Mignot, Kirchner and Wenneberg), is in contrast to the vulgar connection of sport with pornography suggested by the second-rate designers. Sometimes censorious attitudes were expressed by caricature and grotesqueness.

A love of all things modern and an admiration for technological progress are fully expressed in the many postcard series on cars and speed records. Sport represented as an heroic activity, typical of many German series, is, in addition a special variation on the popular need of the time for stars.

SCENERY

The first postcards to illustrate scenery probably appeared in Germany, first of all with little images printed on official *Correspondenz-Karten* intended as advertisements (for hotels, restaurants, etc). At the beginning of the 1890s the first scenic postcards appeared in Germany, Austria and Switzerland. They showed three or four views of cities or holiday resorts combined with decorative motifs and the inscription *Gruss aus* (Greetings from), followed by the name of the place. The image occupied only a small area on the back of the card, leaving plenty of space for a written message. Around 1890 *Gruss* cards were printed in one colour (usually dark brown or blue-brown), but they soon appeared in two colours, usually brown and blue. From the mid-1890s *Gruss* postcards were produced by German firms (especially in Berlin, Saxony and Bavaria) for many other countries as well as their own and by about 1900 they were on sale and very popular world-wide[31]. Once photographic collotype had arrived it seemed certain to become the sole medium for rural scenes and urban views. Faced with competition from this new method of illustration reproduction, some artists initially gave up the genre, with a few exceptions, notably the Germans. Others tried to reassert the artist's role by transforming nature into dreamlike, surrealist creations. This would seem to have been the case with the anthropomorphic mountains invented by Emil Hansen (Nolde) in about 1895. He started a genre which quickly found followers and relaunched landscape as a subject for postcards. The genre enjoyed renewed success, but not only in the German-speaking areas, where many series were produced for export (such as those by Manuel Wielandt, which reproduced watercolours of the great lakes of

31 F. Staff, *op. cit.*, p. 56.

Lombardy, the Ligurian Riviera, Naples and Venice), especially after 1898.

The Flemish illustrator Hendrick Cassiers played an important role in this field. Between 1898 and 1899 he designed such successful series as 'La Hollande pittoresque', 'Costumes hollandais', 'Vichy', and 'Le littoral belge'. shown at international exhibitions, such as the 1899 Venice Biennale, and widely publicized in the specialist press, these series launched the fashion for Dutch landscape with local costume, which even outside Flanders was imitated by many artists (Alfred Ost and Franz Melchers in Belgium and Ethel Parkinson and Florence Hardy in Britain) and almost formed a separate genre.

The transition from landscapes executed in the nineteenth-century watercolour tradition, still evident in the work of Wielandt and in certain designs by Cassiers, to more stylized scenes completed with continuous outlines and flat colours (also influenced by Japanese colour woodcuts) was made by Cassiers himself in his series of Dutch landscapes and by Amédée Lynen in the series 'De-ci, de-là, à Bruxelles et en Brabant'. In Lynen's work the landscape is filled with atmospheric effects depending on the time of day and on the season, and with subtle psychological implications.

There are many artistic postcards of places which were becoming centres of mass tourism, from seaside resorts to spas. Activities of daily life often interested the artist more than the architecture of these places, which were often important centres of the Art Nouveau style. Those reporters of fashionable life for weekly magazines like *Simplicissimus* were the same illustrators who recorded the daily round in fashionable holiday centres on postcards, among them Ferdinand von Reznicek, B. Mars, Marcello Dudovich, and Albert Guillaume.

IMAGES OF THE CITY

City images made by the early postcard artists were generally commonplace. The most trite clichés associated with the *ville lumière*, a place of pleasure and flirtatious adventures, were often passively trotted out by Parisian designers. In the well-known series by Jacques Wely, Paris is the city 'qui danse', it is the world capital of theatre, it is the capital of chic and fashion for Hans Christiansen and Henri Meunier, it is the centre of consumerism, of the greatest concentration of 'Temples des tentations', the department stores, it is Montmartre sparkling with the lights of those shrines of nightlife, where local colour turns its attention to providing a setting for tourists, it is the brightly coloured stage set for the *vie de bohème*, it is the boulevard just right for a chance encounter with a young dressmaker and rendered with the affected ingenuousness and malice by Henri Boutet.

The series 'L'entôlage' by Edouard Bernard 'films' the mishaps of a stockbroker tricked and robbed by two young ladies of easy virtue encountered in a café, all rendered with irony and detachment. Among the interpreters of Parisian life, Alexandre Théophile Steinlen is outstanding. Into postcards he reintroduced social criticism infused with eloquent sympathy for the urban poor; this was the basic theme of his vast graphic output.

Scenes of Vienna in the postcard series produced by the Wiener Werkstätte concentrated on the architecture that gave the city its distinctive character. A similar interest in the architectural profile of a city can be found only in German postcards, in series of lithographs of Hamburg, Munich and Berlin.

As well as the Gothic monuments and great halls of the detached residences of the Vienna Innenstadt, the imperial palaces and baroque monuments, and the colourful spots that typified traditional Viennese life which survived in the suburbs (the old taverns, or Heurige, in Grinsing, the Beethovenhaus, etc), the Viennese series portrayed examples of 'Moderne Architektur', such as the Kirche am Steinhof by Otto Wagner, the 'Villenkolonie' on the Hohe Warte, the 'Kunst-schau' exhibition hall and the 'Fledermaus' cabaret by Josef Hoff-mann. The cafés, the centres of Viennese social life and typical institutions of the Habsburg capital, were another subject frequently illustrated by the Wiener Werkstätte: '[. . .] the Viennese café' – recalled Stefan Zweig – 'is a special institution, which is unique in the world. It is really a kind of democratic club, open to all for the price of a cup of coffee, where each client, once he has fulfilled this modest obligation, is entitled to remain for hours chatting, writing, playing cards [. . .]. In the best Viennese cafés there are all the local papers, all the German ones, not to mention the French, English, Italian and American ones as well as all the literary and artistic magazines of any importance, from *Mercure de France* to *Neue Rundschau*, from *The Studio* to *The Burlington Magazine* [. . .].Possibly nothing has con-tributed more to the intellectual prowess and international awareness of the Austrians than the possibility afforded them of getting them-selves informed of world events at the café [. . .]'[32]. Moriz Jung's scratchy pencil interpreted this microcosm and occasionally ap-proached the level of Karl Kraus's caustic moral criticism.

In the body of work depicting the life of European capitals, the Brussels of Amédée Lynen, a city deeply rooted in the literary culture of Flemish symbolism, holds a special place. Lynen was a friend and admirer of Emile Verhaeren and a collector of his manuscripts, and he was in complete accord with Verhaeren's poetic vision. Like the poet, he perceived that the urban sprawl of Brussels, which he depicted, was an inevitable historical necessity. But this awareness was tinged with nostalgia for the old world that was under sentence of death, for the *villes à pignons*, where the life of centuries followed unchanging rhythms.

'La plaine est morne et morte – et la ville la mange': this verse by Verhaeren might sum up the meaning of the urban scene depicted by Lynen. The crowd he portrayed is not that of a modern metropolis, but a peasant population which lived on the margin of an industrial world. His world is that of local markets, small tradesmen, of tramps and the unemployed, of hostelries in still semi-rural suburbs, of soldiers on

32 S. Zweig, *il mondo di ieri* (1942), in *Opere scelte* edited by L. Mazzucchetti, Milan 1961, Vol. II, pp. 699-700.

leave and of popular amusements. 'Lynen is a true Fleming' – wrote Fernand Khnoff – 'or rather, a true *brabaçon* or rather still, a true *bruxellois* of the old school. He likes the old customs of the *bas de la ville* – the low districts of the city – the windy streets with their gabled roofs and smoky cabarets, where it was possible to meet all the typical Brussels types which he depicts in such a personal, acute, joyous and easy manner. He likes to illustrate his favourite authors too for his own pleasure, to the extent of copying the text and its decoration. He still owns works by Ch. Decoster, Ch. Deulin, and Emile Verhaeren, and continuously adds to the number of these precious manuscripts'[33].

DECORATIVE COMPOSITIONS

Around the turn of the nineteenth century, the stylization of natural forms was the subject of many manuals on ornament by famous Art Nouveau artists, such as *La Plante et ses applications ornamentales* (1898) by Grasset, *Combinaisons ornementales* (c. 1900) by Verneuil, Auriol and Mucha, and *Das Weib in modernen Ornament* (c. 1904) by H. Anker and J. Klinger. It found an obvious outlet in picture postcards, especially greetings cards, where a floral cornice often framed the blank space left for the printed inscription. These postcards sometimes carried a 'famous signature', like the fabric designs of Hoffman and Czeschka, the stylized floral designs by Gustav Marisch for the Wiener Werkstätte, and the series on the days of the week by Somov, but more often the designs were produced by minor or unknown artists. Decorative cards were produced in large numbers and became particularly successful in some countries, such as the United States. Most are classified by collectors as 'fantasy' cards and employ stylized flowers: 'Une avalanche de roses', – wrote Paul Eluard in reference to these postcards – 'de myosotis et de violettes, en soie, en velours, en peluche, en celluloïd, en dentelle, en métal, gaufrées, glacées, pailletées, dorées, nacrées, en relief, des poissons de myosotis, des tanks de violettes, des coeurs de roses. Quelquefois aussi des marguerites, des coquelicots, du muguet, des pensées. La fleur plaît. Mais une tradition détestable impose presque exlusivement la reine des fleurs, le cliché sentimental et la modestie. La fantaisie ne s'exerce pas sur les autres fleurs qui sont toujours reproduites photographiquement ou d'après de misérables aquarelles. Il semble redoutable aux conservateurs jaloux de la médiocrité populaire d'ouvrir ce jardin floribond, féerique où poussent l'anémone pulsatille, la campanule miroir de Vénus, la gueule-de-loup, la marguerite bleue, l'oeillet-de-poète géant, la capucine coccinée, la capucine caméléon, les pieds-d'alouette, l'adonide goutte-de-sang, le perce-neige, la belle-de-jour bleue à la gorge blanche et rose, la belle-de-nuit, belle de rêve au parfum de fleur d'oranger, la calcéolaire tigrée, l'oeuf-de-vanneau, le pas-du-fantôme, le zinnia double nain aux couleurs dégénérées, la centaurée candidissima, la giroflée quarantaine mammouth nuit-d'été, le désespoir-du-peintre, l'amarante queue-de-renard, le chèvrefeuille,

33 F. Khnopff, 'Belgian Pen-drawings'; in *Modern Pen Drawings: European and American*, edited by Ch. Holmes, London-Paris-New York 1901 p. 176.

le cinéraire maritime diamant, la pavot d'Islande, toutes les fleurs rares et, pour cacher les murs, l'aristoloche siphon – d'ouvrir ce jardin féerique ou poussent toutes les fleurs qui baptisent des visions'[34]. Leaving aside the few kitsch examples, decorative postcards form an important record of the spread and use of Art Nouveau as a popular art form.

POLITICS AND WAR

From the last decade of the nineteenth century postcards became an instrument of satire and political polemics. The increased production of political postcards was connected with certain events which inflamed public opinion: 'The Boer war came first' – wrote Wiener – 'and the postcard was used to conduct an anti-British campaign. Series were issued in France, the Low Countries and especially Germany and Belgium. It is amusing to note that at that time they admonished the British for what they would accuse the Germans of twenty years laters [. . .]. Then there was the *affaire Dreyfus*. Postcards which deal with this are so numerous that some people collect only this subject. An incredible number were printed: in France obviously, but particularly in Germany and in Belgium, Spain and Italy [. . .]. The *affaire Dreyfus* [. . .] was used by France's old enemies to try to undermine the state and divide the country. Then there was Clara Ward's escape, which was especially exploited in Germany'[35].

As well as the events cited by Wiener, the Russo-Japanese war (1904–5) and the uprisings by Russian workers (1905) were other major topics that most inspired publishers and designers. Postcards were used not just to send messages of solidarity or condemnation, but also, more appropriately, to address petitions to Queen Victoria in support of Boer women and children or to Tzar Nicholas II on behalf of political prisoners, and here the verbal message was reinforced by the picture on the card.

The 1st May was another occasion for issuing a conspicuous number of picture postcards.

It was above all in France that political postcards were produced in vast quantities and reached the highest quality. This was due to the large number of satirical magazines, such as the *Assiette au Beurre* and *Le Rire,* which educated public taste and reinforced the tradition of satirical drawing, in which the French, through the work of Gavarni and Daumier, had been the leaders in Europe since the end of the nineteenth century. Many of the illustrators working for these magazines also designed postcards. They included Steinlen, Jossot, Henri Gabriel Ibels, Frantisek Kupka, René Hermann-Paul, Felix Vallotton, Adolphe Willette, Jean-Louis Forain, Charles Léandre, Jean Baptiste Roubille, Aristide Delannoy, Gaston Noury, Léal de Camara and the Baron D'Ostoya. The antimilitarism and anticlericalism which stemmed from the anarchist background of some of these artists was expressed in such famous series as 'A bas la Justice Militaire' (1904),

34 P. Eluard, *op. cit.*, p. 86.

35 L. Wiener, *op. cit.*, I (1922-23, no. 26, May 1926) p. 43.

'Pochette de la Paix" (1907) and 'Les Temps Nouveaux', which were signed by artists such as Hermann-Paul, Georges Meunier, Lucien Pissarro, Steinlen, Kupka, Ibels, Jossot, Roubille, Vallotton and Willette. Sometimes the magazines which employed these illustrators themselves published series of political caricatures. The weekly *Le Rire* published the famous 'Le musée des sires' and 'Le musée des souverains', which collected together saucy caricatures of rulers and heads of state from the pencils of such masters of humour as Léandre and Roubille.

In France, political postcards were often issued in luxury or limited editions printed on fine paper by the engraving, etching or screen process or even, in a few cases, drawn by hand. A special type of French card can be called the 'political newspaper postcard'[36]. This appeared in regular series, for which a subscription was taken out, as for magazines. Some appeared with a newspaper headline printed on the front.

A forerunner and a master of this genre was Orens (the pseudonym of Charles O. Denizard), in whose work the element of caricature deftly deformed the subject with a macabre humour close to that of the 'Danza macabra' series of Alberto Martini. Other leading artists in this field were Leal de Camara and Mille.

The Art Nouveau style is not particularly conspicuous in political satire, but it is not entirely absent. The subject matter here precluded any formal refinement extraneous to the polemical thrust of the drawings, which employed more appropriate means of expression: the macabre, grotesque deformation, and frequently uncompromising realism bordering on the sadistic. But some of the features of *fin de siècle* figurative art were nevertheless discernible in some of their compositional and colour schemes. In some countries, moreover, it was precisely in political postcards that the first signs of a change in taste could be seen. In Italy, for example, if the date 1896 is correct for the appearance of the feminist movement's postcard with the motto 'Emancipatevi'[37], this was the first postcard in the Italian Liberty style – and it was a Liberty style that contained reminiscences of the politically committed work of Walter Crane. Also in Italy, the postcards created for the 1st May celebrations by Marcello Dubovich, Roberto Franzoni, G. Crotta, Edmondo Fontana and Osvaldo Ballerio were in the Liberty style. In France, too, we can find, among the political cartoonists, artists who have made a fundamental contribution to Art Nouveau.

After a short decline from the end of the first decade of the century, political postcards began to appear in large numbers again with the First World War, which also saw a more widespread use of picture postcards. All the belligerent countries produced postcards, often reproducing posters asking men to sign up. In Italy they were designed by such artists as Mauzan, Codognato, Girus, Sacchetti, Bonzagni, Borgoni and Carpanetto, in Austria by Maximilian Lenz, and in Germany by Fritz Erler. The German occupation of Belgium stirred world public opinion and gave rise to numerous postcard series

36 The success of political newspaper postcards is charted by the list compiled by L. Wiener, *op. cit.*, I (1922-23, no. 26, May 1923), pp. 44, 45. Useful facts on French political series can be found in the many editions of *Argus Fildier*.

37 This postcard is reproduced in D. Lajolo, *Su fratelli, su campagni*, Cuneo 1983.

expressing support for the displaced populations. Alfred Ost and Arthur Rackham contributed to these series, as did Steinlen who also created a series concerned with Serbian refugees.

In every country the enemy became the target of satirical series. In Italy Antonio Rubino ridiculed the Austro-Hungarian monarchy in the famous series for the newspaper *La Tradotta,* while in Germany the Allies were the targets of illustrators like Diez and Heine in the series published by the magazine *Simplicissimus.*

But most of the rise in the number of picture postcards produced during the war, which reached many millions of copies in different countries, was due to the cards devised for the soldiers at the front. They ranged from regimental cards, which were used to let the men's families or fiancées know where they were, and were usually designed as rhetorically patriotic oleographs, to the 'donnine' or 'little women' genre, which consoled the soldier at the front and helped him to look forward to respite from conflict and the tender attentions of an attractive comforter.

In this way the war gave a new impetus not only to political but also to erotic postcards. The eroticism was generally restrained and depended on subtle allusion rather than explicit nudity.

Printing techniques and materials

THE STUDY AND APPRECIATION of Art Nouveau postcards is incomplete without a knowledge of the technical procedures involved in producing them.

Letterpress (French: typographie or photogravure; Italian: tipografia; German: typographischer-Hochdruck) is a relief printing process, that is, it employs a raised printing surface. To reproduce images drawn in line (with lines and areas of flat colour), a metal block in negative relief, or line block, ready to be inked is directly obtained from a photographic negative. To reproduce images with gradations of tone, this is made up of a regular net of lines which varies in density and translates the design by the photographic process into dots of varying size that reproduce the shading. From the screened negative a negative block is obtained which is called a halftone block. Coloured images can be reproduced by this means, using one block for each colour, as in two-colour, three-colour and four-colour printing.

Collotype (Fr: phototypie; Ger: Lichtdruck; It: fototipia, or photocollografia or collotipia) is also a relief printing process. From the turn of the century to the First World War it was the most commonly used process both for postcards of photographic views and for illustrated 'artistic' postcards. It permitted very faithful reproduction almost as good as photography. Until it was superseded by the offset process from about 1920, most postcards were printed in collotype. The process is based on the property of bichromate gelatine (which is spread on to a glass plate, hence the term glass printing) to accept the oily ink only on the parts exposed to the light through the photographic negative. When greatly enlarged, collotypes can be seen to be composed of black granules of various shapes and sizes, which correspond to the grouping of the photographic granules. The process can reproduce only a limited number of copies up to about 1,000 (30 postcards measuring 9 × 14cm could be printed on one sheet and then cut up; the total for one print run was therefore 1,000 × 30, or 30,000 postcards); but obviously it was easy to remake the plate. Colour printing in collotype uses coloured inks mixed with a varnish, and one plate for each colour. Sometimes a duotone (or duplix) system was used (Fr: double ton; Ger: Duplix-Druck or Duoton; It: a due toni), which required two plates (and two printings), one for the colour and the other for the black, or for two transparent colours, such as light and dark brown. A velvety quality was achieved in this way.

Lithography (Fr: lithographie; Ger: Lithographie or Steindruck; It: litografia) is a planographic printing process – that is, it employs a flat printing surface. It is based on the invention of Aloys Senefelder in 1796. In this process the artist uses an oily crayon. The design can be made directly on a limestone block, or on to paper and then transferred to the stone. A zinc plate can be used instead of the stone. The ink used for printing is also oily and it remains on the moistened plate only on the areas covered by the artist's crayon. This process is also known as autolithography.

Photolithography (Fr: photolithographie; Ger: Photolithographie; It: fotolitografia) is a lithographic printing process obtained by transferring the design on to the stone (or zinc plate) by a photographic process. In colour lithography, also known as chromolithography, each colour requires a separate stone (or zinc plate) and has to be printed separately. In the Art Nouveau period the term chromolithography was commonly used for colour photolithography. Most of the lithographic postcards of the time were printed by photolithography. Chromolithography was replaced by trichromatic printing, first in letterpress and then in offset. Photolithographic postcards could be finished with a lacquer, which gave them a smooth, chamois-like finish. By using a clear varnish they would be given the appearance of an oil painting (as in the 'Oilettes' by the British publisher Raphael Tuck). When processed with an engraved roller, they could acquire relief features resembling the brushstrokes in oil painting.

Colour printing with a *stencil* (Fr: pochoir; Ger: Schablone; It: mascherino), is a means of colouring by hand using a zinc or copper sheet (or a piece of cardboard made waterproof with wax) as the stencil. This is perforated following the outline of the design, and the colour is applied to the paper through it with a pad or brush. This process was used to colour postcards printed in black collotype or in letterpress, and it contributed to the taste for flat colour. A later version of printing with stencils was silkscreen, now known as *screen process* printing.

Colouring by hand in watercolour or tempera was used instead of stencil printing (for example, by the publisher Munk in Vienna) to give richer shading effects.

Photogravure, or photochalcography (Fr: héliogravure; Ger: Photogravüre; It: fotocalcografia) is an *intaglio* printing process – that is, it employs ink-filled grooves cut into the copper printing plate. It is the most perfect of all the photo-mechanical methods. It reproduces by photographic means the traditional process of etching on copper. In photogravure printing, variations in tone are achieved by differences in the depth of the ink-filled depressions in the printing plate.

Woodcut (It: xilografia) is a relief printing process. To obtain colour prints, several blocks have to be cut, one for each colour. Many colours are obtained by using three blocks only, one for each of the primary printing colours (red, blue and yellow), and overprinting to create many combinations of colour. The method has rarely been used for postcards, except in Japan, where it was based on a long tradition and is very common.

Offset, introduced in about 1920, produces similar results to letterpress, but instead of relief blocks it uses a flat (planographic) printing surface and cylindrical plates for rotary printing. The process is based on the principle that oil and water do not mix. By illuminating a photographic positive or negative (screened to reproduce halftones) the design is applied to the surface of a cylindrical zinc plate. The areas of the design are treated chemically so that the ink will stick to them, while the rest, when moistened, will reject it. The design is then transferred, or 'offset', on to a rubber-covered cylinder, which then prints the design on the paper surface. The great advantage of collotype or lithographic printing over letterpress and offset is the absence of screens which allows for better quality reproduction of the original design.

Embossed printing is a revival of an ancient technique, originating in the seventeenth century, which is achieved by pressing the paper between two metal moulds, one positive, the other negative.

Of course there are some postcards which exist in one copy only or in a limited number of autograph copies, such as those by E. Orlik, or by artists belonging to the 'Siebener Club' in Vienna or the 'Círculo Artístico' in Barcelona).

During the period covered by this book the card used for postcards was usually three-ply and weighed between three and five grammes. To encourage collecting and to satisfy the demand for novelty, some publishers put postcards on the market which were made of different materials: leather, aluminium, wood, silk, ivory (or fake ivory); some even had appliqués of feather, hair or cork on their rigid supports. They even experimented with 'mechanical' cards, such as those with moving parts (such as discs or other shapes), translucent postcards which were to be looked at against the light, postcards with a 'stand' (that is, a folding element which opened to support them in a vertical position). Puzzles and series of postcards which could be used to make up one large composition were also in circulation. Finally, postcards

XXXIV

XXXV

XXXIV, XXXV. Examples of German postcards printed in relief (Prägekarte).

came in many shapes: a lozenge, a trapezoid, the shape of a leaf, a shoe, a jug, with open-work, and so on.

National Production

GREAT BRITAIN

IN COMPARISON WITH OTHER COUNTRIES Great Britain was slightly late in beginning to produce picture postcards, but the industry soon grew rapidly. The important study made by Anthony Byatt (1978) on British publishers in this field has shown that there was an impressive concentration of printers and publishers in London, in an area covering about one square mile in the East End from north of St Paul's Cathedral to the Barbican.

Raphael Tuck was the most famous and important British publisher of the 'Modern Style'. He published cards designed, for example, by Evangeline Mary Daniell and by Raphael Kirchner. The 'Modern Style', which anticipated similar movements in Europe, was rooted in the work of the Pre-Raphaelites, and in the style of the artists pioneering the reform of the applied arts after the Great Exhibition of 1851, which led to the Arts and Crafts and Aesthetic movements. In the proto-Art Nouveau movement in England, there are two artists of first rank in the field of graphic art, Walter Crane and Kate Greenaway; they also created postcard designs. In about 1893, Crane designed a series of Christmas cards for M. Ward which were important models for postcards; they were based on a two-dimensional pictorial treatment using light lines on a dark ground. Later series of postcards reproduced by colour lithography graphic work already used by Crane in other types of publications, such as the illustrations from the book *Flora's Feast,* published in 1888.

The fantasy world of Kate Greenaway, which is delicate and charmingly sentimental, found a natural outlet in postcards, especially greetings cards.

In her vast graphic output Jessie Marion King, an exponent of the second generation 'Glasgow School', reinterpreted the stylized linear and geometrical forms of the first generation to create somewhat affected, highly ornate designs which were not, however, devoid of feminine sensitivity.

In his series on female beauties Henry Ryland preferred a more pictorial treatment which skilfully exploited the possibilities of hand-colouring. His work displayed, in a somewhat vague but charming manner, a Pre-Raphaelite approach for neo-Hellenistic subjects associated with the classical form of European Art Nouveau, as in the work of Adolphe Giraldon.

The enormous public success of Kate Greenaway's illustrations justified the special attention paid to her work by imitators such as Millicent Sowerby; as a result, the publisher Misch wanted to use the titles 'Greenaway Girls' or 'In Greenaway Times' for series by Sowerby.

The large number of women illustrators is a typically British phenomenon, and it went on increasing with the emergence of the Art Déco style during the second decade of the century and in the period between the two world wars.

The lithographic poster, which had a long and proven history in Great Britain, found another outlet in the form of picture postcards. In 1903 the publisher Tuck issued the 'Celebrated Posters' series, which contained posters by Cecil Aldin, Dudley Hardy and the Beggarstaff Brothers (William Nicholson and James Pryde).

A particular feature of British (and American) postcards, unlike those of the rest of Europe, is the fact that most of the vast number produced between 1900 and the First World War were in a style that was either quite different from Art Nouveau or simply used some of its features in a very limited way. The same is true of their subject matter; the most popular subjects in postcards produced by the Anglo-Saxon nations are probably caricature and humorous postcards.

Some evidence of the influence of the Modern Style can be seen in Rene Bull's 'Message postcards' (combining an illustration with a simple message) and in the sporting series of Harry Eliott, who, as in his posters, developed his own version or the fluid linear style of international Art Nouveau; it can even be detected in the more personal comic-strip formulae of John Hassal or Philipp May.

A. K. Macdonald and Evangeline Mary Daniell are just two of the outstanding illustrators in Britain who consistently employed stylistic forms close to the spirit of international Art Nouveau, and in particular to French models.

The designs of Ethel Parkinson, which are characterized by their subtle allusion to tradition and their modern style treatment, are internationally recognized as the most delightful of typical idyllic wintry scenes.

Greetings cards designed with exquisite feminine sensibility by designers like Florence Hardy and Margaret Tarrant combine elements of nineteenth-century illustration with a more modern approach to composition.

BELGIUM

At the end of the nineteenth century Belgium was one of the leaders in the production of postcards of high artistic quality that were not reproductions of other forms of graphic art. This reflected the role assumed at the time by Brussels as one of Europe's major artistic centres. The publishing house of Dietrich & Co., in particular, became involved in publishing postcards, in association with well-known Art Nouveau artists and utilizing the great technical achievements of Gossens and De Rycker in colour lithography. With the publication of a poster by Henri Meunier in 1898, the company, which had been engaged until then in publishing posters, produced its first venture into 'Cartes Postales Artistiques', and within two years it published several series signed by Gisbert Combaz, Victor Mignot, Meunier and Hendrick Cassiers, which are justly recognized as classics in the history of Art Nouveau postcards.

Some of these series employed subjects that were to be copied repeatedly; this was true of 'Les Éléments' and 'Proverbes' by Combaz, of the Dutch landscapes and steamboat drawings of the transatlantic liners by Cassiers, and of 'Le Zodiaque' and 'Chic à Paris' by Meunier, which, together with the 'La Mode du Temps' series by Gustave Max Stevens, was, according to Wiener, one of the first series devoted to fashion[38].

A man of many cultural interests and an internationally famous scholar of the art of the Far East, especially Chinese art, Combaz designed three series for Dietrich – in addition to the two mentioned above there was also the 'Pêcheurs' series – which show the profound influence of the Oriental art which he studied on numerous trips. In the

[38] L. Wiener, *op. cit.*, I (1922-23), p. 39.

'Éléments' which borrowed the motifs and bright colours Combaz had already used in sketches for ceramic tiles, the influence of Chinese decorative art is most marked in the compositional design, in which there is a balanced use of figurative and abstract elements, and in which the swirling shapes of the coloured backgrounds are just as important in giving form to the various images as their drawn outlines.

In the 'Pêcheurs' series Chinese influence is filtered through Japanese colour prints and is most noticeable in the cropping of the composition. The unusual subjects of the 'Proverbes' series led Combaz to adopt a more pronounced use of symbolism.

An established illustrator of sports magazines, Victor Mignot was also particularly known for his postcard series 'Les Sports'. Apart from his personal style of draughtsmanship, these designs confirm him as a master of graphic art, with their skilful use of halftones, in finely textured backgrounds alternating with areas of flat colour, to articulate the composition on many planes and to highlight movement by emphasizing effects of depth.

Henri Meunier was particularly involved in designing postcards. He exerted considerable influence internationally, and also probably worked with foreign publishers, some of the series of women's faces for Theo Stroefer's Kunstverlag, in Nuremberg, being attributed to him. Throughout his work, with its great variety and original approach, he constantly fused compositional devices obtained from Japanese prints with a symbolist atmosphere, and this produced an interesting relationship between the figure (often drawn in profile) and the coloured background.

Another prolific designer of postcards was Hendrick Cassiers, who created many series for Dietrich which were reprinted several times by the De Haan Company in Utrecht. Most of his work was inspired by the landscape and costumes of Flanders, in some of his designs his search for atmosphere created impressionistic effects through his mastery of watercolour technique. In others, it produced compositions constructed in straight lines and flat fields of colour, revealing Japanese influence, and for which lithography was the most suitable medium. Both of these aspects of his work exercised a wide influence on postcard art in Belgium: the influence of his watercolours can be seen in postcards of the countryside by F. Coenraets, such as the successful series 'La Meuse de Liège à Dinant', 1899, and by F. Ranot in his 'Belgique pittoresque'. The influence of Cassiers' lithographs is evident in the series 'Types de la Hollande' by Franz Melchers, which, with its picturesque folk realism, seems a long way from the sophisticated, decorative re-working of the 'naif' style used in his famous lithograph 'La Phalène des Iles de la Mer' (1897), which was included in the collection *L'Estampe Moderne*. Evidence of the extensive influence of Cassier's lithographs can also be detected in the vast numbers of postcards produced in Flanders by anonymous Belgian and Dutch designers and by Madeleine Cassiers. It is in various series advertising the 'Red Star Line' shipping company that Cassiers' connection with the Art Nouveau style is most evident. The contrast between two worlds, between an unchanging rural society and a rapidly evolving technological world, was the theme devised by Cassiers for his advertising work. In these postcards, which were sometimes reproductions of *affiches avant la lettre,* or lithographic prints, he often depicted Flemish peasants in typical working dress, standing in the foreground and looking in astonishment at the vessels launched on the sea by modern technology.

Fernand Toussaint's series of ladies of European capitals (all published by Dietrich) show the influence of France. They seem to have started ('seem' is a necessary qualifying term in a field of study where facts have limited reliability) a trend that was internationally successful, a well-known series by Árpád Basch had the same subject.

Around 1900, high-quality Art Nouveau postcards were produced by artists outside the Dietrich 'stable'. In a series of cards for Genval mineral water in that year, the architect Paul Cauchie adapted a type of postcard which was fairly common by then: the photographic scenic view in a decorative Art Nouveau border. Cauchie dispensed with photography, although his graphic technique looked very much like it, and drew landscapes which evoked the faded images of old times, surrounded with floral frames like the carved wooden ones made by Art Nouveau craftsmen. He also made a sketch for a poster, published in the series 'Concours d'Affiches Byrrh', which was remarkable for the elegant calligraphic style of which Mucha and Privat Livemont were masters.

A marginal role in the design of postcards was played by such important Belgian Art Nouveau artists as Henri Van de Velde, Georges Lemmen, Charles Doudelet, Edmond van Offel and Privat Livemont. There is very little information about Van de Velde's contribution, which seems to be limited to the design of postcards with typographical compositions with Art Nouveau borders made to publicize his own work. There are only two known postcards by Georges Lemmen: self-portraits of the artist with his wife Aline, designed in 1893.

Henri Van de Velde and his fiancée Marion Sethe were the recipients of these two greetings cards, which portray family life with a curious symbolist humour[39]. It is, however, possible an artist like Lemmen, who was active in many of the graphic arts, may have made other contributions to postal art.

It seems that Charles Doudelet's production of postcards was limited to reproducing his book and magazine illustrations. Other artists in Belgium, too, used postcards as a means of self-promotion: Louis Titz, for example, used them to make his ex-libris designs known to a wider public, and Armand Rassenfosse issued some engravings as postcards in 1905.

The Flemish artist Edmond van Offel, like Doudelet a leader in the field of book illustration in Belgium, was famous for his series on the seasons. His postcard reproducing the sketch he did for the poster for the 'Byrrh' competition represents his return to the classical themes which were the distinguishing feature of his work. There are very few

39 See *G. Lemmen*, the catalogue of the exhibition edited by F. Aubry, Musée Horta, Brussels 1980, p. 17.

postcards by Privat Livemont. They all have the refined decorative style of his posters, which have often linked his name with Mucha.

The finest Art Nouveau postcards were produced in Belgium between 1898 and 1903, a period so short that authors like Wiener have referred to an early crisis. In effect from about 1905 the Art Nouveau idiom can no longer be traced. That, however, does not justify Wiener's conclusion that Belgium 'après de brillants débuts, [. . .] cessa pendant de longues années de produire autre chose que des cartes médiocres'[40]. Between 1905 and the First World War there was in fact no shortage of postcards of high quality, such as the series by Amédée Lynen entitled 'De-ci de-là, à Bruxelles et en Brabant' (c. 1905) and those designed by the symbolist Fernand Khnopff. Between 1907 and 1914 Alfred Ost was the most prolific illustrator of Belgian postcards. In his series of views of old Flemish cities such as Mechelen, as in the work of Lynen, the influence of Verhaerer's poetry can be felt, with its representation of architecture without any human presence, a metaphor for reality crystallized into a timeless dimension.

FRANCE

Glancing through French catalogues of postcard illustrators, one finds the leading names in this field in Paris at the turn of the century, from Toulouse-Lautrec to Steinlen, from Chéret to Grasset, from Vallotton to de Feure, from Auriol to Rivière, from Denis to Jacques Villon. Very few important names in the Art Nouveau movement are missing. From this it might be assumed that postcards reflected and exhaustively documented the range of personalities involved, the tremendous vitality, and the stylistic variety which characterized the Art Nouveau movement in France. So they did, but in the most literal meaning of the term. They were records only in the sense that they were reproductions of original works of art, but not themselves new creations.

Although France has enjoyed a long and uninterrupted tradition of postcard collecting and developed specialist publications in the form of magazines and catalogues, it is far from easy to find information even about some of the best-known series and the designers who played an important role in the artistic life of Paris. The most recent publications have tended to concentrate on the illustrators active in the capital and to exclude those who worked in other important centres, such as Nancy, where the longest-lived specialist journal was published: *La Revue illustrée de la Carte Postale* (1900-1921).

It would appear also that French postcards, at least the most famous ones and those most closely linked with the Art Nouveau style, generally reproduced designs intended for other purposes (from posters to book and magazine illustrations) rather than those specifically conceived as postcards. It should also be stressed that, with a few exceptions (and these are controversial), the leading artists of the Art Nouveau style do not seem to have created original postcard designs but rather to have used the medium to publicize their own work. The

40 L. Wiener, *op. cit.*, II (1923-24), p. 16.

only postcards known to be by Grasset (four in all) reproduce his posters; those by de Feure reproduce a cover he did for the magazine *Cocorico* and a detail of a lithograph he made for the collection *L'Estampe Moderne*; those by Rivière reproduce his plates in the album *La Marche à L'Etoile*; those by Berthon reproduce his 'decorative panels'; those by Chéret reproduce his posters and lithographs. The lack of documentation makes it difficult to establish whether most of Steinlen's postcards were original designs, as some experts claim, or reproductions of song scores and of some of the several hundred illustrations he did for *Gil Blas illustré*, *L'Assiette au Beurre* and many other magazines. The world he explored in his magazine illustrations also appeared in his best postcards and is clearly described by Anatole France in the preface to a catalogue prepared for an exhibition of the artist's work in 1904: 'A subtle, lively, acute sensibility, an infallible visual memory and a rapid technique destined Steinlen to become a draughtsman and painter of daily life, an artist of the streets. The bright early morning and dark evening rush of the workers, the groups of people sitting at pavement tables, the tramps on the dark boulevards, the streets, the public squares, the distant suburbs with bare skeletal trees, the empty fields—he knows about all these things. Their life is his life, their joy his joy, their sadness his. He has suffered, and laughed with the people passing by. He has received the spirit of the excited or the festive crowd. He has felt its impressive simplicity and grandeur. And for this reason Steinlen's work is epic'[41].

This epic story of city life, which reflected a commited involvement with urban working folk and the underprivileged, was absent in the work of another artist of the boulevards, who, like Steinlen was active from the end of the nineteenth century and produced both reproductions of album illustrations and original postcard designs: Henri Boutet. His boulevards were not inhabited by the proletarian masses, but were the setting for flirtatious adventures, the domain of the 'parisienne', whom he represented more intimately in other postcards, undressing her, covering her in provocative garments, catching her in the intricate ritual of her toilet. Steinlen and Boutet were not the only French artists who, from the end of the last century, became involved with postcards and produced original designs for them. Around 1900, significant contributions to Art Nouveau postcards came from Ernest Louis Lessieux, Jack Abeillé, Léon Cauvy, and Joseph Kuhn-Regnier. Lessieux's varied work explored subjects ranging from pagan mythology to melodrama, and from nineteenth-century historical novels to Parisian night life, and is distinguished by its elegant composition, which sometimes takes on an Oriental kind of richness derived mainly from the combination of figurative and decorative elements. Haziness of line, following the example of Chéret, is the hallmark of Abeillé's postcards, which take Parisian life as their subject. Cauvy and Kuhn-Regnier were particularly known for work which elegantly reinterpreted the recurring compositional features of German greetings cards.

All these designers were more popular with German than with French publishers. This is very revealing if one considers that these

41 cit. in M. Osterwalder, *Dictionnaire des illustrateurs 1800-1914 (Illustrateurs, caricaturistes et affichistes)*, Paris 1983, pp. 1014-1015.

illustrators were particularly interested in the compositional design of postcards—that is, the organization of the image to meet the need to provide a space for the message. It was precisely this aspect which French publishers were least concerned with; they seemed to be more interested in producing postcards which were prints or posters in miniature. Even series of postcards with specially commissioned designs showed a lack of concern for a unified composition incorporating the illustration content and the area for the written message: the message was usually put in a left-over space, or clearly separated from the design.

Market forces evidently had an influence on the publishers. The public for postcards, which around 1900 had still not grown to mass proportions but consisted mainly of collectors, was more interested in the novelties that had become institutionalized and wrapped in an aura of artiness in the process of critical battering, in images already being exploited in other forms of mass communication, and in the artist's signature. Safety in accepted fashion was preferred to risky experimentation according to the viewpoint that considered the postcard to be a sort of substitute for those who could not afford to collect works of art or posters.

The numerous postcard series devoted to posters published in France, beginning with the famous 'Cinos' of 1898, is symptomatic of this attitude. It clearly reflected the immense growth in poster collecting in France and the critical discussions about poster art in widely circulating specialist magazines. Posters guaranteed several things: famous signatures, a high-quality product and a well-known pictorial image. They were also very popular with the public, which flocked to see them in exhibitions, and with the firms and industries advertised in them, which could combine costly advertising on street hoardings with another form of publicity that was less expensive. So there were not only publishers printing posters as postcards, but also companies and printers reproducing their own advertisements as postcards. Most publicity postcards were therefore reproductions of these larger posters, sometimes slightly adapted to allow for the reduction in size (this can be seen on some cards by Cappiello). Postcards are therefore exceptionally valuable research material in the history of posters, especially when they reproduce the ones which remained at the sketch stage. Of particular interest, for example, are those in the series 'Concours d'affiches Byrrh', which collected the 113 entries in the 1906 competition, won jointly by the Spaniard Juan Cardona and Clementine Hélène Dufau[42]. Among the competitors there were several other foreigners, including the Belgians van Offel and Cauchie, the Italian Kienerk, the Bohemian Spillar, the Spaniard Gosé, and the Swiss Carlègle. Other artists who took part, such as Maurice Denis, Adolphe Giraldon and Félix Vallotton, made a limited contribution to this branch of graphic art. In the wide range of work represented by this series, there are clear signs of the crisis which affected poster art in France from about 1905. Poster design became stranded in a mannerism which had its models in the work of Toulouse-

42 All of the postcards in this series are published in A. and F. Baudet, *Encyclopédie Internationale de la carte postale*, vol. 1, Paris 1978, pp. 290-303.

Lautrec, Chéret and Mucha, and which, in spite of its high quality, was incapable of producing the 'surprise effects' and 'talking images' which Cappiello, with his deep understanding of the mechanisms which could catch the distracted attention of city dwellers, was already suggesting. An awareness of the importance of the shock-image could easily have been grasped, without Cappiello, from the example of Toulouse-Lautrec, but it was submerged beneath the notion of the poster as a decorative print. There are few exceptions to this general trend; outstanding among these is the sketch by Kienerk which cleverly reinterpreted the ideas of the Beggarstaff Brothers. The poster was certainly most popular with collectors, but there are also series of postcards in which a high percentage reproduced original designs: the five series of 'Les Maîtres de la Carte Postale', published from 1898 by *La Critique*, using work by artists like Hans Christiansen, Koloman Moser, Jossot, W. H. Bradley, the Swiss Vibert (who designed twelve woodcuts), Léon Lebèque and Lyongrün; the 'Cartes de l'I.P.C.C.' (International Poste Carte Club), published by the essayist, writer and art critic Emile Strauss, who in 1898 founded the magazine *La Carte Postale illustrée*, which aimed at improving French 'artistic postcards' to compete with foreign production; finally the 'Collection des Cent', printed from November 1901 by the publisher Gréningaire. It is uncertain whether this title was adopted because the series was based on the works shown in the 'Salon des Cent', organized by the magazine *La Plume*, or because the publisher intended to make a collection of designs by the hundred most important French artists of the beginning of the twentieth century[43].

Later series which had designs especially executed for them are 'Gala Henri-Monnier' and 'Album Mariani'. The first, published in 1904 for the Gala at the 'Casino de Paris' in honour of the writer, caricaturist, man of the theatre and inventor Joseph Prudhomme, is of particular interest for the contribution of the painter Jacques Villon, who designed seven of the fifty postcards. The second series published around 1910, in spite of the inclusion of such prestigious names as Cappiello, Chéret, Faivre, Giraldon, Girardot, Hermann-Paul, Léandre, A. Lepère, Mars, Mucha, Rochegrosse, Sem, Steinlen and Truchet, contains routine designs and sketches of limited merit.

From the beginning of the twentieth century postcards began to be bought in large numbers, and the number of artists working in the field increased, producing series with original subjects; Gaston Noury and Léopold Lelée were among the most productive. Humorous and caricature postcards, which had a long tradition in France behind them, were greatly in demand. Some humorists, like Albert Guillaume, Charles Léandre, Jean-Baptiste Roubille and Sem, reproduced the illustrations from albums and magazines which had made them famous; others created original designs. Among these, Xavier Sager, the creator of series such as those which satirize women's fashions and hats and which had a whole band of imitators (including Charles Naillod, Roberty, G. Mouton, Robé and Vindier), is outstanding for his invention and variety.

43 The most complete iconographic documentation to date on this series is in A. and F. Braudet, *op. cit.*, pp. 278-289.

The large number of artists involved in postcard design is a characteristic of the French output. The main reason for this was that they regarded it as a means of spreading a style and educating taste. Intellectuals and militant critics like Gustave Kahn, Roger Marx and Frantz Jourdain had insisted on the need to educate the general public if a new art and an art-loving society were to be created. Their ideas were behind groups which favoured 'education for the masses', like 'L'Art pour Tous', founded in Paris in 1901 by the critic Louis Lumet and the mechanical engineer Edouard Massieux. The missionary zeal of this group and of other socialist cultural groups intensified the thrust of 'aesthetic propaganda' through the use of mass communications[44].

Artists who supported such a programme of action, and who regularly opened their studios to visits organized by 'L'Art pour Tous', following a practice begun by Eugène Carrière, Chéret and Steinlen, saw the postcard as a means of promoting 'aesthetic propaganda'. For the most committed, it was also an instrument of political propaganda, with which illustrators like Steinlen, Hermann-Paul, Ibels, Roubille, Vallotton, Kupka and, most biting of all in his work, the anarchist Jossot could launch their criticisms against bourgeois society, and against institutions like the army, the church and the family.

Paradoxically, in spite of their propaganda purpose, the political series were not usually printed in large numbers but in limited editions, often not exceeding 100 copies, and were printed as etchings on fine quality paper, like those of Orens, Leal de Camara and Mille. Circulating them among a small circle of collectors was probably a way of avoiding censorship.

Political postcards were produced in large numbers from the outbreak of the First World War. General mobilization was supported by illustrators like Steinlen, Willette, Ibels, Faivre, Poulbot, Léandre, and the Alsatian Hansi, who was famous for his patriotic allegories featuring children, and his mordant satires on the 'Boches'.

AUSTRIA AND THE HABSBURG EMPIRE
(Hungary, Bohemia and Moravia)

Austria was not only the first country to issue postcards. The Art Nouveau postcards produced in that country, and indeed in the whole of the Habsburg empire, were of particularly high quality and quantity.

Important publishers like M. Munk, Philipp & Kramer, E. Storch, Gerlach & Schenk and Brüder Köhn were active in Vienna. These publishers had at their disposal colour lithography printers of such high quality that they often printed series of postcards in the medium for foreign markets, particularly the British and French. The most important artistic movements and centres for the production of applied art in the history of Art Nouveau in Austria—the Secession, the Hagenbund and the Weiner Werkstätte skilfully used the picture postcard as an important method of promoting and disseminating their work. The major artists of the Secession, among them Koloman

44 L. Lumet, *L'Art pour Tous*, Paris 1904.

Moser, Josef Hoffmann and Joseph Maria Olbrich, all designed interesting postcards. Paintings by Gustav Klimt were also produced in postcard form.

The involvement of Moser in this particular branch of graphic art still appears to be little known and studied, yet it is of primary importance in tracing the stylistic development of an artist who was one of the major figures in international Art Nouveau. While the postcards in the 'Ver Sacrum' series are always included in all the monographs devoted to his work, those that preceded them, designed for not only Austrian but also German publishers, are systematically excluded. The evolution of a style that was essentially graphic invaded all fields of Viennese artistic life, including architecture, as in the work of Otto Wagner, J. M. Olbrich and Josef Hoffmann. Historically, therefore, it is particularly important to note that, in their formative periods, the most important figures in Viennese *fin de siècle* art were always interested in undertaking graphic work together. The well-known collaboration between Hoffmann and Moser, who designed writing paper, magazine covers, illustrations and postcards together, should be seen in the broader context of the 'Siebener Club', established in about 1895 within the ambit of the 'Blauen Freihaus' and the Café Sperl by 'Kolo' Moser, Josef Hoffmann, Leo Kainradl, Adolf Karpellus, Friederich Pilz, Joseph M. Olbrich and Maxmilian Kurzweil. They formed the club because they wanted to design together, and they found the postcard an appropriate means to that end. At first they used postcards designed by themselves in single copies for correspondence between themselves and their friends. Some are dated 1895.

The first five in the famous 'Künstler-Postkarten' series (each with 10 postcards) published by Philipp & Kramer, which together formed a series called by the same publisher 'Artists' Correspondence', were by members of the 'Siebener Club'. They can be dated c. 1896-97; some are not signed, while others bear the mark of the group (C7) or the double monograms of pairs of members (Hoffmann-Moser, Hoffmann-Kainradl, Moser-Kainradl, Moser-Olbrich, Kainradl-Konopa, etc), or even of three members of the club.

The 'Siebener Club' lost its importance after the foundation of the Secession. Even the 'Ver Sacrum' series (comprising twelve postcards), which was issued to promote the magazine of the new group of artists on the occasion of their first exhibition (26 March-15 June 1898), was the result of deliberately combining, within each individual postcard, designs by different artists (Moser-Hoffmann, Moser-Olbrich, Hoffmann-Moser-Roller, etc), most of whom had already appeared in the first numbers of the magazine or in the catalogue of the exhibition.

For the Paris 'Exposition Universelle' in 1900, Philipp & Kramer organized a special publicity campaign. On the front of some of their artistic postcards they published a list of the first 52 series, and on the back, inserted into the design, they printed an order form for the dispatch of free samples. The thirty-third series, entitled 'The New Style', was a compendium of decorative motifs by the architect

Hoffmann. Apart from the members of the 'Siebener Club', there were several interesting artists, among them Maximilian Lenz, Walter Hampel and Raphael Kirchner, who stood out in the first 52 series (about 100 were issued by Philipp & Kramer). Hampel's versatile individuality as a painter enabled him both to revive echoes of the academic style, and to adopt the devices and subjects of Jugendstil without losing fluidity of line, in his series on women cyclists, beach scenes and carnival scenes.

Kirchner's series for Philipp & Kramer, datable to 1898-99, was one of his first attempts in this field. Almost twenty years later, just before his death, he would execute a large number of designs that would make a brilliant contribution to Art Nouveau postcards. He found the most congenial means of expression for his interests and gifts in the field of graphics, in decorative plates, menus, advertisements and particularly postcards. His gift for steering a middle course between the styles of the Viennese Secession, the Munich Jugendstil, and the Parisian Style Moderne; his combination of fantasy subjects and a realistic figurative style; his skilful adaptation of Art Nouveau compositional devices (asymmetry, the dynamic relationships between full and empty fields, and so on to the postcard format; and his coherent exploitation of Secessionist graphic stylization to invent a female type which would become fashionable—all of these factors help to explain the enormous and widespread success of his work, to the extent that it was the first case in history (or at least a simultaneous case to that of Mucha) of the postcard suggesting and creating fashion. It was a fashion to which Paul Eluard paid tribute: 'Et plus idéalisées encore, toutes les femmes de Raphaël Kirchner, les sylphides nacrées, à la lèvre supérieure gonflée, aux yeux grands comme des arc-en-ciel, à la chevelure de liserons, à la taille de guêpe, aux charmes naïfs et pervers'.

We have already discussed the postcard series issued for the first exhibition of the Secession; postcards were often used to advertise various kinds of official exhibitions held in Vienna. The series designed by Hoffmann and published by Philipp & Kramer for the 'Ausstellung' in 1898, which celebrated the Jubilee of Franz Joseph, is only one of the first examples in a long succession which continued until the First World War. In these we find artists like Hoffmann or Olbrich in the forefront, with their young students, and followers of the 'new style', such as Josef Divéky, Remigius Geyling, Hans Kalsteiner, Erwin Puchinger, Kurt Libesny, F. Krenn, Berta Fallrock, Liane Fischer, Sophie Hönig and Mitzi Marbach.

It was certainly no accident that the first four numbers of the long series produced by the Wiener Werkstätte showed views of the 'Kunstschau' of 1908 designed by Emil Hoppe, a student of Hoffmann, in a synthetic stylized manner containing bold areas of flat colour. The 'Kunstschau', the great exhibition organized for the emperor's Jubilee by the group of artists around Klimt who had dissociated themselves from the Secession in 1905, was a showcase above all for the art of Hoffmann and gave ample space to the applied graphic art. In the 'Plakat-Kunst' room, with works selected by Berthold Löffler, was a collection of posters designed by students of the Kunstgewerbeschule and the association of the Wiener Werkstätte, who later designed numerous postcards for the series produced by the 'Viennese laboratory', they included Franz Karl Delavilla, Urban Janke, Moriz Jung, Rudolf Kalvach, Wenzel Oswald and Fritz Zeymer.

The first postcards published by the Wiener Werkstätte preceded the numbered series and were made for particular occasions. Carl Otto Czeschka designed one to send to clients for the New Year in 1906, and Bertold Löffler created another for the 1907 Christmas exhibition at the Wiener Werkstätte shop, opened shortly before at 25 Graben. The numbered series began to be published in 1908; the Künstlerpostkarten were seen both as a new product for sale in the field of graphic art and as a new means of establishing contact between the artist in the workshop and the public. Between 1908 and the First World War about one thousand postcards were printed (the total varies between 200 and 7000 in Traude Hansen's study of 1982), bearing numbers and the mark of the Wiener Werkstätte, which was printed in several forms. They were often but not always signed, and the design was rarely dated. Like most of its products, the postcards produced by the Wiener Werkstätte had an artistic quality that distinguished them totally from most postcards in mass circulation. Graphic designers from different parts of the empire were engaged in creating them—Hungarians (J. Divéky and M. Pranke), Bohemians (M. Alber, U. Janke, B. Löffler, O. Wenzel and R. Teschner) Moravians (M. Jung and K. Schwetz), also Poles (O. Lendecke), Germans (H. Jesser and L. H. Jungnickel) and Russians (E. Makowska-Luksch). The postcards designed by these artists for the Wiener Werkstätte are reproduced in the illustration section for their own country later in this book, unless they deal with specifically Viennese subjects.

Artists trained at the Kunstgewerbeschule, particularly in courses given by Czeschka and, after his departure for Hamburg in 1907, Löffler, were entrusted with the design of the postcard series sold in the organization's many shops. Artists particularly involved with this type of product at the Wiener Werkstätte included Mela Koehler-Broman (about 150 postcards) and Maria Likarz-Strauss (about 80 postcards), the first a pupil of Moser, the second of Hoffmann.

The 1,000 or so postcards in the series designed by 48 artists covering three generations, show all the stylistic tendencies of the Wiener Werkstätte, including constructivist and, geometric tendency (Hoppe, the student of Hoffmann; Kalhammer, the student of Moser) the expressionist tendency (Kokoschka, Schiele, Jung and Kalvach), and the tendency that displayed a playful and non-logical construction of forms rich in fantasy and surreal elements (Peche, Divéky, Wimmer, Lendecke and Likarz). The second phase of their production, from about 1910, is characterized by the dominating presence of women artists like Likarz and Koehler alongside guiding lights who have generally been seen to mark a turning-point in the work produced by the Wiener Werkstätte, like Peche, Wimmer and Lendecke at a time when fashion came to the fore as an important subject. These artists were also in the forefront of the revival of the Biedermeier style.

The subject matter of Wiener Werkstätte postcards was varied. A complex programme of collaboration between the applied and graphic arts was involved in the activities at the 'Fledermaus',—the cabaret opened in 1907 by the Wiener Werkstätte as a culture and leisure centre following Hoffmann's idea and plan—and in it postcards by Löffler, Divéky, Hoffmann, Zeymer, and Jung played a part. Also known because of the 'Fledermaus' are two projects for postcards by Emanuel Margold. As well as the work connected with the 'Fledermaus', there are also postcard reproductions of Löffler's frescoes in the Volkskeller in Salzburg, rebuilt by Hoffmann. Another group which can be distinguished is the series of postcards designed for the emperor's 1908 Jubilee by Löffler, Divéky and Geyling who also participated in planning the settings for the festivities.

Postcards were used as a support for other activities of the Wiener Werkstätte. For example when, at the beginning of 1908, the organization made an agreement with the Deutsche Werkstätten fur Handwerkskunst for the sale of its products in Germany, it began to print postcards with views of German cities, and when, in 1909, it opened a branch in Karlsbad, it reproduced some lithographic views of the city as postcards.

Postcard views, which began in 1908 with a number of designs by Emil Hoppe, included both countryside scenes (C. Krenek) and city views of Vienna (E. Hoppe, U. Janke, G. Kalhammer, K. Schwetz, R. Schmal, J. Divéky and C. Krenek), Berlin (F. Kuhn and G. Kalhammer), Budapest, (F. Kuhn), Prague (J. Divéky), and other places (J. Sika, L. Drexler, A. Leupold and K. Schwetz). Stylistically these vary from strongly stylized architectonic forms (Hoppe) to those more inclined toward the picturesque (Schwetz).

Fashion in all its aspects, from the design of fashion plates, to that of fabrics and accessories, was one of the favourite activities at the Wiener Werkstätte. It managed to set the style until the late 1920s, even outside Vienna and Austria, by exploiting, among other things, the circulation of magazines like *Die Damenwelt*, *Wiener Mode* and *Die Dame*. Postcards were an efficient method of advertising products and forming taste in this area. Eduard Josef Wimmer, the director of the fashion department at the Wiener Werkstätte from 1912 to 1922, designed several postcards in which the slender female figure stands in isolation and is rendered with a feeling for the transparent effects of watercolour. More highly stylized, and forming a bridge between Jugendstil and Art Déco, are those rare but important postcards designed by Otto Lendecke. Maria Likarz-Strauss, who collaborated with the Wiener Werkstätte in many areas of applied and graphic arts, produced compositions and stylizations of particular force and effectiveness, based at times on a skilful popular adaptation of Klimt's style. Mela Koehler-Broman designed not only many fashion postcards but also invitation cards and advertising brochures in a more mannered decorative language than Likarz, but they all had her graceful, personal style. Remigius Geyling and Urban Janke reinterpreted the

Biedermeier fashion, but the most intelligent and balanced exponent of the Biedermeier and Rococo revival was Fritzi Löw, a student of Hoffmann and Strnad. Other fashion postcards were designed by J. Divéky, E. Schmal, F. Berger and S. Singer.

Humour and caricature in Wiener Werkstätte postcards ranged from jokes to satire, from a desire simply to amuse to moral criticism. Moriz Jung's images are outstanding in their rich intellectual and cultural references. Those of Rudolf Kalvach are more original in their expressionist touches, and those of Ludwig Heinrich Jungnickel display acute observations of Viennese life.

Greetings cards formed a significant proportion of the Wiener Werkstätte production. They are designed by many artists: J. Hoffmann, R. Kalvach, O. Kokoschka (showing the transition from his two-dimensional secessionist style to proto-expressionism), J. Divéky (abstract shapes, geometric patterns and colour contrasts), U. Janke, F. K. Delavilla (two-dimensional decorative compositions), W. Oswald, A. Velim, O. Beran, V. Petter, C. Krenek, M. Jung, C. O. Czeschka, K. Koehler, M. Likarz, A. Nechansky (who worked only in this genre), F. Kuhn, S. Singer, J. Sika and F. Löw.

Artists engaged in designing decorative postcards included with their stylized floral themes; G. Marisch, with strong, geometric floral designs; F. Lebisch, the landscape gardener and pupil of Hoffmann; M. Otten, A. Speyer and O. Kokoschka.

The Wiener Werkstätte postcards also included reproductions of drawings by Egon Schiele and of lithographs by Oska Kokoschka, two designs with harlequins by Dagobert Peche, illustrations of Russian proverbs by Elena Makowska-Luksch, and, finally, imaginary visions of the fairy-tale world of childhood by Richard Teschner, Hans Kalmsteiner, Mela Koehler and Carl Krenek.

A means of publicizing the work of the Viennese workshop, postcards also played a mediating role between the various branches of the applied and graphic arts. So, in addition to its better-known series, the Wiener Werkstätte printed a series which reproduced its own collection of fabrics designed by J. Hoffmann, C. O. Czeschka, M. Alber, L. Fochler, A. Popischil, E. Wimmer, M. Riedl, E. Häusler and W. Jonasch.

Not all of the many postcard artists working in Austria are mentioned in this account. The ones listed are certainly the most famous, and the series of postcards published by Philipp & Kramer and the Wiener Werkstätte were important in helping to group and compare their work. To illustrate the tremendous range of this work, it is sufficient to mention Gottlieb Theodor Kempf, a longtime contributor to the Munich magazine *Meggendorfer Blätter* who skilfully steered a middle course between nineteenth-century illustrative styles, and the symbolist and Secessionist idiom, or Alice Wanke, an interesting artist and successful popularizer of Secessionism.

As Leopold Wiener showed in 1923, Hungary had often pioneered printing techniques which were commercially exploited elsewhere. The country's output of postcards too was also notable and was part of the larger, fascinating outburst of symbolist and Art Nouveau applied graphic art in this part of the Habsburg empire. In recent years this has justifiably received more careful critical reappraisal, which has revealed such interesting figures as Lajos Kozma, Sándor Nagy and Attila Sassy. Unfortunately it is not yet known if these artists were active as postcard designers.

In Hungary the dominant influence of the Viennese Secession is obvious, but at the same time there were strong aspirations for the assertion of an independent, national culture, even in postcards. Here versions of the two-dimensional and geometrical style deriving from the Secession are submerged in reinterpretations of themes and decoration in the popular local tradition.

The postcards of Árpád Basch, who trained in Budapest, Munich and Paris, show his desire to steer a middle course between nineteenth-century illustration and Parisian prototypes (possibly via Mucha), while the obvious influence of Raphael Kirchner does not inhibit Károly Józsa's fresh and joyous inventiveness. The work of Basch and Józa is the best known; it made an impression in the specialist press, and in time their cards were circulated internationally. It is probable, however, that there were other interesting artists active in this field of design in Hungary.

Traditional local forms of decoration often receive original treatment in Hungary's vast output of decorative and greetings cards, which are often of a high level in terms of technique and design, although usually anonymous. This decorative element is perhaps less evident in the work of the most important artists, such as those mentioned here.

The versatile personality of József Divéky, who was, among other things, a fine engraver, appeared most clearly in his postcards for the Wiener Werkstätte, but it was also expressed, though in a more mannered way, in the propaganda postcards he produced during the First World War.

Within the general framework of European artistic production, two other parts of the Habsburg empire, Bohemia and Moravia, seem to be particularly rich and noteworthy, both in quality and quantity and at all levels of activity from the graphic arts to architecture. In these areas, however, there is an unfortunate shortage of studies on the history of postcards. It seems unlikely that artists involved in different areas of the graphic arts, like Victor Preissig, did not concern themselves with postal art. Several cultural and formal tendencies can be identified in Bohemian and Moravian graphics: symbolism overlain with elements of the Slav tradition, a revival of popular local traditions, a tendency towards a two-dimensional style clearly influenced by contact with Vienna, and a tendency to develop compositional and figurative forms derived from the culture of Paris.

These diverse components are fused in the outstanding, unique work of Alphonse Mucha, and they were, at least in part, the reason for his success. The elements of symbolism and exotic oriental mystery which he brought to his graphic work, both in the figures and decorative elements, and the sensuality with which he imbued his female figures, of flesh and blood but also idealized in elegant two-dimensional outline and delicate, refined colours, exercised a particular attraction for his contemporaries.

In Paris the 'Mucha style' was synonymous with 'modern', the iris was called a 'fleur Mucha', and Paul Morand defined Art Nouveau as 'style nouille' (vermicelli style), with the work of the Moravian artist in mind. His 'decorative panels', which were large lithographic prints intended to be framed, strongly stamped the Mucha style on all forms of graphic art from posters to postcards. The publisher Champenois exploited the success of Mucha's theatre posters and decorative panels and printed postcards reproducing variations of the same works.

Most of Mucha's vast output of postcards reproduced designs by the artist already used for other purposes. But their reduction to postcard size was carefully and skilfully executed. The image was almost always placed asymmetrically on the rectangle, and the high quality of the colour lithography gave the cards a special quality as miniatures or cameos. This compositional arrangement, first seen in the French 'Cinos' series, was common in Mucha's work and in later series.

Those postcards by Frantisek Kupka so far identified are either political or reproductions of illustrations (such as the cover designed for the magazine *Cocorico*). We do not know whether he also used postcards to express the visionary symbolism, wrapped in abstract geometric forms, which characterized his artistic experiments.

Large numbers of high-quality postcards produced by the Wiener Werkstätte were the work of Bohemian and Moravian artists. The Bohemian artist Berthold Löffler marked the transition in Viennese culture between the religious element in classical mythology and folklore, between bucolic serenity and a taste for decoration, which anticipated aspects of French Art Déco.

For the Wiener Werkstätte the Bohemian Urban Janke and the Moravian Karl Schwetz designed views of Vienna, Karlsbad and smaller cities, and landscapes. Each artist used his own stylistic language – Janke a more colourful, plastic style, Schwetz a more linear and graphic idiom – to explore the possibilities of the two-dimensional designs already created by Hoppe and Hoffmann.

The Moravian Moriz Jung was another outstanding figure. In form, he followed the dominant two-dimensional style of Viennese art, but gave it expressionistic touches; in subject matter, he revealed, in his versatile vein of caricature and satire, aspects of his Moravian culture which joyfully emerged through contact with the more intellectual humour of Viennese satire.

The postcards of another Bohemian artist, Richard Teschner, represented the fairy-tale world of children.

GERMANY

In Germany there was a vast output of picture postcards using both photographs and artists' illustrations. There was a boom in the industry at the turn of the century in both Germany and Great Britain. German publishers usually worked also in other branches of graphic art or book illustration, but there were some specialist publishers, like Stengel & Co. in Dresden and Berlin, who had offices in Great Britain and the United States. The development of the picture postcard was related to lithographic printing. Around 1900 there were some 33,000 people, mainly women, employed in this field. German cities like Berlin, Dresden, Leipzig, Frankfurt, Nuremberg, Stuttgart and Munich were all centres of the printing industry.

It is difficult to establish a date for the first 'artistic postcards' in Germany, but a significant event was the appearance (probably in about 1893-94) of Hans Christiansen's poster for a series of postcard views of Hamburg designed by him[45]. Certainly there were several experiments in this field in the last five years of the century. In Germany the history of postcards is bound up with that of posters and illustrations, and Munich appears to have been a centre of major importance.

In 1892 Franz von Stuck, with Trübner and Uhde, had founded the Munich 'Secession' movement. The name was suggested by Georg Hirth, who started publishing *Jugend* four years later. In the history of Art Nouveau this magazine has always been considered the best guide to Jugendstil graphic art, but it was actually preceded by other similar magazines, which also upheld the importance of the relationship between text and image. Among these were *Die Lustigen Blätter*, published in Berlin, and, even more important, the *Meggendorfer Blätter*, a humorous weekly founded by L. Meggendorfer in 1898 and published by J. F. Schreiber in Munich. Printed on fine paper and with better-quality colour lithographic printing than *Jugend*, the *Meggendorfer Blätter* was illustrated by important designers like Mathilde Ade, Eugen Nanz, the Austrians Gottlieb T. Kempf, Koloman Moser (at times in collaboration with Josef Hoffmann), Mila von Lüttich and Julius Klinger, and the Moravian Ferdinand Staeger. In about 1897-8 Schreiber began to print, using colour lithography or collotype, postcards of the magazine's illustrations in the series 'Künstler-Postkarten der Meggendorfer Blätter'. Among them interesting examples appeared of early work by Moser or by Klinger, an Austrian by birth and training, who in the first decade of the century was to become one of the leading artists in the revival of poster art and applied graphic art in Germany, and in the transition from Jugendstil to German Art Déco.

In January 1896 Hirth, a leading light in Munich cultural life and a tireless promoter of many events, founded *Jugend. Münchner illustrierte Wochenschrift für Kunst und Leben*. The subjects covered ranged from art to fashion, from sport to politics and from music to literature. The high quality of its articles and illustrations, the variety of its ideas and stylistic tendencies, and its versatility, which made the magazine a cross between an art journal and a mass-circulation newspaper, brought it great success with the public, which also approved of its low price. An important feature of the magazine was

45 See *Das Frühe Plakat in Europa und den USA, Band 3: Deutschland, Teil I*, Berlin 1980 p. 42.

the relationship between text and illustration content; the latter ranged from borders to vignettes and full-page plates, and from black and white decorative motifs to full colour lithographic prints. A cover competition held in 1896 revealed typical *Jugend* subjects: 'spring, love, childhood, engagement, maternity, games, pageant, sport, beauty, poetry, music and so on'. The magazine sold the original designs which had been used in the publication, and they were sometimes exhibited in German galleries.

Art prints from *Jugend*, mounted on card, were also offered for sale to readers at very low prices. In his introduction to the 1909 catalogue, *Dreitausend Kunstblätter der Münchner 'Jugend'*, Hirth wrote that by that date two hundred million copies had been bought; this figure gives an idea of the impression *Jugend* made on German taste. But as well as plates which could be framed, Hirth chose another means of spreading the graphic message of the magazine: this was the series of 'Künstler-Postkarten' which reproduced the illustrations and covers of the magazine. The first two series, each of 25 cards, were advertised in number 27 of the magazine on 2 July 1898. Two numbers later an advertisement appeared for the first series of '*Jugend* Reisenpostkarten', with reproduced designs which had already appeared in the magazine by C. A. Bermann, Fidus, F. Hegenbart, A. Jank and O. Kraszenka. Among the artists represented in the first series of 'Kunstler-Postkarten' were Josef Rudolf Witzel, stylistically of great interest for his delightful inventions combining dynamic two-dimensional composition with linear elegance; Ferdinand von Riznicek, with his versatility and facility for conveying aspects of daily life and fashion; Hugo Höppener, known as Fidus, whose work combined abstract and natural forms, and who later reproduced larger graphic works (such as lithographs) as postcards; Robert Engels, who was inclined towards symbolism (with Pre-Raphaelite echoes) in his interpretations of legends and fables; Fritz Erler, who combined symbolism, classical tradition and Germanic culture; Reinhold Max Eichler, the designer of landscapes and genre scenes; Ludwig von Zumbusch, distinguished by his unrestrained and powerful surrealist irony; Ludwig Hohlwein, who was later a leading poster artist during the transition from Jugendstil to Art Déco. There were also Julius Diez, Angelo Jank, Albert Weisgerber and many others.

Still in Munich, and in the same year that *Jugend* was first published, Albert Langen started *Simplicissimus*, a magazine which satirized daily life and politics. He too exploited the success of its illustrations as a sideline to the magazine. He published a large album containing an anthology of illustrations by some of the artists who had worked for the magazine, like Reznicek and Dudovich, and, following the example of *Jugend*, a series of postcards. In this series there were further designs by Reznicek and Dudovich, and by Thomas Theodor Heine (especially his postcards satirizing the politics of the First World War), Brynolf Wennerberg (war propaganda) and others.

The example set by Munich publishers was followed somewhat later in Berlin. The magazine *Die Lustigen Blätter*, founded in 1886, also reproduced illustrations from its pages as series of postcards (c. 1910-14), with designs by Ernst Heilemann, Brynolf Wennerberg and Heinrich Zille. They were mostly scenes from daily life, the subjects and style of which were influenced by Jugendstil.

It is significant that it was in *Pan*, Germany's most prestigious and refined magazine, that one of the first pieces of criticism concerned with postcards appeared in 1898 under the name of Max Lehrs. But it was in Leipzig in May 1898 that possibly the first exhibition of picture postcards was held, to be followed later by many others.

Even though they reproduced magazine illustrations, the postcards of *Meggendorfer Blätter*, *Jugend*, *Simplicissimus* and *Die Lustigen Blätter* are interesting for their varied design and colour and the compositional relationship between the illustration and background, which looked ahead to the space left for the message.

Apart from its involvement with all these magazines, the history of Judendstil postcards is also directly linked to the geographical distribution of the various artists' groups and artistic associations throughout Germany, as well as to the existence of schools of applied arts (and graphic art) throughout the various German states, in Berlin, Munich, Darmstadt, Hamburg, Düsseldorf, Karlsruhe, and so on. For example, in 1897, the Druckerei in Dresden promoted a competition between the students of the local academy to mark the Dresden International Exhibition. The first prize was won by H. J. Hartmann, the second and third by J. V. Cissarz.

One of the first artistic associations to become involved in postcards was the 'Steglitzer Werkstatt für künstlerische Drucksachen' in Berlin, organized by George Belwe, Fritz Helmut Ehmcke and Friedrich Wilhelm Kleukens with the idea of promoting graphic arts. Later, Peter Behrens and Otto Eckmann also worked with the Steglitzer Werkstatt. Around 1900 it published lithographic postcards, greetings cards and publicity material.

Postcards played an important part in the history of the Darmstadt 'Künstlerkolonie', which was without question the most important centre of communication and collaboration between the leading *fin de siécle* artists in Europe. Hans Christiansen, who had already made postcards, designed his famous 'Darmstadt' and 'Paris' series, which reveal his experiments with two-dimensional forms and arabesque line for his highly stylized figures. They in part reflected the 'style', derived from French poster art, which his friend Justus Brinckmann, the director of the Museum of Applied Arts in Hamburg, an admirer of Japanese art, defined as 'Tentakularstil' in the middle of the 1890s. Paul Bürck, Paul Hanstein and later Kleukens also designed postcards during their period at the Künstlerkolonie in Darmstadt. On sale at the colony's exhibitions, there were, in addition to postcards by illustrators, postcards with photographs of designs by J. M. Olbrich, showing the houses on the Matildenhöhe and the temporary exhibition pavilions and bearing special stamps or commemorative labels.

Among the artists of the Künstlerkolonie in Worpswede who were engaged in designing postcards were Heinrich Vogeler, who attempted to fuse German nationalist art with British graphics, and Georg Tappert, whose strongly expressive touches could be seen as an early indication of his adherence to the expressionist movement.

The dominant subject for Worpswede artists and their postcards was landscape, at times idyllic, at others mysterious, but always pervaded by strong emotions, and well defined by Karl Veit Riedel in 1977 as 'Typ Worpsweder Stimmungslandschaften'. However, the design of these cards was generally, except in artists like Sophie Wencke, more inclined toward pictorial representations and rarely adopted, at least in an obvious way, Judendstil devices.

Landscapes and urban scenes had, in any case, an important role in the development of picture postcards in Germany, both before and after the Worpswede era. In about 1897, postcard views which had the pictorial style of nineteenth-century illustrators and which were called 'Aquarellkarten', were in wide circulation. A perfect example of this type is the series by Heinrich Kley, with views of Munich, Berlin, Dresden, Potsdam, Meissen, Hamburg, Lubeck, Bremen and other cities published by Karl Kellner and datable to about 1897. Other publishers active in this field were Ottmar Zieher of Munich (with designs by Zeno Diemer, Paul Hey, Heinrich Kley and others), B. G. Teubner and R. Voigtländer of Leipzig, who published cards in a style in which it is difficult to distinguish between nineteenth-century realism and vague echoes of Jugendstil. Some series of views were sponsored by official bodies, like those published by the railway authorities and Interior Ministries of the various German states. Otto Ubbelohde reproduced his pen-and-ink drawings of German landscapes in the series 'Bildkarten aus Schwaben', published by Fischer Verlag of Tübingen. In response to the interest of collectors and the general public, series of postcard views were printed lithographically by L K H for local publishers.

A special group of scenic postcards comprises the anthropomorphic views of Swiss mountains by Emil Nolde (signed Emil Hansen). These were very popular with the public and were imitated by several artists, some of whom, such as F. Hafs (a contributor to *Jugend* from 1896), even managed to improve the formal quality of the type invented by Nolde.

'Things went better' – wrote Nolde in his autobiography – 'because of a couple of my postcards with views of mountains drawn during my trips, which I sent to my friends with greetings. Dr Hirth in reply wrote me an enthusiastic letter, which in turn excited me. Two of the cards were reproduced, and from then on daily requests arrived from collectors asking for them. What was to be done? I thought about it and decided to have them printed [. . .] They were printed in Munich. Within ten days 100,000 postcards were sold and I earned 1,000 Swiss francs a day. All this was amazing, and my hopes for the future were fired, but when the edition was sold out, hundreds of disgusting, slovenly plagiarized copies appeared which spoilt the original, beautiful idea. It was a strange time. Lots of letters lay on my table awaiting replies. One contained a complete series of postcards with poetry written in rhyme; a postcard of the Matterhorn arrived, signed by the most famous artists in Munich. Artists wrote to me, a dilettante still trying to find my way! [. . .] On my way home, I saw a collection of my postcards in a shop window in Munich next to the Karlstor [. . .] and the same thing happened in Berlin on the Unter den Linden'[46].

Landscape heightened by emotion is a subject which recurs in Heimatkunst. Its first interpreter was Paul Hey, whose work can be seen as the German equivalent of the views of Cassiers or Lynen. But the nationalist element in Hey led to a more intimate, post-romantic *Heimat* emphasis, which tended to submerge the scene in psychological atmosphere. It was no accident that Hey's landscapes did not represent real places, but transformed aspects of the German way of life into idealized emotional (and sentimental) models. Even closer to the limits of symbolism, and at times bordering on fantasy, are the landscapes of Ernst Liebermann, an important book illustrator who was mindful of the symbolist examples of Segantini.

Heimatkunst themes, seen in illustrations of everyday German life, also appeared in the lithographic postcards of Friedrich Kallmorgen and Ferdinand Spiegel; the former was interested in recording the intimate details of contemporary life, the latter in creating fairy-tale transformations of national legends.

Among the postcards produced by the various artistic associations are those published by the Karlruhe Künstlerbund, founded in 1894 by the members and students of the Karlsruhe Academy, some of whom became part of the history of Jugendstil. The Karlsruhe association issued, among others, the 'Deutsche Graphiker' series of cards in which the colour lithographs of members like Gustav Kampmann and Friedrich Kallmorgen were reproduced in small format to increase sales. From the beginning of the century until the First World War, especially in the German-speaking parts of Europe, the custom of printing cards for charity events and the functions of artistic associations was very common; among these are examples by Max Klinger (1911), Otto Gräber and Otto J. Olbertz (1907).

The first picture postcards for an exhibition were the one produced for the Halle exhibition (1881), and the one issued the following year by the Bavarian Post Office for the Bayerische Landes-, Industrie-, Gewerbe und Kunstausstellung in Nuremberg, which had a photograph of the exhibition hall. These were followed by a long series of postcards designed by artists, which often reproduced posters, but on other occasions had designs created especially for them.

Of the publicity postcards, with their obvious relationship to posters, the series produced for the Stollwerksche Chocolade Fabrik and the Keks-Fabrik H. Bahlsen of Hannover deserve particular attention. In 1890 Stollwerk followed the example of Liebig in printing a series of figures, but had the idea of commissioning the designs from reputable artists like Vogeler and Paul and of reproducing them also as postcards (between 1900 and 1910). The ones designed by Vogeler mark the peak of his achievement in applied graphic art. The Keks-Fabrik Bahlsen had a series of war propaganda postcards printed, using the work of

46 E. Nolde, *Das eigene Leben. Die Zeit der Jugend* 1867-1902, Cologne 1967[3].

Julius Diez, Ludwig Hohlwein and Walter Georgi, and a particularly interesting series designed by Carl Otto Czeschka, which popularized the stylized approach which had helped him, during his best years in Vienna, to create a masterpiece in the art of book illustration, his work in the *Die Nibelungen* published by the Gerlach Verlag.

Finally, under the heading of decorative, greetings and other sorts of cards, there were a number of very well-designed series by artists who were particularly distinguished in the field of applied graphic arts, such as Fritz Rehm, Ivo Puhonný, Leo Schnug, F. Nigg and Carl Strathmann.

POLAND

The centre of Art Nouveau in Poland was Cracow, with its 'Sztuka' artistic association, which had Josef Mehaffer and Jan Bukowski, among others, as members.

While working in Germany Ephraim Moses Lilien, a tireless promoter of Jewish culture, created book illustrations which were also reproduced as postcards. In them, he displayed a strong imaginative element, closely linked to the expressive use of black and white, a powerful use of symbolism and overtones that were sometimes epic, sometimes lyrical.

Although they possessed less stylistic unity, the postcards of Wilhelm Wachtel, who also designed a series called 'Typen aus Polen', also reflected Jewish culture. In them he stylized popular Polish traditions using Art Nouveau devices. Franz Laskoff (Laskowski) was of Polish origin, but unfortunately there are few biographical details known about him. We know that he was in Strasburg, Paris and Great Britain in his youth. His work for the publisher Ricordi in Milan is better known, though insufficiently documented and studied. In his postcards, even more than in his posters, Laskoff invented and developed an original graphic style which, although apparently conscious of the work of Toulouse-Lautrec and William Nicholson, did not succumb to it, but on the contrary turned it into something more precisely modern. The image is composed of figures done in silhouette against flat background areas of colour.

At the beginning of the twentieth century a series of postcards depicting musical angels by Kieszkow was very successful with collectors, probably because of their combination of Art Nouveau decorative features and 'realism'.

RUSSIA

In Russia there were two artistic centres, St Petersburg and Moscow, where two different cultural traditions developed. In St Petersburg prevalent thinking, a fusion of neo-romantic and traditional ideas, was concerned with creating a world of elegance that was also often fictitious. The St Petersburg group were well known abroad, in particular in Paris, where artists like Alexandre Benois and Léon Bakst, with their posters, costumes and sets for the 'Ballets Russes' played an important role in the transition from Art Nouveau to Art Déco. The postcards of Alexandre Benois, Eugène J. Lanceray and Constantin A. Somov transformed the rococo tradition into linear rhythms which were pleasingly decorative though occasionally insipid. Ivan J. Bilibin, a notable painter and graphic artist and a member of the 'Mir Iskusstva' group, was particularly well known for his illustrations for storybooks. These are two-dimensional decorative compositions in which static figures, outlined by unbroken lines on areas of flat colour or containing decorative motifs, tend to fill the picture area and submerge into the overall pattern effect. Postcards were a particularly useful means of popularizing this kind of graphic language, the unique result of fusing Art Nouveau devices with popular Russian traditions (the Bilibin collection of craft objects became the nucleus of the ethnographic section of the Russian Museum). The influence of Japanese colour woodcuts is also evident. Bilibin's favourite subjects were the landscape and illustrations of Russian tales and folklore. Whereas these subjects give him the opportunity for powerful psychologically interpretations of relationships between people, and between people and the environment, other artists, such as Eugenij Sokolev, who created many illustrations of nursery rhymes, used them humorously to create relaxed, informal compositions displaying a confident control of line.

Vadim Falilejeff reproduced as postcards his splendid colour lino-cuts of Russian scenes, in which the sense of time and season is comparable to the highest level attained in Japanese colour prints.

In Moscow, which was traditionally the rival of St Petersburg more realistic and progressive tendencies emerged. But it is not known whether the most important artists in the city designed postcards. From Wassily Kandinsky, for example, we know only the postcard he designed for the Bauhaus series.

Little is known about Serge de Solomko, apart from his personal odyssey through German and French culture, which can be seen in his contributions to the magazine *Jugend* and his work for French publishers of illustrated books. Some of his postcards reproduce paintings; others employ subjects and design features drawn from Russian tradition and embellished with elements of fantasy often imbued with symbolism.

HOLLAND

The graphic art of the Dutch Nieuwe Kunst movement occupies a dominant position on the international scene, which has not yet been fully acknowledged in the history of Art Nouveau. Graphic art was an important field of activity for well-known architects like Karel P. C. de

Bazel, Hendrik P. Berlage and Johannes L. M. Lauweriks and for artists like William C. Brouwer, Anton J. Derkinderen, Gerrit W. Dijsselhof, Theodoor van Hoytema, Samuel Jessurun de Mesquita, Chris Lebeau, Carel A. Lion Cachet, Theodorus H. A. Molkenboer, Theodor W. Nieuwenhuis, Wijnand O. J. Nieuwenkamp, Johan Thorn Prikker, Richard N. Roland Holst, Johannes Theodorus Toorop, George Rueter, Willem A. van Konijnenburg and Jacobus G. Veldheer. Some of these graphic artists may also have been interested in postcards, because there were publishers in Holland who were capable of producing the high-quality work required, such as W. de Haan in Utrecht and Roukens & Erhart in Baarn.

The lack of Dutch catalogues makes it difficult to identify artists involved in this area of graphic art. In catalogues from other countries, in the sections relating to illustrators, the only important figures in Dutch art mentioned are Toorop and van Hoytema and those illustrators of children's books, Rie Cramer and Hendrïka Willebeek Le Mair.

Toorop's work in postcards seems to be limited to reproductions of designs of religious subjects (probably cartoons for windows and frescoes). They do not, therefore, belong to his popular symbolist period but to the years following his religious crisis and conversion to Catholicism in 1905, which gave rise to his work for the windows and painted decorations in the Aloysiuskapel in Haarlem cathedral (1906).

Postcards by van Hoytema include a series advertising van Houten cocoa and single items publicizing calendars and children's books which were probably reproductions of the plates drawn directly by him on the lithographic stone. They document very clearly the special interpretation given to Nieuwe Kunst by this unique artist.

There are several series of postcards known to be by Rie Cramer and Hendrïka Willebeek Le Mair, which were published in the second decade of the present century in Holland and Great Britain; nearly all of them reproduced illustrations from children's books or from collections of children's songs.

Influenced during her apprenticeship as an illustrator by Toorop and by the Pre-Raphaelites, Rie Cramer achieved the culmination of her personal style during that decade. In it she frequently returned to the example set by British children's books so that she could understand children better.

In spite of their derivation from Pre-Raphaelite models, her figures retain an almost hieratic, two-dimensional quality, emphasized by the limited but bright colour range which neutralizes her timid effects of chiaroscuro. In this way she achieved a relationship between the perspective of the setting and the outlines of the figures, which in their apparent innocence appeal to a child's sense of drama.

A student of Maurice Boutet de Monvel, a number of whose illustrations she also saw in postcard form, Henrïka Willebeek Le Mair created reinterpretations of the work of illustrators like Arthur Rackham and Edmond Dulac during the second decade of the century. It was precisely these Anglophile touches in her graphic work that appealed to postcard publishers like A. & C. Black and Augener Ltd of London and David McKay of Philadelphia.

THE SCANDINAVIAN COUNTRIES

As in the case of Holland, the lack of catalogues or other means of checking make it difficult to trace the production of postcards (even perhaps by major artists) in Scandinavian countries, where they made a notable contribution to the Art Nouveau movement. Only Finland has adequate records, thanks to recent studies on postcards, which also include monographs on individual artists.

Jugendstil graphic art in Norway, even disregarding an artist like Edvard Munch, is of very high quality. Its variety derives from the fusion of certain features of the International Art Nouveau style (identifiable in the work of illustrators and commercial artists like Thorolf and Othar Holmboe, Gabriel Kielland, Rudolf Krogh, Emil Høye, Olaf Krohn and Jacob Sømme) with aspects of Norwegian figurative art, such as the 'dragon style' of the medieval period reinterpreted by Gerhard Munthe, and the figures from the popular troll sagas given new life by the 'Nordic Fawn' Theodor Kittelson.

From the scant information available it seems that, of the leading figures in Norwegian art at the beginning of the century, only Thorolf Holmboe did designs for postcards, and that Munch and Munthe, whose names are listed in some catalogues, only reproduced their own work, the former paintings and probably woodcuts, the latter items of decorative art. All the graphic work done by Holmboe, which deals with relationship between man and nature in Norway, is steeped in an atmosphere of melancholic lyricism that is alien to the existential anxiety of Munch's work. It is deeply influenced by Japanese prints, which he studied almost exclusively during a youthful visit to Paris. Their influence is visible in his postcards, not only in his use of pronounced outlines and areas of flat colour, but also in his tendency to make details stand out sharply from the design and in his preference for compositions with large white areas in the lower half of the card or between the foreground and background.

In Sweden, several artists reproduced their own work in postcards (especially greetings cards). This branch of graphic design was dominated by Carl Larsson, even though he had only a limited interest in postcards. It appears that he only began to make use of the medium in the second decade of the century, to increase the circulation of his already famous book illustrations in *Ett Hem* (1899) and *Spadarfvet* (1906), which had already become classics in the new Swedish culture, both in the field of figurative art and in architecture. A postcard he designed for a charity event in 1912 belongs to that notable group of rapid sketches (which often cover the text pages in his books) in which he captured, with affectionate pleasure and deliberately childlike strokes, moments in the daily life of his own children.

Childhood, explored with Larssonian humour in a comfortable domestic setting or in life at close quarters with Nordic nature, is the theme of greetings cards by women designers like Signe Aspelin, Elsa Hammar, Aina Stenberg and Hildar Söderberg.

A particularly prolific designer of postcards, Jenny Nyström was imbued with Larsson's optimism and vitality, and celebrated the delights of middle-class Swedish life and the happiness of childhood. Apart from these points in common, Nyström reveals a graphic language which is free of the extravagant mannerism of Larsson and has a greater overall realism and is less inclined toward mere pictorial effect.

The representation of comfortable society is also the theme of Vicke Andrén's postcards. She differed from the other artists mentioned here in her interest in continental Art Nouveau graphics, in particular the work of von Reznicek and the chroniclers of fashionable life who illustrated Munich or Parisian magazines.

Information about the production of artistic postcards in Denmark is scant (one can only point to the work of the humourist Carl Rögind, who developed a form of caricature similar to that made popular in Paris by Xavier Sager, Avis Mertzanoff and Charles Naillod.

The struggle for national independence, which was attained only in 1917, was the major theme of Finnish postcards. In them the spirit of popular nationalism could be seen not only in their explicit propaganda for independence from Russian domination, which involved artists like Eetu Isto, Joseph Alanen and Albert Edelfelt, but also in their very celebration of the Finnish countryside, which was turned into a symbol of the conservation of national values. The elegy on peasant life seen in the postcards of Alexander Paischeff, Oskar Elenius, Ville Musta and Kaapo Virtanen blurred into a *Heimatstil* in which there are echoes of contemporary Swedish and Russian graphic art, from Larsson to Bilibin, filtered through a naive figurative style.

It is a strange fact that only a pale or late reflection can be seen in Finnish postcards of that strongly romantic and nationalistic type of Jugendstil which pervaded the country's decorative arts and architecture and gave birth to the production of postcards whose quality is second to none in Europe. This was probably due to the prevalent view of the postcard as an effective medium for nationalist rhetoric and a method of educating the public. When they made their belated appearance in about 1910, Jugendstil designs tended to have a folkloric flavour even when they were used by artists who had long experience of the language of decoration. Among the illustrators working in the field of postcard design in the second decade of the century, Greta-Lisa Jäderholm-Snellmann stands out. She was trained in Paris and was well known for her work in ceramics. Her work is distinct from that of her compatriots because of its humorous vein, which was refined by the French school where she was trained.

SWITZERLAND

'La Suisse' – Wiener wrote – 'est un des premiers pays où la carte se soit

propagée. Parmi les séries du début, il y eut les montagnes humouristi-
ques de *Killinger*, les grandes séries de vues aux coloris tendres et les
sports de *Clément Tournier* de Genève. Aucun éditeur suisse n'occupe
de place prépondérante, mais beaucoup d'entre eux ont produit des
séries intéressantes. C'est que, quoi qu'on dise, il y a un art suisse
national. Il sort complètement de nos goûts et de notre compréhen-
sion, mais n'en existe pas moins et on le retrouve dans la production
cartophile du pays'[47].

Certainly Swiss artists – at least in the beginning – who made a major
contribution to international Art Nouveau graphics, had no significant
opportunity to work with postcard publishers in their own country.
Such opportunities were denied not only to artists who trained in Paris
and settled there permanently, such as Steinlen, Vallotton, Grasset
(from whom the Swiss Post Office commissioned a stamp) and Charles
Emile Carlège, but also to artists like Richard Ranft and Pierre Eugène
Vibert, who, although they were often active in Paris, maintained
closer working contacts with their own country.

It was also in Munich, and not in Switzerland, that Ernst Kreidolf
found publishers like Otto Gmelin and G. D. W. Callwey, who were
interested in publishing his cards, most of them reproductions of
illustrations in children's books set in a fantastic world of flowers,
insects and personified animals. In them, observations and interpretations of the natural world are recreated in a masterly way and with
simple strokes, in flowers and animals that mimic humans.

A dreamlike fairy-tale atmosphere prevades Kriedolf's postcards
inspired by the war, published by Gmelin, which were not spoilt by the
clichés of patriotic rhetoric seen in German postcards of the time.

Interesting examples of Art Nouveau postcards were published in
Switzerland even though there were no contributions from these
artists, who were already internationally famous in the early years of
the century. In them the influence of the different artistic centres
frequented by Swiss graphic artists is clearly visible.

In the German-speaking cantons the dominant influence was the
Jugendstil graphic art of Munich; in the French-speaking cantons the
Franco-Belgian Art Nouveau style was preferred; in the Tricino canton
there was an interest in the Liberty experiments of Lombardy.

In the Art Nouveau style of Romansch-speaking Switzerland,
French influence is visible not only in the work of masters like Grasset,
de Feure and Chéret, but also in the classical style exemplified by
Adolphe Giraldon. The series of postcards designed by Ernest Biéler
in 1905 for the Vevey 'Festa dei vignaioli', or vine-dresser's festival,
belongs to this group.

More typical of Swiss production, in which those national characteristics referred to by Wiener can be observed, are the numerous
commemorative postcards, particularly those printed from 1910 on-
ward to celebrate the national holiday on 1 August. The proceeds from
the sale of these cards, which were distinguished for the high technical
quality of the colour lithography printing, were used for different
charities each year. Only nationally famous artists took part in the

47 L. Wiener, *op. cit.*, II (1923-24) p. 24.

event, most of them specialists in creating fresco cycles on historical subjects for public buildings, like August M. Bächtiger, Fritz Boscovits Jr., Louis Dunki, Eduard Stiefel, Hans Beatus Wieland, Richard Schaupp and Burkhard Mangold. It was, in fact, a common practice not only in Switzerland for well-known artists to be invited to take part in such charity events.

Ferdinand Hodler, the painter of monumental cycles like *La ritirata a Marignano* (1899), had a dominant influence on these postcard illustrators, who often chose episodes in national history as their subjects, particularly the wars of the Swiss Confederation in the Middle Ages. His influence also played a fundamental role in encouraging the development of a Swiss national style emancipated from nineteenth-century history painting.

Apart from Hodler's considerable influence, there were also traces identifiable in Stiefel of the return to classicism seen in Germany from about 1905 in the graphic work of a number of artists who had already been involved with Jugendstil, like Julius Diez and Johann Vincenz Cissarz, and of which the real master was Franz von Stuck.

ITALY

Italy was one of the leading countries in the production and use of artistic postcards. Proof of the huge growth in collecting is furnished by the superb mail-order catalogues of specialist firms like Fratelli Stoppani in Milan, which at the turn of the century offered clients a wide selection of postcards not limited to those produced in Italy: the company advertised the most important foreign postcard series published by Philipp & Kramer of Vienna and by Dietrich of Brussels (with designs by Combaz, Meunier, Mignot, Cassiers and Toussaint), cards by Kirchner, an artist very popular with the Italian public, 'Jugend-Postkarten', and so on. The extent of the fashion for postcards is also documented by the long list of specialist magazines printed in several cities around 1900 and by the frequency of exhibitions. In 1898 the monthly *La Cartolina Postale illustrata* was published in Milan, followed in 1899 by the fortnightly *Il Raccoglitore di Cartoline Illustrate*, which carried an article in each issue on a new series of postcards, chosen not only from Italian series; one of the artists most often written about was the Belgian Hendrick Cassiers. A succession of magazines then began to appear: in Milan, *L'Indicateur du Philocartiste. Nouveau Journal de Kartophilie et variété pour collectionneurs* (1900), which in 1901 changed its name to *La Rivista della Cartolina*; in Florence, *L'annunzio filatelico e filocartista* (1900); in Modena, *La Cartolina del Progresso Fotografico* (1901); in Turin, *La Cartolina Illustrata, rivista delle riviste* (1902); in Milan, *La Cartolina illustrata, bollettino mensile delle case editrici di cartoline* (1902); in Rome, *Il Filocartista italiano* (1901); and in Caltanissetta, *Il Filocartista Siciliano* (1902). After the great exhibition in Venice in 1899, where single items and sketches by well-known artists were shown as well as printed series of postcards, other exhibitions were held in 1900 in Bologna, Rome and Turin; in 1901 in Leghorn, Monagnana, Lodi and Siena; in 1902 in Genoa and Macerata; in 1903 in Como; and in 1905 once more in Como and in Voghera.

At the end of the nineteenth century, many series of postcards designed by foreign artists on Italian subjects (such as the views of the lakes of Lombardy, the Ligurian Riviera and Venice done by Manuel Wielandt) and printed abroad (mainly in Germany) were being imported into Italy. But graphic studios like Casa Rocordi in Milan and the lithographic printing firm of Gabriele Chiattone in Bergamo, led the way in high-quality postcard production in Italy itself. Their example was followed by other publishers, such as Modiano in Trieste and Armanino in Genoa, and this field of activity took off so rapidly that Aldo Maggioni, writing about the Venice exhibition of 1899, was able to state: 'posters and postcards have become a highly developed industry [. . .] and the public flock to exhibitions of them'[48].

Ricordi, who could count on the artistic contributions of a select band of commercial artists, had already begun to publish postcards in 1897. But it was only in 1898, with the appearance of the first commemorative and publicity cards signed by Leopoldo Metlicovitz, Aleardo Villa and Adolfo Hohenstein and the series devoted to Mascagni's 'Iris' by Giovanni Mario Mataloni and Hohenstein (1898-99) that Milanese publishers showed the distinct preference for the Liberty style which characterised the greater part of Ricordi's postcards until the First World War period.

The first series of postcards produced by Gabriele Chiattone as illustrator and printer appeared in 1898 and were for shipping companies operating on the lakes of Lombardy, especially the Lariana company. With their refined *japonisme* and elegant two-colour combinations of green and gold or blue and gold, these cards marked a radically new concept in postcard views and offered an alternative to the type then fashionable, which were done in watercolour in the nineteenth-century taste.

Equally important in the spread of the Liberty style in postcard design was the work of the publisher Edmondo Chappuis in Bologna. From 1899 he frequently worked with Marcello Dudovich and also, in competition with Ricordi, with illustrators (like Aleardo Terzi) connected with the Milanese firm.

Even before these years Italian postcards revealed the first, sporadic signs of a precocious modernism, which can be related to British sources, in particular the graphic work of Walter Crane. An example is the feminist postcard carrying the slogan 'Emancipatevi!', which seems to date from 1896. When the Venetian exhibition opened in 1899 the national production of postcards was such that, in its range, variety of styles, and quality of printing, it could hold its own with products from any other European country. Contributing to it was Alberto Martini's series of night scenes, which is of particular interest since it provides one of the rare occasions when the artist's excursions into the realm of dreams and symbolism were expressed in a graphic language clearly

48 A Maggiani 'La Prima Esposizione Internazionale di cartoline postali illustrate a Venezia. Note e appunti', in *Emporium*, vol. X (1899), p. 310.

rooted in the Art Nouveau style. In the later 'Carnevale olimpico' series Martini used a surrealist humour not unrelated to illustrations in the magazine *Simplicissimus*. Less successful among his early series is 'Venetia Antiqua', which concedes too much to the medieval revivalism which had run riot in the murals in many neo-Gothic Venetian palaces. Well represented at the 1899 exhibition was Raffaele Tafuri, Venetian by adoption but Neapolitan by birth, who showed alongside series still reflecting the nineteenth-century taste in landscape art, postcards of butterfly-women that are linked to the Liberty style more through their graphic approach. An allegiance to the decorative formulae of Liberty, tempered by a pictorial rather than graphic treatment of the image, can also be seen in the postcards designed by Emilio Paggiaro and Tafuri to publicize the exhibition. A lot of space was given to postcards with views of cities (particularly Venice, of course), which were conceived as small-scale pictures, and executed by such famous painters as Pietro Fragiacomo, Luigi Conconi and Miti Zanetti (who exhibited 24 etchings of views). The modernist type of postcard the 'vero tipo della cartolina illustrata', to use the words of Maggiani[49], was represented not only by Martini and, to a lesser extent, by Tafuri and Paggiaro, but also by the work produced by Chiattone and Ricordi. The latter exhibited several series by Leopoldo Metlicovitz, a commercial artist from Trieste who produced a good deal of work for the company in this field. The popularity of his postcards was due to the peculiar syncretism of his work, his ability to graft post-impressionist stylisations, elegant floral motifs deriving from Jugendstil, and compositional schemes and images recalling Japanese prints on to what are essentially realistic roots. The first postcards of Giovanni Maria Mataloni and Adolfo Hohenstein followed a similar line. While the former placed an emphasis on realism, the latter displayed a more exuberant vein, often creating designs showing a sharp contrast between two areas of the composition, one of them comprising a monochrome frame with pronounced floral decoration and the other the figurative scene itself.

An account of the Venetian exhibition must not omit the humorous postcards and their leading exponents, Agostino Arnani and Vincenzo Nasi (better known under the pseudonym Van Dok), who seem to have their eye on the great school of British humourists. This type of card had a considerable following in Italy, distinguished by artists such as Augusto Majani (otherwise known as Nasica), Luigi Bompard, Golia and Antonio Rubino.

In 1900, after its beginnings in the final years of the nineteenth century, the Liberty postcard entered its Golden Age. The centres with the largest numbers of artists and publishers and which provided the greatest stimulus to the development of modernist postcards were in Lombardy, Piedmont and Emilia-Romagna. The phenomenon was not, however, restricted to these areas, but spread over the whole country, where postcards were produced even in the smaller provincial centres. This cannot be seen as evidence for the widespread adoption of the Liberty style. Some of the finest series published in the first years

49 ibid p. 321.

of the present century were signed by artists who are unknown in the history of Liberty, like G. Crotta, E. Bottaro and Illemo Camelli. Among these illustrators were some who received international acclaim (such as Bottaro) and were invited to work for foreign publishers. Around 1900 the numbers of designers and illustrators interested in postcards increased greatly, and pioneers like Mataloni, Hohenstein, Martini, Metlicovitz and Dudovich were now joined by Aleardo Terzi, Luigi Bompard, Alfredo Baruffi, Giorgio Kiernerk, Aleardo Villa, Rodolfo Paoletti and Aldo Mazza. The lack of exhaustive catalogues of the graphic work of these artists does not allow us to establish how many of their postcards were original designs and not reproductions of posters, or illustrations or covers for magazines. The proportion of reproductions of posters among the publicity and commemorative cards is certainly high, but among other kinds of postcards specially created designs seem to prevail. In any case, whether reproduction or original, the postcard helped to complete our knowledge of some of these artists' work, sometimes revealing aspects of their graphic language which were not visible in other areas of their work.

Despite the complex variety of international Art Nouveau, it is possible to discover some areas of experiment, some graphic features common to different artists, from which the typical characteristics of Italian postcard art can be identified.

Hohenstein's way of laying out a design as a play of contrasting decorative and figurative areas was imitated by artists like Osvaldo Ballerio, Roberto Franzoni, Orfeo Rossato and T. Borsato. Also widely adopted was the device of breaking up the design with elaborate, curvilinear frames, introduced in about 1900 by G. Crotta and Terzi (in the 1901 series 'Omaggio degli editori' Ricordi & C.'. Luigi Bompard showed a masterly use of the frame, when he used it to enclose parts of a woman's face in order to show her state of mind, intense emotions and feelings. In his photographic series, he also showed a mastery of the technique based on the relationship between negative and positive in photography, which has Giorgio Kiernerk as its greatest exponent in Italy and which was greatly exploited by the Viennese. In his postcard reproducing the cover of the magazine *Cocorico* (datable to about 1898), Kiernerk combined the negative-positive device with flat areas of colour, and successfully achieved a three-dimensional effect which was absent in artists like Franz Laskoff, who followed the Beggarstaff Brothers in using a colour-staining technique. This latter technique was also used by Aldo Mazza and Aleardo Villa, but without dispensing with outline or (particularly in the work of the second artist) an emphasis on detail, which opposed the tendency towards abstraction. The influence of the Beggarstaff Brothers on some illustrators was part of the general trend involving turning towards Anglo-Saxon models, which was a feature of the postcards of Aldo Mazza (the publicity series for Agnesi and Giaccone olive oil), Alfredo Baruffi (the series on the months) and later Francesco Nonni. Vittorio Pica's and Rossana Bossaglia's work carries references to

Robert Anning Bell (to whom might be added the American commercial artists William H. Bradley and Louis John Rhead). And for Baruffi as well as for Nonni, it appeared equally fitting, as Pica observed about the former, to substitute a 'pagan serenity' for the Pre-Raphaelite sentimentality of his prototypes. With his series on the Abruzzi, which he published himself by lithography from 1899, Basilio Cascella held a unique position in the history of Italian postcards. With a realism steeped in the vitality and neo-paganism of D'Annunzio, he became the most important artist in Italy of that internationally widespread genre which takes local traditions and customs as its subject. In Cascella's vast output there is no shortage of erotic symbolism, as in the series on the game of billiards with the devil.

In the decade preceding the First World War the postcard recorded the two dominant trends in the Italian Liberty style: a high-flown historic trend, set in a neo-Renaissance framework and interwoven with references to D'Annunzio, which had Adolfo De Carolis as its major interpreter, and the Secessionist trend, with its 'Klimtian finale' (to quote Rossana Bossaglia) marking the end of the Liberty style in Italy. From about 1905 there was a tendency to indulge in a rhetorical type of classicism, sometimes linked to literary symbolism, which ran through the work of such profoundly differing artists as Cambellotti, Terzi, Metlicovitz, Mazza, Hohenstein, Mataloni, Nonni, Glauco Cambon, Plinio Codognato, Mario Borgoni, Giuseppe Palanti and Giovanni Carpanetto. War propaganda postcards then raised the volume of the rhetoric against the classical background, although there were exceptions to the trend. Among these were the satirical anti-Austrian postcards of Antonio Rubino, Arnoldo Bonzagni, Umberto Brunelleschi, and Luciano Achille Mauzan, and the famous series revealing the macabre surrealism of Alberto Martini.

The most significant evidence for a 'Klimtian finale' to modernist Italian postcards is found in the 'Smalti e murrine' series by Vittorio Zecchin, which chronologically marked the end of Liberty postcards: it seems that they were published between 1918 and 1920.

Among the greatly increased number of postcards produced in the war years, the most interesting are not the propaganda cards, but the series of 'donnine' or 'little women', in which artists like Terzi, Dudovich (who here used his experience gained as a social chronicler for *Simplicissimus*), Calderara, Mauzan, Aurelio Bertiglia, Adolfo Busi and Enrico Sacchetti distinguished themselves. In these cards, intended for mass sale, the artists often repeated, with slight variations, the same designs, which were not infrequently imitated outside Italy. These series provide an interesting record of the transition from Art Nouveau to the Art Déco style which would become fashionable in the illustrations and poster art of the 1920s.

SPAIN

In Spain the first picture postcards appeared after the state monopoly was repealed on 31 December 1886. But there was no real industrial and commercial development in this field until after 1892. The main impetus in this development came from important Madrid printing firms like Hauser y Menet and Lacoste, which specialized in the publication and printing of postcards, mostly photographic views, but also 'artistic' postcards. Modernism in postcard art became most widespread in Catalonia from the first years of the century, slightly later than in other European countries.

An important factor in improving the quality of artistic postcards was the work of the postcard society 'Hispania', which was established in Barcelona in 1901 and began to publish its journal *España Cartófila* in the same year. Although appearing later than in other countries, picture postcards were an immediate success in Catalonia. This is borne out by the appearance of specialist printers, the increase in the number of publishers and in the succession of competitions and exhibitions. *Espāna Cartófila*, which was published until 1909, was already joined in 1901 by *El boletín de la tarjeta postal ilustrada* (which was even more short-lived and ceased publication in 1904). It was edited and directed by J. Duran i Bori, the Barcelona representative of the Madrid publishing house of Lacoste. Another specialist magazine, *La Unión Postal* directed by L. Hernando, was published for six months only between 1906 and 1907. In Barcelona in 1902 the first important competition for a series of 10 publicity postcards was held by the syphon-manufacturing firm of F. Clara and was won by Joan Vallhonrat. The work submitted by the competitors was shown in an exhibition at the 'Círculo Artístico'. In the same year the Codorniu company promoted a competition to commemorate the coronation of Alfonso XIII. Other firms used postcards to publicize sketches sent in for poster competitions, as did the cigarette-paper manufacturer Roca, also in 1902. Over the following year there was a stream of postcard exhibitions in Reus (September 1902), Sabadell (January 1903), and Barcelona (one organized in September by the postcard society 'Hispania', another organized in 1903 by the 'Associación gaditana de Caridad' in the Palace of Fine Arts).

Among the publishers most closely associated with the development of modernist postcards was Lluis Bartrina in Barcelona, a founder member and moving spirit behind the postcard society 'Hispania'. He used work by artists like Ramón Casas, Joan Llimona and Alexandre de Riquer. Publishing postcards in a region like Catalonia, where Modernism took on the role of a 'national' art, with its own cultural identity, was not confined solely to publishing houses: there were also business firms, printers (such as L. Tasso, and 'L'Avenç'), political organizations, societies like the 'Círculo Artístico' and the postcard society 'Hispania', magazines like *Catalónia, Joventut, Hispania, Álbum Salón, Hojas Selectas* and *Pel & Ploma*, all of which played an important role in the spread of Modernism in graphic art and illustration.

Casas, de Riquer and Gaspar Camps, three artists who represented different aspects and versions of Catalan Modernism, were among the first to contribute to the development of modernist postcards.

The influence of Mucha characterizes much of the graphic work of Camps, to the extent that he became known as the 'Mucha Catalán'; it is also evident in his first series of postcards (1901) reproducing the illustrations of the Months which he had designed for the magazine *Álbum Salón*. Trained in Paris, where he had the opportunity of studying Mucha's graphic work, Camps was one of the exponents of the international wing of Catalan Modernism, which also included other graphic designers and illustrators who had studied and worked in the French capital, like Juan Cardona and Xavier Gosé. Often employed in recording, in a slightly ironic vein, aspects of the fashionable life of the *belle époque*, these two artists belonged to a long line of pictorial chroniclers who gravitated towards Parisian magazines, such as *Le Rire* or *L'Assiette au Beurre*, or Munich magazines like *Jugend* and *Simplicissimus*. While the work of Gosé shows a marked affinity with the French school, in particular with Sem (in his caricature drawings), the work of Cardona, who for a short time worked on *Jugend*, is basically Parisian in inspiration, but has echoes of ideas derived from Munich illustrators like Ferdinand von Reznicek.

The international cultural roots of Alexandre de Riquer, one of the most important figures of Catalan Modernism were more thoroughly absorbed in his strongly individual idiom. He first appeared as a decorative artist in the neo-medievalist groups nourished by the fervent Catholicism of the circle of Sant Lluc, which he founded in 1893 with the architect Antoni Gaudí, Joan and Josep Llimona, and Dionís Baixeras. In the Pre-Raphaelite movement he found not only artistic models, but also an aesthetic ideology which corresponded with his personal views, so much so that he became a passionate advocate of British art in Catalonia. Just as important as Pre-Raphaelite art in the formation of his style was his discovery of Japanese prints (from which he derived a preference for vertical compositions, areas of flat colour and clearly drawn outlines) and Belgian symbolist painting.

Although his postcards are barely representative of this many-sided artist, and all date from the first years of the century, they are nevertheless of considerable documentary interest. In about 1900 he underwent a profound spiritual crisis which led him to renounce the Jewish-Christian ethic. Through the study of oriental religions and theosophy he arrived at a syncretist mysticism, which found expression in the neo-pagan pantheism and erotic vitality evident in his graphic work. How far he had distanced himself from the Catholic concepts of self-deprivation and continual expiation of sin, adopted by the 'Cercle de Sant Lluc' and the religious fanaticism of Gaudí and which were carried to the extent of wearing penitental clothing and indulging in self-flagellation, can be seen by comparing his series of postcards of allegories of the seasons (designed in 1900, but probably published in 1901) and the decorative panels of 1897, which are the first version of the same subject. The main changes are not so much connected with the female figures, who are dressed in clothes woven with brightly coloured flowers but in the character of the landscape. Beneath the emphasis in the panels on the frailty of existence and the repetition of *memento mori*, a theme running through the gloomy symbolism of certain Catholic artists in the Catalan symbolist movement, there is an underlying feeling that nature is a continuous process of regeneration, which is expressed in a formal hedonism which links Japanese elegance with the attenuated refinement of certain Belgian Art Nouveau artists (such as Privat Livemont, whose name is often associated with that of de Riquer). Before 1900, in his publicity work, de Riquer had already begun to develop a more decorative manner close to Belgian poster artists like Adolphe Crespin and Privat Livemont: an example is the design he sent to the poster competition held by the industrialist Vicente Bosch in 1898 for 'Anís del Mono', which was later published as a postcard.

Symbolism nourished by the fervent Catholic faith of the 'Cercle de Sant Lluc' can be seen in some of the postcards published by the group, consisting of reproductions of the work of its members, and in the series 'Ave Maria Purissima' by Juan Llimona which show signs of degenerating into religious oleographs.

Among the leading artists of Catalan Modernism, Ramón Casas was the most prolific in the field of postcards. His postcards show the two main directions of his art: 'synthetic realism', typical of his work as a poster artist, and a realism which derived from impressionism, and which can be found in French illustrators like Jean-Louis Forain and Hermann-Paul, with whose work his series on Spanish ladies can be compared (with excursions into Andalusian folklore). In these and in the hundreds of illustrations designed by Casas for magazines like *Quatre Gats* and *Pel & Ploma* there are clear reminiscences of youthful visits to the cabaret clubs of Montmartre. With his Bohemian friends Santiago Rusiñol and Miguel Utrillo, and with Pere Romeu, Casas tried to recreate the Parisian atmosphere in Barcelona by opening the cabaret-bar 'Quatre Gats', which was frequented by the young Pablo Picasso and was involved in the development of postcards in the first years of the century.

The synthetic realism of Casas is seen in some of his postcards reproducing posters. Here, the use of some Art Nouveau features (like the unnatural use of colour in flat areas, the Japanese technique of cropping the composition and the accentuation of line) was resolved in a way which does not destroy their realism. Postcards by Antoni Utrillo, Richard Opisso and Lluis Labarta are in direct succession to those great masters of the style, Toulouse-Lautrec and Steinlen.

The 'happy fusion of a modern decorative style and an archaic Gothic style' which Trenc Ballester[50] defined as the distinctive mark of some of the book illustrations of Josep Triado, can also be found in his series of postcards 'Lo Zodiaco'.

Politics was at the forefront of modernist postcards, which were used as a means of popularizing the Catalan nationalist movement (the cards designed in 1906 by Apelles Mestres and Jaume Llongueras for the 'Fiestas de la Solidaritat Catalana' are an example of this) and even as political satire. Llorenç Brunet was distinguished in this genre with his

50 E. Trenc Ballester, *op. cit.*, p. 58.

series of caricatures and his unique series of 'Ex Libris políticos' devoted to well-known figures in Catalan politics, in which the allusions are difficult for us to decipher today.

Brunet was one of those outstanding humorous draughtsmen who also designed postcards. Others worthy of mention of Lluís Bagaria, Gaietá Cornet, Picarol and Vallhonrat, the designer of the famous series with a syphon personified as a night reveller, which won the competition sponsored by the firm of F. Clara.

The period of the modernist postcard was fairly short in Catalonia, the first signs of a decline in its popularity already appearing in 1907. In that year there were scarcely any entrants for the competition sponsored by the Sociedad Cartófila Española, while the magazine *Unión Postal* had to suspend publication because of the lukewarm response of publishers, dealers and collectors. In the March – April 1909 number of *España Cartófila*, the president of the 'Hispania' society defined the crisis in the artistic postcard market. 'Hoy por hoy la postal vista sigue reinando y la postal artística ha degenerado en un terreno que ni vale la pena de ocuparse de la misma, pues en general en nuestro país sólo es adquirida por modistillas y criadas, o sea por gente que atribuyen el arte a los colores y brillantinas, lo que convierte a la postal en verdadero cromo de pésimo gusto. [. . .] La postal ilustrada muere por falta de buen gusto y muy principalmente por haberla apartado du su veradero carácter (that is, as a means of aesthetic education)[51]. A short time later (in August) *España Cartófila* ceased publication, and with it the *belle époque* of modernist postcards was at an end.

THE UNITED STATES

American production of picture postcards at the beginning of the twentieth century was high in quantity, but less consistent in quality and certainly less rich in invention than other cultural activities of the time.

Two kinds of cards seem to be dominant: those celebrating women, and greetings cards or decorative compositions.

The postcard, with its clever use of design as a means of mass communication, played a role in popularizing the female type created by Charles Dana Gibson. The 'Gibson Girl' was the first in a long line of American female types who took the name of the illustrator who invented her. The 'American Girl' of Philip Boileau, the 'Christy Girl' of Howard Chandler Christy, the 'Fisher Girl' of Harrison Fisher, and so on, then appeared and were publicized throughout the printed media, from magazines to decorative prints – the American equivalent of the *panneau décoratif* of Mucha-Champenois – and from the poster to the postcard. The 'American Girl' of Boileau was created as a rival to the 'Gibson Girl'; her image, widely publicized through the pages of the *Associated Sunday Magazines* and through postcards, was the east-coast equivalent of the Gibson girl, who was publicized through the

51 ibid p. 204.

Saturday Evening Post and through postcards in the Atlantic coast states. The 'pin-ups' invented by these gifted American designers differ not only in the standard of the draughtsmanship, but also in the different conception of the figure and the compositional layout. Gibson, for example, preferred different settings, placing the figure sometimes in the foreground, sometimes in more distant views, while Boileau almost exclusively used the foreground, and Christy and Fisher preferred the middle ground and softened, broken outlines.

Some recent and up-to-date postcard catalogues, like that of Neudin, include famous commercial artists such as William H. Bradley and the architect and graphic designer Claude Bragdon in the list of illustrators involved in postcard design. Presumably these lists include publicity postcards, or cards reproducing posters, magazine covers, or illustrations from the magazines to which these artists contributed.

In the United States, as elsewhere, picture postcards reflected developments in the art of illustration. Towards 1908 there was the beginning of a transition from a type of graphic art still based on nineteenth-century illustration or even more closely linked to international Art Nouveau to a new style characterized by its special combination of Art Nouveau features with the realism typical of traditional American art. This transition could be seen in illustrated American magazines like *Scribner's Magazine*. Interesting versions of this new stylistic phase in applied graphic art are the series of postcards designed by Ethel Franklin Betts and Anne Whelan Betts.

There is a tremendous variety in American greetings and decorative cards, which include Valentine postcards, Christmas postcards, Easter postcards, Birthday postcards, Halloween postcards, Thanksgiving Day postcards, and so on. The number of cards produced was enormous compared to that in other countries. Some typical kinds of design can be distinguished: compositions with areas of decorative writing or stylized floral decoration, which at times reflected the American Arts and Crafts movement; compositions with isolated figures set against plain, flat backgrounds, which at times resemble a popular version of designs by Bradley; and individualized figurative compositions which derive to some extent from British caricatures (as in the postcards of C. W. Dwiggins).

JAPAN

The relationship between Art Nouveau picture postcards and developments in the pictorial traditions of the Far East, in particular Japan, is a subject of special interest meriting a separate study. The importance of Japanese colour woodcuts as a model and source of inspiration for the linear style and colouring of Art Nouveau graphic art has already been studied and generally recognized and is easily seen in postcards. But the production of picture postcards in Japan during the same period has not been studied, at least in the West.

Japanese postcards are very rarely seen in commercial use or in collections. The few examples which we have been able to examine, some of which are reproduced in these pages, allow us nevertheless to hazard the suggestion that the Japanese postcard illustrates a phenomenon of considerable historic interest in that it shows Japanese art unusually being influenced by the West, in this case by the Art Nouveau style.

It should be noted that the production of postcards in Japan was able to exploit the country's long tradition of reproducing works of art, in which, thanks to popular colour printing, Japan seems to have been ahead of the West. Japanese cards reproduced the masterpieces of the most celebrated artists of the Ukiyo-e school, using the finest colour printing techniques. Other postcards, following the same stylistic traditions, celebrate contemporary events, such as the Russo-Japanese war (which was also widely depicted in woodcuts).

Another kind of Japanese postcard, the humorous postcard, seems to employ stylistic effects that were current in Europe.

The 'decline' after the First World War

IT IS AGREED BY MOST WRITERS on postcards that, with the end of the First World War, the design of postcards tended to decline because of several factors: a decline in the artistic standard of the designs and the quality of printing, halftone letterpress becoming more widely used than colour lithography; the loss of interest in postcards by the best graphic designers; and the gradual waning of enthusiasm among collectors.

Although these explanations are generally true, they need comment. The war was a major stimulus to the production of postcards, but by the time it ended, some kinds of cards (such as the 'donnine' and those depicting engaged couples), which are often somewhat insipid in comparison with pre-war designs, had become the most popular with the public. Some illustrators who continued to produce postcards between 1915 and 1918 were active until the middle of the 1920s, using an approach attuned to a changed market; it was no longer geared towards educated collectors but to a wider public more susceptible to bad taste. The fact that artists, such as Aurelio Bertiglia, often concealed their identity behind a pseudonym was symptomatic of their distancing themselves from an activity that had become merely commercial. Their declining interest was reflected in the falling number of designs made especially for postcards. The names of the most committed illustrators and commercial artists of the 1920s, like A. M. Cassandre, René Vincent, Paul Iribe, Umberto Brunelleschi, Paul Colin, Leonetto Cappiello, Icart and Lucien Achille Mauzan, do appear on postcards of the period, but these are almost always reproductions of posters or prints.

It is true that there is an interesting group of Art Déco postcards, at times executed in unusual techniques (such as stencil, drypoint, and so

XXXVI

XXXVII

XXXVIII

XXXIX

XL

XLI

on), which are of high quality and have original though often anonymous designs, but here it is no longer possible to record the involvement of the elite group of graphic artists who had worked in this field before the war.

From the end of the war to the 1930s, artists and designers of the avant-garde movement, from the futurists to the expressionists and surrealists, as well as centres of artistic achievement like the Bauhaus, were interested in postcards and published some series, or even designed autograph examples in single copies.

XXXVI-XLVII. Japanese postcards, some of which reproduce colour woodcuts by Ukiyo-e artists, chromolithographs and woodcuts.

XLII

XLIII

XLIV
BY UTAMARO

XLV

XLVI

XLVII

One cannot therefore talk in general terms of a decline in the artistic quality of postcards after 1918, but only of a sharp distinction between mass-produced cards, which tended to degenerate into kitsch, and more elite productions made up limited editions for small intellectual circles or even of single items for private correspondence.

What came to be clearly lacking was precisely that widespread pursuit of high aesthetic standards which from Spain to Russia and from Scandinavia to Italy, had been the principal quality of the international Art Nouveau style.

The Illustrations

Great Britain

*1, 2. W. Crane, postcards from the series
reproducing with variations the illustrations
from the book* Flora's Feast *(1888), without
publisher's marks c. 1900, chromolithography.*

THE·QUEEN·OF·HEARTS·SHE·BAKED·SOME
TARTS·ALL·ON·A·SUMMER·DAY·

3

4

3. E. M. Daniell, 'Art Post-Card' series 2524, I.
publ. R. Tuck & Sons, London, chromolithography.
4. J. M. King, 'The Queen of Hearts', 'The
National Series', publ. Millar & Lang, c. 1904,
chromolithography.

5

6

5, 6. *A. K. Macdonald, 'At the Theatre' and 'Autumn', without publisher's name, chromolithography.*

7

8

7, 8. *E. Parkinson, series without publisher's name post-marked 27.12.1904, chromolithography.*

9

10

11

9-11. Anonymous, 'Clifton Happy Thought Postcard' series 689, publ. E. W. Savory Ltd, Bristol, chromolithography.

12-18. H. Eliott, postcards from the series
entitled 'La vie sportive', publ. S., Paris,
chromolithograph.

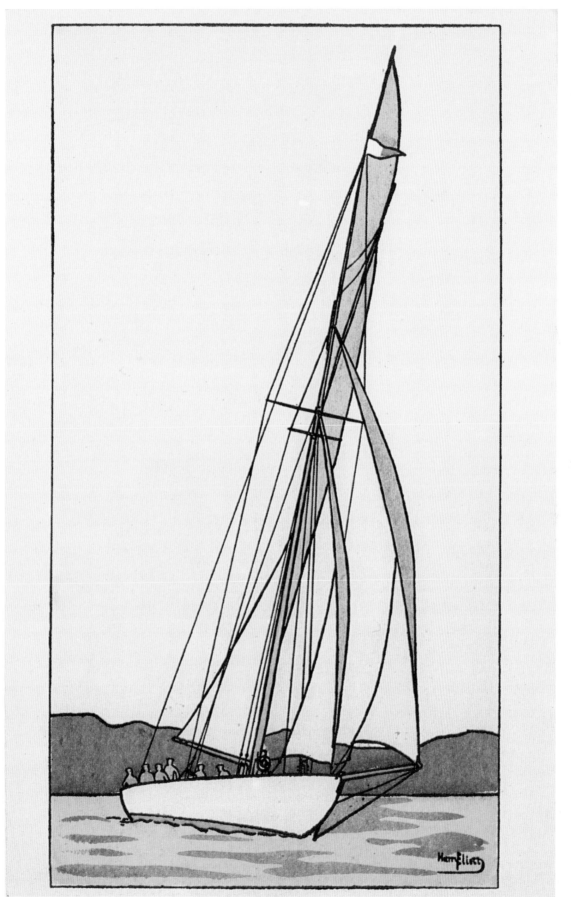

19

20

21

19. M. Sowerby, postcard, post-marked; 1906, chromolithography.

20. F. Hardy, postcard from series 382 by the publisher M. Munk, Vienna, chromolithography.

21. F. Hardy, postcard no. 390, Druck und Verlag B. Dondorf G.m.b.H., Frankfurt a/M., chromolithography.

22, 23. S. M. Evans, postcards of a series of proverbs, N.V. v.h. Roukens & Erhart, Baarn, chromolithography.

24. L. Govey 'The Spinning-wheel flies . . .', publ. Humphrey Milford, London, halftone letterpress.

25. Anonymous, The 'Ellanbee' Dutch Art Series 111, publ. Landeker & Brown, London, printed by M. Munk, Vienna, after 1902, chromolithography.

26. M. Sowerby, 'To swing over poppies . . .', publ. Humphrey Milford, London, halftone letterpress.

A STITCH IN TIME SAVES NINE.

G.M.EVANS

Lucinda sits and sighs and sews,
Her children do so tear their clothes;
They are so very strong and healthy.
Lucinda wishes she was wealthy.
And "oh my children dear"
∽∽∽ says she.

Pray bring your clothes straight in
∽∽∽ to me,
When on the garden gate they catch,
Or else upon the nursery latch;
Remember now dear children mine,
A little Stitch in Time Saves Nine."

22

THERE ARE NONE SO DEAF AS THOSE WHO WON'T HEAR.

S.M.EVANS.

Oh Master Pat and Master Paul,
This really will not do at all.
I've called you once, I've called you twice,
And yet you lie as still as mice;
And if like mice you both had tails,
I'd pull them - then there'd be some wails!

Now Master Paul 'tis after eight,
Now Master Pat, you'll both be late,
So rise like little gentlemen.
Please recollect at half past ten,
With lesson books you have to be,
At Dr. Smart's Academy.

23

THE SPINNING-WHEEL FLIES ROUND AND SINGS,
THE OWLS WORK HARD FOR HOURS.
THEY'RE MAKING FAIRIES' FROCKS AND WINGS
FROM SPIDER-WEBS AND FLOWERS.

24

25

TO SWING OVER POPPIES IS NICE –
ON THE TAILS OF TWO JOLLY DORMICE.
THE DORMICE DON'T MIND IT AT ALL,
AND THEY WONT LET THE FAIRYKIN FALL.

M. Sowerby

26

27

28

29

30

31

32

33

34

27, 28. H. Ryland, postcards from a series printed by M. Munk, Vienna, hand-coloured collotype.
29. H. Ryland, postcard printed by M. Munk, Vienna, collotype (?).
30. Anonymous, postcard without publisher's name, c. 1900, chromolithography.

31. Anonymous, postcard from series 308, publ. C. W. Faulkner & Co. Ltd., London, halftone letterpress coloured by hand.
32, 34. R. Bull, postcards from a series 'Message-postcards', chromolithography.
33. Anonymous, postcard belonging to the 'Message-postcards' group.

35

36

35. *Anonymous, postcard (no. 172) printed by*
M. Munk, Vienna, hand-coloured woodcut.
36. *J. Hassal, 'Returned from Klondyke', a*
publicity card for Colman's Mustard, chromo-
lithography.

Belgium

37

38

*37, 38. G. Combaz, 'Le feu' and 'L'eau', from
the series 'Les Eléments', publ. Dietrich & Cie,
Brussels, 1898, chromolithography.*

39

40

41

42

43

39. *G. Combaz, 'Droit au but' from the series 'Proverbes', publ. Dietrich & Cie, Brussels, c. 1899, chromolithography.*

40-43. *G. Combaz, 'L'Air', 'La Terre', 'La Terre' and 'Le Feu', for the series 'Les Eléments', publ. Dietrich & Cie, Brussels, 1898, chromolithography.*

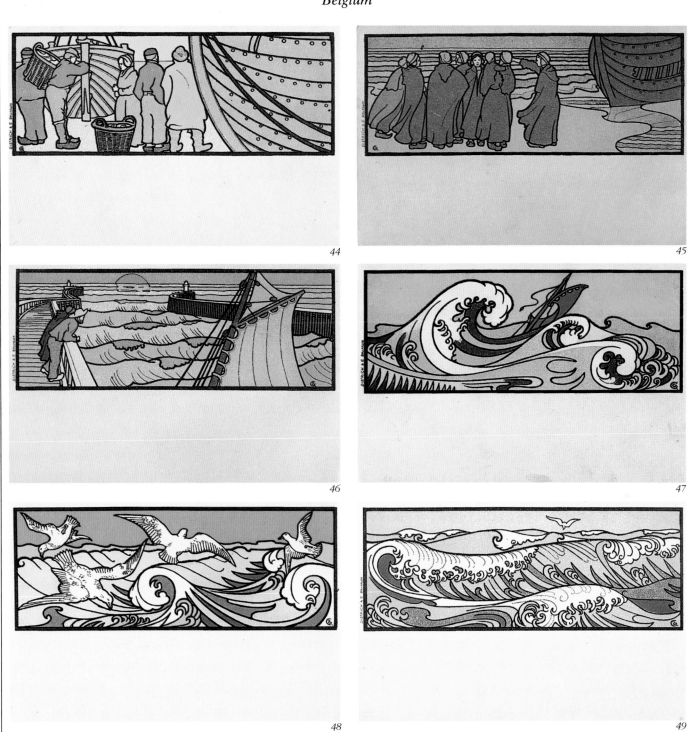

44-49. *G. Combaz, postcards from the series*
'Les Pêcheurs', publ. Dietrich & Cie, Brussels,
c. 1899, chromolithography.

50

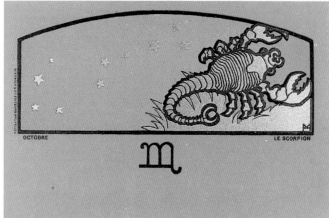

51

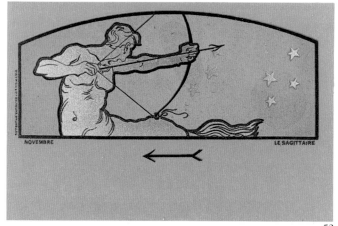

52

50-52. H. Meunier, 'Août', 'Octobre' and 'Novembre', from the series 'Le Zodiaque', publ. Dietrich & Cie, Brussels, c. 1898, chromolithography.
53. H. Meunier, postcard from the series 'grandes femmes', 1900, chromolithography.

HENRI
MEUNIER

53

54, 55. H. Meunier, 'Le Printemps' and 'Bonsoir', c. 1900, chromolithography.
56, 57. H. Meunier, from the series 'Femmes-
fleurs', publ. Dietrich & Cie, Brussels, c. 1898,
chromolithography.
58, 59. H. Meunier (?), publicity postcards
(some of this series are stamped 'Biscuits &
Desserts Victoria Bruxelles—Dordrecht'), c.
1900, chromolithography.

*60, 61. G. Gaudy, postcards from the series
advertising the newspaper* The Sportsman,
without publisher's name, chromolithography.

62-67. *V. Mignot, 'pochette' and postcards from the series 'Les Sports', publ. Dietrich & Cie, Brussels, c. 1899, chromolithography.*

68-73. V. Mignot, postcards from the series 'Les Sports', publ. Dietrich & Cie, Brussels, c. 1899, chromolithography.

74

75

76

77

78

74. *Privat Livemont, 'Automobile Club de France-Sicième Exposition Internationale de l'Automobile', halftone letterpress.*

75-78. *F. Toussaint, 'A Londres', 'A Paris', 'A St. Peterbourg' and 'A Constantinople' from*

the series of ladies from European capital cities, publ. Dietrich & Cie, Brussels, c. 1899.

79. *Anonymous, publicity postcard for 'Vino Vermouth Cinzano' lith. De Rycker & Mendel, Brussels, chromolithography.*

80. *E. van Offel, postcard from the series 'Concours d'Affiches Byrrh', Paris 1906, screenblock phototypography.*

81. *P. Cauchie, 'Concours d'Affiches Byrrh', Paris 1906, halftone letterpress.*

79

80

81

82

83

84

85

82. *P. Cauchie, 'Genval-Les Eaux', from the publicity series for the mineral waters of Genval, Dricot & Cie, 1900, chromolithography.*

83. *A. Ost, 'De Meijsbrug', from the series 'Oud Mechelen', tip. van den Bossche, Mechelen, 1912, chromolithography.*

84. *H. Cassiers, 'Woudrichem' from the series 'Pays-Bas', publ. Dietrich & Cie, c. 1900, Brussels, chromolithography.*

85. *A. Ost, 'Olifantbrug-Sluisbrug', from the series 'Oud Mechelen', tip. van den Bossche, Mechelen, 1912, chromolithography.*

86-88. *H. Cassiers, 'Goes', 'Zuid-Beveland', and 'Terneuzen', publ. Dietrich & Cie, c. 1900, Brussels, chromolithography.*

GOES

ZUID-BEVELAND

86

87

TERNEUZEN

88

89

90

91

92

93

89-91. *H. Cassiers, 'Westcapelle', 'Vlissingen' and 'Omstreken van Goes', publ. Dietrich & Cie, c. 1900, Brussels, chromolithography.*
92. *H. Cassiers, 'Terugkeer van de Markt', publ. W. de Haan, Utrecht, c. 1904, reproduced from a lithographic print, chromolithography.*
93. *H. Cassiers, publicity postcard for the 'Red Star Line Antwerp—New York', lith. De Rycker & Mendel, Brussels, 1903, reproduced from a lithographic print, chromolithography.*

94

95

94-95. A. Lynen, 'Bruxelles, Autour de la Bourse' and 'Soir d'été' from the series 'De-ci, de-là, à Bruxelles et en Brabant', c. 1905, chromolithography.

96

97

98

99

100

101

96-101. A. Lynen, 'La Senne à Molenbeek-St. Jean', 'Impasse du Tabernacle-Louvain', 'Gare du Midi', 'Etterbeek', 'Poste Centrale', 'Bruxelles, Cabaret aux Trois Couleurs', from the series 'De-ci, de-là, à Bruxelles et en Brabant', c. 1905, chromolithography.

102

103

104

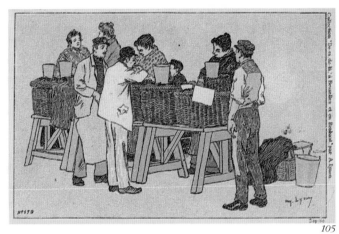

105

106

107

102-107. A. Lynen, 'Carabiniers et Nounou', 'En ballade', 'Au Jeu de Balle', 'Les Moules', 'Les Affiches', 'Marchand de parapluies', from the series 'De-ci, de-là, à Bruxelles et en Brabant', c. 1905, chromolithography.
108. A. Ost, 'Aux Bals Masqués de la Monnaise-Carnaval 1914', lith. J. Goffin Fils, Brussels, drawing dated 1913, chromolithography.
109. A. Rassenfosse, postcard from the 'Collection Job' series, 1914, reproduced from a poster, 1910, chromolithography.
110. Mars, publicity postcard for Nestlés powdered milk, chromolithography.

Aux Bals Masqués de la Monnaie

108

109

Nourrissez les enfants à la farine lactée Nestlé,
contenant le meilleur lait suisse.

110

France

111

112

111. H. Rivière, postcard from the series 'La
Marche à L'Etoile', no publisher's name, c.
1899, reproduced from a plate in the album.

112. A. Vignola, postcard from the series 'Le
Sphinx', no publisher's name, c. 1899, reproduced from a plate in the album.

113

114

113, 114. E. Crasset, postcards from the series 'Cinos', Paris, 1898, reproduced from the posters for the newspapers The Century Magazine *and* The June Century, *chromolithography.*

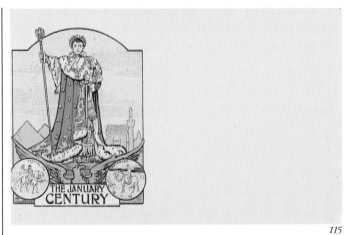

115

116

117

118

119

120

115-120. *Postcards from the series 'Cinos', Paris, 1898, reproduced from posters by L. Métivet, M. Réalier-Dumas, H. de Toulouse-Lautrec, Pal, Japhet, A. Truchet, chromo-lithography.*

121

122

123

124

125

121, 122. Th. A. Steinlen, postcards with scenes of Parisian life, chromolithography.
123. Th. A. Steinlen, postcards from the series 'Cocorico', c. 1898, reproduction of the design for the cover of the magazine, chromolithography.
124, 125. Th. A. Steinlen, postcards with scenes of Parisian life, chromolithography.

126

127

128

129

130

126. *E. Grasset, postcard from the 'Collection des Cent', publ. Gréningaire, Paris, c. 1901, reproduction of the poster, collotype coloured with stencils.*

127. *J. Chéret, postcard from the 'Collection des Cent', publ. Gréningaire, Paris, c. 1901, collotype coloured with stencils.*

128. *J. Chéret, postcard from the series 'Cinos', Paris, 1898, reproduction of the poster, chromolithography.*

129. *H. Boutet, postcard of a Parisian scene, design dated 1891, chromolithography.*

130. *J. Abeille, postcard from a series of the seasons, publ. P. Süss A.-G., Dresden, design dated 1898.*

131

132

133

134

131. H. Thomas, postcard advertising the news-paper L'Eclair, lith. G. Bataille, Paris, design dated 1898, chromolithography.

132. H. J. F. Bellery-Desfontaines, 'Exposition Universelle et Internationale de Liège. . . 1905', printed Charles Verneau, Paris, reproduction of the poster, chromolithography.

133. P. Berthon, postcard from the series 'Affiches des chemins de fer', halftone letterpress.

134. J. A. Grün, postcard from the series 'Affiches des chemins de fer', design dated 1892, letterpress.

135. P. Berthon, 'Etude de femme (1)', publ. J. S. Paris, reproduction of a decorative panel, chromolithography.

ETUDE DE FEMME (1)

136

137

138

139

140

141

142

136. L. Cappiello, 'Grands Magasins des Cordeliers. Lyons Nouveautés', printed P. Vercasson & Cie, Paris, c. 1904, chromolithography.
137. G. -H. Jossot, postcard advertising the Parisian tailor Lejeune, printed P. Vercasson & Cie., Paris, 1903, chromolithography.
138. A. Roubille, postcard from the series Musée des Sires', published by the newspaper Le Rire, Paris, chromolithography.
139-142. Postcards from the series 'Concours d'Affiches Byrrh', c. 1906, by F. Vallotton, M. Leenbardt, M. de Thoren, L. André, halftone letterpress.

Concours d'Affiches « BYRRH » — 112 Lauréats
3e Prix (6 lauréats ex-æquo) ADOLPHE GIRALDON

143

Concours d'Affiches « BYRRH » — 112 Lauréats
6e Prix (66 lauréats ex-æquo) MAURICE DENIS

144

Concours d'Affiches « BYRRH » — 112 Lauréats
5e Prix (31 lauréats) ARTHUR FOACHE

145

Concours d'Affiches « BYRRH » — 112 Lauréats
5e Prix (31 lauréats ex-æquo) VAVASSEUR

146

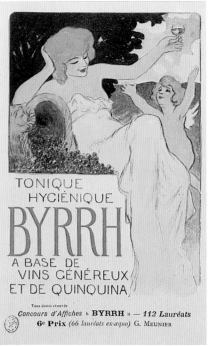

Concours d'Affiches « BYRRH » — 112 Lauréats
6e Prix (66 lauréats ex-æquo) G. MEUNIER

147

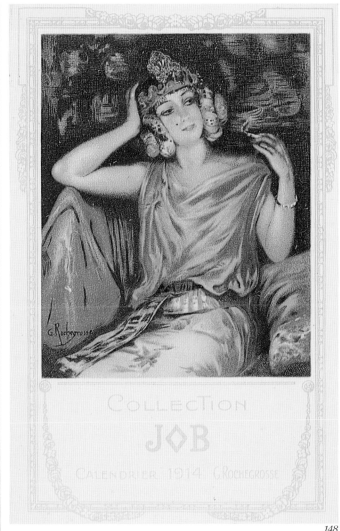

148

149

143-147. Postcards from the series 'Concours d'Affiches Byrrh', c. 1906, by A. Giraldon, M. Denis, A. Foache, E. Ch. P. Vavasseur, G. Meunier, halftone letterpress.
148, 149. Postcards from the series 'Collection Job' by G. Rochegrosse (1914 series, reproduction of a 1914 claendar) and by J. Atché (1914 series, reproduction of a 1897 poster), chromolithography.

150

151

150. *L. Cauvy, postcard n. 2 from series 10 of
Künstlerkarten, publ. Stengel & Co, Dresden u.
Berlin, chromolithography.*
151. *J. Kuhn-Regnier, postcard from series 103,
publ. Stengel & Co. Dresden, chromolithography.*

152

153

154

152. *E. L. Lessieux, 'Moderne' design dated*
1900, chromolithography.
153. *E. L. Lessieux, 'Bacchanale' design dated*
1900, chromolithography.
154. *E. L. Lessieux, 'Bellona', Theo Stroefer*
Kunstverlag, Nürnberg, series 137, n. 10, c.
1900, chromolithography.

155

156

157

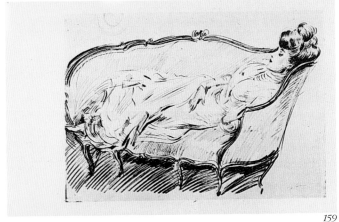

158

159

155-157. *L. Lelée, postcards from a series of ladies' faces, c. 1901, chromolithography.*
158. *L. Lebègue, postcard from the 'Collection des Cent', publ. Gréningaire, c. 1901, collotype coloured with stencils.*
159. *P. C. F. Helleu, postcard of a woman lying on a sofa, photogravure.*

160, 162. *E. L. Lessieux, 'Esclarmonde' and 'Salammbô', postcards from a series of heroines of literature and melodrama, designs dated 1900, chromolithography.*
161. *E. L. Lessieux, 'Venus', postcards n. 5 from series 137, Theo Stroefer Kunstverlag, Nürnberg, c. 1900, chromolithography.*

Nürnberg, Theo Stroefer's Kunstverlag, Serie 137, No V.

160

161

162

163

164

165

166

167

163. *G. Bonnet, postcard from the 'Collection des Cent', publ. Gréningaire, Paris, c. 1901, collotype coloured with stencils.*

164. *C. Henrida, postcard from the 'Collection des Cent', publ. Gréningaire, Paris, c. 1901'*

165. *M. P. Verneuil, postcard from the 'Collection des Cent', publ. Gréningaire, Paris, c. 1901, collotype coloured with stencils.*

166. *A. Cadiou, postcard from the 'Collection collotype coloured with stencils.*

des Cent', publ. Gréningaire, Paris, c. 1901, collotype coloured with stencils.

167. *A. Cadiou, postcard from the series 'Concours d'Affiches Byrrh', Paris, c. 1906, half-tone letterpress.*

168-173. E. Bernard, series 'L'entôlage', P. F.
res, chromolithography.

174

175

176

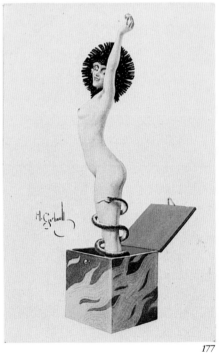

177

174. L. Morin, postcard from the 'Collection
des Cent', publ. Gréningaire, Paris, c. 1901,
collotype coloured with stencils.
175. L. Max, postcard without series or publisher's name, photogravure.
176, 177. H. Gerbault, 'Le papillon amoureux'
and 'Le Diable Parisien', nos 3 and 7 from
series 36, publ. R. & Cie Imp., screen-block
phototypography.

178. L. Lelée, postcard from the 'Collection des Cent', publ. Gréningaire, Paris, c. 1901, collotype coloured with stencils.
179. H. Morin, postcard advertising the postcard publisher A. Girard, collotype coloured with stencils.

180

181

180. F. Bac, postcard from the 'Collection des
Cent', publ. Gréningaire, Paris, c. 1901, collotype coloured with stencils.
181. G. Auriol, postcard from the 'Collection
des Cent', publ. Gréningaire, Paris, c. 1901,
collotype coloured with stencils.
182. A. Barrère, postcard advertising the bicycle gear factory, A. Brossard, no publisher's
name, 1903, chromolithography.
183. J. Wely, postcard from the 'Collection des
Cent', publ. Gréningaire, Paris, c. 1901, collotype coloured with stencils.
184. Sem, postcard advertising 'Tournées Ch.
Baret', chromolithography.
185. Géoft, 'Le Bal Bullier', collotype coloured
by hand.
186. A. Guillaume, 'La valse', Imp. Camis,
Paris, chromolithography.
187. Caran d'Ache, postcard advertising the
periodical Le Journal, 1904.
188. X. Sager, humorous postcards on ladies,
hats, publ. K. F., Paris, chromolithography.

182

183

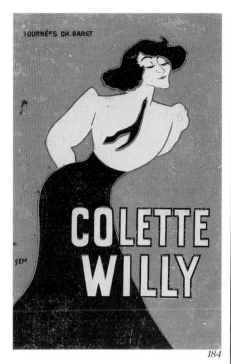

184

185

186

187

188

189. Hansi, 'Gosses d'Alsace', P. J. Gállais et Cie, éditeurs, Paris, reproductuion of a print of 1916, chromolithography.

190. Hansi, 'Saverne, Dernière page de l'Histoire d'Alsace', P. J. Gallais et Cie, éditeurs, Paris, reproduction of a print of 1914, chromolithography.

191. A. Roubille, postcard from the series 'Cocorico', c. 1898, reproduction of the design for a magazine cover, chromolithography.

On attend le Général.. *(d'après l'estampe.)*

189

HANSI - Saverne. Dernière page de l'Histoire d'Alsace. *(d'après l'estampe).* — Lt von Forstner back from schopping *(after the drawing).*

190

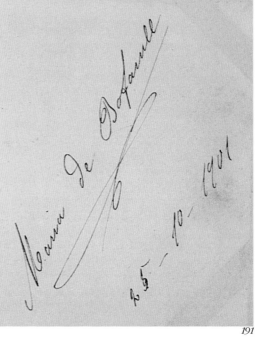

191

Austria and the Habsburg Empire
(Hungary, Bohemia and Moravia)

192. K. Moser, 'Wiener Künstler-Postkarten'
series V, n. I. Philipp & Kramer, Vienna,
chromolithography.

DRUCK u. VERLAG v. PHILIPP & KRAMER, WIEN. WIENER KÜNSTLER-POSTKARTE SERIE V/1.

192

193

194

195

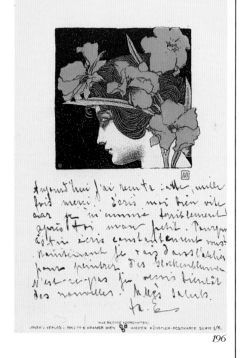

196

193. K. Moser, 'Künstler-Postkarten der Meggendorfer Blätter', n. 510, Verlag J. F. Schreiber, Esslingen, post-marked: 22.12.1898, collotype.

194. K. Moser, 'Künstler-Postkarten der Meggendorfer Blätter', n. 8, Verlag J. F. Schreiber, Esslingen, written 25.9.1899, halftone letterpress.

195. K. Moser, J. Hoffman, 'Ver Sacrum. Erste grosse Kunstausstellung der Vereinigung bildend Künstler Oesterreichs. Secession', n. I, Verlag Gerlach & Schenk, Vienna, 1898, chromolithography.

196. K. Moser, 'Wiener Künstler-Postkarten' series I, n. 5, Philipp & Kramer, Vienna, 1897, chromolithography.

197. K. Moser, 'Sommernacht', 'Künstlerpostkarte' n. 90, F. A. Ackermann Kunstverlag, Munich, c. 1897, collotype.

198, 199. K. Moser 'Wiener Künstler-Postkarten' series I, n. 9 and series IV, n. 7, Philipp & Kramer, Vienna, 1897, chromolithography.

197

198

199

200

201

202

203

204

205

206

207

208

200. 'Wiener Künstler-Postkarten' series III, n. 10, Philipp & Kramer, Vienna, 1897, chromolithography with the monograms (from the top) of A. Karpellus, K. Moser, J. Hoffmann, F. Pilz, M. Kurzweil, A. Pock (?), L. Kainradl.

201. K. Moser, J. Hoffmann and others (on the man's chest there are four monograms), 'Wiener Künstler-Postkarten' series IV, n. 5, Philipp & Kramer, Vienna 1897, chromolithography.

202. K. Moser, 'Wiener Künstler-Postkarten' series III, n. 7, Philipp & Kramer, Vienna, 1897, chromolithography.

203. K. Moser, F. Kruis (?), J. Hoffmann, 'Wiener Künstler-Postkarten' series II, n. 9, Philipp & Kramer, 1897, Vienna, chromolithography.

204. K. Moser, 'Wiener Künstler-Postkarten' series n. 10, Philipp & Kramer, Vienna, 1897,

chromolithography.

205. J. Hoffmann, L. Kainradl, 'Wiener Künstler-Postkarten' series IV, n. 10, Philipp & Kramer, Vienna, 1898, chromolithography.

206. L. Kainradl, 'Wiener Künstler-Postkarten' series V, n. 8, Philipp & Kramer, Vienna, 1898, chromolithography.

207. K. Moser, J. Olbrich, 'Ver Sacrum, Erste-grosse Kunstausstellung der Vereinigung bildender Künstler Oesterreichs. Secession', n. 7, Verlag Gerlach & Schenk, Vienna, 1898, chromolithography.

208. A. Böhm, 'Ver Sacrum. Erste grosse Kunstausstellung er Vereinigung bildender Künstler Oesterreichs, Secession', n. 2, Verlag Gerlach & Schenk, Vienna, 1898, chromolithography.

Variété. XXX/1 Wiener Künstler-Postkarte. — Alle Rechte vorbehalten. Druck und Verlag PHILIPP & KRAMER, Wien, VI.

209

210

VI/6 Wiener Künstler-Postkarte. — Alle Rechte vorbehalten. Druck und Verlag PHILIPP & KRAMER, Wien, VI.

Fahrendes Volk. XVI/7 Wiener Künstler-Postkarte. — Alle Rechte vorbehalten. Druck und Verlag PHILIPP & KRAMER, Wien, VI.

XIII/6 Wiener Künstler-Postkarte. — Alle Rechte vorbehalten. Druck und Verlag PHILIPP & KRAMER, Wien, VI.

211

212

213

214

215

209. W. Hampel, 'Variété', 'Wiener Künstler-Postkarten', series XXX, n. 1, Philipp & Kramer, Vienna, c. 1899, halftone letterpress.
210. W. Hampel, 'Wiener Künstler-Postkarten' series LXII, n. 6, Philipp & Kramer, Vienna c. 1900, halftone letterpress.
211. W. Hampel, 'Wiener Künstler-Postkarten' series VI, n. 6, Philipp & Kramer, Vienna, 1898, halftone letterpress.
212. M. Lenz, 'Fahrendes Volk', 'Wiener Künstler-Postkarten' series XVI, n. 7, Philipp & Kramer, Vienna 1898, halftone letterpress.
213. R. Konopa, 'Wiener Künstler-Postkarten' series XIII, n. 6, Philipp & Kramer, Vienna, 1898, halftone letterpress.
214. C. O. Czeschka, postcard published by Gerlach & Schenk, Wien, design dated 1898, chromolithography.
215. R. Konopa, 'Wiener Künstler-Postkarten' series XLVI, n. 2, Philipp & Kramer, Vienna, c. 1900, halftone letterpress.

216

217

216. *A. Wanke (?), Verlag M. Munk, Vienna,*
Druck S. Czeiger, Vienna, c. 1900, chromo-
lithography.
217. *F. Bayros, 'Erster Morgengruss!', series*
'O, das Ewig Weibliche!', Verlag M. Victor,
Cologne, design dated 1898, halftone letter-
press.
218–220. *G. Th. Kempf, series 165, nos. 8, 7, 3,*
no publisher's name, c. 1900, chromo-
lithography.

218

219

220

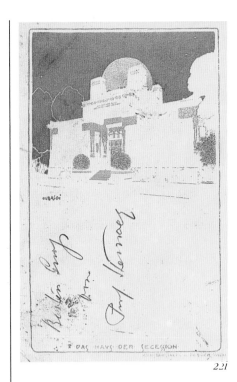

221

222

223

224

221. J. M. Olbrich, 'Das Haus der Secession', Kunstanstalt A. Berger, Vienna, c. 1898, chromolithography.
222. J. Heinisch, 'Entwurf einer monumentalen Bank', a single-copy postcard, pen with black Chinese ink, postmarked: 9.12.1918.
223, 224. J. Hoffmann, series 'Jubiläums-Ausstellung Wien 1898', postcards n. 18 e n. 14, Druck u. Verlag Philipp & Kramer, Vienna, 1898, halftone letterpress.
225. R. Kirchner, 'Auf Sommerfrische', 'Wiener Künstler-Postkarten' series XVIII, n. 10,

Philipp & Kramer, Vienna, 1899, halftone letterpress.
226. R. Kirchner, untitled and no publisher's name, post-marked: 10.9.1901, chromolithography.
228. R. Kirchner, untitled and no publisher's name, c. 1901, chromolithography.
227, 229. R. Kirchner, series 99, nos. 3, 1, Theo Stroefer's Kunstverlag, Nürnberg, Druck Meissner & Buch, Leipzig, 1900, chromolithography.

Auf Sommerfrische. XVIII 10 Wiener Künstler-Postkarte. — Alle Rechte vorbehalten. Druck und Verlag PHILIPP & KRAMER, Wien, VI.

225

226

227

228

229

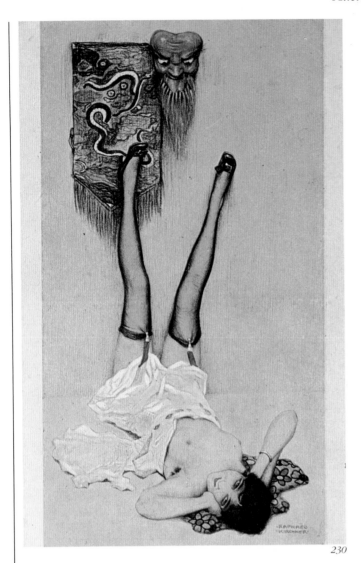

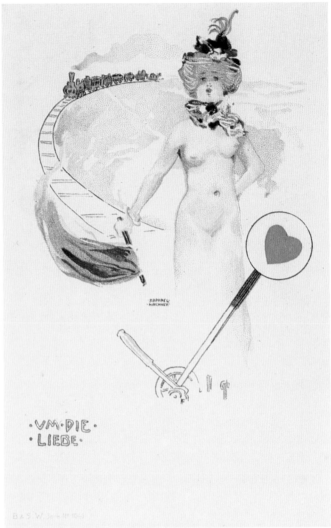

230

231

232

233

234

230. *R. Kirchner, 'Le masque impassible', a variation on an illustration in the volume* Le Bandeau, *by F. Champsaur (1916), postcard n. 15 in a series published by Librairie de l'Estampe, Paris, Imprimerie A. Leroy et R. Grémieu, Paris, halftone letterpress.*
231. *R. Kirchner, 'Um die Liebe': series 1040,* Back & Schmitt, Vienna, chromolithography.
232. *R. Kirchner, 'Flussnixe', J. Gerson, Paris, before 1901, chromolithography.*
233, 234. *R. Kirchner, 'A'ala' and 'Estramadura', series 'Les Cigarettes du monde', nos. 2, 4, E. Storch, Vienna, 1900, chromolithography.*

235

236

237

238

235. J. Divéky, 'Wien. Steinhof-Kirche', series by the Wiener Werkstätte, n. 405, chromolithography.

236. J. Hoffmann, 'Cabaret Fledermaus, Wien, Karntnerstrasse 33', series by the Wiener Werkstätte, n. 74, chromolithography.

237. G. Kalhammer, Restaurant Staatsbahnhof in Vienna, series by the Wiener Werkstätte, n. 408, chromolithography.

238. E. Hoppe, the garden at the Kunstschau 1908, series by the Wiener Werkstätte, n. 4, chromolithography.

239–243. M. Jung, series by the Wiener Werkstätte, nos. 510, 66, 339, 529, 530, chromolithography.

ZWISCHEN 3 UND 4 UHR FRÜH!

239

NAECHTLICHES GESPRAECH

240

UNBLUTIGE JAGD AUF GIRAFFEN

241

WIENER CAFE: CARAMBOL.

242

WIENER CAFE: IM LESEZIMMER.

243

244

245

246

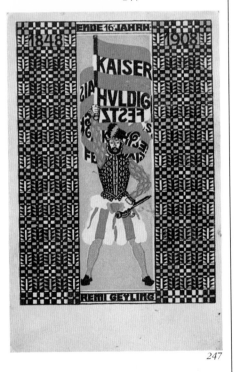

247

244. K. Moser, official postcard for the Jubilee of emperor Franz Josef, published in Prague by Staatsdruckerei, Vienna, 1908, photogravure.
245–247. R. Geyling, postcards for the Jubilee of emperor Franz Josef in 1908, series by the Wiener Werkstätte, nos. 164, 173, 177, chromolithography.
248–250. B. Löffler postcards reproducing the designs for the murals in the Volkskeller in Salzberg, series by the Wiener Werkstätte nos. 907, 914, 916, chromolithography.

248

249

250

251

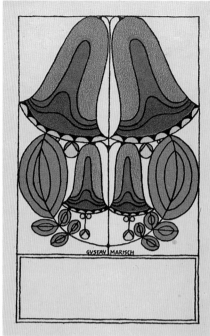

252

253

254

255

256

251, 253. *C. Krenek, series by the Wiener Werkstätte, nos. 253, 256, chromolithography.*
252. *G. Marisch, series by the Wiener Werkstätte, n. 610, chromolithography.*
254. *V. Petter-Zeis, Easter postcard, series by the Wiener Werkstätte, n. 153, chromolithography.*
255. *L. Kolbe, series by the Wiener Werkstätte, n. 36, chromolithography.*
256. *A. Velim, Christmas postcard, series by the Wiener Werkstätte, n. 875, chromolithography.*

257. *L. H. Jungnickel, series by the Wiener Werkstätte, n. 380, chromolithography.*
258. *G. Marisch, postcards published by B. R., Vienna, chromolithography.*
259. *F. K. Delavilla, Christmas postcard series by the Wiener Werkstätte, n. 19, chromolithography.*
260. *F. Löwensohn, New Year greetings postcard, series by the Wiener Werkstätte, n. 962,*
261. *R. Kalvach, series by the Wiener Werkstätte, n. 148, c. 1908, chromolithography.*

257

258

259

260

261

262

263

264

265

266

267

262. U. Janke, view of the cake-shop Demel in the Kohlmarkt, series by the Wiener Werkstätte, n. 402, chromolithography.
263. J. Divéky, 'Wien. Laimgrubenkirche', series by the Wiener Werkstätte, n. 402, chromolithography.
264. E. Schmal, 'Wien Am Hof. Christkindlmarkt, series by the Wiener Werkstätte, n. 239, chromolithography.
265. U. Janke, 'Wien. Belvedere', series by the Wiener Werkstätte, n. 136. chromolithography.
266. F. Lebisch, series by the Wiener Werkstätte, n. 12, c. 1908, letterpress.
267. J. Divéky, 'K. K. Hofburg in Wien', series by the Wiener Werkstätte, n. 262, chromolithography.
268. F. Süsser, 'Kunsthistorisches Hofmuseum', Kilophot A 104, chromolithography.
269. K. Schwetz, the Gloriette in the park of Schönbrunn in Vienna, Kilophot A 128, chromolithography.
270. K. Schwetz, Schönbrunn, Vienna, Kilophot A 127, chromolithography.

268

269

270

271

272

271. *E. Schiele, series by the Wiener Werkstätte,*
n. 288, design dated 1910, chromolithography.
272. *E. Schiele, series by the Wiener Werkstätte,*
n. 77, c. 1908, chromolithography.

273

274

273. *O. Kokoschka, series by the Wiener Werkstätte, n. 77, chromolithography.*
274. *O. Kokoschka, series by the Wiener Werkstätte, n. 152, chromolithography.*

275

276

277

278

279

280

275, 277. M Koehler, publishers Brüder Kòhn, Vienna, series 131, nos. 1 and 5, halftone letterpress.

276. M. Koehler, publishers Brüder Köhn, Vienna, series 481, n. 3, chromolithography.

278. O. Lendecke, series by the Wiener Werkstätte, n. 853, chromolithography.

279. A. Nechansky, New Year greetings postcard, series by the Wiener Werkstätte, n. 893, chromolithography.

280. D. Peche, series by the Wiener Werkstätte, n. 626, design dated 1912, chromolithography.

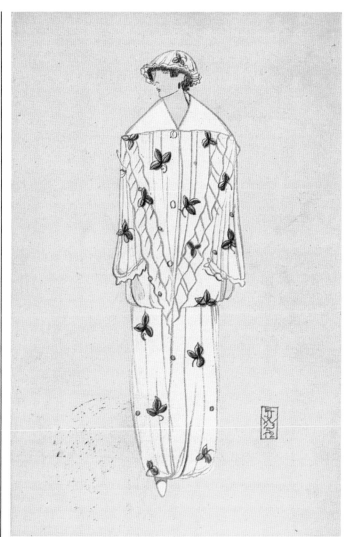

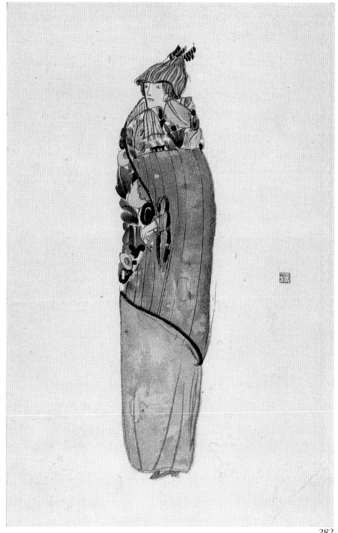

281

282

281. *E. J. Wimmer, fashion plate, design dated
23.5.1912, series by the Wiener Werkstätte, n.
870, chromolithography.*
282. *E. J. Wimmer, fashion plate, series by the
Wiener Werkstätte, n. 864, chromolithography.*

283–288. *Postcards from the special series by the Wiener Werkstätte, with fabric designs by C. O. Czeschka, M. Alber, L. Fochler, W. Jonasch, E. Wimmer, M. Riedl. chromolithography.*
289. *F. Löw, series by the Wiener Werkstätte, n. 1001, design dated 1910, chromolithography.*
290, 291, 293. *M. Likarz, series by the Wiener Werkstätte, nos. 768, 832, 769, chromolithography.*
292. *C. O. Czeschka, New Year greetings card, series by the Wiener Werkstätte, n. 252.*

289

290

291

292

293

294

295

296

297

294. *L. Fischer, '1. Internationale Jagdausstellung Wien 1910', halftone letterpress.*
295. *A. Wanke, design dated 1909, n. 452 publ. M. Munk, Vienna, chromolithography.*
296. *M. Lenz, postcard for the war loan, lith. A. Berger, Vienna, 1917, chromolithography.*
297. *R. Wichera, publisher M. Munk, n. 336, postmarked: 28.12.1907, collotype coloured by hand.*

298

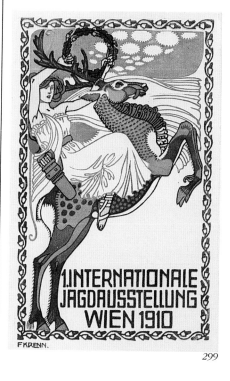

299

300

301

298. *K. Libesny, 'Ost Adria Ausst. 1913, Wien', chromolithography.*
299. *F. Krenn, '1. Internationale Jagdausstellung Wien 1910', halftone letterpress.*
300. *E. Puchinger, 'Erste Internationale Jagdausstellung Wien 1910 Mai-Oktober', halftone letterpress.*
301. *S. Hönig, '!. Internationale Jagdausstellung Wien 1910', halftone letterpress.*

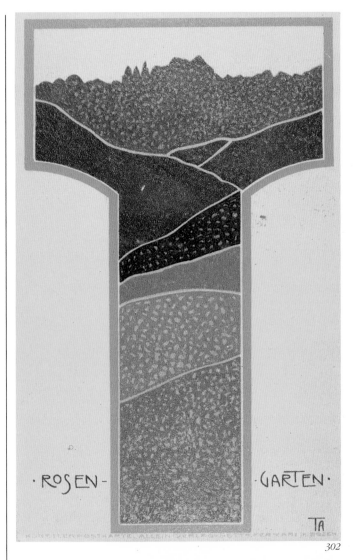

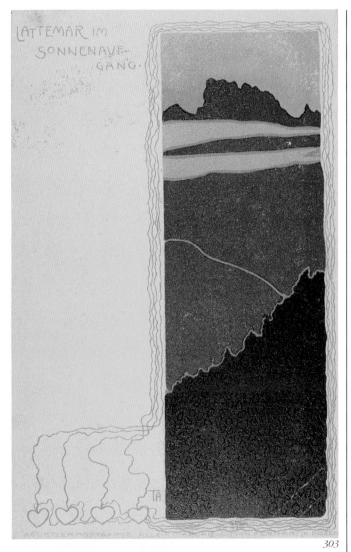

302

303

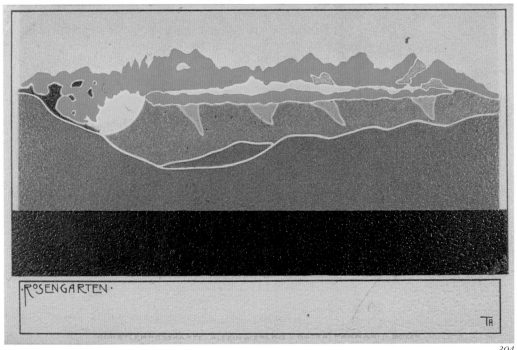

304

305

306

302–304. *TA (unidentified monogram), three postcards in a series of at least eight, 'Künstlerpostkarten. Allein-Verlag v. Gotth. Ferrari jr. Bozen'.*

305, 306. *A. Basch, 'La suédoise', 'L'espagnole', series of women of different nationalities, no publisher's name, c. 1900, chromolithography.*

307

308

*307, 308. A. Basch, series of women warriors,
no publisher's name, c. 1900, chromolithography.*

309

310

309. *C. Józsa, postcard from a series with women's heads, c. 1900, chromolithography.*
310. *C. Józsa, 'Sirenen und Circen' series VII, n. 40, publ. A. Sockl, Vienna, c. 1900, chromolithography.*

311

312

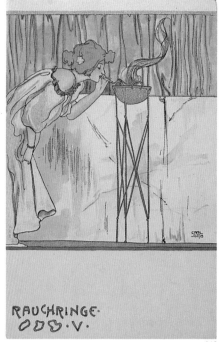

313

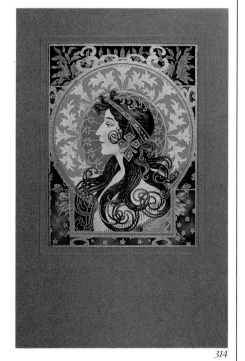

314

311. *C. Józsa, 'Sirenen und Circen' series VII,*
n. 32, publ. A. Sockl, Vienna, c. 1900,
chromolithography.
312. *(Unidentified monogram), no publisher's*
name, c. 1904, hand-coloured halftone letter-
press.
313. *C. Józsa, series 'Rauchringe', n. 5, c. 1900,*
chromolithography.
314. *Anonymous, no publisher's name, c. 1902,*
chromolithography.

315

316

317

318

315. (Unidentified monogram), no publisher's
name, c. 1910, chromolithography.
316–318. Postcards from a series by the Hungarian National School for Applied Arts, publ.
J. E. Rigler, Budapest, c. 1911, chromolithography.

ESPOSIZIONE·INTERNAZIONALE.
TORINO·APRILE—NOVEMBRE·1911
PADIGLIONE·UNGHERESE
ARCHITETTI·PROGETTORI
Prof.E.TÖRY&M.POGÁNY

319

ESPOSIZI
ONE·INTER
NAZIONALE
TORINO
APRILE
NOVEMBRE
1911

PADIGLI·
ONE-UNG·
HERESE
ARCHITET·
TI-PROGET·
TORI· Prof
E·TÖRY&
M·POGÁNY

320

ESPOSIZIONE·INTERNAZI NALE.
TORINO·APRILE·NOVEMBRE·1911
PADIGLIONE·UNGHERESE·ARCHI-
TETTI·PROGETTORI·Prof·E·TÖRY&·M·POGÁNY

321

EXPOSITION·INTERNATIONALE
·TURIN·1911·
·HONGRIE·

ESPOSIZIONE·INTERNACIONALE
·TORINO·1911·
·UNGHERIA·

322

ESPOSIZIONE·INTERNAZIONALE
TORINO·APRILE×NOVEMBRE×1911
PADIGLIONE×UNGHERESE×××ARCHI-
TETTI·PROGETTORI PROF·E.TÖRY&M·POGÁNY

323

324

325

319–323. E. Töry and M. Pogány, postcards
from the series in the Hungarian pavilion at the
'Esposizione Internazionale' in Turin, 1911,
halftone.

324. A. Mucha, postcard advertising the 'Slavia' bank, Prague, 1909, reproduction with
variations of the poster, halftone letterpress.

325. A. Mucha, Spring, publ. F. Champenois,
Paris, c. 1902, reproduction of a decorative
panel 1899, chromolithography.

326

327

328

329

330

326. A. Mucha, Sunset, series 'Cartes postales artistiques', publ. F. Champenois, Paris, c. 1902, reproduction of a decorative panel, chromolithography.

327. A. Mucha, Byzantine head: Brunette, series 'Cartes postales artistiques', publ. F. Champenois, Paris, c. 1902, reproduction of a decorative panel, c. 1897, chromolithography.

328. A. Mucha, Zodiac, series 'Cartes postales artistiques', publ. F. Champenois, Paris, a design previously executed in several mediums, chromolithography.

329, 330. A. Mucha, The arts of Poetry and of Painting, series 'Cartes postales artistiques', publ. F. Champenois, Paris, reproductions

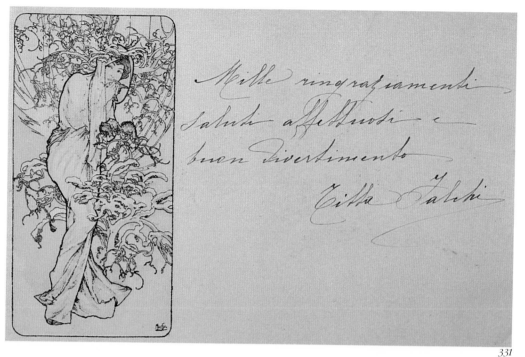

331

332

333

334

335

from decorative panels 1908, chromolithography.
331. A. Mucha, Winter, series, 'Cartes postales
artistiques', publ. F. Champenois, Paris, repro-

duction of a decorative panel 1896,
chromolithography.
332-335. A. Mucha, April, January, July,
March, series of the months, 'Cartes postales

artistiques', publ. F. Champenois, Paris, reproductions with variations on the monochrome
lithographs in Le Mois Littéraires et Pittores-
ques in 1899-1900, chromolithography.

336

337   *338*   *339*

336. A. Mucha, Iris, series 'Cartes postales artistiques', publ. F. Champenois, Paris, reproduction of a decorative panel 1897, chromolithography.
337-339. A. Mucha, Adolescence, Maturity, Old Age series, publ. F. Champenois, Paris, reproductions from the plates in a calendar for Chocolat Masson, chromolithography.
340. F. Kysela, 'Všestudentská Slavnost', reproduction of the poster, chromolithography.

341. K. Spillar, postcard from the series 'Concours d'Affiches Byrrh', 1906, design dated 1883, halftone letterpress.
342. Anonymous, 'Národní Beseda. 24.1.1900. T. Zofin', halftone letterpress.
343. Anonymous, 'Presěrnov Sonetni Venec', chromolithography.
344. S. Kulhanek, 'Veselé svatky velikonoční, Kladno, chromolithography.

340

341

342

343

344

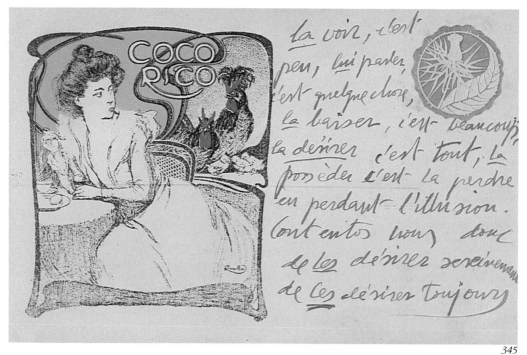

345

346

347

345. *F. Kupka, postcard from the series 'Coco-*
ico', c. 1989, chromolithography.
346. *A. Brázda, 'Ustrední matice školská, half-*
tone letterpress.
347. *W. A. Hablik, 'Ortsgruppe Brüx des*
deutschen Schulvereines', design dated 1902,
letterpress.

Germany

348

349

348, 349. J. R. Witzel, untitled postcards, H. C.
Wolf Editeur, Paris, Lith. E. Nister, Nuremberg, c. 1902, chromolithography.

350

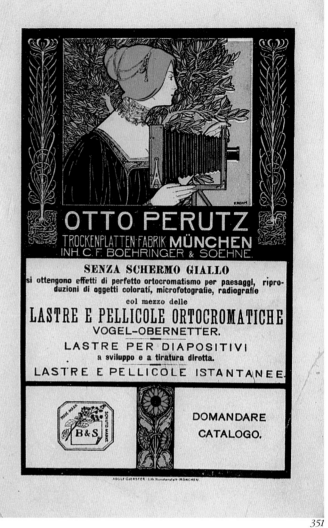

351

352

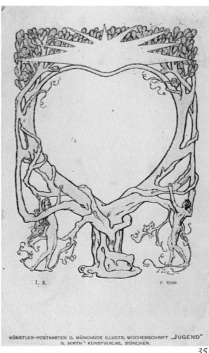

353

354

355

356

357

350. F. Rehm, 'Hexerei' (Sorcery), no publisher's name, c. 1900, chromolithography.

351. F. Rehm, publicity postcard 'Otto Perutz Trockenplatten-Fabrik München', Adolf Gierster, Lith. Kunstanstalt, Munich, c. 1900, chromolithography.

352. J. Klinger, 'Künstler-Postkarte der Meggendorfer Blätter. N. 514', Verlag J. F. Schreiber, Esslingen, postmarked: 1898, letterpress.

353. F. Erler, 'Künstler-Postkarten d. Münchner Illustr. Wochenschrift Jugend', series I, n. 8, G. Hirth's Kunstverlag, Munich, 1898.

354. F. W. Kleukens, Easter greetings postcard from the series by the Steglitzer Werkstatt; E. S., Berlin, post-marked: 1902.

355. G. Tappert, 'Karlsruher-Kunstlerfest'. J. Schober (Inb. Karl Obrist), Karlsruhe, postmarked: 1901, chromolithography.

356. E. Hansen (Nolde), 'Rigi u. Pilatus', Kunstverlag F. Killinger, Zurich, c. 1898, half-tone letterpress.

357. Anonymous, postcard published by Druck u. Verlag von B. Dondorf G.m.b.H., Frankfurt a.M., n. 422, c. 1908, chromolithography.

358. Fidus (H. Höppener), Vor dem Angesichte', design dated 1914.

358

359

360

362

363

359. *Fidus (H. Höppener), Dornröschen',*
1919.
360. *Fidus (H. Höppener), 'Lenzweben', re-*
production of a large plate, Römmler & Jonas
Dresden, halftone letterpress.
361. *H. Christiansen, postcard from a series,*
publ. J. Ph. Leuthner, Darmstadt, Lith. Korn-
sand & Co., Frankfurt a.M., c. 1902,
chromolithography.
362, 363. *H. Christiansen, postcards from the*
series 'Paris', publ. Wolfrum & Hauptmann,
Nürnberg, 1900, chromolithography.
364, 365. *H. Christiansen, postcards from the*
series 'Darmstadt', Kunst-Anstalt Kornsand &
Co., Frankfurt a.M., c. 1902, chromo-
lithography.
366. *O. Eckmann, 'Künstler-Postkarte' from*
Jugend, series i. n. 6, G. Hirth's Kunstverlag,
Müchen, c. 1902, chromolithography.

DARMSTADT

364

DARMSTADT

365

367

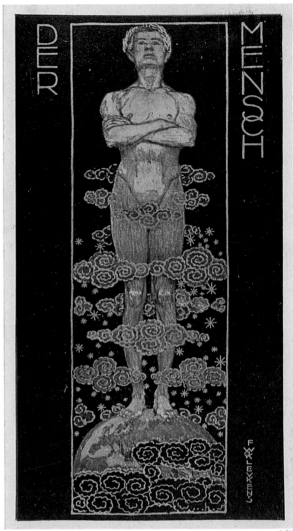

368

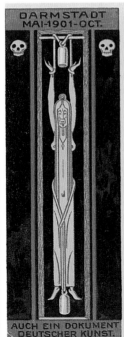

369

370

371

HAVS DEITERS.

372

KVNSTLER· KOLONIE· DARMSTADT· AVSSTELLVNG 1904
ECKHAVS· ERBAVT· VON· PROFESSOR J.M·OLBRICH·

373

367. *P. Haustein, 'Ausstellung der Künstler-Kolonie Darmstadt 1904', chromolithography.*
368. *F. W. Kleukens, 'Ausstellung Der Mensch, Darmstadt 1912', chromolithography.*
369. *Anonymous, parody of the poster by P. Behrens for the exhibition of the artists' colony in Darmstadt in 1901, Verlag K. Kneib, Munich, chromolithography.*
370. *F. W. Kleukens, 'Hessische Landes-Ausstellung für freie angewandte Kunst Darmstadt 1908', chromolithography.*
Anonymous, parody of the poster by M. Olbrich for the exhibition of the artists' colony in Darmstadt in 1901, Verlag Georg Hof, Darmstadt, chromolithography.
371. *Anonymous, parody of the poster by M. Olbrich for the exhibition of the artists' colony in Darmstadt in 1901, Verlag Georg Hof, Darmstadt, chromolithography.*
372, 373. *J. M. Olbrich, series of postcards for the exhibition of the artists' colony in Darmstadt 1901: views of the Deiters house, and of the house at the corner of a group of three, Kunstanstalt Lautz & Jsenbeck, Darmstadt, chromolithography.*

374

375

376

377

378

379

380

381

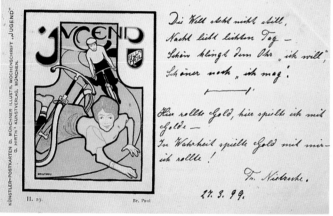

382

383

374. *W. Oertel, Künstlerkarte, series 10, n. 131, ed. Stengel & Co., Dresden-Berlin, c. 1900, chromolithography.*

375. *G. A. Stroedel, Künstlerkarte, Stengel & Co., Dresden, c. 1900, chromolithography.*

376. *P. Ebner, Christmas postcard, publ. M. Munk, Vienna, post-marked: 25.12.1914, chromolithography.*

377. *L. Schnug, New Year greetings card, 'Wiener Künstler-Postkarte' series XLV ('Neujahrs-Humor'), n. 4, Philipp & Kramer, Vienna 1899, chromolithography.*

378. *J. v. Kulas, Christmas greetings card, chromolithography.*

379. *Anonymous, decorative postcard, chromolithography.*

380. *O. Gräber, 'Gruss vom Schlusskommers der Kunstgewerbeschüler in Karlsruhe', chromolithography.*

381. *Th. Th. Heine, 'Berliner Secession', reproduction of the poster, M. Fischer Kunstverlag, Berlin, 1901, chromolithography.*

382. *B. Paul, 'Künstler-Postkarte' from Jugend, series II, n. 19, G. Hirth's Kunstverlag, Munich, 1898, chromolithography.*

383. *L. v. Zumbusch, 'Künstler-Postkarte' from Jugend, series II, n. 25, G. Hirth's Kunstverlag, Munich, 1898, chromolithography.*

384, 385. *H. Vogeler, 'Stollwerck-Postkarten'. Gruppe 17: Gänsemädchen-Königssohn', n. 5: 'Gefunden', n. 4: 'In den Krieg', c. 1906, chromolithography.*

386, 388. *O. Eckmann, 'Stollwerck-Postkarten'. Gruppe 14: Gefiederte Welt', n. 1: 'Schwanenlied', n. 4: 'Schwarze Schwâne', c. 1906, chromolithography.*

387. *J. Gerdes, 'Worpsweder Künstlerkarten', Eigent. u. Verlag d. Nordwestd. Antiquariat, Bremen, Lith. Anstalt H. Bosking, Bremen, post-marked: 1900, chromolithography.*

389. *R. Engels, 'Künstler-Postkarte' from Jugend, series II, n. 11, G. Hirth's Kunstverlag, Munich 1898, chromolithography.*

390. *M. Klinger, 'Margueritentag, Leipzig 11 Februar 1911', Druck Meissner & Buch, Leipzig, chromolithography.*

391. *E. M. Lilien, 'Sturm', reproduction from the illustration in the book* Lieder des Ghetto *by M. Kolenfeld (1902), letterpress.*

Stollwerck-Postkarten. — Gruppe 17. Gänsemädchen-Königssohn. Von: H. Vogeler. No. V. Gefunden.

Stollwerck-Postkarten. — Gruppe 17. Gänsemädchen-Königssohn. Von: H. Vogeler. No. IV. In den Krieg.

384

385

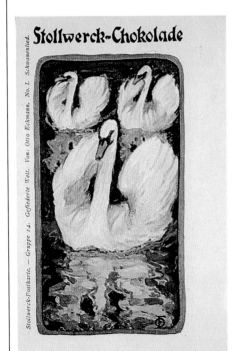

Stollwerck-Postkarte. — Gruppe 14. Gefiederte Welt. Von: Otto Eckmann. No. I. Schwanenlied.

Stollwerck-Postkarte. — Gruppe 14. Gefiederte Welt. Von: Otto Eckmann. No. IV. Schwarze Schwäne.

386

387

388

KÜNSTLER-POSTKARTEN D. MÜNCHNER ILLUSTR. WOCHENSCHRIFT „JUGEND"
G. HIRTH'S KUNSTVERLAG, MÜNCHEN.

II. 11.   Rob. Engels

389

390

STURM

E. M. LILIEN

391

392

393

394

395

396

397

398

399

400

392. A. Konrad, publicity postcard. 'Künstler-karte' series 10, n. 137, publ. Stengel & Co., Dresden-Berlin, chromolithography.

393. E. Döcker jr., 'Modern' series 29, Kunst-verlag R. Neuber, Vienna, c. 1900, chromolithography.

394. H. Anker, 'Sternthaler', postcard from the publicity series 'Märchen-Postkarte', for the company Jünger & Gebhardt, Berlin: Kunstan-stalt Etzold u. Kiessling A. G., Crimmitschad i.S., chromolithography.

395. V. Lauer, 'Künstlerpostkarte', series 10, n. 141, publ. Stengel & Co., Dresden-Berlin, chromolithography.

396, 398. J.S. (unidentified monogram), 'Jung-gesellen-Postkarte', nos. 7 and 2, Philipp & Kramer, Vienna, post-marked: 1899, chromolithography.

397. H. C. Starcke, 'Coeur-Dame', no publish-er's name, c. 1900, chromolithography.

399. B. Wennerberg, 'Lawn-tennis', 'Künstler-Postkarten' series 1039, Meissner & Buch, Leipzig, chromolithography.

400. P. O. Engelhardt, New Year greeting postcard 'Künstlerpostkarte' series 10, n. 32, publ. Stengel & Co., Dresden-Berlin, post-marked: 1899, chromolithography.

401

402

401. C. Zander, 'Winter', no publisher's name,
c. 1900, chromolithography.
402. O. Beyer, greetings postcard for the feast,
of St. Nicholas (6 December),
chromolithography.
403. E. Heilemann, 'Simplicissimus-karte', series XII, n. 5.
404. F. v. Reznicek, 'Simplicissimus-karte',
series I, n. 12, publ. A. Langen, Munich, c.
1900, chromolithography.
405. F. v. Reznicek, 'Madame Vervier', 'Jugend-Postkarte' series XV, n. 3, G. Hirth's
Verlag, Munich, halftone letterpress.
406. F. v. Reznicek, 'Blumenkorso in Ostende',
'Jugend-Postkarte' series XV, n. 5. G. Hirth's
Verlag, Munich, Druck Knorr & Hirth, Munich, design dated 1896, published in Jugend, *I*
(1896), n. 36, p. 585, halftone letterpress.
407. E. Thöny, 'Der Landesvater', 'Simplicissi-
mus-Postkarte'. n. 33, design published in the
magazine, vol. IV (1899/1900), n. 42.

403

404

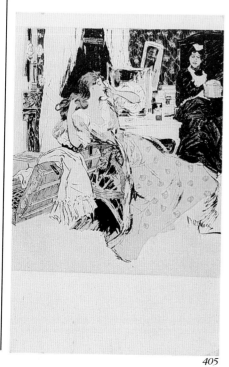

405

406

407

408

409

410

411

412

413

414

408. *J. Diez, 'München 1908 Ausstellung angewandte Kunst – Handwerk – Industrie – Handel – Öffentlich Einrichtungen – Sport', reproduction of the poster Künstler-Karten, Herst. v. Vertr. Ges. m.b.H. Munich, chromolithography.*

409. *G. Triebe, '26. Mitteldeutsches Bundesschiessen 1911 Leipzig', chromolithography.*

410. *A. Weisgerber, 'II Offizielle Ansichtskarte der bayerischen Jubiläums-Landesausstellung, Nürnberg 1906', Kunstverlag Martin, Nürnberg, Lith. & Druck Fritz Schneller & Co. Nürnberg, chromolithography.*

411. *J. Klinger, 'Grosse Berliner Kunst-Ausstellung 1909', Kunstanstalt Arnold Weylandt, Berlin, chromolithography.*

412. *P. Behrens, 'Offizielle Postkarte der Deutschen Werkbund Ausstellung Cöln 1914', reproduction of the poster, Verlag Georg Stilke, Berlin, series I, n. 1, chromolithography.*

413. *(Unidentified monogram), postcard from a series of Hamburg views, publ. Kumm Gebr. Kunstverlag, Hamburg, lith. L.K.K.*

414. *C. Kunst, 'Ausstellung Munchen 1908' chromolithography.*

415

416

415. *P. Hey, 'Herbstmorgen', Lith. Anstalt Hubert Kohler, Munich, chromolithography.*
416. *P. Hey, 'Dämmerung', Lith. Anstalt Hubert Kohler, Munchen, post-marked: 1910, chromolithography.*
417-419. *E. Liebermann, three postcards from a landscape series: 'Kapelle', 'Mühle', 'Bergeshöh', Lith. Anstalt Hubert Köhler, Munich, chromolithography.*

417

418

419

friedr. Kallmorgen, Der erste Schnee

420

421

420. Ost (O. Petersen), ice-skating.
421. F. Kallmorgen, 'Der erste Schnee', post-card from the series 'Deutsche Graphiker', reproduction of a lithographic plate, Verlag der Kunstdruckerei Künstlerbund Karlsruhe G.m.b.H., chromolithography.
422-424. F. Spiegel, three postcards from the series 'Aus goldener Zeit'; 'Im Lenz', 'Das versunkene Schloss', 'Lueg in's Land', Druck H. Köhler, Munich, chromolithography.

422

423

424

Guſt. Kampmann, Abendzug

425

Friedrich Lissmann   Nr. 1. Dreizehenmöwen

426

425. *G. Kampmann, 'Abendzug', 'Deutsche Graphiker' series VIII, n. 3, reproduction of a lithograph, Verlag der Kunstdruckerei Künstlerbund Karlsruhe G.m.b.H., chromolithography.*
426. *F. Lissmann, 'Dreizehenmöwen', Hanseatischer Kunstverlag, Hamburg, reproduced from a woodcut, chromolithography.*

427

428

427, 428. C. O. Czeschka, postcards from a
series for the military post, advertizing H.
Bahlsen's Keks-Fabrik, Hannover, 1915,
chromolithography.

429

430

431

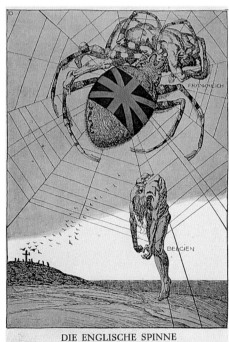

DIE ENGLISCHE SPINNE

432

429. *C. O. Czeschka, postcard from a series for the military post, advertising Bahlsen's Keks-Fabrik, Hannover, 1915, chromolithography.*
430. *K. Schulpig, 'Die Bäder und der Krieg', J. C. König & Ebhardt, Hannover, chromolithography.*
431. *L. Hohlwein, 'Zur Erinnerung an die Volksspende für die deutschen Kriegs- und Zivilgefangenen', 1916.*
432 *J. Diez, 'Die Englische Spinne', postcard published by Simplicissimus, Munich, c. 1915.*

Poland

433

434

433, 434. F. Laskoff, postcard from a series of
women, chromolithography.

435

436

437

438

439

440

435-440. *F. Laskoff, postcards from a series on sports, chromolithography.*
441. *F. Laskoff, publicity postcard for Cioccolato Talmone, publ. Ricordi, Milan, c. 1900, chromolithography.*
442. *Kieszkow, postcard from the series of musical angels, design dated 1900, no publish-er's name, halftone letterpress.*
443. *W. Wachtel, 'Typy swojskie-Typen aus Polen', H. Alterberg, Lwów, Verlag f. Deutschl. M. Kimmelstiel & Co, Hamburg, sent 23.10.1899—halftone letterpress.*
444. *Kieszkow, Christmas greetings card, sent 19.12.1903, chromolithography.*

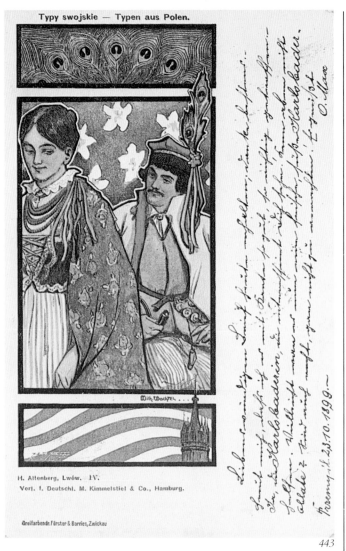

442

443

444

Russia

445

446

445. *I. Bilibin, Poduzen'e village in the Kepsk district, design dated 1904, chromolithography.*
446. *I. Bilibin, The windmills in the Vologda district, Lith. A. Il'ina, St Petersburg, design dated 1904, chromolithography.*

447

448

449

450

451

452

453

447. *I. Bilibin, postcard published in 1904, Lith
Il'ina, St. Petersburg, design dated 1901,
chromolithography.*
448. *I. Bilibin, 'Il'ja Muromec', heroes of
Russian epic songs, Lith. Il'ina, St. Petersburg,
design dated 1902, halftone letterpress.*
449. *I. Bilibin, 'Vol'ga', Russian folk song.
Lith. Il'ina, St. Petersburg, design dated 1903,
chromolithography.*
450. *I. Bilibin, 'Michajlo Potyk', design dated
1902, halftone letterpress.*
451. *I. Bilibin, 'Curilo Plenkovic', design dated
1902, halftone letterpress.*
452. *I. Bilibin, 'Christ is risen', published by the
Russian Red Cross, 4 ed., Lith. A. Il'ina, St.
Petersburg, design dated 1901, chromolithography.*
453. *I. Bilibin, untitled postcard; published by
the Russian Red Cross, 3 ed., Lith. A. Il'ina, St.
Petersburg, design dated 1901, chromolithography.*

454

455

454. *(Unidentified signature), postcard printed by Lith. A. Il'ina, St. Petersburg, chromolithography.*
455. *B. Z., postcard printed by Levenson Typography, Moscow, chromolithography.*
456. *F. Charibine, 'A l'Art Russe, Av. de l'Opera 7', Publicité Wall, Paris, chromolithography.*
457. *G. Narbut, the emblem of Moscow, design dated 1904, chromolithography.*
458. *M. Villir, decorative postcard, Lith. Litografia Il'ina, St. Petersburg, post-marked: 26.1.1899, chromolithography.*
459. *E. Luksch-Makowska, Russian proverb: 'He who gives parties has many friends and brethren', postcard n. 395 from the series by the Wiener Werkstätte, Vienna, chromolithography.*
460. *B. Sippin, Ukraine nationalist propaganda postcard, chromolithography.*

456

457

458

459

460

461

462

461. S. Solomko, The favourite, design dated
1914, I. Lapina, Paris, halftone letterpress.
462. S. Solomko, Vanity, publ. Théo Stroefer,
Nürnberg, halftone letterpress.

463

464

463, 464. *E. Sokolev, Russian nursery rhyme postcards, Lith V. O. Kubinova, Moscow, chromolithography.*

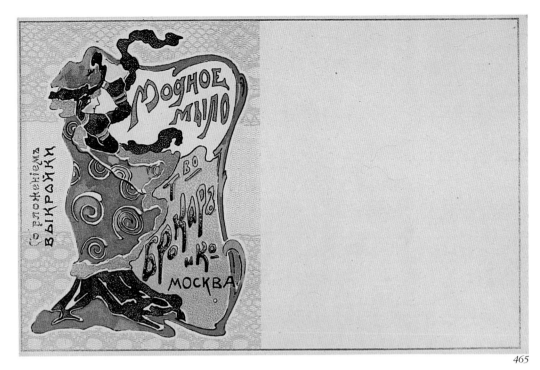

465

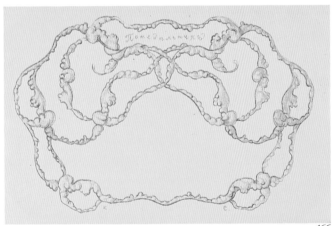

466

467

468

469

465. *Anonymous, publicity postcard for 'fashionable soap' made by Brokar & Co., Moscow, chromolithography.*

466-469. *C. A. Somov, postcards from a series of weekdays ('Monday' 'Tuesday', 'Thursday', 'Sunday').*

470

471

470. *V. D. Falilejeff, 'S. Petersbourg. Le Palais de Biron', chromolithography.*
471. *I. Bilibin, 'The River Kem', Lith. A. Il'ina, St. Petersburg, chromolithography.*

472, 473. *L. S. Bakst postcards printed by Lith. A. Il'ina, St Petersburg, chromolithography.*
474. *A. N. Benois, 'Dancing bears', design dated 1904, chromolithography.*

7.

1.

472

473

474

Holland

475

476

475, 476. R. Cramer, postcards from the series
134 of the months, publ. Roukens & Erhart,
Baarn, halftone letterpress.

477

478

477. *R. Cramer, postcard from series 134 of the months, publ. Roukens & Erhart, Baarn, half-tone letterpress.*

478. *A. Vlaanderen, Easter greetings card, publ. Boekuil en Karveel, Antwerp, line block letterpress.*

H. Willebeek Le Mair.   Al de eendjes.—The Ducks.

479

Vintage.   Weinlesezeit.

480

479. *H. Willebeek Le Mair, postcard from the series 'Old Dutch Nursery Rhymes', publ. Augener Ltd., London, and David McKay, Philadelphia, halftone letterpress.*
480. *H. Willebeek Le Mair, postcard from the series 'Schumann's Children's Pieces', publ. Augener Ltd., London, and David McKay, Philadelphia, 1915, halftone letterpress.*

481, 482. *H. Willebeek Le Mair, postcards from the series 'Schumann's Children's Pieces', publ. Augener Ltd., London, and David McKay, Philadelphia, 1915, halftone letterpress.*
483. *H. Willebeek Le Mair, postcard from the series 'Little songs of long ago', publ. Augener Ltd., London, and David McKay, Philadelphia, halftone letterpress.*

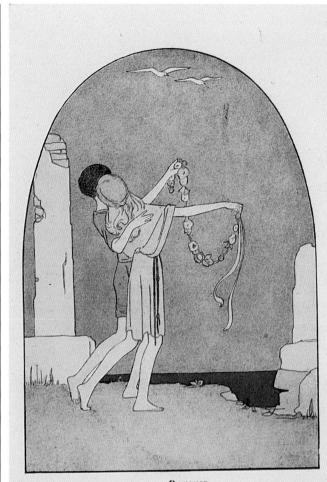

Romance.

Perfect happiness.   Glückes genug.

481

482

H. Willebeek Le Mair.   I saw three ships a sailing.

483

Scandinavia
(Sweden and Finland)

Efter V. Andréns väggmålningar å Hôtel du Nord. Stockholm.

484

Efter V. Andréns väggmålningar å Hôtel du Nord. Stockholm.

485

*484, 485. V. Andrén, publicity postcards for the
Hotel du Nord, Stockholm, Central Tryckeriet,
Stockholm, chromolithography.*

486

487

488

489

490

491

492

493

494

486, 487. S. Aspelin, 'Happy July' and 'Happy Easter' postcards, Axel Eliassons Konstförlag, Stockholm, post-marked: 1908 (fig. 487).

488. (Unidentified monogram) 'the past year will never return, the girl whom you did not appreciate will never by your friend', Granbergs Konstindustri – Aktiebolag, Stockholm, halftone letterpress.

489. V. Schonberg, greetings postcard, Svenska Litografiska, Stockholm, chromolithography.

490. M. Lindmann Jan, 'Happy July' greetings postcard, Axel Eliassons Konstförlag, Stock-holm, post-marked: 1916, chromolithography.

491. Anonymous, 'Happy July' greetings post-card, Skånska Lith. Akt. Bol., Malmö, chromolithography.

492. E. Hammar, 'Happy New Year 1905' greetings card, no publisher's name, chromolithography.

493. A. Stenberg, 'Happy July' greetings card, Förlag Eskilholm, Stockholm, chromo-lithography.

494. J. Nyström, postcard, no publisher's name.

495

496

497

498

499

495. C. Larsson, postcard for a charity event for poor children, design dated 1912, chromolithography.

496-499. C. Larsson, postcards reproducing book illustrations, some (nos. 497-499) taken from Ett Hem (1899), c. 1912, screen-block phototypography.

500

501

500. *A. Paischeff, postcard with a skier, line and halftone letterpress.*
501. *V. Blomstedt, Christmas greetings postcard, chromolithography.*

502

503

504

505

502. G. L. Jäderholm-Snellman, 'Bain de Soleil', chromolithography.
503. V. Musta, Christmas greetings card (a
couple going to the sauna), c. 1918,
chromolithography.
504. V. Musta, postcard of a lady writing a
letter, c. 1918, chromolithography.
505. G. L. Jäderholm-Snellman, 'Patinage',
series C, n. 201, chromolithography.
506, 507. O. Elenius, postcards with scenes of
peasant life, line and halftone letterpress.
508. A. Paischeff, postcard of a sledge in a
farmyard, c. 1917, line and halftone letterpress.

506

507

508

509

510

511

512

509. *V. Blomstedt, Christmas greetings post-card, chromolithography.*
510, 511. *J. Alanen, patriotic postcard, photography.*
512. *C. Rogind, humorous postcard, no publisher's name, 1901, hand-coloured letterpress.*

Switzerland

513. F. Boscovits jr. 'Offizielle Festpostkarte Sechseläuten – 18 April Zurich 1910', Lith. Anst. Gebr. Fretz, Zurich, chromolithography.
514. E. Stiefel, 'Offizielle Festpostkarte Sechseläuten - 18 April Zurich 1910', Lith. Anst. Gebr. Fretz, Zurich, chromolithography.
515. E. Bieler, 'Vevey 1905 – Le Char de Pales – Fête des Vignerons', Chromotypographie Sauberlin et Pfeiffer, Vevey, chromolithography.

513

514

515

516

517

518

519

516. *B. Mangold, '1315 – Un pour tous – Tous pour un – 1915 – Fête Annivers.re de la Bat. de Morgarten en Faveur d'Uri', Graph. Anstalt J. E. Wolfensberger, Zurich, chromolithography.*

517. *A. M. Bächtiger, postcard for the National Holiday 1st August 1913, Graph. Werkstätten Gebr. Fretz, Zurich, chromolithography.*

518. *H. B. Wieland, postcard for the National Holiday 1st August 1912, for the Red Cross, Graph. Anstalt J. E. Wolfensberger, Zurich, chromolithography.*

519. *B. Mangold, 'Offizielle Künstlerpostkarte der Schweiz, Landes – Ausstellung in Bern,*

1914', series A, Graph. Anstalt W. Wassermann, Basel.

520. *E. Kreidolf, 'Eine Feste Burg ist unser Gott', publ. O. Gmelin, Munich, halftone letterpress.*

521. *A. Marxer, 'Offizielle Postkarte, 30 September bis 3 Oktober, Gordon Bennett – Wettfliegen, Zurich 1909', Graph. Anstalt J. E. Wolfensberger, Zurich.*

522. *Ch. E. Carlègle, postcard in the series, 'Concours d'Affiches Byrrh', Paris, 1906, halftone letterpress.*

520

521

522

523

524

525

526

523. *L. Dunki, postcard for the National Holiday 1 August 1911, Graph. Anstalt J. E. Wolfensberger, Zurich, chromolithography.*

524. *R. Schaupp, 'Offizielle Postkarte, 30 September bis 3 Oktober, Gordon Bennett – Wettfliegen, Zurich 1909', Graph. Anstalt J. E. Wolfensberger, Zurich.*

525. *E. Cardinaux, 'Offizielle Postkarte, 30 September bis 3 Oktober, Gordon Bennett – Wettfliegen, Zurich 1909', Graph. Anstalt J. E. Wolfensberger, Zurich.*

526. *B Mangold, 'Offizielle Postkarte, 30 September bis 3 Oktober, Gordon Bennett – Wettfliegen, Zurich 1909', Graph. Anstalt J. E. Wolfensberger, Zurich.*

Italy

527-529. *A. Martini, 'Plenilunio', 'Musa Sil-vestre' and 'Ore Notturne', series 'Notti serene – Notti stellate', Stab. Longo, Treviso, 1899, chromolithography.*

PLENILVNIO

TREVISO - STAB. LONGO

527

MVSA SILVESTRE

TREVISO - STAB. LONGO

528

ORE
NOTTVRNE

TREVISO - STAB. LONGO

529

530

531

530. *A. Martini, 'Beneficenza e divertimento - Treviso Carnevale 1899', Lith. Longo, Treviso, chromolithography.*

531. *A. Martini, 'Carnevale Olimpico. I Carnevale inebbria il mondo', Lith. Longo, Treviso, c. 1900, chromolithography.*

532-534. *G. Mataloni, postcards from the series 'Iris' by Mascagni, publ. Ricordi, Milan, 1898, chromolithography.*

532

533

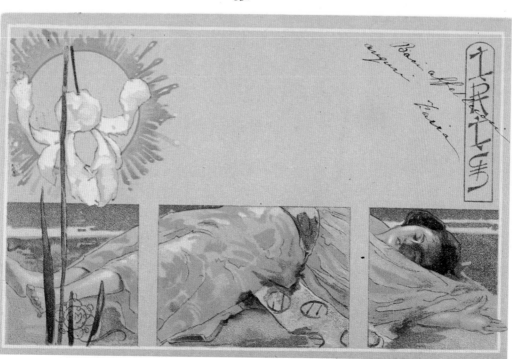

534

535

536

535. *G. Chiattone (?), 'Lariana – Navigazione Lago di Como', publ. G. Chiattone, Bergamo, 1898, chromolithography.*
536. *A. Hohenstein, 'Sempione 1906', Arti Grafiche T. Termali, Milan, typ. Ronchi & Roncoroni, chromolithography.*
537. *G. Kienerk, postcard from ther series 'Concours d'Affiches Byrrh', Paris, 1906, half-tone letterpress.*

Concours d'Affiches « BYRRH » — 112 Lauréats
6e Prix (66 lauréats ex-æquo) G KIENERK

538

539

538. A. Villa, publicity postcard 'Cioccolato
Talmone', publ. Ricordi, Milan, 1905,
chromolithography.
539. G. Kienerk, postcards in the series 'Cocorico', Paris, c. 1899, chromolithography.
540-543. L. Bompard, 'La Positiva', 'La Nega-
tiva', 'La Camera Oscura' and 'L'Obbiettivo',
series 'La Fotografia', publ. G. Mengoli, Bologna, chromolithography.
544. L. Bompard, 'Stupidité', no publisher's
name, c. 1901, chromolithography.

540

541

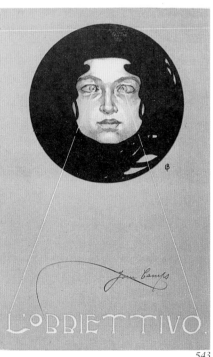

542

543

544

545

546

547

548

549

550

545. O. Ballerio, publicity postcard 'Lampada C', publ. Fumagli, Milan, chromolithography.

546. G. Crotta, 'Ispirazione', publ. A. Guarneri, Milan, c. 1900, chromolithography.

547. A Terzi, 'Omaggio degli Editori G. Ricordi & C.', publ. Ricordi, 1901, chromolithography.

548. R. Franzoni, 'Teatro Comunale – Gran Veglione di Beneficenza (. . .) Bologna 20 February 1904', Lith. Sordomuti, Bologna, chromolithography.

549. A. Hohenstein, 'Cassa Nazionale Mutua Cooperativa per le Pensioni', c. 1900, chromolithography.

550. T. Borsato, 'Feste Lariane – Como 1905, agosto-settembre', chromolithography.

551. M. Dudovich, 'Bianco e Nero, Veglione della Famiglia Artistica, Teatro Dal Verme (. . .)', publ. Ricordi, Milan, 1908, letterpress.

552. M. Dudowich, 'Citta di Bologna – Feste di primavera – maggio 1903-Società per il Risveglio della vita cittadina', typ. C. A. Pini, Bologna, letterpress.

553. L. Metlicovitz, publicity postcard for the store 'E & A Mele & C – Magazzini italiani Napoli', publ. Ricordi, Milan.

551

552

553

554

555

*554-555. E. Bottaro, postcards from a series of
ladies with lamps, series 443 A.D.G.,
chromolithography.*

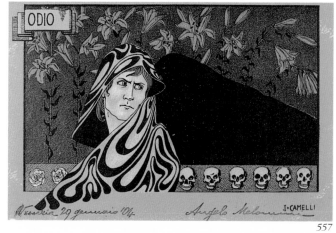

556

557

558

559

560

561

556-561. I. Camelli, 'Sorriso', 'Odio', 'Ira', 'Paura', 'Dolore', 'Quiete', chromolithography.

NOVEMBRE

Dr. Trenkler & Co., Lipsia. Serie P 11

562

GENNAIO

Dr. Trenkler & Co., Lipsia. Serie P 1

563

OLIO D'OLIVA
AGNESI &
GIACCONE
ONEGLIA

564

565

566

562, 563. A. Baruffi, 'Novembre' and 'Gennaio', series 'I mesi', Dr Trenkler & Co, Leipzig, series P, designs dated 1900, chromolithography.

564. A. Mazza, publicity postcard for 'Olio d' Oliva Agnesi & Giaccone – Oneglia', 1902, chromolithography.

565, 566. P. Zaretti (?), postcards printed by Heinrich & Schlesler, Dresden, 1902-03, chromolithography.

567

568

567. *B. Cascella, from 'Fuoco' by G. D'Annunzio', II series Abruzzo', lithography.*
568. *B. Cascella, 'Sosta di pellegrini', II series
'Abruzzo', lithography.*

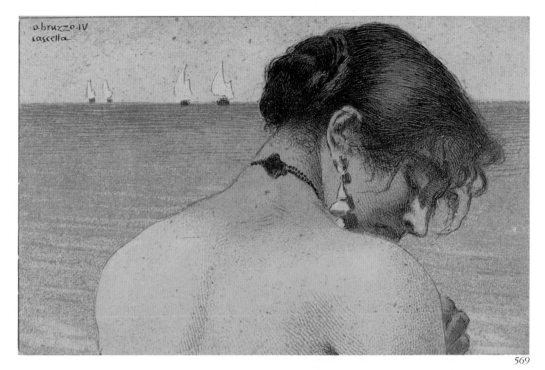

569

570

569. B. Cascella, postcard from the IV series
'Abruzzo', lithography.
570. B. Cascella, 'Il rito delle serpi', from the
series 'Cartoline abruzzesi' (people and customs), lithography.

571

572

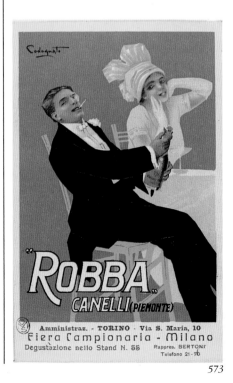

573

574

575

576

577

571, 572 R. Paoletti, publicity postcard for the magazine *Natura ed Arte*, publ. Villardi, Milan.

573. P. Codognato, publicity postcard 'Robba Canelli (Piemonte)', no publisher's name, chromolithography.

574. L. Metlicovitz, publicity postcard 'Calzaturificio di Varese', publ. Ricordi (?), Milan, reproduction of the postcard 1913, line and halftone letterpress.

575. E. Sacchetti, publicity postcard for the newspaper *Verde e Azzurro*, no publisher's name, c. 1904.

576. A. Rubino, publicity postcard 'Sorelle Dell'Acqua – Via Manzoni 22 Milano', halftone letterpress.

577. Golia (E. Colmo), 'Omaggio della stampa sportiva, ai visitatori della IV esposizione internazionale d'automobili – Torino 1907', chromolithography.

578

579

580

581

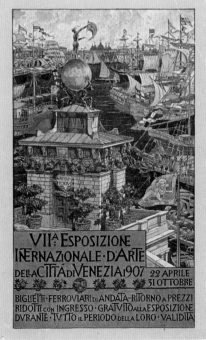

582

583

584

585

586

587

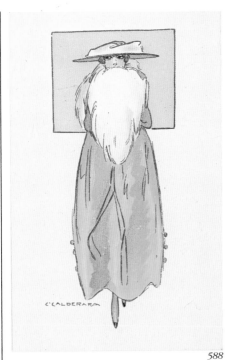

588

589

590

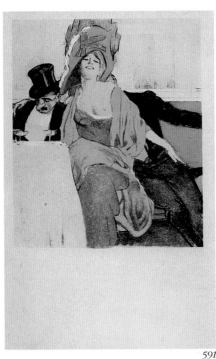

591

592

593

578. *A. Magrini, 'Città di Parma-settembre 1907-Congressi-Inaugurazioni-Corse-Spettacoli-divertimenti popolari', reproduction of the poster, chromolithography.*
579. *A. Magrini, 'Mostra Segantini – Padiglione A. Grubicy – Esposizione Milano 1906', reproduction of the poster, chromolithography.*
580. *G. Guerrini, 'Esposizione di Faenza, III Centenario della nascita di Evangelista Torricelli 1908', halftone letterpress.*

581. *Bevilacqua, 'Primo esperimento di Posta Aerea Palermo – Napoli' edited by Soc. Anon. Industrie Aviatorie meridionali di Napoli.*
582. *A. Sezanne, 'VII Esposizione Internazionale d'Arte della Città di Venezia 1907', Instituto Italiano d'Arti Grafiche, Bergamo, reproduction of the poster, halftone letterpress.*
583. *G. Palanti, 'Esposizione Nasionale di Belle Arti dell'Accademia di Brera – Palazzo della Permanenta – Via P. Umberto 32 –*

settembre-novembre 1912', Unione Zincografi, Milan, halftone letterpress.
584. *U. Boccioni, 'Brunate (Como) maggio-giugno 1909. Esposizione di Pittura e Scultura promossa dalla Famiglia Artistica e dalla Patriottica di Milano', Off. Chiattone, Milan, chromolithography.*
585. *A. Terzi, 'Rome 1911 – Exposition Internationale . . .', publ. E. Chappuis, Bologna, reproduction of the poster, chromolithography.*

594

595

586. D. Cambellotti, 'Rome février – novembre 1911. Fêtes Commemoratives de la Proclamation du Royaume d'Italie . . .', publ. E. Chappuis, Bologna, reproduction of the poster, chromolithography.

587. G. Chini, 'Roma 1911 – Exposition Etnographique . . .', reproduction of the poster, halftone letterpress.

588. C. Calderara, postcard from series n. 4118, entitled 'donnine invernali', c. 1918.

589. R. Tafuri, postcard from the series of butterfly-women, 1899, halftone letterpress.

590. A. Busi, 'Adolfo Busi, un fiore sconoscieto', publ. C.A.B. (Bologna), halftone letterpress.

591. M. Dudovich, postcard n. 4 from series XVI of 'Simplicissimus-Karten', 1912-14, reproduced from a plate in the **Corso Album**, chromolithography.

592. M. Dudovich, postcard n. 1 from series 'Zenit', post-marked: 1917.

593. M. Dudovich, postcard n. 6 from series VI 'Al mare', publ. Arte Eureka, c. 1917.

594, 595. A. Terzi, postcards, from series n. 215, no publisher's name, c. 1917, chromolithography.

596

597

598

599

600

596. A. De Karolis, 'Feste della città di Faenza,
MCMVIII, publ. Albonetti, Faenza.
597. F. Nonni, postcard from the series for the
'Esposizione Nazionale del Bianco e Nero',
Bologna, June 1912.
598. F. Nonni, postcard reproducing a woodcut, no publisher's name.
599. P. Codognato, 'Avanti! Quotidiano socialista esce in Milano', publ. La Zincografica,
Milan, c. 1910, reproduction of the poster,
halftone letterpress.
600. P. Nomellini, 'Municipio di Genova inaugurazione del monumento ai Mille, 5 maggio
1915', publ. Ricordi, Milan, reproduction of
the poster, chromolithography.

601

ROMA · 4 · LVGLIO · 1918

602

« Abbiamo ricomperato la tua bellezza a misura di baionette; e nelle nostre vene rimporporato il tuo stendardo.» Gabriele d'Annunzio

603

604

FRATELLI SALVATEMI! SOTTOSCRIVETE !

605

606

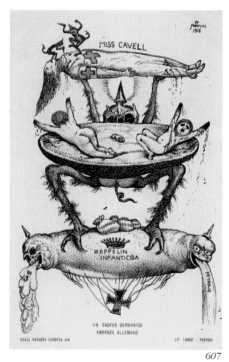

607

608

609

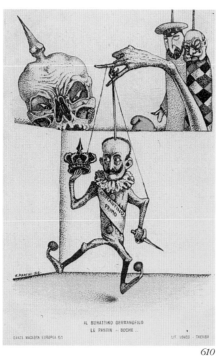

610

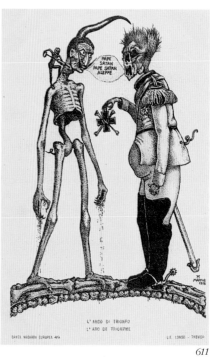

611

601. A. Rubino, an infantryman who crosses the Piave and prepares to crush the Habsburg eagle, publ. Ricordi, Milan 1918.

602. V. Grassi, 'Roma – 4 luglio 1918', publ. Bestetti e Tumminelli, Milan, line-block letterpress.

603. U. Brunelleschi, cartolina di progaganda di guerra con citazione di D'Annunzio, c. 1918, halftone letterpress.

604. L. A. Mauzan, 'Aurora di Pace', Dell'Anna e Gasparini, Milan, c. 1918, halftone letterpress.

605. A. Bonzagni, propaganda postcard for the national loan, Cromogliptica A. Marzi, Rome, c. 1916, halftone letterpress.

606-611. A. Martini, six postcards from the series 'Quinta danza macabra europea', publ. D. Longo, Treviso, 1915-16, lithography.

612

613

612, 613. V. Zecchin, postcards from the series
'Smalti e Murrine', 'Zenit', publ. F. Polenghi &
C., Turin, c. 1918, chromolithography.

Spain

614

615

614. A. de Riquer, 'Ivern', allegorical series of
the seasons, c. 1901, designed 1900,
chromolithography.
615. A. de Riquer, postcard commemorating
the 'Fiesta de la Merced', publ. L. I. Bartrina,
Barcelona, 1902, chromolithography.
616, 617. A. de Riquer, 'Tardor' e 'Istiu',
allegorical series of the seasons, c. 1901, designed 1900, chromolithography.
618. A. de Riquer, 'Hispania Sociedad Cartófila Española', membership card, typ.
L'Avenc, Barcelona, 1901, halftone letterpress.
619. G. Camps, postcards from ther series
'Cabezas y Flores', typ. L. Tasso, Barcelona,
typography.

616

617

618

620

621

622

623

624

625

626

627

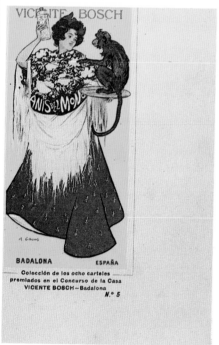

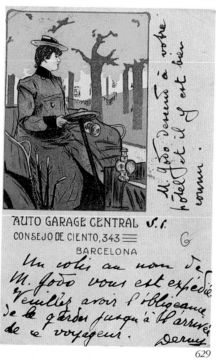

628

629

630

620. *G. Camps, publicity calendar postcard for Henri Garnier cognac, typ. Thomas, Barcelona, 1902, halftone letterpress.*
621. *G. Camps, 'Noviembre', from ther series of allegories of the months, publ. L. Artiaga, Havana, c. 1904, halftone letterpress.*
622, 624. *G Camps, postcards from the series 'Cabezas y Flores', typ. L. Tasso, Barcelona, 1904, halftone letterpress.*
623. *G. Camps, publicity postcard for 'Cosme Puigmal Barcelona', 1902, halftone letterpress.*

625. *A. de Riquer, 'Anis del Mono-Vicente Bosch-Badalona', a reproduction of the sketch for the poster exhibited at the 1898 competition, chromolithography.*
626. *A. de Riquer, 'Commemorativa de la Exposición de postales-Mayo-Junio 1903', Soc Cartófila Hispania, halftone letterpress.*
627. *Anonymous, 1902 New Year greetings card for 'Sociedad Española de Incandescencia E. Candis Y C.ª', lith. Labielle, Barcelona, chromolithography.*

628. *R. Casas, 'Vicente Bosch-Anis del Mono-Badalona', reproduction of the sketch for the poster exhibited in the 1898 competition, chromlithography.*
629. *R. Casas, publicity postcard 'Auto Garage Central - Consejo der Cinto, 343', c. 1902, reproduction of the poster, chromolithography.*
630. *R. Lorenzale, 'Papeles Roca para Fumar. . .', typ. Thomas, Barcelona, 1902, reproduction of the sketch for the poster sent to the competition, letterpress.*

631

632

633

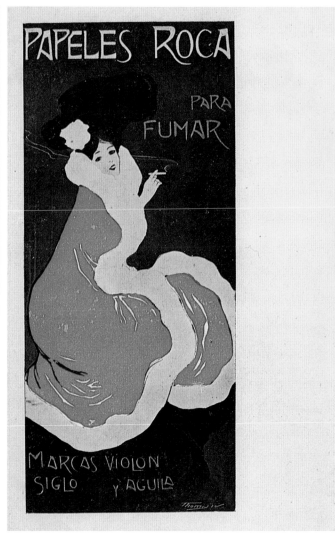

634

635

631, 632. *Ll. Labarta, 'Enero' and 'Febrero',*
series 'Los Meses', lith. M. Pujadas, Barcelona,
c. 1902, chromolithography.
633. *R. Opisso, publicity postcard for the*
'Farmacia Novellas', 1902, chromolithography.
634. *J. Cardona, 'Papeles Roca para Fu-*
mar. . .', typ. Thomas, Barcelona, 1902, repro-
duction of the sketch for the poster sent to the
competition, letterpress.
635. *Anonymous, 'Papeles Roca para Fu-*
mar. . .', typ. Thomas, Barcelona, 1902, repro-
duction of the sketch sent to the competition,
halftone letterpress.

636

637

638

639

640

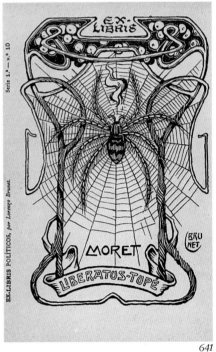

641

636. *J. Llongueras, '1906 Visca la Solidaritat Catalana-La Unio fa la forsa', typ. J. Horta, Barcelona, line and halftone letterpress.*

637. *J. Triadó, 'Papeles Roca para Fumar. . .', typ. Thomas, Barcelona, 1902, reproduction of the sketch for the poster sent to the competition, letterpress.*

638. *F. de Cidon, publicity postcard 'La Tribuna-Diario Independiente Barcelona',*

chromolithography.

639. *Ll. Brunet, postcard from the series 'Ex libris politicos', line-block letterpress.*

640. *J. Llimona, postcard from the series 'Ave Maria Purissima', publ. Ll. Bartrina, typ. Thomas, Barcelona, halftone letterpress.*

641. *Ll. Brunet, postcard from the series 'Ex libris politicos', line-block letterpress.*

642

643

642. *J. Vallhonrat, postcard from the humorous publicity series for syphons made by F. Clara y Cia, Lith. Barral Huos, Barcelona, 1902.*

643. *Anonymous, postcard from a series of 6 on flaménco dancing, publ. Mencia y Paquet, Gijón, c. 1906, chromolithography.*

644

645

646

647

648

649

644. *A. de Riquer, postcard reproducing the cover of the score of the popular song* Sant Ramon *by Enric Morera.*

645. *S. Rusiñol, postcard reproducing the cover of the score of the popular song* El Rossinyol, *line-block letterpress.*

646. *Apel-les Mestres, publicity postcard for the magazine* Joventut, *letterpress.*

647. *P. Picasso, postcard announcing the birth of Pere Romeu's first son, typ. Pere Romeu, typ. La Académica, 1902, letterpress.*

648. *O. Junyent, single-copy postcard, pen and watercolour.*

649. *Ll. Masriera, single-copy postcard with the imprint of the 'Circulo Artistico' of Barcelona, 1902, watercolour.*

650. *R. Casas, postcard from the publicity series 'Wertheim', typ. Thomas, Barcelona, leterpress.*

651. *R. Casas, postcard from the series 'Chauffeuses', publ. Ll. Bartrina, typ. Thomas, Barcelona, 1903, halftone letterpress.*

652. *R. Casas, postcard from the series, 'Cabezas femeninas a la sanguina', publ. Ll. Bartrina, typ. Thomas, Barcelona, 1904, letterpress.*

653. *R. Casas, 1902 New Year greetings postcard for the magazine of the Review Pel & Ploma, typ. L'Avenc, Barcelona 1901, line and halftone letterpress.*

654. *R. Casas, publicity postcard 'Fayans Catalá, parfumerie aux fleurs Barcelona', typ. Thomas, Barcelona, c. 1906.*

650

651

652

Pèl & Ploma

Barcelona, 10 pessetes any; fóra, 12; Unió postal, 12 francs
96, Passeig de Gracía (interior)
BARCELONA

Felís Any 1902

653

654

655

656

655, 656. J. Cardona, postcards from series
XVIII of the 'Künstler-Postkarten' of Jugend,
publ. G. Hirth, Munich, c. 1908.
657, 658. A. Utrillo, postcards from the series
'Costumbres populares catalanas', c. 1902, lith.
A. Utrillo S. C. Barna, chromolithography.
659. A. Utrillo, postcard from the series 'Carmen', c. 1902, chromolithography.

657

658

659

660-663. *J. Triadó, postcards from the series 'Lo Zodiaco', chromolithography (?).*
664, 665. *P. Torné Esquius, postcards from a series of five for the French market, typ. Tobella, Barcelona.*

The United States of America

Under the Microscope.

666

The Rubicon.

With love
may.
6. V. 1911
BvR

667

666, 667. C. D. Gibson, postcards 788 and 795
from the series 'The Gibson Post Cards', publ.
James Henderson & Sons Ltd., London, printed in Saxony, photogravure.

Five ways of expressing it when you are bored.

668

The Image of his Father.

669

At a Comedy.

670

Accident to a young man with a weak heart.

671

Their First Quarrel.

672

The Parting Wall.

673

668-673. C. D. Gibson, postcards from the series 'The Gibson Post Cards', publ. James Henderson & Sons Ltd., London, printed in Saxony (some are reprinted by the Hamburg publ. Alfred Schweizer), photochalcography.
674, 675. Ph. Boileau, postcards from the series by the publisher Reinthal & Newman, New York, c. 1907, halftone letterpress.
676. Wiles, 'Are You ready?', publ. Carlton Pubs., London, series 702, n. 2, halftone letterpress.
677. L. Mayer, 'Broilers', postcard 508, publ. Reinthal & Newman, New York, halftone letterpress.
678. C. A. Gilbert, 'Miranda', postcard 106 from the series 'Pictorial Comedy', publ. James Henderson & Sons Ltd., London, postmarked: June 1908, collotype.

"RINGS ON HER FINGERS"

© REINTHAL & NEWMAN, PUBS., N. Y.

674

MY CHAUFFEUR...

675

ARE YOU READY?

676

BROILERS

© REINTHAL & NEWMAN, PUBS., N. Y.

677

Miranda.

678

DO I INTRUDE?

PAINTED BY HARRISON FISHER   © REINTHAL & NEWMAN, PUBS., N. Y.

679

PLEASANT REFLECTIONS.

© REINTHAL & NEWMAN, PUBS., N. Y.

680

MY LADY DRIVES

PAINTED BY HARRISON FISHER   © REINTHAL & NEWMAN, PUBS., N. Y.

681

ISN'T HE SWEET?

PAINTED BY HARRISON FISHER   © REINTHAL & NEWMAN, PUBS., N. Y.

682

"THE THIRD PARTY"

Painted by Harrison Fisher

© REINTHAL & NEWMAN, N. Y.

683

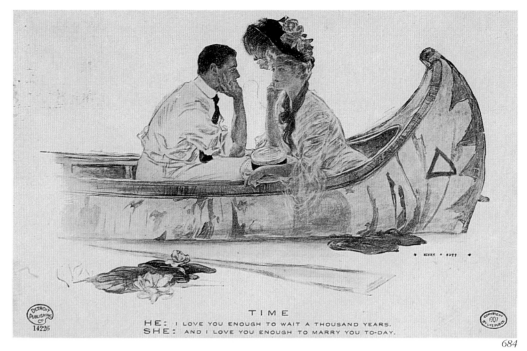

TIME

HE: I LOVE YOU ENOUGH TO WAIT A THOUSAND YEARS.
SHE: AND I LOVE YOU ENOUGH TO MARRY YOU TO-DAY.

684

695

686

687

679, 681-683. H. Fisher, postcards 415 ('Do I intrude?'), 417 ('My Lady drives'), 409 ('Isn't he sweet?' post-marked: 1915), 770 ('The third Party', 1916), publ. Reinthal & Newman, New York, halftone letterpress.
680. C. F. Underwood, 'Pleasant Reflections', postcard 350, publ. Reinthal & Newman, New York, halftone letterpress.
684. H. Hutt, 'Time' postcard 14226, Detroit Publishing Co., 1907, screen-block letterpress.
685, 686. FRK (unidentified monogram), postcard from a series of the months, chromolithography.
687. J. Willcox Smith, postcard from the series which reproduces illustrations from The Child in the Garden (1903), publ. Reinthal & Newman, New York, c. 1909, screen-block letterpress.

688

689

688, 689. *E. F. Betts, postcards from series 290 printed by M. Munk, Vienna, c. 1912, chromolithography.*

690

691

*690, 691. A. W. Betts, postcards from series 291
printed by M. Munk, Vienna, c. 1912,
chromolithography.*

692

693

694

695

696

697

692. *Anonymous, 'Laugh', The Gibson Art Co., Cincinnati, copyright 1912, chromolithography.*
693. *Anonymous, Valentine-card, The Gibson Art Co., Cincinnati, chromolithography.*
694. *Anonymous, 'Thanksgiving', copyright S. Bergman, New York, 1912, chromolithography.*
695. *E. Weaver, Valentine-card 'Greetings from Dover, New Hampshire', series 2372, no pub-* *lisher's name, chromolithography.*
696. *Anonymous, Easter greetings postcard, series 3603 ('Easter'), ed. Raphael Tuck & Sons, London, printed in Saxony, chromolithography.*
697. *(Unidentified monogram), Christmas greetings postcard n. 734, publ. P. F. Volland Co., Chicago, copyright 1912, chromolithography.*

698

699

700

701

698. H. B. Griggs, birthday greetings postcard, printed in Germany L. & B., series 2232, no publisher's name, chromolithography with gold printing.

699. C. V. Dwiggins, 'Fortune Teller', series 55, copyright R. Kaplan 1909, chromolithography printed in relief.

700. W. Wellmann, 'Need a Doctor? Try Dan Cupid, M.D.', copyright 1908, chromolithography.

701. (Unidentified monogram), postcard from a series of proverbs, post-marked 1911.

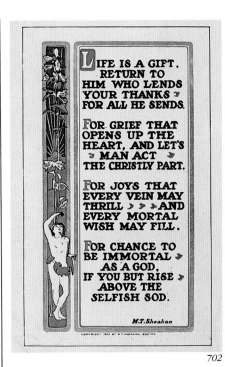

702

703

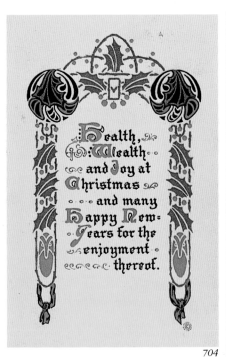

704

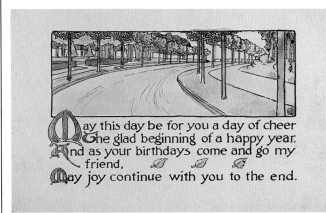

705

706

707

708

702. *Anonymous, postcard from the series 'Sheahan's Good Mottos', publ. M. Y. Sheahan, Boston, 1907, chromolithography.*
703. *Anonymous birthday greetings postcard, no publisher's name, halftone letterpress.*
704. *Anonymous greetings postcard, copyright 1912 S. Bergman, New York, halftone letterpress.*

705. *Anonymous, postcard from the 'Desk Motto Series', publ. G. K. Prince, Buffalo, copyright 1910, two-colour print with gold printing.*
706. *(Unidentified monogram), postcard from the series 'Birthday Post Card', publ. M. T. Sheahan, Boston, copyright 1911, chromo-*

lithography.
707. *(Unidentified monogram), birthday greeting postcard, 6520, copyright 1910, by The Rust Craft Shop, Kansas City (Mo.), hand-coloured letterpress.*
708. *Anonymous, greetings postcard, P. C. 212, chromolithography with raised printing.*

Biographical Dictionary

A

Louise ABBEMA
Etampes, 30.10.1858 – Paris, 1927
Painter, watercolourist, sculptress, etcher, writer.
A student of Ch. Chaplin, J.-J. Henner and E.-A. Carolus-Duran. A friend of Sarah Bernhardt; when she was very young she painted her portrait. She exhibited regularly at the Salon des Artistes Français, where in 1881 she received a mention of honour for her 'panneaux decoratifs' (decorative panels). She won the bronze medal at the 1900 Paris Exposition Universelle. She made decorative panels for the town halls of the VII, X and XX *arrondissments*, for the Hôtel de Ville, for the Musée de l'Armée, for the Théâtre Sarah-Bernhardt and for the hall of the Sociéte Ñationale d'Horticulture de France in Paris and for the Governor's palace in Dakar. She illustrated the book *La Mer* by René Maizeroy. She worked on *La Gazette des Beaux-Arts* and on *L'Art* as an art critic.
Postcards: several with portraits of Sarah Bernhardt ('Sarah Bernhardt dans la Sorcière'); the series 'Home Décor'; several French landscapes.
Bibl.: Zeyons 1979; Neudin 1980.

Jack ABEILLE
Varenne-St. Hilarie, St Maur, 27.5.1873 (or 1875)
Cartoonist, illustrator, commercial artist.
He exhibited at the Salon des Humoristes and in the exhibition of humorous drawings in Copenhagen. He worked on several French humorous magazines. He illustrated books in the series 'Modern-Bibilothèque' published by Fayard. He is also famous for a series of designs on the first world war.
Postcards: series of 4 'Les Saisons', publ. P. Süss A-G, Dresden, 1898 (date of the designs); series 'Les Baigneuses', 1898; series on the times of the day ('Le Matin', etc.), publ. P. Süss A-G, Dresden, c. 1898, a series on hairstyles through the centuries c. 1899; 'Chaperon rouge', 1899; series on flowers ('La Rose', 'Le Chrysanthème', 'L'Oeillet', 'La Violette', etc.), publ. W. H. à B., 1900; series on the 1900 Exposition Universelle; series 'Monaco'; series 'Paris'; several propaganda

anti-German. Bibl.: Baudet 1978, 1980; Bartoli-Mataloni 1979; Zeyons 1979; Holt 1981, 1983.

Joseph ALANEN
Tampere 2.11.1885 – Helsinki 16.5.1920
Painter, decorator.
He attended the School of Industrial Design in Helsinki and finished his studies in Stockholm and Berlin (1907-08). His painting belongs to the symbolist school and shows the influence of the Dutch artist J. Th. Toorop.
Postcards: several patriotic propaganda p. done during the civil war in 1917.

Martha ALBER
Rumburg, Bohemia 15.1.1893 – ?
Fabric designer.
She studied at the School of Applied Arts in Prague and from 1908 in Vienna (O. Strnad, J. Hoffmann). She worked with the Wiener Werkstätte designing fabrics.
Postcards: some cards in the special Wiener Werkstätte series of fabric designs, Brüder Kohn, Vienna.

Cecil Charles Windsor ALDIN
Slough 28.4.1870 – Mallorca 6.1.1935
Watercolourist, commercial artist, illustrator.
He studied at South Kensington School of Art and then with the animal painter F. W. Calderon. He established himself as a humorous draughtsman. For some time he lived at Bedford Park, where other artist friends lived, including Dudley Hardy and Lance Thackeray. He worked on several papers and magazines: *Black and White, The Graphic, The Poster, Punch*, etc.
Postcards: 'Celebrated Posters', R. Tuck, London c. 1903, series 1500 ('Cadbury's Cocoa'), series 1502 ('Colman's Blue', Colman's Starch').
Bibl.: Holt 1980, 1983.

Frederic-Hugo d'ALESI
Rumani, 1849 – Paris, 11.11.1906
Commercial artist, painter, graphic designer (song scores).
Born in Rumania (his father was the official instructor to the Turkish army), he settled in

1876 in Paris. From 1882 he began working intensively as a commercial artist for the railway company (Paris-Lyon-Mediterranée, Chemins de fer d'Orléans, Chemins de fer de l'Est. In 1901 the Galerie Georges Petit in Paris held an exhibition of his work.
Postcards: many p. reproducing posters and picturesque places in France and other countries.
Bibl.: Zeyons 1979.

Edmond AMAN-JEAN
Chevry-Cossigny (Seine et Marne), 14.11.1858 – Paris 1936 or 35
Painter, engraver, tapestry designer, commercial artist, art critic.
A student of H. Lehmann, E. Hébert and L. O. Merson at the Ecole des Beaux-Arts in Paris. From 1885 he exhibited at the Salon de la Société des Artistes Français and in the same year he won a grant to go to Rome. He was a member from 1893 of the Société Nationale des Beaux-Arts, where he was given a gold medal in 1900. He was one of the founder members with Albert Besnard of the Salon des Tuileries. In the 1890s he made several lithographs and worked on *L'Estampe Moderne*. He published some art-historical essays in *L'Artiste* (1892) and in the magazine *Revue de l'art ancien et moderne*. He designed the poster for the Salon de la Rose-Croix (1893). He was one of the most representative figures of French symbolist painting.
Postcards: several in the series 'Künstler-Postkarten' from *Jugend*, G. Hirth, Munich c. 1910.
Bibl.: cat Altonaer Museum, Hamburg 1970.

Vicke (Anders Victor) ANDRÉN
Gothenburg 7.12.1856 – Uddevalla 11.11.1930
Painter, commercial artist, illustrator, decorator, stage designer.
From 1875-1879 he attended the Stockholm Academy, and then studied sculpture in the workshop of F. Kiellberg. As an illustrator he worked on the magazines *Ny illustrerad tidning* (1890-97) and *Puck* (1890-1916). He designed the illustrations for the album *Från Stockholm teatrar* (1889) and for several books: *Nya Stockholm* by C. Lundin (1890), *Kärlekssagan*

på Björkeberga by AA.U. Bååths (1892, *Kung Orres saga* by I. Lundström (1892), *Stockholm och skargarden* by D. Fallström (1908).
Postcards: series of publicity p. for the 'Hotel du Nord in Stockholm, typ. Central Tryckeriet, Stockholm.

Hans ANKER
Berlin 30.10.1873 – Hannover 1950
Painter, engraver, illustrator, graphic designer.
He studied at the school of the Kunstgewerbemuseum and at the Berlin Academy, then at the Académie Julian in Paris. He was the author, in collaboration with Julius Klinger, of the album *Die Grotesklinei und ihre Spiegelvariation im modernen Ornament und Dekorationsmalerei*, Berlin, c. 1903.
Postcards: for the series 'Märchen-Postkarten', publicity p. for the company Jünger & Gebhardt in Berlin.

A. P. A., pseudonym for Feliu ELIAS
Barcelona, 9.10.1877 – Barcelona, August 1948
Writer, journalist, painter, illustrator, graphic-designer (book design, commercial graphics, publicity graphics, menus).
A man of many interests, he combined writing and journalism with painting (with divisionist tendencies) and with work in graphic art. As an illustrator he worked on the Catalan magazines *Calendari del Cu-Cut, Garba, Or y Grana*. As a writer of articles he took the pseudonym Joan Sacs and Dimoni Verdi. He was the author of the books: *La catedral de Barcelona, La Escultura Catalana moderna, El moble xinès, L'Escenògraf Francesc Soler i Rovirosa*.
Postcards: 'Esperanto 5 Internacio Kongreso 5-11 septembre Barcelona'.
Bibl.: Fildier 1980.

Signe ASPELIN
Stockholm, 22.10.1881 – ?
Watercolourist, illustrator, fabric designer.
She studied at the School of Industrial Arts in Stockholm. Between 1904 and 1905 she made many fabric designs for the Nordiska Kompaniet. She was above all active as an illustrator of children's books.
Postcards: many greetings cards published by Axel Eliassons Konstförlag, Stockholm.

Jane (or Jeanne) ATCHÉ
Toulouse, ? – ?
Painter, lithographer, graphic designer (menus, publicity graphics, commercial art).
The author of a series of black and white lithographs (*L'Abbesse, Méditation*). She was a friend of Mucha, whose work influenced her.
Postcards: 1 p. in the series 'Collection Job', the series of 1905, 1911, 1914, reproduction of a poster of 1905; several publicity p.
Bibl.: Baudet 1978.

Georges AURIOL pseudonym of Jean-Georges HUYOT
Beauvais, 1863 – Paris, 1938
Illustrator, engraver, graphic designer (ex libris, book design, lettering, theatre programmes, song scores), commercial artist, designer of fabrics, carpets, screens, furniture ornament, cartoonist, lyricist, writer.
With Steinlen and Willette he was part of a group of artists at the cabaret 'Chat Noir' and he was the editor of the magazine of the same name. He designed the 'Auriol' alphabet, which was exceptionally successful in Art Nou-

veau typography. Full documentation of his work as a graphic designer is collected in three volumes of the *Livre de cachets, marques et monogrammes*, published from 1901 to 1924. He collaborated on the periodicals: *Le Chat Noir* (1886-1889), *La semaine illustrée, L'Image, Scribner's*. He illustrated *Chansons naïves et perverses* by G. Montoya and, in collaboration with others, the volumes: *Combinaisons ornementales* c. 1900; with A. Mucha and M. P. Verneuil; *Pour passer une heure* by H. Valbel (1904); *Bastille et Latude; Chansons fleuries; Contes du Chat noir* by Salis; *Contes pour bibliophiles; L'embarquement pour ailleurs*. He wrote the lyrics of several songs and designed the scores for the publisher Enoch & Co. He was the author of the book *Divan japonais . . . Pourvu qu'on rigole* (1891).
Postcards: 1 p. in the 'Collection des Cent', publ. Greningarie, Paris, c. 1901.
Bibl.: Baudet 1978.

B

Ferdinand Sigismand BAC, also BACH
Stuttgart, 15.8.1859 – Paris 18.11.1952
Cartoonist, illustrator, engraver, commercial artist, writer.
He went to Paris when he was young and c. 1880 he started work on the magazines *La Caricature* and *La Vie Parisienne*, becoming famous under his pseudonym, Cab. He also worked on *Le Rire, Le Journal amusant* and *Gil Blas illustré*. His illustrations are collected in the albums *Fantaisies Féminines; Elégances Parisiennes* (1893); *Les Enfants du XVIIIe siècle; La Parisienne à travers les âges; L'amour contemporain; Le Triomphe de la femme; Vieille Allemagne; Nos petits aïeux* (c. 1900); *La Comédie féminine*. He wrote the text of several books and designed the illustrations: *La volupté romaine; Odysseus; Jardins enchantés; Les Colombières; Le Pélerin Amoureux; L'Extra-Planétaire; L'aventure italienne; Le Mystère vénitien; Le Fantôme de Paris; Chez Louis II de Bavière; Souvenirs d'exil*. He took French nationality.
Postcards: 2 p. in the 'Collection des Cent', publ. Gréningaire, c. 1901.
Bibl.: Baudet 1978.

Domenico BACCARINI
Faenza, 16.12.1883 – Faenza, 29.1.1907
Painter, woodcut artist, etcher, ceramist, illustrator.
He studied in Faenza at the School of Art and Trades directed by A. Berti. He was established very young as a ceramist decorating plates, jugs and vases for the Fabbriche Riunite. He soon became the leading figure in a group of modernist artists in Faenza which included D. Rambelli, F. Nonni, E. Drei, and later G. Guerrini, G. Ugonia and O. Toschi. In 1901 he went to Florence, with a grant to attend the life classes at the Accademia. During his stay he met R. Dal Molin Firenzona, G. Viner, G. Costetti and L. Vaini. In 1903 he moved to Rome, where he was in touch with the group who had their headquarters in the studio of G. Prini. In the capital he worked on the paper *La Patria*. In 1905 he exhibited at the Venice Biennale and in the following year in Milan. In his last years he won the Milan prize and then in Rome, he found a job with the 'Casa del Pane' a charitable institution, for which he made a series of designs with work in the fields as the subject. His painting was at

first influenced by the Macchiaioli, then turned towards symbolism and reflected in its technique and subject matter, G. Previati, G. Segantini, G. Pellizza di Volpedo, and later even F. Khnopff and G. Klimt.
Postcards: a series of 6 greetings p. for the 'Casa del Pane', publ. Pilade Rocco, Milan, c. 1906; several reproducing his designs and engravings.
Bibl.: Mordente 1982; Arrasich 1984.

August Meinrad BACHTIGER
Mörschwil, near St. Gallen, Switzerland, 12.5.1888-?
Painter, designer, xylographer, lithographer, commercial artist, graphic designer (ex libris), illustrator, stained glass window designer, wall paper designer.
He studied at the Academy in Munich with P. Halm and A. Jank. He executed painted decorations and stained glass in churches in St. Gallen, Neu St. Johann, Henau, Arlesheim, Amden, Goldach, Mels, Ebikon and Rabius. He designed illustrations for school and religious books.
Postcards: P. for the national holiday, 1 August 1913, Graph. Werkstätten Gebr. Fretz, Zurich, 1913.

Lev BAKST, pseudonym of Lev ROSENBERG
St. Petersburg, 10.5.1866 – Paris, 28.12.1924.
Painter, illustrator, commercial artist, graphic designer, theatre and costume designer.
He studied at the Academy in St. Petersburg. He began as a designer of theatrical costumes. In 1898 he was one of the founders of 'Mir Iskusstva'.
In 1906 he exhibited in the Russian section of the Salon d'Automne in Paris; two years later he designed the costumes for the Ballets Russes for Diaghilev. His graphic work is important for the transition from Art Nouveau to Art Déco. He worked on the magazines *Mir Iskusstva, Jugend,* Αpollon, etc.
Postcards: series of theatrical costumes, published in Russia; series for the Ballets Russes 1908.
Bibl.: Fildier 1979; Bandet 1980; Holt 1980, 1983.

Osvaldo BALLERIO
Milan, 1870 – Azzate, 1942
Painter, commercial artist, illustrator.
He spent his formative years at the Accademia di Brera in Milan, where he was a pupil of G. Bertini. In the first years of the twentieth century he was active as an illustrator and commercial artist (from the second decade of the century he designed posters for the publisher Chappuis in Bologna). He painted altarpieces and decorative painting in several churches in the Val d'Intelvi.
Postcards: 'Mese di Maggio ai giardini pubblici-Grande Esposizione sport e allevamento . . . -1901', Stab. Lith: Fraschini, Milan; P. celebrating the birth of the Prince of Savoy, 1904; 'Società Dante Alighieri, comitato di Milano – Inaugurazione della bandiera, 28.5.1905', Tricromia Unione Zincografi; 'V Esposizione di Automobili, Torino', 1908; 'Esperimenti di aviazione, Bologna', 1910; 'Feste di Maggio – Cremona – 1910'; 'Centenario della nascita di G. Verdi, Parma, 1913'; several war propaganda p, 1915-18; publicity P. Soc. Anonima Incandescenza a Gas 'Auer'; publicity p. for 'Lamparda C.', publ. Fumalli, Milan.

Bibl.: Gaibazzi 1979, Mordente 1982; Arrasich 1984.

Adrien BARRÈRE
Paris, 1877 – Paris, 1931
Painter, lithographer, cartoonist, illustrator, commercial artist.
He made his debut as a caricaturist with the series 'Têtes de Turos' published in the magazine *Fantasio* (1920). He worked on the papers *Courrier Français Cri de Paris, Nouvelle Revue parisienne*. He designed posters for the Grand Guignol. He published a series of 6 colour lithographs *Professeurs de la Faculté de Médecine et de l'Ecole de Droit*, which were very successful (420,000 copies sold). He also designed albums inspired by the great war. He exhibited at Salon des Humoristes.
Postcards: publicity for 'Salon du Cycle. L'Idéal du Touriste', c. 1903; 1 p. in the series 'Les Voeux de la France, Rire Rouge', 1914; several publicity and humorous p. on sport.
Bibl.: Lebeck 1978; Baudet 1980; Drago 1981; Lebeck 1981.

Alfredo BARUFFI
Bologna, 13.12.1873 – Bologna, Nov 1948.
Woodcut artist, illustrator, commerical artist, graphic designer (ex libris, publicity graphics, calendars, diplomas), designer of fabrics, ceramic vases, furniture.
He finished his studies as an accountant and got a job with the Cassa di Risparmio in Bologna. He was a self-taught artist, matured by contact with the 'bohemian' circle of artists at the Palazzo Bentivoglio, whose life he described in the book *I Giambardi della Sega* (1940). Above all interested in graphic design, from 1897 he designed several ex libris and illustrations for magazines. In 1898 he took part in the exhibition of the Bolognese society promoting the Fine Arts 'Francesco Francia', later he became its secretary. His work on magazines like *Il Tesoro* (1897), *Bologna che dorme* (1889-99) and *Italia ride* (1900) made him one of the most representative illustrators of the Bolognese Liberty. In 1902 he worked on the *Divina Commedia* published by Alinari, in 1903 he illustrated the book *Il malato d'Asia* by P. L. Occhini and from 1904 he executed 35 designs for the *Vita Nova* of Dante and 49 for the *Aminta* of Tasso, which were never published. He worked on the magazines *Lo Scappellotto* (1902-05), *Novissima* (1904-13), *Emporium* (1905), *Vita d'Arte* (1908), *La Casa* (1909). He also illustrated the books - *Ofelia* (1906) and *Desdemona* (1906) by P. O. Occhini, *Nonna Felsina* (1906), the only number of *Bologna la grassa* (1907), *La Secchia rapita* by Tassoni (1908), *Le Canzoni di Re Enzo* (1908-09) and *I Poemi italici* (1911) by G. Pascoli, the *Novelle* by A. Fiorenzuola (1913) by *La civiltà musicale di moda* by F. Vitielli (1913). He took part in the Turin exhibition in 1902, in the Venice Biennales of 1905 and 1914, at the 1906 Milan exhibition, and of the 50 anniversary of national unity in Rome 1911.
Postcards: Charity event. The nuns' orphan shelter in Bologna, publ. Chappuis, Bologna, 1899; a series of 12 'I Mesi', publ. Trenkler & Co., Leipzig, 1900.
Bibl.: Mordente 1982; Arrasich 1984.

Árpád BASCH
Budapest, 16.4.1873 – ? 1944
Painter, commercial artist, illustrator, graphic designer (book design, ex libris).
He studied in Budapest (B. Karlovsky), in

Munich (S. Hollósy), in Paris (L. Bonnat, J.-P. Laurens). In 1896 he returned to Hungary. He illustrated a lot of books, almanacs and Hungarian magazines. He was the artistic director of *Magyar Genius*.
Postcards: series of 10 of women of different nationalities 'L'allemande', 'La russe', 'L'Italienne', 'La suédoise' etc., series n. 785 of cities, large views; series of cities, small views; series of female warriors, c. 1900, several decorative cards.
Bibl.: Gaibazzi 1979; Baudet 1978, 1980; Bobba 1979; Holt 1980; 1983; Lebeck 1980; Drago 1981.

Franz von BAYROS
Agram (Zagreb), 1866 – Vienna, 3.4.1924
Painter, engraver, illustrator, graphic designer (ex libris).
He was the son of a Spanish father and a Viennese mother. He was well known above all for his engravings and illustrations of erotic subjects. He was an original interpreter of Beardsley's graphic language and on the Rococo revival.
Postcards: several for the publisher M. Victor, Cologne, 1898: 'O, das Ewig Weibliche!', 'O, die Männer!', 'O, die Väter!'.

BEGGARSTAFF BROTHERS, pseudonym for James PRYDE and William NICHOLSON
Postcards: 'Charitas', Venice, May c. 1901; some in the series 'Celabrated Posters', R. Tuck & Sons, London.

Peter BEHRENS
Hamburg, 14.4.1868 – Berlin, 27.2.1940
Painter, architect, graphic designer (book design, lettering, publicity graphics), commercial artist, illustrator, designer of furniture, fabrics, glass, metalwork, everyday objects and ceramist.
He studied at the Kunstgewerbeschule in Hamburg, from 1886 to 1889 at the Academy in Karlsruhe; then at the Academy in Düsseldorf (F. Brütt). From 1890 he was in Munich; in 1892 he was one of the founder members of the Munich Secession and in 1893 he was one of the Vereinigten Werkstätten für Kunst im Handwerk. In 1900 he was invited to join the Künstlerkolonie in Darmstadt, where he built his studio-house, his first architectural project. From 1902 to 1903 he taught at the Gweerbemuseum in Nürnberg. From 1903 to 1907 he was the director of the Kunstgewerbeschule in Düsseldorf. He worked on the magazines *Pan* (from 1898) and *Jugend*. He was one of the founders of Deutscher Werkbund (1907). From 1907 he was artistic adviser to A.E.G., he designed their industrial buildings in Berlin.
Postcards: 'Deutsche Kunstausstellung, Cologne, 1906, 'Tonhaus'; several reproducing his posters.

Henri Jules Ferdinand BELLERY-DESFONTAINES
Paris, 1867 – Petites-Dalles, 6.10.1909 (or 1910)
Painter, lithographer, illustrator, graphic designer (banknotes, stamps, lettering), commercial aartist.
A student of Galland and of J. P. Laurens, with whom he worked on the decorative paintings in the Paris Panthéon, and for paintings for the Hôtel de Ville, for which he did the architectural perspectives. He exhibited at the Salon de la Société Nationale des Beaux-Arts. He worked on the magazines: *L'Assiette au*

Beurre (for which he executed the monographic number 180, '*Grandes et petites superstitions*'), *L'Image, Almanach du Bibliophile, L'Estampe moderne, Art et Décoration*. He illustrated the books: *Jean Gutenberg* by A. France (1900); *Poèmes en prose* by M. de Guérin (1901); *La Prière sur l'Acropole* by E. Renan (1901); *Le Roi des Aulnes* by Goethe (1904); *Ode à la lumière* by A. France (1905); *Le Génie Latin* by A. France (1909); *Ode on a Grecian Urn* by Keats; *Faust* by Goethe.
Postcards: 'Exposition Universelle et Internationale de Liège 1905', typ. E. Verneau, reproduction of the poster.

Achille BELTRAME
Arzignano, Vicenza, 19.3.1871 – Milan, 19.2.1945
Illustrator, painter and commercial artist.
He was a student of Giuseppe Bertini at the Academy at the Brera. In 1890, while still a student he won the Mylius prize. He exhibited at the Brera Triennales (1891, 1894), at the group exhibition of the Società per le Belle Arti, and at the Milan Permanente, and at the Esposizione Nazionale in Turin in 1898. From 1896 he began intense activity as an illustrator, first for *Illustrazione italiana* (1896-98), then for *domenica del Corriere* (1899-1944); his fame is particularly tied to this magazine. From the first years of the twentieth century he worked as a commercial artist for Officine Grafiche Ricordi.
Postcards: 'Il Francobollo e la Cartolina', publicity p. for the magazine, 1899; series 10 p. 'La Colonia Libera', publ. Ricordi, Milano, 1899; series 10 of 'Opere e balli moderni', publ. Ricordi, Milan, 1900; series of 6 'Esposizione Nazionale d'allevamento cani, gatti, animali da cortile', publ. Ricordi, Milano, 1901; 'Esposizione annuale della società degli Artisti e Patriottica', 1902; 'Pro Sicilia', c. 1903; '1906 Coppa d'Oro Automobil Club Milano'; 'Loden Dal Brun, Schio-Stabilimenti', coloured publicity card on tin; p. for the war loan ('Fuori i barbari!'), c. 1915; several war propaganda p. 1915-18.
Bibl.: I. V. Brusa, 'La Colonia Libera', Il Raccoglitore di cartoline illustrate, 1 (n. 7, 20.10.1899), p. 80-82; Gaibazzi 1979; Bartoli-Mataloni 1979; Mordente 1982; Arrasich 1984.

Giovanni BELTRAMI
Milan, 26.2.1860 – Milan, 31.1.1926
Painter, stained glass designer, mosaic artist, art critic.
From 1878 he studied at the Academy at the Brera with R. Casnedi, B. Giuliano and G. Bertini. The last artist inspired his interest in mosaic art and painting on glass, which were his principal areas of activity. In 1894 he won the Mylius prize. In 1900 with the painters G. Buffa, I. Cantinotti and G. Zuccaro he opened a glass factory, their products were shown in many national and international exhibitions: in Turin in 1902, in Venice in 1903 and 1905. As an art critic he worked on the *Corriere della Sera*. In 1914 he succeeded Camillo Boito as president of the Brera Academy. In 1916 he became co-director with G. Treves, of *Illustrazione italiana*.
Postcards: publicity p. for 'Il Corriere della Sera', several regimental p. 1915-18.
Bibl.: Mordente 1982; Arrasich 1984.

Georg BELWE
Berlin, 12.8.1878 – Ronneburg, near Gera, 12.5.1954

Painter, commercial artist, lithographer, illustrator.
He went to the Kunstgewerbeschule in Berlin (E. Döpler). from 1906 he taught at the Akademie für graphische Künste und Buchgewerbe in Leipzig. In 1900 he founded with F. H. Elmcke and F. W. Kleukens the 'Steglitzer Werkstätte', which promoted important developments in applied graphic art.
Postcards: several decorative postcards.
Bibl.: Cat. Altonaer Museum, Hamburg 1970.

Alexandre BENOIS
St. Petersburg, 1870 – Paris, 1960
Painter, illustrator, graphic designer, theatrical designer and costumier, writer and critic.
After beginning legal studies, he became involved in art. He studied painting from 1897 to 1899 in Paris. He was a member of the circle which founded the magazine *Mir Iskusstva*. He worked on the Diaghilev's Ballets Russes. He worked on *Mir Iskusstva*, Απολλον, *Zolotoe Runo*.
Postcards: several decorative p.
Bibl.: Baudet 1980.

Fritzi BERGER
Probably a woman. Her biographical details are unknown. She seems to have had a fashion salon with her sister Hilde in Vienna.
Postcards: 4 of fashion in the series of the Wiener Werkstätte nos 764, 787-89.
Bibl.: Gaibazzi 1979; Baudet 1980; Hansen 1982; cat Vienna 1984.

Edouard BERNARD
Dates of birth and death unknown.
Illustrator, cartoonist, painter.
He worked on the magazine *L'Assiette au Beurre*, for which he completed several monographic volumes. He exhibited at the Salon des Humoristes.
Postcards: a series of 6 'L'entôlage', publ. P. Frères, publicity p. for 'Tourné Polin'.
Bibl.: Fildier 1979.

Max BERNUTH
Leipzig, 22.7.1872 – ?
Painter, lithographer, commercial artist, illustrator, graphic designer (ex libris).
From 1886 to 1890 he learnt lithography with J. Klinkhardt in Leipzig. He attended the Academy in Munich from 1886 to 1890. (S. Liezen-Mayer and C. v. Marr). From 1902 to 1932 he taught at the Kunstgewerbeschule at Elberfeld. He worked on the magazines *Jugend* and *Jungbrunnen*.
Postcards: in the first series of 'Künstler-Postkarten' of *Jugend*, G. Hirth, Munich 1898-99.

Paul Emile BERTHON
Villefranche, Rhône, 14.3.1872 – Paris, 1909
Painter, lithographer, commercial artist, graphic designer (book designer), designer of furniture and ceramics.
He studied at the Ecole Guérin and he followed L.-O. Merson's course on painting and E. Grasset's course on decorative arts. In 1895 he exhibited for the first time at the Salon of the Société Nationale des Beaux-Arts, and in 1897 he exhibited at the Salon de la Rose-Croix. He was mainly active as a designer of posters and decorative panels (lithographic prints). From 1897 to 1901 he made a series of decorative panels of musical instruments ('La Viole', 1897; 'La Femme àla Harpe', 1899; 'La Viole de Gambe', 1899; 'La Lyre', 1901;

'Mandore', 1901; and the series 'Six Petits Nus', which was reproduced in postcards. He designed ceramics for Villeroy & Boch and covers for magazines (*L'Image*, 1897; *Les Maîtres de l'Affiche*, 1897; *Revue d'Art Dramatique* 1898; *The Poster*, (1899). He worked on the magazines *L'Ermitage* (1898) and *Les Hommes d'aujourd'hui*.
Postcards: series of musical instruments; series 'Etudes de nu'; 1 in the series 'Affiches des Chemins de fer'.
Bibl.: Kyrou 1966; Baudet 1978, 1980; Mordente 1982.

Aurelio BERTIGLIA
Turin, 23.6.1891 – ?
Illustrator, commercial artist, caricaturist, graphic designer (musical scores, commercial and publicity graphics), fashion design, painter.
Self-taught. From the age of fourteen he was very active in producing postcards, also in working for German publishers.
Postcards: several series of children; several series of little women; several anti-Austrian caricatures 1915-18.
Bibl.: Bartoli-Mataloni 1979; Gaibazzi 1979; Mordente 1982; Arrasich 1984.

Anne Whelan BETTS
Painter, illustrator.
Biographical details are unknown. The American artist was born in Philadelphia. A student of H. Pyle in Wilmington and of Vonnoh, and later of Courtouis in Paris. She was active in Philadelphia. She worked for the magazines *The Century, Harper's* etc.
Postcards: series n. 291, M. Munk, Vienna.

Ethel Franklin BETTS
Biographical details are unknown. The American artist was active in Philadelphia c. 1909. She worked on *Scribner's* Magazine.
Postcards: Series n. 290, M. Munk, Vienna.

Otto BEYER
Kattowitz, Silesia (now in Poland) 20.10.1885 – ?
Painter and graphic designer.
He studied at the art school in Bratislava and at the Academy in Königsberg. He spent summer holidays in Belgium from 1910 to 1914. He was influenced by L. Corinth and M. Pechstein.
Postcards: several decorative p.

Maurice BIAIS
Dates of birth and death are unknown.
Painter, lithographer, cartoonist, commercial artist.
He designed several posters for the Folies-Bergère and other parisian theatres and cabarets. There are many posters for the shows of his wife, the dancer Jane Avril. He also designed 'panneaux decoratifs'.
Postcards: 1 in the IV series of the collection 'Les Maîtres de la Carte Postale, c. 1899.

Alberto BIANCHI
Rimini, 10.9.1882 – Milan, 23.2.1969
Painter, illustrator.
The nephew of Mosè Bianchi, he was a student of Mancini at the Accademia di Belle Arti in Rome. Mainly active as an illustrator and portrait painter, he also executed important fresco cycles (Theatre of King Fuad in Egypt; Teatro Comunale in Rimini). He began to be very involved in postcards from the early years of the century.

Postcards: 'Esposizione Antica Arte Senese', 1904; 'Associazione Artistica Internationale e Comitato Romano per la Flotta Aerea d'Italia – Roma, 2 giugno 1912'; 'Date Ali all 'Italia, 1912'; several series 'donnine', 1915-18; several series of war propaganda 1915-18; several anti-Austrian satirical series, 1915-18.
Bibl.: Forissier 1978; Bartoli-Mataloni 1979; Mordente 1982; Arrasich 1984.

Ernest BIÉLER
Rolle, Vaud, 31.7.1863 – Lausanne, 1943
Painter, watercolourist, woodcut artist, furniture designer, mosaicist, glass painter.
From 1880 he studied at the Ecole des Beaux-Arts in Paris with J. Lefebvre and Boulanger. He painted murals in several churches and public buildings in Switzerland (Stadttheater in Bern, the Ariana Museum in Geneva).
Postcards: series 'Fête des Vignerons – Vevey 1905', chromotypographie Sauberlin and Pfeiffer, Vevey, 1905.

Vespasiano BIGNAMI (known also under the pseudonym VESPA)
Cremona, 18.8.1841 – Milan, 29.2.1929
Painter, lithographer, caricaturist, illustrator, commercial artist, art critic.
From 1852 to 1862 he studied at the Accademia Carrara in Bergamo under the guidance of Enrico Scuri. He moved to Milan in 1862, and quickly gained notoriety as an illustrator and caricaturist in newspapers like *Uomo di pietra Mefistofele, Spirito folletto*. In 1872 he was a founder member of 'Famiglia Artistica' in Milan. In 1881 he organized the exhibition 'L'Indisposizione di Belle Arti'. In the last years of the century he designed several posters printed by the Officine Grafiche Ricordi. He worked as an art critic on the *Corriere della Sera*. He painted portraits, genre scenes and decorative cycles in several Italian and foreign theatres.
Postcards: '9° Congresso Nazionale Commercianti Industriali, Bologna', 1910; publicity p. 'Marsala Depa; ul', c. 1910; 'Veglionissimo della Stampa. Teatro Comunale Bologna', 1911; several war propaganda p. 1915-18.
Bibl.: Mordente 1982; Arrasich 1984.

Ivan J. BILIBIN
Tarkhovkov, nr St. Petersburg, 16.8.1876 – Leningrad, 7.2.1942
Painter, illustrator, graphic designer, theatre designer and costumier.
After starting university courses in law, he studied painting with Ilja Répin. He travelled in Switzerland and Italy (1898), England and Ireland (1908). He belonged to the group 'Mir Iskusstva'. From 1925 to 1936 he remained in France and worked with Ballets Russes. Already in 1899 he had started to work in the graphic arts. Of particular interest is his activity as the illustrator of several books for children (1902-1937).
He designed many series of postcards, in Russia at the beginning of the century, among them several for the Red Cross, which had as subjects, rural life (1901), heroes (1902), villages in the Russian provinces (1904), customs (1905), plays (1908), proverbs (1909), popular tales (1912).
Bibl.: Fildier 1979; Neudin 1979; Baudet 1980; Lebeck 1980; Mordente 1982.

C. BISHOP
Biographical facts are unknown. An American artist who was the author of several greetings,

humorous and glamour cards.
Postcards: series of Valentine cards A. H. & Co., series 'What do you know about that', a satirical series.
Bibl.: Lyons 1975; Holt 1983.

Vaino Alfred BLOMSTEDT
Nyslott, 1.4.1871 – Helsinki, 1947
Painter, illustrator, designer.
He studied in the School of Industrial Art in Helsinki and then went to the Académie Julian in Paris (1891, 1893-94, 1897-98, 1903, 1905-06, 1912), where he had Gauguin as his teacher. In 1900 he executed decorative paintings for the Finnish pavilion at the Paris Exposition Universelle. Around the turn of the century he became one of the Finnish symbolist painters. In 1902 he became the director of the Finnish Association of Friends of Craft.
Postcards: several from the period 1900-20, in which themes from bourgeois family life predominate.
Bibl.: Johanson-Termonen 1983.

Umberto BOCCIONI
Reggio Calabria, 19.10.1882 – Verona, 16.8.1916
Painter, sculptor, commercial artist, illustrator, art theorist.
Unlike Balla, Boccioni in the period before his allegiance to Futurism, when he was involved in various fields of applied graphic art, does not seem to have paid much attention to postcards. The only one known to date is 'Brunate (Como) – Maggio-Giugno 1909 Esposizione di pittura e scultura promossa dalla Famiglia Artistica e dalla Patriottica di Milano', off. Chiattone, Milan, which reproduced the poster.
Bibl.: M. Scudiero, 'Futurismo', *La Cartolina*, V (1985, n. 2) pp. 3-34.

Hans BÖHLER
Vienna, 11.9.1884 – Vienna, 17.9.1961
Painter, graphic designer.
The son of the industrialist Otto he studied painting at Jaschke's private art school. After the first world war he went to live in the Ticino and in 1936 in the United States, where he stayed until 1950. He worked on the magazines *Erdgeist* and *Muskete*. He exhibited at the 1909 Kunstschau in Vienna.
Postcards: 7 in the series of the Wiener Werkstätte of women and children, in which there are echoes of his journey to the Far East, nos 647, 648, 650, 653, 801.
Bibl.: Baudet 1980; Hansen 1982.

Adolf BOHM
Vienna, 25.2.1861 – Klosterneuberg, 20.2.1927
Painter, commercial artist, graphic designer (calendars), stained glass window designer, ceramist, designer of glass and furniture.
The son of a painter, from 1876 he went to the academy in Vienna (C. Wurzinger, A. Eisenmenger). From 1900 he taught at the Kunstschule für Frauen und Mädchen. A member of the 'Hagen-Gesellschaft'.
A founder member of the Vienna Secession, which he left in 1905 with the Klimt group. He worked on the magazine *Ver Sacrum*.
Postcards: in the series 'Ver Sacrum' published for the 1st exhibition of the Vienna Secession, Verlag Gerlach & Schenk, Vienna 1898.
Bibl.: Pabst 1984.

Philip BOILEAU

Québec, 1864 – ?, 1917
Painter, commercial artist, illustrator, graphic designer (calendars and decorative prints).
He studied art and music in 1887 in Milan, where he married. After his wife's death, he travelled across Europe and moved to Baltimore (1897) where he married his second wife Emily Gibbert, who was often his model. He created a female type the 'American Girl' – who rivalled the 'Gibson Girl' – who was very successful and was imitated by many artists like A. Heinze, etc. His many postcards were widely available in the United States and in Europe. He worked for *Associated Sunday Magazines*.
Postcards: several publicity p. ('Contrary Mary Book', 'Flood & Conklin', 'Metropolitan Life Ins. Co.,', 'Nat. Suit and Cloak Co.'); several series on the theme 'American Girl' (heads of women, couples and three women etc), or of children, Reinthal & Newman, New York, 1900-1914, reproduced in the first decade, and later by other publishers, like Charles Hauff & Co., London.
Bibl.: Klamkin 1974; Lyons 1975; Holt 1981, 1983; D. Ryan, *Philip Boileau: painter of fair women,* New York 1981.

Luigi BOMPARD
Bologna, 8.9.1879 – Rome, 24.2.1953
Illustrator, painter, commercial artist, watercolourist, engraver, fashion designer.
He established himself in Bologna with illustrations from 1900 for *Italia ride*. He worked successively on the magazines *L'Illustrazione italiana* and *Illustration française*. He also did illustrations for books like *The conquest of the South Pole* by E. H. Shackleton. He lived for a long time in Paris, where he was influenced by Boldini. This is particularly evident in the series of engravings of fashionable life exhibited in Italy and abroad (Mostra nazionale dell'Incisione, in Rome 1915, at the Exhibition of the Association of Italian Etchers and Engravers in London 1916). As a painter he exhibited at the Venice Biennale in 1905, 1912, 1920, and at the Salon d'Automne in Paris 1909. After the first world war he worked on the papers *Il Travaso, La Stampa* and *Il Giornale della Domenica*.
Postcards: 'Teatro Filodrammatico di Ravenna – Festa di Beneficenza del patronato dei bambini poveri', publ. Chappuis, Bologna 1901; 'Mostra nazionale ventagli, bambole, giocattoli', 1901; series of female faces in floral frames 'Modestia', 'Ricchezza', 'Stupidità', etc., c. 1902; 'Ricordo Pasqua di Carità', 1906; humorous series about exams ('S' avvicinano gli esami', 'Sciopero!', 'Fiasco', etc.), c. 1908; humorous p. 'Chasse au mari', c. 1909; series of 'donnine', publ. Ricordi, c. 1917; publicity p. 'Al vino del Chianti', publ. Minarelli, Bologna; series of 7 'La fotografia', publ. G. Mengoli, Bologna.
Bibl.: Bartoli-Mataloni 1979; Bobba 1979; Neudin 1981; La Cartolina, I (1982, n. 4), p. 23; Mordente 1982; Arrasich 1984.

Gigi BONFIGLIOLI
Bologna, 9.3.1874 – ?
Painter, illustrator.
He attended the Accademia di Belle Arti in Bologna where he was a student of Ferro and Puccinelli. He exhibited at the Venice Biennale in 1899 and 1901. Postcards: 'Città di Bologna, Ricordo delle Feste di Primavera, 1901', lith. Thumb.
Bibl.: Emilia Romagna, supplement to n. 4,

1982 of *La Cartolina*; Arrasich 1984.

Aroldo BONZAGNI
Cento, 24.9.1887 – Milan, 30.12.1918
Painter, caricaturist, fashion designer, commercial artist, illustrator.
From 1906 to 1909 he attended the Academy at the Brera, where he followed C. Tallone's courses in painting, G. Mentessi's and A. Lorenzoli's courses in decoration. Through Boccioni he came into contact with the Futurist movement, and signed the first edition (11.2.1910) printed on the flyleaf of the review *Poesia*, of the *Manifesto dei pittori futuristi* and he took part in some Futurist parties. In 1910 he designed fashion plates for a Milanese fashion house. In 1912 he took part in the Esposizione dei Rifiutati in Milan (Palazzo Covo) and in the Venice Biennale. In 1913 he showed a series of satirical posters of mostly political subjects at the Mostradella Caricatura in Bergamo. In 1914 he moved to Buenos Aires, where he did the frescoes in the Hippodrome, had a one-man show, and began to work for the humorous magazine *El Zorro*. In 1915 he returned to Milan.
Postcards: series of caricatures of the Italian-Turkish war, publ. Pilade Rocco, Milan 1911; several p. for the subscription to the national loan for the war ('Fratelli salvetemi! Sottoscrivate', Cromoglliptica, A. Marzi, Rome) and of anti-Austrian satire, 1915-18.
Bibl.: Bobba 1979; Mordente 1982; Arrasich 1984.

Mario BORGONI
Pesaro, 24.7.1869 – ?
Painter, commercial artist.
He attended the Instituto di Belle Arti in Naples, where he was a pupil of I. Petricci. He was professor of ornament at the same Institute.
Postcards: commemorating the fiftieth anniversary of the southern plebiscite, 1910; publicity p. for 'Birra Milano', 1901; 'Esperimenti d'aviazione Piazza d'Armi Bologna', 1910; 'Mostra floreale e orticola, Napoli 1911'; 'Fiera Campionaria di Napoli, 1911'; 'Pro Espulsi', 1915; several for the national loan, 1915-16; several war propaganda p., 1915-18; 'Primo viaggio di Posta Aerea Napoli – Palermo, 1917'.
Bibl.: Gaibazzi 1979; Mordente 1982; Arrasich 1984.

Fritz BOSCOVITS
Zurich, 13.11.1871 – ?
Painter, illustrator, caricaturist, commercial artist.
The son of the Hungarian painter Friedrich. He studied at the Academy in Munich with H. Knirr, L. v. Löfftz, P. Höcker and F. von Defregger. From 1895 to 1897 he lived in Florence. From 1900 he lived in Zurich, where he designed several lithographic sheets. He illustrated the book by B. Meinecke *Ein Kleines Märchenbuch* (1918). He executed frescoes at the main post office in Schaffhausen, in the Landwirtschaftliche Schule and in the Zurich Polytechnic.
Postcards: 'Offizielle Festpostkarte Sechseläuten, 18 April, Zürich, 1910', Lith. Anst. Gebr. Fretz. Zurich, 1910; p. for charity for the Swiss Red Cross, 1917.

Etienne – Maurice – Firmin BOUISSET
Moissac, Tarn et Garonne, 2.9.1859 – Paris, 19.3.1955

Painter, engraver, illustrator, commercial artist, graphic designer (menus, calendars, song scores).

A student of Garrepuy and A. Cabanel at the Ecole des Beaux-Arts in Paris. From 1880 he exhibited portraits and scenes of childhood at the Salon. He was intensely active as an illustrator, with a predilection for childhood subjects. (*La Journée* de Bébé, 1885; *Les Bébés d'Alsace et de Lorraine*, 1886, by M. Arnaud), which are also the subject of his posters. He collaaborated on the magazines *Le Capital* (1883) and *L'Estampe moderne* (1899). He illustrated books: *N'a-qu'un-oeil* by L. Cladel (1882); *Contes* by E. Pouvillon (1888); *Le Roman d'un dé à coudre* by O. Gevin-Cassal (1902).
Postcards: in the series 'Album Mariani', c. 1910; 1 p. in the 'Collection Job', series 1911, 1914, reproductions of a poster of 1895.

Henri BOUTET
Sainte-Hermine (Vendée), 24.3.1851 – Paris, 11.6.1919 (1920 or 1921)
Painter, engraver, commercial artist, illustrator, graphic designer (ex libris, menus, programmes).
He exhibited at the Salon of the Société des Artistes Français and at the Salon d'Automne. He worked on the magazines *Paris-Croquis* (1888-89), *L'illustration* (1891), *Le Courrier français* (1894), *Paris-Artiste, Paris-Médaillon, Revue artistique, L'Art et l'Idee, L'Art Moderne*. He was the author of many albums: *Autour d'elles* (1898), *Les modes féminines du XIXe siècle* (1902), *Filles de joie et de misère de Phryné à Margot* (1913), *Etude illustrée de la Môme* (1913), *Le Petit Café blanc* (1914), *Le Lever, Les modèles*.
He designed illustrations for the 1887, 1888, 1890, 1893 Almanac and for the books: *Calendrier Parisien* by E. d'Hervilly (1886); *Une partie de campagne* by G. de Maupassant (1892); *Les Déshabillés au théâtre* (1895) and *Les Parisiennes d'à présent* (1896) by G. Montorgueil; *Femmes de mer* by H. H. Devillers (1904) + *Le Manchon de Francine* by H. de Murger; *L'année féminine* by G. Montorgueil.
In 1895 he exhibited at the Salon des Cent works to which the magazine *La Plume* dedicated a monographic issue.
Postcards: 126 c. published by A. D. Motot and by Librairie Charles, 1898-1902 (20 p. 'À la fleur' 10 p. 'Auto d'eles', 10 p. 'À la tête de femme', 5 p. 'Scénes parisiennes', 4. p. 'L'hiver', 4 p. 'Silhouettes parisiennes', 5 p. 'Scénes parisiennes', 4 p. 'Silhouettes parisiennes', 5 p. 'Scénes parisiennes', 4 p. 'Le Printemps', 4 p. 'Silhouettes parisiennes', 4 p. 'Sur la plage', 4 p. 'L'été'. 4 p. 'Aux bains de mer', 4 p. 'En automobile', 4 p. 'A bicyclette', 4p. 'Paysages parisiens', 4p. 'Ouvrières parisiennes', 4 p. 'Où elles vont', 4 p. Croquis d'enfants', 4p. 'Coulisses de théâtre', 4 p. 'Têtes de femmes', 4 p. 'Liseuses', 4 p. 'Blanchisseuses', 4 p. 'Le sommeil', 4 p. 'Sur les quais', 4 p. 'au piano', 4 p. 'Les omnibus'); 52 p. for Editions de l'atelier d'art, executed in dry-point (12 p. 'Le lever de la parisienne', 8 p. 'Les corsets', 6 p. 'La fête des fleurs', 8 p. 'La vie féminine', 12 p. 'Les douze heures de la parisienne', 4 p. 'Le mauvais temps'); 32 p. for Editions Kunzli Frères (8 p. 'Le coucher', 12 p. 'Le bain', 12 p. 'Modèles d'artistes') + a series of 18 p. 'Les déshabillés'; 4 series of 6 p. 'Modes féminines du 19 siecle'; 2 series of 4 and 8 p. 'Danseuses'; series of 12 publicity p. 'Ph. Fallières: chansons de grand'mère'; 12 of

military p. (one dedicated to Marchal Foch and one to Clemenceau); 1 p. in the 'Collection des Cent', publ. Gréningaire, Paris; 1 p. 'Denise Fille de l'artiste, 1902; 1 p. 'Naissance Jean F.', c. 1894; 1 p. 'Calendrier', 1903; 1 p. 'Communion: Jean F.', 1903; 1 p. 'Noces d'argent, 1881; 1 p. 'Changement de domicile personnel', 1902; 1 p. 'Charles Fontane'; 1 p. 'Association Philocartiste Nancéenne-nouvelle année 1902'.
Bibl.: Kyrou 1966; Forissier 1976; Weill 1977; Baudet 1978, 1980; Forissier 1978; Bobba 1979; Neudin 1979; Rostenne 1979; Holt 1983.

William H. BRADLEY
Boston, Massachusetts, 10.7.1868 – La Mesa, California, 25.1.1962
Commercial artist, illustrator, graphic designer (book design, commercial graphics, lettering).
He learnt to draw from his father, the caricaturist Aron. Basically self-taught. From 1881 he worked for printers in Marquette (Michigan) and Chicago. In the 90's he became one of the most important graphic artists. In 1895, in order to create works of the highest possible craftsmanship, he founded his own studio, the Wayside Press in Springfield (Massachusetts), which printed his magazine *Bradley, His Book, A Monthly Magazine*, published by the University Press of Cambridge, of which he became artistic director. He worked on several American magazines *The Inland Printer* (1894-95), *The American Chap Book* (1904), *Collier's Magazine* (of which he was the director 1907-1909), *Good Housekeeping* (1911-13), *Metropolitan* (1914-16), *The Century*, etc.
Postcards: 1 c. in the first series 'Les Maîtres de la Carte Postale', published by the paper *La Critique*, Paris, 1898; p. reproducing his graphic work.
Bibl.: Rostenne 1979, Baudet 1980.

Adolf BRÁZDA
Rícanech, 16.6.1875 – ?
Painter commercial artist, illustrator.
He completed his artistic studies in Prague.
Postcards: 'Ústredni Matice Skolská'.

Umberto BRUNELLESCHI
Montemurlo, 21.6.1879 – Paris, 16.2.1949
Illustrator, painter, sculptor, scenographer.
He studied painting and sculpture under the guidance of B. Sorbi and E. Ciaranfi at the Accademia di Belle Arti in Florence. In 1901 he moved to Paris with A. Soffici and there he continued his studies with L. Gérôme. In 1902 he exhibited a self-portrait in the Salon des Indépendants. During his stay in France he worked on several Italian magazines like *Il giornalino della Domenica* (1906, 1907, 1909), and on French magazines like *La Gazette du bon ton, Fantasio, Flirt, Le Rire* and others. He also illustrated books: *Satanello* by G. Lipparini (1909); *Contes* by Mme d'Aulnoy (1912); *Fantasio, Les Caprices de Marianne, La Nuit Vénitienne* by A. de Musset (1913); *Journal des Dames* (1914) and others.
In 1912 he made his debut as a scenographer with the sets for the ballet 'Légende du clair de lune' by Madame Rasini at the 'Les bouffes parisiens' theatre, which launched him as a scenographer of music-hall. His studio in Paris became a meeting-point for personalities from the world of art and culture: Modigliani, Soutine, Picasso, Van Dongen, Derain, Boldini, D'Annunzio. At the outbreak of war he returned to Italy and joined the army. In this period he worked on *L'illustrazione Italiana*.

After the war he settled in Paris, where he worked as a scenographer for the Folies-Bergère, the Casino, the Mogador, the Châtelet, for the Marigny and for the Théâtre de Paris. He was also intensely active as a book illustrator for French and Belgian publishers.
Postcards: series of 6 p. 'Le Coraggiose', published in honour of the III Armata, publ. Ricordi, Milan, 1915-16; series of 6 p. special edition for the *Traddota* publ. Milan, 1917; p. with the motto by D'Annunzio 'Abbiamo recomperato la tua bellezza a misura di baionette; e nelle nostre vene rinsanguato il tuo stendardo', c. 1918; p. of an infantryman with 'a helmet against a background of St Mark's, Venice', c. 1918; series of women and jobs (the postwoman, the sweeper etc), 1915-18. Bibl.; Fildier 1979; Gaibazzi 1979; La Cartolina, n. 4, 1982; Mordente 1982; Arrasich 1984.

Llorenç BRUNET i TORROLL
Badalona, 1873 – Barcelona, 1939
Caricaturist, illustrator, commercial artist, graphic designer (ex libris, visiting cards, calendars, commercial and publicity graphics), watercolourist.
A student of A. Caba, c. Lorenzale and E. Planas at the school of Belle Arti in Barcelona and of Mercier in Paris. He is well-known for his work in the field of ex libris, posters and caricature. He worked as an illustrator on the Catalan magazines *Almanach de la Campana de Gracia, Almanach de la Esquella de la Torratxa, Calendari del Cu-Cut, La Ilustració Llevantina*.
Postcards: series of 10 p. 'Ex Libris Politicos'.
Bibl.: Trenc Ballester 1977.

Giovanni BUFFA
Casale Monferrato, 10.10.1871 – ?, June 1964 (or 1956)
Painter, illustrator, sculptor, etcher, designer of glass, furniture and furnishings.
He was trained at the Academy at the Brera. He designed windows for Officina Beltrami in Milan. He made designs for furnishings for the firm Richard Ginori and for the Famiglia Artistica Milanese. In 1906 he won the Città di Milano prize with a series of designs inspired by the *Divina Commedia*.
Postcards: 'Fiera di beneficenza pro cieche e sordomute, deficienti e offanelle ricoverate in Borgo Vico', publ. G. Chiattone, Milan 1901.
Bibl.: Arrisich 1984.

René BULL
Dublin c. 1870 – ?, 1942
Illustrator.
He studied engineering in Paris, where he met Caran d'Ache. From 1892 he began working for illustrated magazines in London: *Black and White, The Graphic, The Illustrated London News, The Sketch* and many others. He made a vast number of humorous and caricatural postcards, in which one can recognize an unsystematic and therefore limited use of Art Nouveau devices. He invented the so-called 'Messagepostcard', where a sentence was combined with a design.
Bibl.: Holt 1980, 1983.

Paul BÜRCK
Strasbourg, 3.9.1878 – Munich, 18.4.1947
Painter, engraver, commercial artist, graphic designer (ex libris, menus etc)
During his time as a painter's apprentice with a painter and decorator in Munich, he attended the Kunstgewerbeschule from 1896-1897.

From 1899 to 1902 he was a member of the Künstgewerbeschule in Darmstadt. From 1903 he taught at the Kunstgewerbeschule Magdeburg, then he moved to Munich.
Postcard: for the Künstlerkolonie Ausstellung Darmstadt 1901.

Jean-Léonce BURRET
Bordeaux, 20.4.1866–Paris, 1915
Cartoonist, lithographer, illustrator, commercial artist, graphic designer (song scores).
He studied at the Ecole des Beaux-Arts in Bordeaux
He worked on the magazines *Le Rire, Le Sourire, Le Chat Gris, Fantasio, La vie Parisienne, L'Assiette au Beurre*. He illustrated the book *La Petite Marquise* by Cremnitz (1910).
Postcards: 1 p. in the 'Collection des Cent', publ. Gréningaire Paris, c. 1901.
Bibl.: Baudet 1978; Neudin 1983.

Adolfo BUSI
Faenza, 6.1.1891 – Bologna (?), 1977 (or 1978)
Painter, commercial artist, illustrator, graphic designer (publicity graphics).
He got his diploma at the Accademia di Belle Arti in Bologna. He took part in the II exhibition of the Rome Secession (1914) and at the international exhibition in San Francisco, where he won the silver medal. In 1914 he had a one-man show at the Hotel Baglioni in Bologna. He was particularly active in the fields of publicity graphics, book illustration and posters. He also designed several postcards, above all in the Twenties of the 'donnine' genre.
Postcards: series of 'donnine', publ. Ricordi, Milano, c. 1918.
Bibl.: La Cartolina, n. 4, 1982; Arrasich 1984.

Gaston BUSSIÈRE
Cuisery, Saône-et-Loire, 24.4.1862 – Paris, 1929
Painter, engraver, illustrator.
A student of a. Cabanel and Puvis de Chavannes. From 1886 he exhibited at the Salon des Artistes Français. He painted pictures and made decorative panels with Wagnerian themes. As an illustrator he worked on the magazine *Monde Moderne*. He made engravings for several books, mainly published by Ferroud.
Postcards: several inspired by R. Wagner's melodramas.

C

Arsène – F. P. CADIOU
Morlaix, Finistère ? – 1906
Painter.
A student of L. O. Merson. He exhibited in 1903 and in 1905 at the Société des Artistes Français.
Postcards: 1p. in the 'Collection des Cent', publ. Gréningaire, Paris, c. 1901; 1p. in the series 'Byrrh', 1906.
Bibl.: Baudet 1978.

C. CALDERARA
?, 1883 – ?
Illustrator, cartoonist.
Born in Lombardy. He went on study trips to Paris. From 1903 he worked on several Milanese illustrated papers. From 1912 he began to design postcards, but at the beginning of the war his series of 'donnine' became very successful.
Postcards: series 139 of 6p. ('Ma il tram non si ferma', 'Vita nuova', 'Cercando la via', 'Come comincia un flirt', etc), D.G.M.; series n. 149 of 6p., women's faces, D.G.M.; series n. 191 of 6 p., donnine; series 328 of 6p., donnine, F.P.M., unsigned; series n. 399 of 6p., women in winter, Ars Parva; series n. 347 of 6p., women's faces with French inscriptions, ('Sporteuse', 'Reveuse', etc), Ars Parva; series n. 348 of 6p., women's faces with French inscriptions ('Touquette de la Toque' 'Simplicie de Saint-Plipsy', etc), Ars Parva; series n. 363 of 6p., charms with Italian and French inscriptions ('Birichina/Fripeuse', 'Fotografia particolare/Photographie intime', etc.), Ars Parva; series n. 378 of 6p., women in winter, Ars Parva, series 379 of 6p., women's faces, Ars Parva; series n. 1005 of 6p., charm, F.L.M.; series n. 2840 of 6p. 'donnine', series n. 3058, (UFF. Rev. Stampa, Milan) of 6p., 'donnine'; series n. 3062 of 6p., women in winter fashions, series n. 3066 of 6p. Happy Easter greetings, unsigned series n. 3126 (UFF. Rev. Stampa, Milan) of 6p., Red Cross nurses, woman and a car, two ladies; series n. 3128 (Uff. Rev. Stampa, Milan) of 6p. faces in a circle; series n. 3203, of 6p., walking; series n. 322 of 6p., 'donnine' unsigned; series n. 3225 (Uff. Rev. Stampa, Milan) of 6p., 'donnine', series n. 3226 of 6p., 'donnine'; series n. 3241 of 12p., charm; series n. 3328 (Uff. Rev. Stampa, Milan) of 6p., charm; series n. 3338 (Uff. Rev. Stampa, Milan, charm; series n. 4118 (Uff. Rev. Stampa) of 6p. women with a panel in the background; series n. 4144 (UFF. Rev. Stampa) of 6p. 'military women', 1918; '159° Regg. Fanteria M.M. – Brigata di Milan', F.P.M. Bibl.: F. Arrasich, 'Le donnine di Calderara', **La Cartolina**, IV (1984, n. 15), pp. 22-23.

Achille CALZI
Faenza, 1873 – Faenza, 1919
Ceramist, painter, graphic designer (publicity graphics), designer of furniture and wrought iron.
He completed his early studies in the School of Design and Plastic Arts directed by A. Berti in Faenza, and then at the accademia di Belle arti in Faenza, where he attended A. Burchi's course on decorative art. He made several study trips to France and England. He had many interests, and taught at the art school 'T. Minardi' in Faenza (he later became the director there); He directed the Pinacoteca Comunale in Faenza, he established in 1917 his own ceramic factory, and he designed furniture for the Casalini company. He designed wrought iron for Matteucci and also continued painting and making designs in graphic art.
Postcards: 'Esposizione Regionale Romagnola, 1904, Typ. Lavagna, Ravenna; 'Ebanisteria Casalini all' Esposizione di Ravenna, 1905'; 'Faenza, 29 giugno 1905'; 'Faenza 1905, Societa per il Risveglio cittadino', Lith. A. Morgagni, Faenza; 'Festeggiamenti del 1908. Faenza', publ. A. Albonetti, Faenza; 'Terzo centenario della nascita di Evangelista Torricelli, Faenza', publ. A. Albonetti, Faenza, 1908; publicity card for the book *Faenza nella storia e nell'arte* by A. Calzi e A. Messeri, 1909
Bibl.: Bartoli-Mataloni 1979; *Emilia-Romagna* supplement of no 4 of *La Cartolina*, 1982, pp. 58-60; Arrasich 1984.

Tomás Júlio Leal de CAMARA
New Goa, 30.11.1877 – Rinchoa, 21.7.1948
Painter, designer, caricaturist.
He completed his early studies in Portugal, and moved to Paris, where he perfected his artistic studies. His work for *L'Assiette au Beurre* gave him notoriety as a political caricaturist. Political satire was the subject matter of nearly all of his postcards. After his stay in Paris he worked in Madrid and Lisbon.
Postcards: series of 25 p. 'Leurs statues', publ. B.C.I., 100 copies issued; series of 6p. 'La guerre Russo-Japonaise', publ. B.C.I. 1904, issue of 10 copies; series of 16p. 'Méli-Mélo', publ. F. Jackl, 100 copies issued; series 6p. 'Fallières I', publ. F. Jackl, 50 copies issued; series 'Le Carillon', B.C.I.; series 'Le nouveau carillon', publ. B.C.I. 100 copies issued; series of 6 c. 'Le Knout', publ. B.C.I. 50 copies issued; series 'Les organisateurs de la paix', publ. F. Jackl, 100 copies issued; series 'Les organisateurs de la guerre', publ. B.C.I. 100 copies issued; series of 14 or 20 p. 'Nos Ministres', publ. B.C.I. 100 copies issued; series (?) 'Conference d'Algesiras', publ. B.C.I.; series 'Valets-Dames Rois' (p. in the form of playing cards), publ. B.C.I. series of 8p. 'Masques et visages', publ. F. Jackl; series of 6 p. 'Leurs bobos', publ. F. Jackl; series of 8 p. 'Dis-moi ce que tu bois et tu manges, je te dirai qui tu es', publ. F. Jackl; series of 6 p. 'Les écraseurs', publ. P. Lamm; series of 6 p. 'Cyclistes', publ. P. Lamm; series of 6 p. 'Patinage', publ. P. Lamm; series of 6 p. 'Election législative – la Nouvelle Chambre'; series of 12 p. 'Nos littérateurs', publ. P. Lamm; series of 10 p. 'A propos du couronnement', publ. P. Lamm; series of 15 p. 'Les Souverains', publ. P. Lamm; series of 15 p. 'Nos Souverains', Publ. P. Lamm; series of 6 (?) p. 'artistes', publ. P. Lamm; series of 22 p. 'Hommes politiques', no publisher's name.
Bibl.: Wiener 1922-23; Weill 1977; Fildier 1979, 1980.

Duilio CAMBELLOTTI
Rome, 10.5.1876 – Rome, 31.1.1960
Scenographer, engraver, illustrator, commercial artist, painter, sculptor, architect, designer of furniture, mosaics, stained glass windows, ceramics, jewellery, lighting, mirrors, jewel caskets, buckles, graphic designs (ex libris, commercial and publicity graphics).
He got a diploma in accountancy, and from 1893 attended the Museo Artistico Industriale in Rome, under the direction of A. Moroni and R. Ojetti, and in 1897 he received the 'licence' to teach in art schools. From 1896 he was active as a commercial artist and furnishing designer. In 1898 he exhibited in the exhibition of the Società Promotrice di Belle Arti in Turin and in 1899 he was in Constantinople with R. D'Aronco. In 1900 he promoted with the socialist A. Marucci the popular 'Letture Dantesche' and he illustrated the books. In 1900 he worked on the Bolognese magazine *Italia Ride*, and in Rome in 1902 he published socially satirical illustrations – in *Fantasio*. From 1902 to 1909 he worked on *Avanti della Domenica* and from 1903 to 1907 on *Novissima*. In 1904 he joined the revolutionary socialist party and worked on their Roman paper *Divenire sociale*. From 1905 he designed stage sets for the Stabile Romana, and this activity became his main interest for the rest of his life. From 1908 he was a professor of ornament at the Rome Istituto d'Arte and collaborated on the magazine *La Casa*, in which he published his project for worker's housing. He took part with Marcucci and Cena in the socialist movement

'Scuole Rurali', rural schools for the peasants from the Roman plain, which on the occasion of the 1911 Rome Exhibition organized the Mostra delle Scuole dell'Agro, which was assembled in a hut designed by Cambellotti and decorated with paintings by Balla. As a painter he was active with the group 'XXI della campagna romana' and he painted works with a distinctly populist character. Between 1911 and 1914 he executed frescoes, tempera paintings and decorative ceramics in the schools of Casal delle Palme, Torre di Fuori, Scauri and Torre Spaccata. He worked as an illustrator until the end of the war on the magazines *Italia!* (1913), *La Lettura* (1914), *Il Soldato* (1916), *Il Piccolissimo* (1916-19), *L'Arte* (1917) and *Rapiditas* (magazine of the Florio competition) and the book illustrations: *La Divina Commedia* (ed. Alinari 1902-03); *La Nave* by D'Annunzio (1908); *L'ultima fata* by Cordelia (1909); *I racconti di sorella Orsetta* by Térésah (1910); *Nel regno dei nani* by A. France (1913); *Mille e una notte* (1913); *I racconti della foresta e del mare* by Térésah and Ezio Maria Gray (1914); *La leggenda d'oro di Mollichina* by Camille Mallarmé (1915). Postcards: Targa Florio, 1908. 'Istituto Coloniale Italiano. Il Congresso degli italiani all'estero, Roma-Torino 1911'; Roma 1911 Esposizione Internazionale', publ. E. Chappuis, Bologna, reproduction of the poster (there are other editions of this p. with the inscription 'Feste Commemorative della Proclamazione del Regno d'Italia' in many languages; Rome XXII Congresso Dante Alighieri, 1911; 'Società Nazionale Dante Alighieri XXIII Congresso, Catania 27-31 ottobre 1912', publ. E. Chappuis, Bologna; series Battaglione aviatori, per aspera ad astra', 1913; 'Sanctus Georgius – Equitum – Patronus. Modena, Squadrone Allievi, 1917', several for the national loan; several war propaganda p., several in the series 'Divina Commedia', publ. Alterocca, Terni; publicity for the magazine '*La Casa*'. Bibl.: *La Cartolina*, n. 2, 1981; Mordente 1982; Arrasich 1984.

Glauco CAMBON
Trieste, 13.8.1875 – Biella, 7.3.1930
Painter, commercial artist, graphic designer (magazine covers, publicity graphics, ex libris). He began his artistic studies in Trieste, while he was still at school. From 1892 to 1895 he studied at the Academy in Munich. In 1897 he took part for the first time in the international exhibition in Venice, followed by his presence there in 1907, 1909, 1910, 1912, 1914, 1920, 1922, 1924. In 1900 he gained the 'pensionato romano' from the Rittmeyer Foundation and he moved to the capital, where he stayed for five years. He returned to Trieste in 1905 and following this he worked both as a painter and commercial artist.
Postcards: 'Veglia campestre Soc. M.S. Barbieri, Bologna', 1903; 'Esposizione Regionale dilettanti fotografi Trieste 1905', reproduction of the poster 'Torneo Internazionale di Scherma, Trieste 1906'; 'Mostra d'arte Pisino, 1907'; 'Concerto di Beneficenza', 1907; 'Il Palvese, giornale letterario della Domenica, Trieste', c. 1907; 'Settimana aviatoria, Trieste Aerodromo di Zaule, 1911'; series of views of Trieste, c. 1915; 'Occupazione Italiana, Pisino, 1918'; 'Dio che si midollo . . .', c. 1918, Bibl.: Mordente 1982; Arrasich 1984.

Illemo CAMELLI
Cremona, 1.5.1876 – Cremona, 4.1.1939

Painter, illustrator, writer.
He studied at the Istituto Ala Ponzone in Cremona and at the Academy at the Brera in Milan. He took part in the Turin exhibition in 1902 showing his illustrations of the *Divina Commedia*. He illustrated stories by Poe (1900) and other works as well as his own volume of fables: *Le fiabe della vita*. He worked on the magazine *La Riviera Ligure* (1904). At the age of thirty he was ordained as a priest. In spite of this new commitment he continued to be involved in artistic and literary activity, as the director he took charge of the arrangement of the Museo Civico in Cremona. In 1935 he held a one-man show in Cremona.
Postcards: series of 6 p. with the subjects 'Dolore', 'Quiete', 'Odio', 'Ira', 'Sorriso', 'Paura', c. 1904.
Bibl.: Arrasich 1984.

Gaspar CAMPS i JUNYENT
Igualada, 1875 – Barcelona, 1942.
Illustrator, commercial artist, designer, graphic designer (calendars).
He studied at the Escuela de Lonja. In 1894 he moved to Paris, where he studied with P. Constant and P. Laurens. During his stay in the French capital he worked both as an illustrator and commercial artist. In 1896 and 1898 he exhibited at the exhibition of art in Barcelona. He worked on the Catalan magazines Álbum Salón, *Pluma y Lápiz*, *Hojas Selectas*, *Catalunya Artística*. He illustrated the volumes in the collection 'Ambos Mundos' published by the Editorial Artística Española and the book *Valentina* by E. C. Price (1904). The obvious influence of Mucha in his graphic work has given him the nick-name 'Mucha catalán'.
Postcards: series of 12 p., the months, publ. Album Salón, Barcelona, and publ. L. Miguel, Havana (Cuba), 1901; two series of 6 p. 'Cabezas femeninas', publ. Tasso, Barcelona; publicity p. for the firm Cosme Puigmal, Barcelona, 1902; postcard – calendars for the brand of cognac Henri Garnier, Typ. Thomas, Barcelona, 1902; publicity p. 'Bengaline Peinture Email', Paris.
Bibl.: Trenc Ballester 1977.

Leonetto CAPPIELLO
Leghorn 9.4.1875 – Cannes, 2.2.1942
Commercial artist, caricaturist, illustrator, scenographer, theatrical costumier, painter.
Self-taught. In 1896 he published his first album of caricatures: *Lanterna Magica* in Leghorn. In 1898 he moved to Paris, where he began to work on the magazines *Le Rire* and *Le Cri de Paris*. His caricatures and illustrations appeared successively in '*Le Cri du Mois* (1899), *Les Feux de la Rampe* (1899), *la Revue Blanche* (1899), le *Souvire* (1899-1900), *La Rampe* (1899-1901), *Le Frou-Frou* (1901), *L'Assiette au Beurre* (1901-02), *Le Figaro* (1901-04), *Le Gaulois du Dimanche* (1902-03), *Femina* (1903), *Le Canard Sauvage* (1903), *Le Théâtre* (1903), *La Baîonette* (1915-17). In 1898 he designed his first poster. In 1900 his collaboration with the typographer and publisher P. Vercasson marked the beginning of intense activity as a commercial artist, which made Cappiello one of the leaders of the revival of posters which was destined to exert a major influence until the end of the 20's. He exhibited at the Salon des Humoristes (1908) and at the Société Nationale des Beaux-Arts (1909, 1910). In 1930, he took French nationality.

Postcards: 'Livorno stagione balneare', publ. Ricordi, Milan, 1901; 1 p. in the 'Collection des Cent', publ. Gréningaire, Paris, c. 1901; publicity p. 'Cachou Lajaunie', c. 1901; publicity p. 'Grands Magasins des Cordeliers, Lyon', publ. Vercasson & Cie, Paris c. 1904; publicity p 'Portofino-Kulm', c. 1906; publicity p. 'Thermogène, c. 1907; publicity 'Lampe Osmine', publ. Vercasson & Cie, Paris, c. 1910; 1 p. in the series 'Album Mariani', c. 1910; publicity p. 'Cinzano Vermouth', c. 1910; reproduction of the famous poster of 1910 showing a man in white on an orange zebra; publicity p. 'Je ne fume que le Nil', c. 1912; publicity p. 'Bitter Campari', c. 1913; 1 p. in the 'Collection Job', 1914; several war propaganda p. 1914-18.
Bibl.: Baudet 1978, 1980; Neudin 1979, 1983; Mordente 1982; Arrasich 1984.

CARAN D'ACHE, pseudonym of Emmanuel POIRÉ Moscow, 1852 (or 1858 or 1859) – Paris, 25.2.1909.
Illustrator, caricaturist, commercial painter, designer of wood games.
Born in Russia, he moved to Paris to do his military service and to gain his ancestors' nationality. He attended erratically the Ecole des Beaux-Arts in Paris. Encouraged by E. Detaille he started working as an illustrator, and he worked on the newspaper *Chronique parisienne*, where he signed his work Caran D'Ache (transliteration of the Russian word which means 'pencil'). He worked on several magazines: *L'Assiette au Beurre*, *L'Album* (1900), le *Courrier français*; *La Caricature*; *Le Chat Noir*, *Le Figaro*; *Die Fliegenden Blätter*, *The Graphic*; *L'Illustration*; *Journal amusant*; *Punch*; *Revue illustrée*; *Le Rire*; *Tout-Paris*; *Vie militaire*; *Vie parisienne*. He founded with J. L. Forain, the paper *Psst!* (1898-99), the organ of the nationalist antidreyfus movement. His illustrations are collected in several albums: *Physiologies parisiennes* (1888); *Le Courses dans l'Antiquité* (1888); *Nos soldats du siècle* (1889); *Trois albums Caran d'Ache* (1889, 1890, 1892); *Carnet de Cheques* (1892); *Bric à Brac* (1893); *Les lundis de Caran d'Ache* (1896); *C'est à prendre ou à laisser* (1898); *Les lundis du Figaro* (1898); *Pages d'histoire* (1904); *La découverte de Russie* (in coll. with A. Guillaume); *Comédie du jour*; *Comédie de notre temps*. He illustrated the books: *Historie de Marlborough* by J. Marthold (1885); *L'Amour en garnison* by R. Maizeroy (1886); *Les Gaietés de l'année* by Grosclaude (1886, 1887); *Nuit blanche d'un hussard rouge* by A. Allais (1887); *La Comédie du jour dans la république athénienne* by A. Millaud (1887); *Fantasia* by Grimsel (1888); *Le joies du plein air* by Grosclaude (1889); *Le prince Kozakokoff* by Bernardaky (c. 1893); *Hâtons-nous d'en rire* by Grosclaude. In collaboration with others *La gomme* by F. Champsaur and *Rire & Grimaces* (1892). For the theatre 'Le Chat Noir' he inspired the shadow pantomime '1809' and 'L'Epopée'. He exhibited at the Salon des Humoristes and at the Fine Art Society.
Postcards: 1 p. in the 'Collection des Cent', ed Gréningaire, c. 1901; several p. of political satire against Dreyfus and his supporters; publicity for *Les Journal*, 1904.
Bibl.: Neudin 1977; Baudet 1978; Zeyons 1979; Holt 1981.

Emil CARDINAUX
Bern, 11.11.1877 – Bern, 2.10.1936
Painter, lithographer, illustrator, commercial artist, graphic designer (ex libris, publicity

graphics).

He studied at the Academy in Munich with F. von Stuck and Schmidt-Reuth. In 1903 and 1904 he completed his artistic studies in Paris. He was mainly active in Bern. He illustrated books by L. Meyer and H. Bloesch.
Postcards: p. in the series 'Gordon Bennett-Wettfliegen 30. Sept. – 3. Okt., Zurich 1909', Graph Anstalt J. E. Wolfensberger, Zurich.

Juan CARDONA i TIO
Date of birth and death unknown.
Illustrator, commercial artist and painter.
A student of C. de Haes and of the Madrid School of Art. He was active in Paris, where he exhibited at the Salon of the Société Nationale des Beaux-Arts (1906) and worked on *Le Rire* and *Jugend* (1908). His illustrations appeared in Catalan magazines *El Gato Negro* and *Almanach de L'Esquella de Torratxa*. In 1906 he won the first prize in the competition for the tonic drink Byrrh.
Postcards: 1 p. in the series 'Byrrh', 1906; several from the series XVIII of 'Künstler-Postkarten' for *Jugend*, p. 1908; publicity p. 'Mechero Luz' publicity series for 'Paeeles Roca para fumar', typ. Thomas, Barcelona, c. 1902.
Bibl.: Trenc Ballester 1977; Baudet 1978; Forissier 1978.

Charles Emile CARLÈGNE
Aigle, Vaud, 30.5.1877 – ?, 1940
Illustrator, cartoonist.
From 1909 he exhibited at the Salon des Humoristes. He worked on *L'Assiette au Beurre* and other humorous magazines. He was above all active as a book illustrator: *Roi Pausole* by P. Louys; *Lysistrata* by Aristophanes; *Contes* by La Fontaine; *Discours sur les passions de l'amour* by Pascal (1920); *Les plus jolies roses de L'Anthologie grecque; La Muse de Ronsard; Ode à la bien-aimée* by Sappho; *La Fille d'auberge* by Virgil; *Lettres de la Religieuse Portugaise; Oeuvres complètes* of A. France (some volumes); *L'Alleé des Philosophes* by C. Maurras; *La Bonne Chanson* by Verlaine; *Florilegè des Ballades Françaises* by P. Fort; *La Relève du matin* by H. de Monterlant; *Les Contrerimes; Une femme pleure* by P.-J. Toulet; *Lettres à un ami* by P. Valéry; *Les Recontres de M. de Bréhot* by H. de Régnier; *Des Riens* by G. Soulages; *Le Nouvel Anacharsis* by A. Hermant; *Gerbes et mosaiques* by A. Lebey; *Les Amants de Tibur* by J. Benda, *Premiers et vingt-troisième* by M. Donnay.
Postcards: 1 p. in the series 'Gala Henry Monnier', 1904; 1 p. in the series 'Byrrh', 1906.
Bibl.: Weill 1977; Baudet 1978.

Giovanni CARPANETTO
Turin, 30.9.1863 – Turin 26.7.1928
Painter, lithographer, illustrator, commercial artist, graphic designer (paper money)
He studied at the Accademia Albertina in Turin with Andrea Castaldi and Enrico Gamba. He first showed work at the Promotrice in Turin, with a painting of a history subject (*Fanfulla*). In successive years he was always included in exhibitions of the Promotrice and of the Circolo degli artisti in Turin. In 1895 he exhibited at the Venice Biennale and in 1896-97 at the Nazionale in Florence. He worked on several theatrical events and worked on the magazines *La Domenica del fanciullo* and *Vita d'arte*. In 1902 he won the competition held by the commission which organized the festivities for the Turin Exhibition of decorative arts. In

1904 he prepared sketches for the new five lire notes. In 1914 he worked with the architect Pietro Betta on the reorganization project for the piazza S. Carlo in Turin.
Postcards: Photographic exhibition 1900; 'Torino 1902 Festeggiamenti. I Esposizione internazionale d'arte decorativa moderna', 1902; 'Convegno concorso mondiale dei pompieri, Torino' 1911; series 'Valore italiano. Diorama della guerra italoturca', Lith. Doyen, Turin, 1911; 'Esposizione Internazionale delle Industrie e del Lavoro in Torino-1911'; series for the anniversary of the proclamation of the unification of Italy, several war propaganda p., 1915-18; 'Per la Patria-Omaggio ai valorosi feriti in guerra'; 'IV Esposizione Internazionale d'Automobili'.
Bibl.: Mordente 1982; Arrasich 1984.

Ramón CASAS i CARBÓ
Barcelona, 5.1.1866 – ivi, 29.3.1932
Commercial artist, illustrator, designer, painter, graphic designer (book designer, commercial graphics, menus, festival programmes).
A student of the painter and decorator Joan Vicens, he moved in 1882 to Paris where he studied with Carolus Duran and he attended the free academies Gervex and de la Palette, directed by Puvis de Chavannes and E. Carrière. Until 1894 he lived mainly in Paris where he formed a Catalan brotherhood with Miguel Utrillo and Santiago Rusiñol whose book *Desde el Molina* (1890) he illustrated. In 1887 he founded with Pere Romeu, Utrillo and Rusiñol the tavern-theatre-artistic centre the 'Quatre Gats' which was modelled on the Parisian cabaret 'Le Chat Noir'. This artistic centre published the magazines *Quatres Gats* (1898-99) *Pèl & Ploma* (1899-1903) and *Forma* (1899-1908) in which C. was the art director and co-owner, and he published many designs and humorous vignettes. For the tavern 'Quatre Gats' he produced his first commercial art work, he designed with M. Utrillo the poster 'Sombras chinescas'. He won many prizes in poster competitions. First prize in the competition 'Anís del Mono' (1898). Second prize in the competition 'Champagne Cordorniu' (1898); and third prize in the competition 'Cigarillos París' (1901). He won important awards in several art exhibitions: first class medals at the Esposición Internacional (1904) and at the V Esposición de Bellas Artes e Industrias (1907) in Barcelona.
Postcards: 3 p. in the series 'Anis del Mono-Vicente Bosch, Badalona', reproducing sketches for the posters sent to the competition; publicity p. 'helius material para fotografia', 1901; series Pèl & Ploma', publ. Catalonia Barcelona 1901; p. n. 1 and n. 2 of the series by the magazine *España Cartofila*, Barcelona, 1901; 1 p. in the second series by the magazine *España Cartofila*, reproduction of the painting 'Moulin de la Galette', 1902; publicity for Sard wine, 1902; series of 4 p. with female figures drawn in charcoal, publ. Miró, typ. J. Thomas, 1902 (the fifth card of the series was published in 1905); series 'Chulas', publ. Ll. Bartrina, typ. Thomas, Barcelona, 1902; 'Felix año nuevo', typ. Cunill, Barna; series of 6 p. 'Rêveuses', publ. Ll. Bartrina, 1903; series of 6 p. in colour and 5 p. in black and white 'Chauffeuses', publ. Ll. Bartrina, typ. Thomas, Barcelona, 1903; series of 5 p. 'Cabezas femeninas a la sanguina', publ. Ll. Bartrina, typ. Thomas, Barcelona 1904; publicity p. 'Auto Garage Central, Barcelona', 1905 ca.; 1 p. in the 'Collection Job', designed in 1906; several New

Year greetings p. (1902, 1903) etc, for the Pèl & Ploma; for the magazine Hispania, several for the magazine reproduction of the covers; series of 6 humorous p. on motoring, with self portraits of the artist inspired by popular Catalan engraving of the XVII century; p. commemorating the 'Sociedad Cartófila Española'; 2 series of 5 publicity 'Wertheim'; publicity p. for the tavern 'Quatre Gats'; publicity p. for the paper *L'Avenç*; for the brothers Palleja; publicity p. 'M. Furster Grandes Hornos de Vidrieria'; p. for the Wedding of Pere Romeu and Corinna Jauregui.
Bibl.: *Esposición Ramon Casas*, cat. of the exhibition Palacio de la Verreina, Barcelona, 1958; Trenc Ballester 1977: Fildier 1979, 1980; Mordente 1982.

Basilio CASCELLA
Pescara, 1.10.1860 – Rome 24.7.1950
Painter, lithographer, illustrator, graphic designer (visiting cards, commercial labels, publicity graphics), commercial artist, ceramist, fashion designer.
At fifteen he went to Rome where he was taken on as an apprentice in the lithographic press 'Salomone'. Later he moved to Naples where he completed several jobs in graphics, he designed fashion plates and visiting cards. During his military service in Pavia he met Medardo Rosso and Vincenzo Irolli who inspired him to paint. He moved to Milan and was introduced to the A. Villa's artistic family, and he perfected his lithography at Borsino's factory. In 1883 he returned to the Abruzzo, and painted frescoes in the Council Chamber of the Town Hall in Ortona a Mare and he exhibited in important national and international exhibitions (Venice 1887, London 1888, Naples 1893, Milan 1894, Rome 1895). In 1899 he opened in Pescara a chromolithographic press, and founded with V. Bucci's collaboration, the artistic and literary magazine *L'Illustrazione abbruzzese*, of which only 10 issues appeared until 1905. In 1900 he was also the art director of *Illustrazione meridionale*, published in Naples. He designed (drawing directly on to the lithographic stone) postcards for his own press in Pescara, plates for illustrations of the *Divina Commedia*, for operas, for novels, labels for liqueurs and typical Abruzzi sweets. Much of this production was exhibited in 1905 in the exhibition of art held in Chieti. From 1910 to 1912 he lived in Milan, where he worked on the magazine *Natura e Arte*. In 1914 he founded a new magazine *La Gande illustrazione*, which in style was anti-D'Annunzio, anti-futurist in literature and anti-impressionist in art. Between 1917 and 1918, he moved to Rapino, where he began to get interested in ceramics, he pursued this interest in the following years. Established in Rome in 1928 he was involved in monumental public works, which were in celebration of the regime, and which rewarded him with fame and a nomination as a deputy. In Parliament he was above all involved in efforts to improve schools of applied arts, and to create schools of fashion and of cinematography.
Postcards: (a) Printed series of 12 p. (?) Abruzzo I, costumes and habits; series of 12 p. Abruzzo II ('Dal Fuoco di D'Annunzio', 'Due pescatori sulla riva', 'Falciatrici', 'il cieco dei campi', 'Il farro', 'L'indovina', 'L'organetto', 'La passagallia', 'Raccolto delle olive', 'Sosta di pellegrini', 'Uomo e donna nella neve', 'Veglia al focolore'); series of 12 p. Abruzzo III (woman with a child in her arms, Woman

with a flowered kerchief on her head, Woman in a red shawl, Woman with grapes, Pettorano, Profile of a woman with a yellow collar, Profile of a woman with a red kerchief on her head, Nude torso of a girl, A stall, An old man with a hat etc.); series of 12 p. Abruzzo IV at the sea (A child holding an ox, nude woman with a child, A nude with a goat, The back of a nude, A girl drying her foot, Portrait of the back of a woman, Sleeping girl, Little boys making sand-castles, Naked Child with an umbrella, Naked girl with a veil in the rocks; series of 12 p. Abruzzo V. habits and beliefs, Tattooing, 'The use of Rue and wormwood against worms', 'The treatment of wounds with milk and flour', 'To destroy the evil eye', 'To cure lumbago, etc.); series of 12 p. Abruzzo VI, Castelli ('Avezzano', 'Capestrano', 'Celano', 'Crecchio', 'Gagliano', 'Magliano dei Marsi', 'Ortona', 'Ortucchio', 'Pacentro', 'Ponte levatoio, Castello di Magliano', 'Roccascalegna', 'Ruderi del Castello de Contelmi Popoli'); series of figurative adverbs ('Costantemente', 'Soavemente', etc.); series of 12 p. (?) 'Cartoline abruzzesi' ('Afilaretto', 'Contadina di Rapino', 'Contadino della Maiella', 'Corpus Domini: Ortona a mare', 'Danza Campestre', 'Eco dei monti', 'Il rito delle serpi', 'La cantarice di San Vito', 'La grazia del latte', 'Marinaio di Ortona', 'Partenza di emigranti'. ?); untitled series, customs and habits of Abruzzi ('Il fieno', 'La fattura', 'L'esorcismo', 'Per far rinsavire uno scemo', etc.); series of flowers ('fiore del cardo', 'Il melo florito', etc.); series off fruits ('Il firasole', 'L'arancio', 'Le ciliege', 'Le pesche', 'L'oliva', 'Il grano', 'L'uva', 'Melograno', 'Pomi d'autunno', etc.): series with roman numbers; 'La cartolina del Natale' (Pivaro e bambinello); series 'Storia banditesca' ('Al mulino', 'Il Fischio', 'L'aresto', 'La sete', L'ultimo bacio', 'Nella casa', 'Una vendetta'). (b) Postcards published by G. G. A. M. (Milan?), with *pochettes* in french; series of 8 p. 'Une partie au billard' 'I. Il gessetto', "II. L'Acchitto', 'III. Di dorso', 'IV. Colpo sotto', 'V. Filotto', 'VI. Alla sponda', 'VII. Palla a giro', 'VIII. Partita'); series of 12 p. Mystical series ('Alleluja', 'Andantino', 'Declamazione', 'Fuori uffizio', 'In fa maggiore', 'L'incenso', 'L'uccellino'; 'Meraviglia', 'Offerta', 'Ultima flammella', 'Una tiratina', untitled; a series of musical women ('Bach', 'Elegia', L'Arietta', 'Meditazione', 'Mozart', 'Schopin' (sic!)., 'Souvenir', ?); series of 16 p. 'Napoli' ('A capera', 'Alla marinella', 'E maruzze', 'Il tamburello', 'L'acquaiolo', 'Mercato di gallinacci', 'O capitone', 'O cecato', 'O dichiaramento', 'O mozzonaro', 'O sfreggio', 'Polecenelle', 'Ritorno da Montevergine', 'Scrivano publico', 'Tre guagliune', 'Venditrice di limoni'). (c) Postcards published by several publishers: 'Mostra d'arte antica abruzzese, Chieti 1905', lith. 'Ripamonti Pitgliani, Rome, 'ricordo delle feste maggio-giugno, Chieti 1905', lith. 'Ripamonti Pitigliani, Roma; series 'Eruzione del Vesuvio, Napoli 1906', publ. Pilade Rocco, Milan; series of 12 p. 'Mietitrici' ('Abruzzo', 'Calabria', 'Campania', 'Lazio', 'Liguria', 'Lombarrdia', 'Piemonte', 'Prov. Venete', 'Romagna', 'Sardegna', 'Sicilia', 'Toscana'), publ. Pilade Rocco, Milan, 1906-07, there is also a series of the same subject, but with different designs, no publisher's name; several series of lover's faces, some without publisher's name, others with the monograms L.G.M. and P.C.G.F.; series (?) of Abruzzi customs n. 2034 publ. Stampa, Milan; series 2203 of lovers in Abruzzi costume, publ. ? f.b;

series (?) on Abruzzi, publ. La Grande Illustrazione, Pescara; series n. 1031 of 6 c. (?) 'Sogno . . . e realità' no publisher's name; series n. 1054 of 6 p. (?) 'Profumi . . .', publ. CCM; series 2001 of 6 p. 'Il primo amore', no publisher's name; 'Frammento' (mother embracing her son), two editions with different patriotic inscriptions for 'Istituto Britannico, Publ. Modiano, Trieste; series 'Nudi di donna e piante' publ. G. Citterio & C. Milan.
Bibl.: Bartoli-Mataloni 1979; Bobba 1979; Gaibazzi 1979; Baudet 1980; E. Sturani-M.C. La Porta-C. Vicario, *Gli illustratori. Basilio Cascella* (1860-1950), *La Cartolina*, XII (1982, n. 6), pp. 23-26; Mordente 1982; Arrasich 1984.

Walther CASPARI
Chemniz, 31.7.1869 – Munich, 19.7.1913
Painter, commercial artist, illustrator, graphic designer (ex libris).
He went to the art school and academies in Munich, Leipzig and Weimar. He worked on the magazines *Jugend, Simplicissimus, Lustige Blätter, Gartenlaube*.
Postcards: p. in the first series of 'Künstler-Postkarten' for Jugend, G. Hirth, Munich, 1898-99.

Hendrick CASSIERS
Antwerp, 11.8.1858 – Brussels, 1944
Watercolourist, engraver, commercial artist, illustrator, graphic designer (calendars, menus).
He studied at the Academy of Fine Arts in Antwerp. After a seven-year apprenticeship in an architectural office in Antwerp, he dedicated himself to painting, and he perfected his watercolour technique under the guidance of H. Stacquet. He went on several study trips to England, Scotland, France, Italy and he stayed a long time in Holland, where he met the English painter C. W. Bartlett who exercized a considerable influence on his work. The landscape and popular customs of Holland and Flanders became a recurrent theme in his graphic work, in book illustration (*Trois femmes de Flandre* by C. Mauclair and *Contes des Pays Bas* by C. Buysse) and in the watercolours of C. which were very successful through many reproductions in postcards and in chromolithographic prints published in Brussels by Dietrich & Cie and by the printers De Rycker & Mendel. From 1898 he made several posters for shipping companies ('Red Star Line' later 'American Line', 'Ostende-Dover'), which were often put on the market in issues without inscriptions. He took part in important international art exhibitions: Venice (1899, 1907, 1912); Buenos Aires (1910), President of the Société Royale Belge des Aquarellistes.
Postcards: 4 series of 6 p. (numbered A1-A6, B1-B6 or BB1-BB6, C1-C6, H1-H6) 'Red Star Line', lith. De Rycker & Mendel, Brussels, 1898 and following years several series 'Red Star Line/Paquebots', 1898 and following years postcard menus 'Red Star Line' in several years; series of 12 c. 'La Hollande Pittoresque', Dietrich & Cie, Brussels, 1898, reproduced from watercolours: 'Scheveningen', 'Rotterdam', 'Dordrecht', etc.); series of 12 p. 'Delft', Dietrich & Cie, Brussels, 1898; series of 12 p. 'Costumes Hollandais', Dietrich & Cie, Brussels, 1898, Dutch publ. W. De Haan, Utrecht (reproductions of watercolours 'Axel', 'Goes', 'Katwijk', 'Laren', 'Marken', 'Scheveningen', 'Urk', 'Volendam', 'Volendam', 'Walcheren', 'Walcheren'); series of 6 p. 'An-

vers', Dietrich & Cie, Brussels, c. 1899 (reproduced from watercolours: 'Les Bassins', 'L'Escaut', 'La Grande Place', 'L'Ancienne Boucherie', 'La Ronde', 'La Cathédrale'); series of 6 p. 'Bruxelles', Dietrich & Cie, Brussels, c. 1899; (reproduced from watercolours: 'Rue de la Régence', 'La Bourse', 'La Grande Place', 'Rue au Beurre', 'Rue Chair et Pain', 'Saint Gudele'); series of 12 p. 'Vichy', Dietrich & Cie, Brussels, c. 1899; (reproduced from watercolours: 'Le Pont sur l'Allier', 'L'Allier à Vichy', 'Une rue à Vichy', 'Le Sichon à Vichy', 'Soleil couchant sur l'Allier', 'Le pont à Vichy', 'L'ardoisière', 'Le Parc et le Casion', 'L'établissement thermal', 'Chateldon', 'Cusset', 12 unknown); series of 12 p. 'Moulins et voiles' in one colour (blue), publ. Dietrich & Cie, Brussels, c. 1899; series of 12 p. 'Le Littoral Belge', Dietrich & Cie, Brussels, c. 1899; (reproduced from watercolours: 'La Panne', 'La digue à Blankenberghe', 'La plage à Ostende', 'Pêcheurs de Nieuport', 'Mariakerke', 'La plage a Blankenberghe', 'Ostende', 'La plage de Heyst', 'Vieille ru à Blankenberghe', 'Ostende-les Bassins', 'Middelkerke', 'Village de Knocke'); series of 12 p. 'Londres', publ. Dietrich & Cie, Brussels, c. 1900; (reproduced from watercolours: 'Tower of London', 'Houses of Parliament', 'Piccadilly Circus', 'Westminster', 'National Gallery', 'Hyde Park', 'London Bridge', 'Strand', 'Ludgate Hill', 'Royal Exchange', 'Trafalgar Square', 'Tower Bridge'); series of 12 (?) p. 'Paris', no publisher's mark or artist's signature, c. 1900; series of 12 (?) p. with Flemish landscapes with figures in regional costumes, publ. Dietrich & Cie, Brussels, c. 1900, publ. W. De Haan, Utrecht (there is also an issue without a publisher's mark, the subjects: 'Domburg', 'Goes', 'Omstreken van Goes', 'Westcapelle', 'Vlissingen', 'Middelburg', 'Omstreken van Middelburg', 'Zuid Beveland', 'Terneuzen', 'Veere'); series of 24 p. 'Pays-Bas', publ. Dietrich & Cie, Brussels, publ. W. De Haan, Utrecht, published with the mark D. & Cie (Dietrich), c. 1900; (reproduced from watercolours: 3 'Amsterdam', 2 'Arnhem', 'Delft', 'Domburg', 2 'Dordrecht', 'Edam', 'Haarlem', 'Katwijk', 'La Haye', 'Leiden', 2 'Nijmegen', 'Rotterdam', 'Scheveningen', 'Utrecht', 'Woudrichem', 2 'Zaandam', 2 unknown); series of Dutch costume (reproduced from lithographs); several reproducing posters ('La Royale Belge, Société Anonyme d'Assurances sur la vie et contre les accidents', Imp. De Rycker & Mendel Brussels, c. 1910; etc.); series Venice and 'Glasgow', in black and silver by De Rycker & Mendel Brussels, but they were unpublished.
Bibl.: Lehrs 1898; Joletta, *'Il Litorale belga', Il Raccoglitore di cartoline illustrate*, I (n. 5, 20.9.1899), pp. 57-58; Joletta, *Vichy e suoi dintorni', Il Raccoglitore di cartoline illustrate*, I (n. 3, 20.8.1899), pp. 33-34; Maggioni 1899; F. Steno, *'Red Star Line', Il Raccoglitore di cartoline illustrate*, I (n. 7, 20.10.1899), pp. 78-79; Stoppani 1900; F. Khnopff, *'A Belgian Painter. M. Henry Cassiers', The Studio*, XXVI, June 1902, p. 13; Wiener 1922-23; Philippen 1977; Fildier 1979; Rostenne 1979; Baudet 1980; Neudin 1980, 1983; Fanelli 1981, 1983.

Paul CAUCHIE
Ath, Hainaut, Belgium, 1875 – Brussels, 1952
Architect, painter, decorator, graphic designer (calendars).
He studied at the Académie Royale des

Beaux-Arts in Brussels. With the building of his own house at no. 5 rue des Francs (1905) he became one of the foremost Art Nouveau architests in Brussels. He did fresco decoration for buildings in rue Malibran (1900) and in rue du Tyrol (1902) in Brussels.
Postcards: series of 6 p. (?) publicity c. 'Eaux minerales de Genval', typ. f. Dricot & Cie, 1900; 1 p. in the 'Byrrh', c. 1906.
Bibl.: Baudet 1978.

Emile CAUSÉ
Porrentruy, Switzerland, 1867 – ?
Painter, commercial artist.
He was born in Switzerland of French parents. A pupil of De la Rocque, he developed his art at the Ecole Nationale des Arts Décoratifs in Paris. He is known above all for his posters.
Postcards: 1p. in the 'Collection des Cents', publ. Gréningaire, Paris, c. 1901.
Bibl.: Baudet 1978.

Léon CAUVY
Montpellier, 12.1.1874 – ?.?.1933
Painter, engraver, commercial artist, designer of fabrics, furniture, leather goods, graphic designer (lettering).
A pupil of A. P. R. Maignan and E. Mickel, he exhibited at the Salon of the Société des Artistes Français, where he won a second class medal in 1911. His engravings were published in the *Gazette des Beaux-Arts* and in *Art et Décoration*. He did decorative murals in the Palais d'été in Algiers. He was the director of the Ecole des Beaux-Arts in Algiers.
Postcards: several greetings p. in the series 10 and 13 of the 'Künstlerkarten', publ. Stengel & Co., Dresden-Berlin, 1899-1900.
Bibl.: cat. Altonaer Museum, Hamburg 1970; Bobba 1979; Lebeck 1980.

Ludovico CAVALERI
Milan, 1867 – Cento, Ferrara, 1942 (or Milan, 1941)
Painter, etcher, lithographer, commercial artist, illustrator.
He abandoned his medical studies to follow courses at the Academy at the Brera. He was widely recognised as a painter, even internationally and had one-man shows in Montevideo and São Paulo. He produced some posters for Officine Grafiche Ricordi. *I modi – Anima e simboli* (1896) by R. Quaglino is among the books illustrated by him.
Postcards: 'Società Dantesca di Varese, 1908'; 'Manciano-Ricordo della Inaugurazione dell'acquedutto di S. Fiora, 1913'.
Bibl.: Arrasich 1984.

Frédérick-Auguste CAZALS
Paris, 31.7.1865 – ivi, 1914
Illustrator, commercial artist, painter, lithographer, designer, poet, song writer.
He exhibited at the Salon of the Société Nationale des Beaux-Arts (1899, 1905) and at the Salon des Cent. He worked on the magazines *La Plume* and *La Vie franco-russe*. He illustrated *Le Moutardier du Paper* (1907) by A. Jarry and his own collection of songs *Le Jardin de Ronces*. He is especially famous as the portraitist of Verlaine.
Postcards: several portraits of Verlaine.
Bibl.: Fildier 1979.

Jules CHÉRET
Paris, 31.5.1836 – Nice, 23.9.1932
Commercial artist, lithographer, painter, illustrator, graphic designer (publicity graphics, musical scores).
After his first experience with a lithographer he went to London in 1854 for the first time, he returned there in 1859 and remained there until 1866. In England he broadened his knowledge of new technical advances in colour lithographic printing. In 1858 his three colour poster for 'Orphée aux enfers', by Offenbach, was very successful. He returned to Paris in 1866 and he opened his own lithographic press and made the first posters: 'la Biche au bois' and 'Bal de Valentino'. He began an intensive activity as a commercial artist making more than one thousand posters. He handed over his press in 1881 to the typographers Chaix, C. remained there as artistic director. He did illustrations for several magazines (*L'art et l'idée*, *Gil Blas illustré*, *Le Courrier Français*, *Figaro illustré*, *L'Image*, *Paris illustré*, *L'Assiette au Beurre*, *Revue illustrée*, etc.) and for books: *Le livre des Parfums* by E. Rimmel (1870); *Les soirées parisiennes* by A. Mortier (1877); *Pierrot sceptique* by Henrique e Huysmans (1881); *Mon petit premier* by A. Monselet (1887); *Les Bohemiens* (1887), *Lulu* (1888) and *La Gomme* (1899) by F. Cahmpsaur; *La Fée du rocher* by Sylvestre Thomé (1894); *La Songe d'une nuit d'hiver* by L. Henrique (1903); *Sonnets antiques et modernes* by P. Dandicolle (1906). He was also the author of some mural cycles: in the Baron Vitta's Villa 'La Sapinière' in Evian (1895-96); in the Hôtel de Ville in Paris (1898-1902); in the dining room of the industrialist N. Fenaille's villa in Neuilly (1901). In 1905 he decorated the 'Taverne de Paris'.
Postcards: 8 p. in the series 'Cinos', 1898, reproducing the posters 'Palais de Glace' (two), 'Musée Grevin Pantomimes Lumineuses', 'Musée Grevin Les Dames Hongroises', 'Musée Grevin Les Coulisses de l'Opera', 'Bal du Moulin Rouge', 'Au Joyeux Moulin Rouge', 'Casino de Paris'; 1 p. in the 'Collection des Cent', publ. Gréningaire, Paris c. 1901; 1 p. 'Collection Job', series 1905, 1907, 1911, 1914, reproducing the poster of c. 1896 in the series 'Les Affiches Celèbres' publ. Tuck, London.
Bibl.: Forissier 1976; Weill 1977; Baudet 1978, 1980; Holt 1981, 1982; Arrasich 1984.

Galileo CHINI
Florence, 2.12.1873 – ivi, 23.8.1956
Painter, ceramist, decorator, commercial artist, scenographer, illustrator, graphic designer, designer of glass windows, of mosaics.
He was an orphan at eight years of age, and he was taken on as an apprentice with his paternal uncle Dario, the decorator and restorer. In 1890 with his uncle he collaborated on the restoration of the church of S. Trinità in Florence and in the same year he enrolled in the free school of the nude at the Accademia di Belli Arte in Florence, where he met P. Nomellini, L. Tommasi, G. Graziosi, L. Andreotti. In 1896 he made his first works as a ceramist and between 1896 and 1897 he set up with his friends V. Gianti, G. Montelatici, and G. Vannuzzi a ceramic factory 'Arte della Ceramica' which was quickly recognised and won many important recognitions: the gold medal at the exhibition of decorative art in Turin 1898, *Grand Prix* at the Paris Exposition Universelle in Paris 1900, and in St. Petersburg in 1901. In 1901 he took part in the Venice Biennale for the first time, he was invited again in 1903, 1905, 1907, 1914, 1920. In the first decade of the century he extended his activities to commercial art, to illustration, to scenography and important decorative cycles. After the first poster for 'Arte della Ceramica' (c. 1901), he designed posters for 'Cena delle Beffe' (1909) and for the Rome ethnographic exhibition in Rome 1911. In 1901 he made the illustrations for S. Benelli's book on the Biennale sculptors; in 1906 he made vignettes for the *Giornalino della Domenica* and in 1910 he illustrated *L'Amore di tre re* by S. Benelli. in 1903 with his painted wall and ceiling decorations in the Cassa di Risparmio in Pistoia and the Hotel Pace in Montecatini and with the furnishing of the Tuscan room at the Biennale in Venice he began important decorative cycles which included the Cassa di Risparmio in Anezzo (1906), the 'L'Arte del Sogno' room at the Biennale (1907), the frescoes in the room with the dome at the Biennale (1909), the decorative panels for the Italian pavilion a the Brussels exhibition (1910) and several works for the exhibitions celebrating the fiftieth anniversary of national unity in Rome, Turin and Florence (1911). In 1907, with his cousins Pietro and Chino he founded 'Manifattura Fornaci S. Lorenzo – Chini and Co.', Borgo S. Lorenzo - a Ceramiche e vetri d'arte', which was active until the end of the second world war and of which he was artistic director. In 1909 he first worked as a scenographer, designing the sets for *Maschera di Bruo* by S. Benelli, *La Cena delle Beffe* (1909), *Sogno di una notte di mezza estate* (1909), *L'Amore dei tre re* (1910) and for *Orione* by E. L. Morselli (1910). In 1908 he held the chair in decorative painting at the Accademia di Belle Arti in Rome and 1911 he was nominated to the chair of decorative arts at the Accademia in Florence. From 1911 to 1914 he lived in Bangkok, where he decorated the Royal Palace. He returned to Italy and held a one-man show at the Biennale in Venice in 1914, where he exhibited paintings and ceramics which showed oriental influences mixed with echoes of Klimt. In 1917 he launched the magazine *Rinnovando rinnoviamoci* sponsored by a group of artists belonging to the Associazione di propaganda artistico-industriale. After the first world war he executed in Salsomaggiore a decorative cycle in the Terme Berzieri and in several Hotels and private villas. In 1925 he won two 'Grands Prix' at the Paris exhibition, one for ceramic materials, and the other for vases. Towards the end of the '20s he distanced himself from the pictorial formulae of late secessionist Déco and returned to a naturalism belonging to the post-macchiaiola tradition.
Postcards: 'Florentia-Ars-Manifatture ceramcine, Firenze', 1903; commemorative p. for the ethnographic exhibition in Rome, 1911, reproducing the poster; publicity p. for the Regie Termi di Salsomaggiore, 1913; several p. for exhibitions of his paintings 1900-14.
Bibl.: Bartoli-Mataloni 1979; Mordente 1982; Arrasich 1984.

Hans Heinrich CHRISTIANSEN
Flensburg, 6.3.1866 – Wiesbaden, 5.1.1945
Painter, graphic designer, commercial artist, designer of glass windows, metal work, jewellery, fabrics, carpets, furniture, ceramist.
He studied painting in Hamburg. He studied at the Kinstgewerbeschule in Hamburg from 1887 to 1888. In c. 1890 he established a Geschäft für Dekorationsmalerei in Hamburg. He participated in the efforts of the association 'Volkskunst' to reform applied arts. He attended from 1896 to 1899 the Academémie Julian

in Paris. From 1899 to 1902 he was a member of the Künstlerkolonie in Darmstadt. Until 1911 he was active both in Paris and Darmstadt, then he settled in Wiesbaden. He was the author of the text *Neue Flächenornamente* (Altona, 1892). He worked on the magazine *Jugend*.

Postcards: series 'Hamburger Postkarten', with views of Hamburg, publ. Gebr. Harz, Altona, c. 1893 (to publicize the series he made a poster); 2 p. in the *series* 'Les Maîtres de la Carte Postale', published by the paper *La Critique*, Paris 1898-1900; several p. in the first three series for '*Jugend*', 1898-99, 1900-1910, publ. G. Hirth, München; series 'Les Femmes du XXme Siècle', '6 cartes postales artistiques d'après Christiansen', 1899, republished in Germany 1900 by Wolfrum & Hauptmann, Nürnberg (on each c. there is the inscription 'Paris'); series 'Darmstadt', heads of women with roses, 4 p. c. 1902, Kunst-Anst. Kornsand & Co, Frankfurt c. M. (the preparatory drawings are conserved at the Stadt-Museum, Flensburg); series of at least 4 p. heads of women, c. 1902, lith. Kornsand & Co, Frankfurt a.M., Kunstverlag J. Ph. Leuthner, Darmstadt.

Bibl.: *Deutsche Kunst und Dekoration*, 1900; E. Redlefsen, '*Hans Christiansen*', in *Nordelbigen*, 27, 1959, pp. 93-111; cat. Altonaer Museum, Hamburg 1970; cat. Darmstadt 1977; Neudin 1978, 1980; Baudet 1980; Lebeck 1980; Drago 1981; Holt 1981, 1983; Mordente 1982; Arrasich 1984.

Howard Chandler CHRISTY
Morgan County, Ohio, 10.1.1873 – New York, 4.3.1952.
Painter, commercial artist, illustrator.
He went to the Academy and Art Students' League in New York, he was a student of W. M. Chase. He took part in the conflict between the United States and Cuba and sent drawings of the war to American magazines. He created the feminine type the 'Christy Girl', the elegant society lady, was also reproduced in decorative designs. His poster for the first world war of a young woman dressed as a sailor, was famous. He worked on the magazines: *Scribner's Magazine, Leslie's, Harper's Collier's Weekly*.
Postcards: several series with variations on the theme of the 'Christy Girl' (heads, whole figures couples).
Bibl.: Lyons 1975; Holt 1980, 1983.

Francisco de CIDON i NAVARRO
Barcelona, 1871 – Tarragona, ?
Painter, commercial artist, graphic designer (ex libris, calendars, commercial and publicity graphics).
He took part in the exhibition of fine arts in Barcelona in 1894 and in the national exhibition in Madrid in 1904, where he won a second class medal. He was nominated professor of design at the Institute in Tarragona, where he spent the last years of his life. His posters are reproduced in the magazine *Pluma y Lapiz*.
Postcards: publicity for 'La Tribuna diario independiente Barcelona', 1903.
Bibl.: Trenc Ballester 1977.

Johann Vincenz CISSARZ
Danzig, 22.1.1873 – Frankfurt a.M., 23.12.1942
Painter, commercial artist, illustrator, engraver, graphic designer, designer in applied arts, interior designer.

He attended the Academy in Dresden (L. Pohle, H. Freye, F. W. Pauwels). From 1903 he was a member of the Künstlerkolonie in Darmstadt. In 1906 he moved to Stuttgart, where he taught book design at the Lehr- und Versuchsverkstätte. In 1916 he moved to Frankfurt and was nominated director of the Meisterklasse für Malerei at the Kunstgewerbeschule.
Postcards: in 1897 he won 2nd and 3rd prize in the competition promoted by the Dresdner Druckerei Arnold between the students of the Dresden Academy for postcards designed to commemorate the international Kunstausstellung in Dresden; p. reproducing plates in the calendar *Kunst und Leben*.

Plinio CODOGNATO
Verona, 1878 – Milan, 30.9.1940
Commercial artist, illustrator, painter cartoonist.
A student of M. Bianchi. He was principally active in the field of posters, publicity graphics and illustration. In 1905 he took part in the Prima Esposizione d'Arte nella Pubblicità' winning the gold medal and the first prize in the G. Ricordi competition. He worked as an illustrator on *La Lettura, L'Illustrazione Italiana, La Tradotta*. He did publicity work for several companies; Pirelli, Atlala, O. M. Liebig, Campari, Cinzano. for twenty years he was the official commercial artist for FIAT and he did the graphic design for *Rivista FIAT*.
Postcards: Commemorative p. "Fiera dei Cavalli, Verona 1905", PUBL. Chappuis, Bologna; series of 10 p., 'Esposizione di Milano 1906' ('Architettura', 'Acquario', 'Agraria', 'Aereonautica', 'Automobilismo', 'Belle Arti', 'Galleria del lavoro', 'Marina', 'Salone Concerti', 'Trasporti', publ. Pilade Rocco, Milan, 'Grande Fiera dei Cavalli Verona 1907', Off. Franehini, Verona; 'Concorsi Aeriei di Milano 1910'; 'Valico del Sempione 1910', Stab. Grafico Frizzi e Bresciani, Milan; 'Grande Riunione Aviatoria di Rimini, 1911' 'Fiera di Cavalli – Municipio di Verona', 1912; 'Ristorante Italia – con giardino sul mare' – Tripoli Soc. Anonima Suvini Zerboni – Milano', publ. Pilade Rocco, Milan, 1912; 'I Mostra Industriale Italiana in Tripoli', 1913; 'Centenario Verdiano, Verona-Grande Arena-Anfiteatro Romano–1913', publ. G. B. Virtuani & C., Milan. b) publicity p. 'Avanti! Quotidiano socialista esce a Milano', publ. La Zincografica, Milan c. 1910; 'Robba Canelli' 'Radda di Giacomo Orefice'; 'Prestito Nazionale, La guerra oltre che col sangue', publ. Virtuani, Milano; 'Prestito Nazionale, VI, tutto il nostro risparmio alla patria'. c) Military p. 'Auto Parco', 1917; 'Soldato Codognato – Dovrà essere cosi'; 'Preso dal Vero ai nostri confini', publ. Passero, Udine' 'Buone Feste!', satirical; several war scenes. d) Little women series p. 1173, 1174, 1185, 1189, publ. A. D. M.
Bibl.: Mordente 1982; '*Codognato tra cicli e motori*', La Cartolina, III (1983, n. 11), pp. 19–23; Arrasich 1984.

Gisbert COMBAZ
Antwerp, 23.9.1869 – Brussels, 18.1.1941 Lithographer, commercial artist, graphic designer (publicity and commercial graphics, calendars, lettering, theatre programmes), illustrator, painter, designer of fabrics, carpets, wallpaper, ceramic tiles, sculptor.
He completed his studies in law and left the profession after one year in practice as a lawyer to study art. He attended the Academie Roy-

ale des Beaux-Arts in Brussels. From 1895 he taught intensively: professor of design at the Institute of agronomy in Grembloux (1895-1900); professor of decorative arts at the school of decorative and industrial art at Ixelles (1898-1940); professor of art history at the Institut Belge des Hautes Etudes; and at the Institut Belge des Hautes – Etudes Chinoises (from 1905); professor of ornamental composition at the Académie Royale des Beaux–Arts in Brussels (from 1913). From 1897 he took part in the exhibitions 'Libre Esthétique' (1898, 1899, 1901, 1903, 1908, 1912, 1914), for which he designed several posters. He was employed in wide–ranging types of work and he was also well known as a student of the arts of the Far East, particularly China. He was one of the founder members of the Société Belge d'Etudes Orientales.
Postcards: series of 12 p. 'Les Eléments', Dietrich & C., Brussels, 1898; series of 12 p. 'Les Pêcheurs', Dietrich & C., Brussels, c. 1899; series of 12 p. 'Proverbes et devises', Dietrich & C., Brussels, c. 1899.
Bibl.: Lehrs 1898; Maggioni 1899; Stoppani 1900; Neudin 1977, 1980; Baudet 1978, 1980; Wittamer–De Camps 1980–81; Fanelli 1981, 1983; Holt 1983.

Dante COMELLI
Bologna, 21.7.1880 – Bologna 1958
Painter.
He trained at the Accademia di Belle Arti in Bologna. His early paintings, with divisionist tendencies, showed the influence of G. Segantini.
Postcards: publicity p. for the seaside resort Pesaro, c. 1910.
Bibl.: Arrasich 1984.

Tito CORBELLA
Pontgremoli, 1885 – Rome, 20.1.1966
Illustrator, commercial artist, painter.
He got a degree in chemistry at the University of Padua. He attended the Accademia di Belle Arti in Venice, where he was a student of G. Ciardi and E. Tito. Until the 20's he was especially active as an illustrator and commercial artist (he made posters for Ricordi). He became very famous for his postcards which had women and engaged couples as their subject, and which he began designing at the beginning of the first world war and continued to produce until the 20's.
Postcards: several series of 'little women' and 'fiancés' 1912(?)–18; several series for the national loan, 1915–16; series 'Miss Cavell' printed in Great Britain.
Bibl.: Bartoli–Mataloni 1979; Mordente 1982; Arrasich 1984.

Aurelio CRAFFONARA
Callarate, 15.9.1875 – Genoa, 5.2.1945
Watercolourist, illustrator, commercial artist, ceramist, painter.
He attended the Accademia di Belle Arti in Genoa. He was at first active as a commercial artist and postcard designer. He worked on the humorous Genoese magazine *Il Successo*. He illustrated several books (including novels by E. Salgari). He designed serveral caricatures, signing them often with the pseudonym Lelo.
Postcards: series of 6 p. women and flowers ('Anemone', 'Crisantemi', 'Iris', 'Rosa dei campi', 'Garofano rosso', 'Robinie'), Publ. Sciutto, Genoa; p. for the national loan, 1915–16; several war propaganda p. 1915–18; several 'Little women', series, 1915–18.

Bibl. Mordente 1982; Arrasich 1984.

Rie (Marie) CRAMER
Soekaboemi, Dutch East Indies, 10.10.1887 – ?, 1977.
Illustrator, commercial artist, painter, fashion designer, theatrical costumier, graphic designer (calendars, book design).
She was trained at the Academy in The Hague. Her first work showed the influence of Dutch Nieuw Kunst and in particular of artists like W. A. van Kinijnenburg, J. G. Veldheer and Th. van Hoytema. In 1903 with the first volume of the series *Het Karnen van den oceaan des tijds* (1903–20), she began an intense activity as an illustrator, which made her popular in Holland. Among the books illustrated by her are: *Voor Meisjex en Jongetjes* (1906); *Olof de Vondeling* by I. Heyermans (1912); *Prentjes bij versjes* (1913); *Lentebloemen* (1914); *Nieuwe prentjes en versjes* (1915); *Sprookjes van Hans Andersen* (1915).
Postcards: series 'Lentebloemen', series 0124 by publ. C. H., London c. 1918, reproducing book illustrations of 1914; series of 8 p. 'Vieilles Chansons', series 131 by publ. W. de Haan, Utrecht; series of 8 p. 'Oudt Nederlandsche Minneliedjes', series 138 by publ. W. Haan, Utrecht; series of 12 p. of the months, series 134 by publ. Roukens & Erhart, Baarn; series of 12 p. 'Kinderdeuntjes uit Grootmoeders Tijd', series 137 by publ. Roukens & Erhart, Baarn.
Bibl.: Cope 1978.

Walter CRANE
Liverpool, 15.8.1845 – London 14.3.1915
Painter, graphic designer (books, calendars publicity graphics, ex libris), commercial artist, illustrator, designer of fabrics, tapestries, carpets, embroidery, glass windows, jewels, objects of daily life.
He attended from 1859 to 1862 the studio of the painter and engraver W. J. Linton and then the Heathrey School of Fine Art. He studied on his own, old prints, Japanese woodcuts and the Pre-raphaelites. He joined the Arts and Crafts movement of W. Morris, with whom he collaborated in the production of the Kelmscott Press. From 1893 to 1896 he was the director of Reading College and from 1898 to 1899 of the Royal College of Art, South Kensington. He was the author of fundamental texts on design, on applied arts, and graphic design including *The Claims of Decorative Art* (1892), *The Bases of Design* (1898), *Line and Form* (1900), *Of the Decorative Illustration of Books Old and New* (1901). Some of the most famous books illustrated by him are: *The Baby's Opera* (1877), *The Baby's Bouquet* (1878), *Flora's Feast* (1888), *Queen Summer* (1891), *Rumbo Rhymes* by A. C. Calmour (1911). From c. 1893 he designed some Christmas greetings cards for Marcus Ward & Co. He is considered to be one of the leading Art Nouveau figures.
Postcards: series reproducing, with variations, plates from the volume *Flora's Feast* (1888), no publisher's name, c. 1900.
Bibl.: White 1894; Lebeck 1980; Drago 1981.

Carl Otto CZESCHKA
Vienna 22.10.1878 – Hamburg, 10.7.1960.
Painter, xylographer, commercial artist, illustrator, graphic designer (books, lettering, ex libris, publicity and commercial graphics, calendars, paper money), designer of fabrics, furniture, objects of daily use, furnishing, enamel, jewellery, toys, glass, metalwork, ceramist, interior designer, scenographer and theatrical costumier.
From 1894 to 1899 he attended the Akademie der bildenden Künste in Vienna (C. Griepenkerl). From 1902 to 1907 he taught at the Kunstgewerbeschule in Vienna (his students were R. Kalvach, M. V. Uchatius, O. Kokoschka, etc.) and from 1907 to 1943 at the one in Hamburg. From 1900 he was a member of the Viennese Secession. He worked with the Wiener Wekstätte from autumn 1905 and also after his move to Hamburg, in 1907 designing postcards, graphics (for the cabaret 'Fledermaus', 1907), fabrics, jewellery, metalwork, furniture, toys, enamel, carving. His book designs for several Viennese and German publishers is important for the field of applied graphic art. (*Nibelungen*, Gerlachs Jugendbücherei 1908). He designed postcards of posters, calendars, prints, commercial graphics for firms like: Chwala, Reisser, the Austrian State Printer, Gerlach & Schenk, Gerlach & Wiedling. He worked on the magazines *Erdgeist, Die Kunstwelt, Moderne Stickereien*.
Postcards: series for Gerlach & Schenk, c. 1899, series of German sagas for New Year greetings p. Deutsch-Völkischer Scherer-Verlag. Innsbruck-Leipzig, c. 1900; n., 252, from the series for the Wiener Werkstätte, Vienna; c. special series for Wiener Werkstätte with fabric designs, Brüder Köhn, Wien; p. with women and roses (preparatory design in the Historisches Museum der Stadt Wien); series of 6 p. for the military post (Feldpostkarten) with pochette, Keks-Fabrik H. Bahlsen Hannover, c. 1915.
Bibl: cat. Wien 1964; Carl Otto Czeschka, Aspekt seines Lebenswerkes, cat. della mostra a cura di H. Spielmann, B. A. T.-Haus, Hamburg 1978; Hansen 1982; Schweiger 1982; Till 1983 (n. 506).

D

Evangelin Mary DANIELL
?, 1880 – ?, 1902
Biographical details are unknown.
Postcards: series 'Modern Art', R. Tuck, London; 'F. Marquis, passage des Panoramas, Paris', R. Tuck, London.
Bibl.: Neudin 1978; Fildier 1979; Baudet 1980; Holt 1980, 1983.

Adolfo DE CAROLIS
Montefiore dell'Aso, Ascoli Piceno, 6.1.1874 – Rome, 7.2.1928
Painter, woodcut artist, illustrator, scenographer, commercial artist.
He completed his early studies at the Accademia di Belle Arti in Bologna (1888-92), under the guidance of D. Ferri. He then moved to Rome, where with the Collegio Piceno grant he attended the Scuola di Decorazione Pittorica attached to the Museo Artistico Industriale. In Rome he met N. Costa, who introduced him to the group 'In Arte Libertas', founded by him in 1886. In 1893 he won first prize in the final year entries to the Regio Istituto di Belle Arti in Rome, and the Gold Medal and diploma from the Museo Aristico Industriale. In 1897 he became officially a member of 'In Arte Libertas' and took part in their exhibition of that year. About 1897 he began a fresco cycle in Villa Brancadoro at San Benedetto del Tronto, which he worked on until 1904. In 1899 he was present for the first time at the Venice Biennale, where he also exhibited in 1901. In 1901 he moved to Florence, where he gained the chair in ornament at the Accademia di Belle Arti. From 1901 he began his collaboration with D'Annunzio for the illustrations of *Francesca da Rimini* and with Pascoli, for whom he designed the illustrations of *Mirabile visione*. In 1913 he made the woodcuts for the magazine *Leonardo*. Between 1903 and 1904 he began intensive activity as a magazine illustrator (*Novissima, Il Regno, Hermes, Ebe*) and of the books: *Le Fiale* by Govoni, *Myricae, I Canti di Castelvecchio, Primi poemetti* and *Poemi conviviali* by Pascoli; *La Figlia di Jorio* (1904) by D'Annunzio. From 1905 he designed the sets for *La fiaccola sotto il moggio* by D'Annunzio and from the following year for *La Figlia di Jorio*, for which he designed the poster. Between 1907 and 1909 he frescoed the walls and ceiling of the Salone del Consiglio Provinciale di Ascoli Piceno. In 1908 he won the competition for the decorations of the Salone dei 400 in Palazzo del Podestà in Bologna, a great fresco cycle on which he continued to work until his death. At the same time he continued illustrating books: *La serenata delle zanzare* by M. Moretti (1908); *Laudi and Fedra* (1909) by D'Annunzio; *I Nuovi Poemetti, Odi ed Inni* (1911) and *Carmina* (1914) by Pascoli; *Alcyone* (1911), *Le canzoni delle gesta d'oltremare* (1912) and *Notturno* (1917) by D'Annunzio. From 1911 to 1914 he worked on the magazine *L'Eroica*. Between 1916 and 1920 he frescoed the Aula Magna of the University of Pisa. In 1917 he moved to Bologna to teach at the Accademia di Belle Arti and in 1922 he moved to the one in Rome, where he held the chair in scenography.
Postcards: series of 12 p. 'La Figlia di Jorio', publ. Ricordi, 1901; 'Feste della Città di Faenza 1908', publ. Albonetti, Faenza; 'VIII Esposizione Internazionale d'arte di Venezia', 1909; 'Esposizione Internazionale di Torino', 1911; 'Esposizione Marchigiana 1915'; 'Comitato Dame Bolognesi Romagnole, 1916'; several war propaganda p.1915-18; p. in the series of the 'Divina Commedia', publ. Alterocca, Terni.
Bibl.: Bartoli-Mataloni 1979; Gaibazzi 1979; *La Cartolina*, n. 4, 1982; Mordente 1982; Arrasich 1984.

Eugene DELÂTRE
Paris, 10.12.1864 – ?
Engraver.
A student of his father, the engraver Auguste, and of Lewis Brown. From 1871 to 1876 he lived with his father in England. He is the author of several engravings on picturesque aspects of Montmartre. He exhibited at the Salon of the Société Nationale des Beaux-Arts and he was a member of the Society of Colour Engravers.
Postcards: 1 p. in the I series (1898) and 1 p. in the II series (c.1898) 'Les Maîtres de la Carte Postale' publ. by the paper *La Critique*.

Franz Karl DELAVILLA
Vienna, 6.12.1884 – Frankfurt a.M., 2.8.1967
Graphic designer (books, commercial graphics, illustrations), woodcut artist, commercial artist, illustrator, designer of carpets, tapestries, jewellery, scenographer.
He attended Fachschule für Textilindustrie

and from 1903 to 1908 the Kunstgewerbeschule in Vienna (C. O. Czeschka, R. v. Larisch, B. Löffler). From 1908 he taught at the Kunstgewerbeschule in Magdeburg, from 1908 in Hamburg, from 1913 to 1922 in Frankfurt a.M., where he coninued to teach until 1950. He worked with the Wiener Werkstätte designing postcards, decoration and posters for the cabaret 'Fledermaus'. He worked on the periodicals *Jung Wien*, *Die Fläche* etc. Exhibitions Kunstschau, Vienna 1908, Bugra, Leipzig 1914.

Postcards: 6 p. in the series of the Wiener Werkstäte, all greetings p. nos. 19, 20, 149, 154 ?, 158, 517.

Bibl.: Dichand-Martischnig 1978; Baudet 1980; Hansen 1982.

George DELAW
Sedan, Ardennes, 1874 – 8.12.1929
Painter, cartoonist, illustrator, decorator.
He worked on *Le Rire* and other illustrated papers. He was the author of the album *Sur les chemins de France* (1920). He illustrated the books: *Le Roman du Lièvre* by F. Jammes; *La Comédie de celui qui épousa une femme muette* by A. France; *Contes* by Andersen; *Contes* by Perrault; *Contes de Nourrices*; *Histoires de Brigands*; *Camembert-sur-Ourcq* by M. and A. Fischer. He made decorative panels for the children's play-room on the transatlantic liner 'Paris' and others for the steamboat 'Aramis'.

Postcards: 1 p. in the 'Collection des Cent', publ. Gréningaire, Paris, c. 1901; 1p. in the series 'Les Voeux de la France, Rire Rouge', 1914.

Bibl.: Baudet 1978.

Maurice DENIS
Granville, Manche, 25.11.1870 – St. Germain-en-Laye 13.11.1943.
Painter, engraver, illustrator, commercial artist, art theorist, scenographer.
He studied at the Ecole des Beaux-Arts in Paris, where he was a student of G. Moreau, and then he joined the Académie Julian, where his companions were Bonnard, Vuillard, Ranson, Sérusier, R. Piot. He joined the Pont-Aven group and Gauguin, becoming their theorist: his text was *Manifeste du Mouvement Nabi* published in 1890 in the magazine *Art et Critique*. From 1890 he exhibited at the Salon des Indépendants. In 1891 he opened a studio with Bonnard, Lugné-Poë and Vuillard, and he started book illustrations and scenography (for the Théâtre d'Art and the Théâtre de l'Oeuvre). Between 1895 and 1898 he made several journeys to Italy, where he studied the early Sienese and Florentine schools. This marked an important change in his work. In 1895 he exhibited religious paintings for the first time at the Salon of the Société Nationale des Beaux-Arts. He was a founder member of the Salon d'Automne (1903) and of the Société des Amis des Cathédrales (1912). In 1919 he founded with G. Desvallières the 'Atelier d'Art Sacré'. He illustrated the books: *Sagesse* by P. Verlaine (1891-1911); *Voyage d'Urien* by A. Gide (1893); *Imitation de Jésus-Christ*, for which he also wrote the text (1903); *Vita Nova* by Dante (1907); *Fioretti* by S. Francis of Assisi (1913); *Sainte Thérèse* by P. Claudel (1916); *Eloa* by A. Vigny (1917); His main theoretical works are collected in *Théories* (1912) and *Nouvelles Théories* (1921).

Postcards: 1p. in the series 'Byrrh', 1906; several before 1914 reproducing paintings.

Bibl.: Baudet 1978; Zeyons 1979.

Henri-Julien DETOUCHE
Paris, 10.1.1854 – Paris, 1913
Painter, engraver, commercial artist, watercolourist, graphic designer, decorator, writer, cartoonist.
He received his first artistic training from his father, the painter Laurent-Didier and studied afterwards with the painter U. Butin. He was the author of collections of engravings *Souvnirs d'Espagne*, *Les Péchés Capitaux*, *Les Cinq Sens*. He exhibited at the Société de l'Estampe en Couleurs, the Société Royale des Aquarellistes Belges (1896), at the Salon des Peintres-Graveurs and at the Salon des Humoristes. He collaborated on the magazines: *Courrier français*, *La Chronique parisienne*, *Le Panurge*, *L'Art moderne*, *Le Parisien de Paris*, *La Plume*, *Le Journal*. He illustrated the books: *Entrée de Clowns* by Champsaur and *Les Clés de Saint Pierre* by H. Rebell. He wrote the books *Propos d'un peintre* (1895); *De Montmartre à Monserrat* (1899); *Les Peintres de la femme intégrale*, *F. Rops and A. Willette* (1906); *Sous la dictèe de sa vie* (2 vols, 1906-08).

Postcards: 1 p. in the II series of 'Les Maîtres de la Carte Postale', c. 1898; 1 p. in the series 'Gala Henri Monnier', 1904; 1 p. in the series 'Byrrh', 1906; 2 p. in the series 'Cartes de I'I.P.C.C.'.

Bibl.: Neudin 1978; Baudet 1978.

Fritz DIETL
Vienna, 19.10.1880 – ?
Graphic designer, fabric designer, ceramist.
He attended the Kunstgewerbeschule in Vienna (J. Hoffmann, F. Metzner). He worked with the Wiener Werkstätte in the decoration of the cabaret 'Fledermaus'. He worked on the magazines *Der Liebe Augustin*, *Die Fläche* etc.

Postcards: There is a famous unnumbered p. in the series of the Wiener Werkstätte.

Bibl.: Hansen 1982.

Julius DIEZ
Nürnberg, 18.9.1870 – Munich 13.3.1957
Painter, graphic designer (ex libris, playing cards), commercial artist, illustrator, designer of works of applied art.
He attended from 1888–1892 the Kunstgewerbeschule (Barth) and the Academy (G.V. Hackl, R. V. Seitz) in Munich. From 1907 to 1927 he taught at the Kunstgewerbeschule, then until 1938 at the Munich Academy. He worked on the magazines *Jugend* (from 1896) and *Meggendorfer Blätter*.

Postcards: several in the series of the 'Künstler Postkarten' for *Jugend*, 1898, and the later series 1900-1910, publ. G. Hirth, Munich; 'München Ausstellung 1908', lith. Köhler, Munich, reproducing the poster; 'Paul Brann's Marionetten-Theater. Münchner Künstler'; series 90 Geburtstag des Prinzregenten Luitpold', Druck O. Consée, Munich, 1911; 'Appels Delikatessen'; Feldpostkarten of the Keks-Fabrik H. Bahlsen, Hannover; several p. of propaganda for the first world war.

Bibl.: Neudin 1980, 1983, Till 1983.

Henri Patrice DILLON
San Francisco, 1851 – Paris, 1909
Lithographer, painter, commercial artist, illustrator, graphic designer (calendars, menus, books).
He was a student in Paris of I. Pils, H. Lehman, E.-A. Carolus-Duran and J. Frappa. From 1876 he exhibited at the Salon. From 1882 he wsa principally involved in lithography, he took part in the exhibitions of the Société des Peintres-Graveurs. He was nominated president of the Société des Lithographes. He worked on the magazines: *L'Artiste*, *L'Estampe moderne*, *Magazine of art*, *Revue de l'Art*, *Revue illustrée*. He illustrated with 13 lithographs the album *Calendrier parisien* by H. Le Roux (1892). He did the illustrations for *Nouvelle Bibliopolis* by O. Uzanne (1897) and for *Ninette* by L. Robert (1900) and, in collaboration with others, *Rêve d'un viveur* by Dubut de Laforest (1884); *Pirouettes* by Coquelin Cadet (1888) and for the *Album des Peintres-Lithographes*.

Postcards: 1 p. in the series 'Gala Henri Monnier', 1904; series (?) 'Au Cirque', typ. H. C. Paris.

Alphonse-Étienne DINET
Paris, 28.3.1861 – Paris, 20.2.1929
Painter, illustrator, commercial artist.
He attended the Académie Julian, where he was the pupil of A. Bouguereau and the orientalist painter T. Robert-Fleury. He then went to the Ecole des Beaux-Arts in Paris. In 1882 he exhibited for the firt time at the Salon. In 1884 he went with a grant to Algeria, where the discovery of the Arab world made a fundamental change in his work. From 1890 he exhibited at the Salon of the Société Nationale des Beaux-Arts, and he became one of the most appreciated orientalist painters. He illustrated the books: *Antar, poème héroïque arabe* (1898); *Rabia El Kouloub, ou le Printemps des coeurs* (1902); *Mirage, scènes de la vie arabe* (1906); *El Fiafi ou El Kifar ou le Désert* (1911); *La Vie de Mohammed* (1918). He worked on *L'Estampe moderne*.

Postcards: 1 p. in the 'Collection des Cent', publ. Gréningaire, Paris, c.1901; 1 p. in the series 'Album Mariani' c.1910.

Bibl.: Baudet 1978.

Josef DIVÉKY
Farmos, Hungary, 28.9.1887 – Sopron, Hungary, Sept. 1951
Etcher, commercial artist, illustrator, graphic designer (books, commercial graphics, ex libris), glass designer.
He attended the Academy in Vienna (A. Dehug) and from 1906 the Kunstgewerbeschule (R. v. Larisch, C. O. Czeschka, B. Löfler). From 1910 to 1914 he worked in Zurich and Brussels. From 1919 to 1941 he lived in Switzerland, where he taught book illustration. In 1941 he was nominated professor at the School of Applied Art in Budapest. He worked as an illustrator for several Viennese, German and Swiss publishers and for the Wiener Werkstätte. He worked on the magazines *Der Ruff*, *Die Muskete*, *Figaro*, *Donauland*. Exhibitions: Bugra, Leipzig 1914; Secession, Vienna 1914.

Postcards: 38 p. in the series of the Wiener Werkstätte; 6 for the Emperor's Jubilee of 1908 (nos 160, 162, 169, 171, 173, 183), 8 fashion p. (nos. 229-234, 236, 237), 13 views of Prague and Vienna (nos. 261-267, 316, 317, 402-405), 10 greetings p. (nos 141, 142, 168, 180, 184, 189, 192, 238, 247, 248), 14 with subjects from childhood and fables (nos. 240-246, 494, 496-501); p. of war propaganda c.1917.

Bibl.: Mrazek 1978; Trost-Martischnig 1978; Baudet 1980; Lebeck 1980; Drago 1981; Fanelli 1981, 1983; Hansen 1982; Schweiger 1982.

Georges DOLA, pseudonym for Edmond VERNIER
Dôle, Jura, 2.11.1872 – Bricquebec, Mandre, 9.7.1950
Painter, lithographer, commercial artist, graphic designer.
A member of the Société des Artistes Français, he took part in the Salons of this society, receiving an honourable mention in 1909. He was known above all as a commercial artist and a painter of actors' portraits and for several designs for song score covers. He was a member of the Union des Artistes dessinateurs and professor at the Cercle international des Arts.
Postcards: 1 p. in the 'Collection des Cent', publ. Gréningaire, Paris, c.1901; publicity p. 'Le Diabolo', several publicity c.
Bibl.: Baudet 1978; Neudin 1979.

Leopold DREXLER
Vienna, 3.8.1888 – ?
Graphic designer, jewellery designer.
He studied at the Graphische Lehr – und Versuchsanstalt and from 1907 the Kunstgewerbeschule (B. Löofler, O. Prutscher).
Postcards: 2 p. in the series of the Wiener Werkstätte, with views of a Karlsbad café (nos. 214, 219).
Bibl.: Baudet 1980; Hansen 1982.

Marcello DUDOVICH
Trieste, 21.3.1878 – Milan, 31.3.1962
Commercial artist, graphic designer, painter.
Self taught, he attended from the age of fifteen the Circolo di Trieste artists and he knew the painters Guido Grimani and Arturo Rietti, who were his first influences. Between 1893 and 1895 he made a study trip to Munich. In 1897 he was sent by his father to Milan to be an apprentice at the Officine Grafiche Ricordi, under the guidance of L. Metlicovitz. At the same time he was a member of the Società artistica and patriottica and he studied design. In 1899 he moved to Bologna where he worked intensively for the publisher Edmondo Chappuis. In 1900 he won the competition for the poster 'Feste pri-maverile' in Bologna, he worked on the magazine *Italia Ride* and he won the Gold Medal at the Exposition Universelle 1900 (poster section). In the first years of the twentieth century he worked on the magazines *La lettura, Norissima, Varietas*. From 1906, after a short stay in Genoa where he worked for the Graphic Studio 'Armanino', he returned to Officine Grafiche Ricordi for whom he designed until 1915 several posters (above all for the fashion house 'Mele' in Naples). In 1911 he won the competition for the poster 'Borsalino' and he was invited to replace Reznicek as a draughtsman for the society page in *Simplicissimus*. From 1911 to 1914 he was the special correspondent for *Simplicissimus* reporting on European Society; the illustrations made for the magazine were collected in *Corso album* and they were reproduced as postcards. In 1914 he won the poster competition for DAG. At the outbreak of war he returned to Milan. Between 1917 and 1919 he worked in Turin where he designed posters for the cinema.
Postcards: 'Club Alpino Italiano, Sezione de Milano', 1898; 'Teatro Comunale Bologna, Stagione Lirica', publ. Chappuis, Bologna, 1899, reproducing the poster 'Città di Bologna, Feste de Maggio 1899', publ. Chappuis, Bologna, reproducing the poster 'Teatro Sociale Trento', publ. Chappuis, Bologna, 1900;

'Esposizione Nazionale de Floricultura, Bologna', publ. Chappuis, Bologna, 1900, reproducing the poster 'Ricordo della Festa del Ventaglio, Padova', Feb 1901, publ. Chappuis, Bologna; 5 Congresso Concorso Nazionale Federale Ginnastica, Bologna', publ. Chappuis, Bologna, 1901; 'Al vino Chianti', publ. Chappuis, Bologna, 1902; 'Feste de Maggio, Bologna 1902', publ. Chappuis, Bologna; 'Feste de Primavera, Bologna 1902', publ. Chappuis, Bologna; 'Fisso l'idea. Federazione italiana chimico industriale . . . Ricordo dell 'Esposizionne di Udine', publ. Chappuis, Bologna, 1903; 'Società Anonima Forniture Elettriehe', publ. Chappuis, Bologna, 1903; 'XVII Congresso Nazionale della Società Dante Alighieri, 1903, Teatro La Fenice, Venezia'; 'Città di Bologna-Feste de Primavera 1903', publ. C. A. Pini, Bologna; publicity p. 'Fernet Branca', publ. Chappuis, Bologna, 1903, it also exists as a menu-postcard, 'Esposizione italiana dell 'industria e dell' arte turistica, Bologna, estate, 1904', publ. Chappuis, Bologna; 'Esposizione dell Industria italiana per il materiale turistico, Bologna', publ. Chappuis, Bologna, 1904, reproduced from the poster 'Ravenna Esposizione regionale romagnola maggio-giugno 1904', publ. Chappuis, Bologna, reproduced from the poster; publicity p. 'Cognac Stock Trieste', publ. Chappuis, Bologna, c. 1904; 'Miniere Solfuree Trezza Romagna', publ. Chappuis, Bologna, c. 1904-05; 'Ferrarelle, Veglione di beneficenza, Teatro Contavalli Bologna', publ. Chappuis, Bologna, 1906; 'Feste autunnali verbanesi, Teatro Sociale de Pallanza', 1906; publicity for the department store 'Mele' in Naples, 1906, and in the following years; p. commemorating the Fuenza exhibition reproduced from the poster 'Bianco e Nero, Veglione della Famiglia Artistica, Teatro dal Verme', publ. Ricordi, Milan, 1908; 'Esposizione Universale di Bruxelles 1910', publ. Ricordi, Milan, reproduced from the poster; publicity p. 'Zenith-Borsalino', publ. Ricordi, Milan 1911, reproduced from the posters; series XVI of 'Simplicissimus-Karten' (nos. 3, 4 and others), 1912-1914, reproduced from Corso Album; p. for the plays at the Teatro del Corso in Bologna, 1915; 'Italia ansioso lo sguardo sul mare fidente nei giovani figli', 1915; publicity p. for the liqueur 'Strega', 1917; at least 15 series of 6 p. 'Zenit', 1917; at least 14 series of 6 p. 'Eureka', 1917 (III, la lettera; VI, A1 mare; VII, Flirt, VIII, Colloqui; IX, L'attesa; X, Sport d'hiver; XI, Regard); 'S.I.A. Società Italiana di Aviazione', 1918; circa 10 series of 6 p. of 'donnine' 'little women', no publisher's mark, c. 1918; publicity p. 'Giornale d'Italia', c. 1918; 'Teatro del Corso, Bologna, Stagione Lirica', publ. Chappuis, Bologna s.d.; 'G. A. Coppoli-Premiata Calzoleria, Bologna', publ. Chappuis, Bologna, s.d.
Bibl.: Bartoli-Mataloni 1979; Bobba 1979; Gaibazzi 1979; 'Gli illustratori. Marcello Dudovich', *La Cartolina*, I (1981, n. 1), p.n.n.; *La Cartolin*, I (1981, n. 2), p. 9, I (1981, n. 3), p. 19-22, I (1982, n. 4), p. 12, II (1982, n. 7), p. 12, III (1983, n. 12), p. 13; *Emilia Romagna*, special supplement to n. 4 of *La Cartolina*, 1982; Mordente 1982; Arrasich 1984.

Clementine Hélène DUFAU
Quinsac, Gironde, 1869 – Paris, 1937
Painter, lithographer, commercial artist, illustrator.
A pupil of A. Bouguereau, T. Robert-Fleury and G. Ferrier at the Académie Julian in Paris.

From 1893 she exhibited at the Salon of the Société des Artistes Français. She illustrated the books; *Basile e Sophia* by P. Adam (1898); *Les Femmes de Setné* by J. H. Rosny (1903); *L'Amour par principes* by P. Valdagne. She did the symbolist murals for the Sorbonne (1908) and for the house of Edmond Rostand in Cambo (1909). She designed posters for the feminist magazine, *La Fronde*.
Postcards: series of p. for the Exposition Universelle, Paris, 1900; 1 p. in the series 'Les Affiches Célèbres'; 1 p. in the series 'Byrrh', 1906; 1 p. in the series 'Album Mariani', c.1910.
Bibl.: Baudet 1978.

Louis DUNKI
Geneva 5.4.1856 – ?, 1915
Painter, illustrator, designer.
He trained at the art school in Geneva. From 1873 to 1876 he was a student of B. Menn for painting and of E. Mayor for enamelling. He studied illustration with G. Roux (1876-77). In 1878 he moved to Paris to work in the studio of F. Th. Lix. He collaborated as an illustrator on various French magazines: *Almanach du Bibliophile, L'Illustration, L'Image, Lecture pour tous, Monde illustré, Paris illustré, Univers illustré*. He illustrated for French publishers the books: *Petits contes à ma soeur* by H. Moreau (1896); *Servitude et Grandeur militaires* by A. de Vigny (1898); *La Maison du chat qui pelote* by H. Balzac (1899); *Jean Louis* by Bachelin. For Swiss publishers he illustrated *Histoire de Suisse* by Gobat and *Petites chroniques genevoises*. He painted historical, military and oriental subjects.
Postcards: p. for the national holiday, 1st August, 1911 Graph. Anstalt J. E. Wolfensberger, Zurich, 1911.

Clare Victor DWIGGINS (DWIG)
Wilmington, Ohio, 1873 – ?, 1958
Illustrator, graphic designer.
She worked on several newspapers and magazines. In 1903 she designed her first postcard for the London publisher R. Tuck. To date 350 cards have been identified as her work, some are not signed, they were designed between 1903 and the second world war for several publishers, like R. Tuck, R. Kaplan, Ch. Rose, W. P. Anderson etc., mainly of humorous subjects. Only part of her production has devices which relate more or less directly to the idiom of Art Nouveau. Among the series which were most successful is 'Fortune Teller' (copyright 1909).
Bibl.: Lyons 1975; B. Miller, *All about Dwig*, Palm Bay, Florida, 1976; Holt 1980, 1983.

E

Pauli EBNER
Biographical details are unknown.
She designed several series of p. for many publishers including M. Munk, Wien, A. Pökl etc. Her decorative and greetings cards from before and after the first world war were popular all over Europe until the 30s.
Bibl.: Gaibazzi 1979; Till 1983.

Otto ECKMANN
Hamburg, 19.11.1865 – Badenweiler, 11.6.1902
Painter, woodcut artist, commercial artist (books, ex libris calendars, lettering, commer-

cial and publicity graphics), designer of fabrics, furniture, objects of daily use, interior designer.

He attended the Kunstgewerbeschule in Hamburg, and Nürnberg and the Academy in Munich. From 1897 he taught ornamental painting at the Kunstgewerbemuseum in Hamburg. He worked on *Pan, Jugend* (from 1896), *Simplicissimus* (1896-98). He is considered to be one of the leading figures of Jugendstil.
Postcards: p. in the first series of the 'Künstler-Postkarten' for *Jugend*, G. Hirth, Munich 1898; p. in the publicity series 'Stollwerck-Postkarten'.
Bibl.: Neudin 1977; Baudet 1980; Arrasich 1984.

Albert Gustav-Aristides EDELFELT
Helsinki, 21.7.1854 – Borga, 18.8.1905
Painter and illustrator.
He attended the Academy of Fine Arts in Antwerp, and then from 1874 the Ecole des Beaux-Arts in Paris, where he was a pupil of V.-L. Gérôme. In 1889 he exhibited at the Salon of the Société des Artistes Français and, from 1890 to 1903 at the Société Nationale des Beaux-Arts. He was active at the Russian court, where he was employed by Alexander II to paint the portraits of his sons. In Finland he executed several fresco cycles in important public buildings. Between 1894 and 1904 he illustrated several books. He also played an important role in Finnish politics: in 1899 he was at the head of a movement protesting against constitutional changes and he was a deputy.
Postcards: several inspired by the history of Finland, which in the main reproduce book illustrations.

Helmuth EICHRODT
Bruchsal, 27.2.1872 – ?
Painter, commercial artist, graphic artist (book, publicity graphics), applied arts designer.
From 1890 to 1903 he attended the Academy in Karlsruhe (L. V. Kalckreuth, H. Thoma). He was a member of the Karlsruher Künstlerbund. He worked on *Jugend*. In 1930 he was still active in Karlsruhe.
Postcards: series II, Verlag Gebr. Knauss, Karlsruhe, Kunstdruckerei Künstlerbund Karlsruhe, c. 1898.
Bibl.: Lebeck 1980; Drago 1981.

Oskar ELENIUS
Valkeala, 16.5.1885 – Helsinki, 1965.
Painter, illustrator.
He studied at the School of Industrial Art (1904-07) and at the School of Fine Arts in Helsinki, where he later taught.
Postcards: several from the period 1910-20 which have Finnish countryside, its customs and peasant life as their subjects.
Bibl.: Johanson-Termonen 1983.

Harry ELIOTT
Born in Great Britain. His biographical details are unknown.
Commercial artist, graphic designer (menus, publicity graphics).
Postcards: two series each of 10 p., 'La vie sportive', Coll. Ed. S., Paris, c. 1900; series of humorous p.
Bibl.: Baudet 1980.

Paul Otto ENGELHARDT
Offenbach a. M., 1872 – ?
Commercial artist, illustrator.
Biographical details are unknown. He worked on the magazines *Meggendorfer Blätter*, *Jugend*.
Postcards: p. in the 'Künstlerpostkarten', series 10, Stengel & Co., Dresden.

Robert ENGELS
Solingen, 9.3.1866 – Munich, 24.5.1926
Commercial artist, illustrator, graphic designer, painter.
He attended the Academy in Düsseldorf from 1886 to 1889 and until 1898 Fehr's private school in Munich. From 1910 he taught at the Kunstgewerbeschule in Munich. He worked on the magazine *Jugend* from 1896. Among the many books illustrated by him *Tristan und Isolde* is the most famous.
Postcards: series 'Tennisspielerin', Schwannschenkarten, Düsseldorf, c. 1897; p. in the first three series 'Künstler-Postkarten' for *Jugend*, G. Hirth, Munich, 1898-99.
Bibl.: Lehrs 1898.

Fritz ERLER
Frankestein, Silesia (now in Poland), 15.12.1868 – Munich 11.7.1940
Painter, illustrator, commercial artist, graphic designer (ex libris), scenographer.
He studied in Breslau (A. Bräuer) and from 1892 to 1894 at the Académie Julian in Paris. In 1899 he formed with others the group 'Die Scholle' in Munich. He worked on *Jugend* from the first appearance of the magazine (he also designed the first cover).
Postcards: p. in the first three series of 'Künstler-Postkarten' for *Jugend*, G. Hirth, Munich, 1898-99; p. for the war loan 'Kriegsanleihe', C. Woll & Son, Munich.
Bibl.: Baudet 1980; Till 1983.

Georges d'ESPAGNAT
Paris, 14.8.1870 – 1950
Painter, engraver, illustrator.
He worked on the newspapers *Courrier Français* and *L'Image*. He exhibited at the Salon des Indépendants, at the Salon of the Société Nationale des Beaux-Arts, at the Salon d'Automne, at the Libre Esthétique in Brussels, at the Berlin Secession and at the 1st exhibition of the Société de la gravure sur bois.
Postcards: 1 p. in the I series (1898) and 1 p. in the II series (c. 1898) 'Les Maîtres de la Carte Postale' publ. by the newspaper *La Critique*.

F

Fabio FABBI
Bologna, 18.7.1861 – Casalecchio di Reno, 1946
Painter, sculptor, illustrator.
He was a student of the painter Rivalta. From 1893 he taught in Florence. He made several journeys abroad, to Paris, Warsaw and Germany. Above all a long study trip to Egypt left significant traces on his work. He took part in the international exhibition in Munich in 1889, at the exhibition of Sempione in Milan in 1906 (where he showed models of medals) and at the international exhibition of sacred art in Paris in 1911. He illustrated the *Iliad*, the *Odyssey* and the *Aeneid* as well as novels by Salgari.
Postcards: 'Onoranze centenarie a Paolo Toscanelli e ad Amerigo Vespucci, Città di Firenze', 1898; 'Regio Teatro della Pergola, Firen-

ze, Serata di Beneficenze', 1901; 'Esposizione di Beneficenza pro asili infantili, Firenze', 1904; 'Cinquenario del colera a Firenze', 1905; 'Circolo degli artisti di Firenze, Pro Calabria', 1905; p. in the series 'Divina Commedia', publ. Alterocca, Terni; 'Finis Saeculi XIX', series of 'little women'.
Bibl.: Gaibazzi 1979; Arrasich 1984.

Jules Abel FAIVRE
Lyon, 30.3.1867 – Paris, 1945
Cartoonist, illustrator, commercial artist, painter.
He studied at the Ecole des Beaux-Arts in Lyon, and then in Paris with J. Lefébre and B. Constant. He made study trips to Greece, to Italy and the Orient. From 1892 he exhibited portraits and paintings of figures at the Salon in Lyon and Paris. He was a member with Grün, Léandre, Steinlen and Willette of the artistic group at the cabaret 'Taverne de Paris'. From 1895 he worked on several magazines: *Le Rire, L'Assiette au Beurre, Le Figaro, Le Journal, L'Echo de Paris, Candide, La Baïonnette, Gazette du Bon Ton*. In 1902 he published his album of caricatures *Médecins*. During the first world war he designed several posters for the national loan, which were reproduced as postcards.
Postcards: 1 p. in the series 'Gala Henry Monnier', 1904; series 'Les Médecins', publ. by the magazine *L'Assiette au Beurre*, c. 1906; reproduced from plates published in 1902 n. 51 of the magazine; 1 p. in the series Album Mariani, c. 1910; 1 p. in the series 'Les Veoux de la France, Rire Rouge', 1914; 1 p. in the series 'Le Rire Rouge', 1915; 1 p. in the series 'Journée du Secours National'.
Bibl.: Baudet 1978; Forissier 1978; Zeyons 1979.

Vadim FALILEJEFF
Penza, 1.11.1879 – ?
Etcher, woodcut artist, lino-cutter.
He went to the Princess M. A Teniśeva's laboratory of applied arts in St. Petersburg then to the academy in the same city.
Postcards: series for the Red Cross with lithographic reproductions of his woodcuts of the landscape along the Volga.
Bibl.: Baudet 1980.

Alexander Thiodolf FEDERLEY
Abo, Turku, 1864 – Helsinki, 15.11.1932
Painter, designer, illustrator
He completed his artistic studies in Helsinki and Paris, where he attended the Académie Julian (1891-93). He was one of the leaders in the revival of illustration in Finland.
Postcards: several mainly of nationalistic political propaganda, from the last decade of the nineteenth century.
Bibl.: Johanson – Termonen, 1983.

Lyonel FEININGER
New York, 17.7.1871 – ivi, 13.1.1956
Illustrator, lithographer, etcher, xylographer.
In 1887 he moved to Germany where he attended the Gewerbeschule (P. Woldemar) and then (1888) the academy (E. Hancke) in Hamburg and the Kunstschule in Berlin (A. Schlabitz). In 1912 he came into contact with the expressionist group 'Die Brücke'; he designed wall decoration for the 'Fest der Berliner Secession 1912'. In 1919 and 1933 he was a lecturer at the Bauhaus, the school of W. Gropius, for which he designed the first poster (1919). He did important work as a satirical

illustrator and as the designer of 'bandes dessinées' for German, American and French magazines, like *Harper's Young People* (1894-95), *Ulk* (from 1896), *Lustige Blätter* (from 1896, *Das Narrenschiff, Berliner Illustrierte Zeitung, Der liebe Augustin, Chicago Sunday Tribune, Le Témoin, Licht und Schatten.*
Postcards: 'Ball der Lustigen Blätter. 24 Januar 1905. Five o'clock in der Hölle'; several of the series Lustige Blätter.
Bibl.: *Lyonel Feininger, Karikaturen, Comic strips, Illustrationen*, 1888-1915, cat. by several authors, Museum fur Kunst und Gewerbe, Hamburg 1981.

Fernand FERNEL
Brussels, 1872 (?) – Paris, 1934 (?)
Commercial artist, illustrator, cartoonist.
He exhibited at the 1903 Salon d'Automne and from 1907 to 1914, from 1920 to 1923 at the Salon des Humoristes. He worked on the papers: *La Caricature, Le Rire, Le Sourire.* He was the author of the albums: *Mr Bob et son Rataplan no. 1, Estampes sportives, Les Enfants s'amusent* (1913), *Les Jolies poupées.*
Postcards: 1 p. in the series 'Collection des Cent', publ. Gréningaire, Paris, c. 1901; series of 6 p. 'Les Humbert à la mer'; 2 series of 10 p. 'Les Sports'; humorous p. 'Marche des midinettes'; caricatural 'Jacques 1 Empereur du Sahara'; publicity 'Cirque d'hiver'; publicity 'Les Fratellini'; series of 6 p. 'Cake Walk'; series of 5 p. 'Paris-Madrid, course automobile'.
Bibl.: Weill 1977; Baudet 1978; Rostenne 1979; Fildier 1980.

Georges de FEURE, pseudonym for Georges Joseph van SLUIJTERS
Paris, 6.9.1868 – Paris, 26.11.1943
Decorator, painter, illustrator, lithographer, commercial artist, scenographer, designer of furniture, fabrics, tapestry, glass windows, ceramics, furnishings, graphic designer (books).
He was the son of a Dutch architect. He had his first experience as a scenographer in Amsterdam and moved to Paris in 1890, where he designed the sets for several spectacles at the cabaret 'Chat Noir' and worked as an illustrator on the magazines *Le Boulevard* and *Le Courrier Français.* He attended the studio of J. Chéret, who introduced him to poster design. In 1892 he exhibited some watercolours at a symbolist exhibition in the gallery 'Le Barc de Boutteville'. From 1894 he took part in the exhibitions of the Société Nationale des Beaux-Arts. Collaboration with S. Bing's gallery 'L'Art Nouveau' founded in 1896 made him one of the foremost artists in the revival of the decorative arts in France. Above all, his furniture, mostly manufactured by the company Fleury in Paris, received immediate critical acclaim. While designing fabrics, tapestries, ceramics, glass windows, furnishings, he continued to do graphic design and illustrations. In 1899 he illustrated *La porte des rêves* by M. Schwob. For Bing's 'L'Art Nouveau' pavilion at the Exposition Universelle in Paris 1900 he designed the decoration for the façade and the interior design. In 1902 he exhibited in Turin a series of porcelain objects manufactured by G. Dufraisse in Limoges. With the architect from Aachen Th. Cossmann, he established in Paris in the first years of the twentieth century the 'Atelier de Feure', which became the main centre for the production and sale of his furniture. In 1903 he held an important one-man show at Bing's gallery. After the first

world war he was mainly active as a scenographer and as a fashion designer (for the Parisian fashion house Madeleine Vionnet).
Postcards: 1 p. in the series 'Cocorico', c. 1898; 1 p. reproducing a detail of the lithographic print made for the collection *L'Estampe Moderne* c. 1898.
Bibl.: Baudet 1978; Neuden 1979.

FIDUS, pseudonym for Hugo Reinhold Karl Johann HÖPPENER
Lübeck, 8.10.1868 – Schonblink, near Woltersdorf, Berlin, 23.2.1948
Painter, graphic designer (books, ex libris), illustrator, commercial artist.
After a period studying at the Gewerbeschule in Lübeck he was the student of K. W. Diefenbach, who lived in the hermitage at Hollrigelskreuth in the valley of the Isar from whom he got the name of Fidus. From 1889 to 1892 he went to the academy in Munich (N. Gysis). Later he settled in Berlin. He was a member of Verband Deutscher Illustratoren, of the Vereinigung Junst im Leben des Kindes, of the Verein für Körpelkultur, of the Deutsche Gartenstadt-Gesellschaft, of the Richard Wagner Gesellschaft. He worked on *Jugend* (dal 1896), *Pan, Sphinx, Berliner Illustrierte Zeitung.*
Postcards: p. n. 2 in the series '*Jugend* Reisenpostkarten', G. Hirsh, Munich 1898; several p. mainly reproducing his graphic work (lithography, drawings, et.) or also publicity p. for his graphic series (e.g. the one for the *Naturkinder* Maps, c. 1910) or of books illustrated by him.
Bibl.: Lebeck 1980; Neudin 1980; Drago 1981; Holt 1983.

Harrison FISHER
Brooklyn, New York, 22.7.1877 – ??, 19.1.1934.
Painter, illustrator, graphic designer.
The son of the painter Hugh Antoine, he attended the Mark Hopkins Institute of Art in San Francisco and at only sixteen he began working for the city's newspapers. After moving to New York, at the end of the 90's, he became the member of staff of *Puck* who was most appreciated by the public. He created a female figure known as 'Fisher Girl' (heads, groups) which was close to the prototypes by Ph. Boileau and H. C. Christy, although she was less strongly characterized. He worked on the magazines *San Francisco, Call & Examiner, Puck, Scribner's, Cosmopolitan, Life, The Saturday Evening Post, McClure's.*
Postcards: several series with variations on the theme of the 'Fisher Girl', for different publishers, including Reinthal & Newman, New York (series 'American Beauties', etc). Detroit Pubs (series 14000), etc.
Bibl.: Lyons 1975; Holt 1980, 1983; D. Bowers, E. and G. Budd, *Harrison Fisher*, Iola, Wisconsin, 1984.

James Montgomery FLAGG
New York, 18.6.1877 – ivi, 27.5.1960
Illustrator, commercial artist, painter.
He studied at the Art Student League in New York, in Great Britain, and in France. He began working at twelve years of age, and he was noted for his humorous, satirical touch. His graphic language, which was often influenced by Gibson, modified Art Nouveau devices. He was famous for his poster of Uncle Sam in the first world war 'I Want You for the US Army'. He worked on the magazines *St Nicholas* (1890), *Scribner's, Cosmopolitan,*

Life etc.
Postcards: several of female figures, couples etc.
Bibl.: Holt 1980, 1983.

Arthur FOACHE
Janzé, Ille-et-Vilaine, ? – ?
Painter, commercial artist, illustrator.
He was a pupil of B. Constant. He worked in Toulouse. He designed the posters for the magazine *La Dépêche* and for L'Imprimerie Cassan Fils. He exhibited at the Salon des Artistes Français.
Postcards: 1 p. in the series 'Byrrh', 1906.
Bibl.: Baudet 1978.

Edmondo FONTANA
Ferrara, 16.8.1861 – Ferrara, 31.10.1929
Illustrator, caricaturist, cartoonist, graphic designer (commercial and publicity graphics, diplomas, brand marks), commercial artist, photographer, painter.
The facts regarding his early training are uncertain and scarce. From the last decade of the nineteenth century he supplied several Ferrarese magazines with caricatural drawings: *Chichett de Frara; L'Ippogrifo* (1890); *Il Resto del Sigaro* (1892-93); *L'Usel Grifòn* (1894); *Ferrara a 100; Sal-in-guerra* (1896-97); *Il Pupazzetto Anatnof* (1897); *L'Omnibus* (1900-01); *La Macchietta Ferrarese* (1908); *L'Analfabeta* (1913). He designed covers for different commemorative publications and he did illustrations for books (*Il simbolismo dell'arte* by O. Novi, 1900). A large part of his production in applied graphic art (including postcards) was printed by the lithographic press which he owned. In 1905 he took part in the Mostra Umoristica Nazionale in the Palazzo Diamanti in Ferrara.
Postcards: 'Ricordo della escursione nel Ferrarese degli Ingegneri e Artchitetti Italiani al IX congresso di Bologna', 1899; 'Ricordo Esposizione Artistica Ferrara', 1899, numbered issue; 'Circolo Ferrariola, Ferrara', 1899; 'Teatro Comunale-Farrarariola, Ferrara', 1899; 'Teatro Cómunale-Ferrara – Grande veglia dei fiori', 1901; 'Ricordo della bandiera sociale – Società di Mutuo soccorso fra i Carabinieri in congedo', 1901; 'Società di Mutuo Soccorso, Frande Veglia mascherata', 1901; 'Grande Veglia dei fiori a favore della Dante Alighieri', 1901; 'Ultimo estinto dell'ostaggio austriaco. Anton Francesco Trotti', 1901; 'Convegno delle Ferrovie di carattere locale', 1902; 'Convegno ciclistico femminile', 1902; 'Convegno Turistico Nazionale, Ferrara', 1902; series of 15 p. with views commemorating the 'Convegno Turistico Nazionale', 1902; 'Fiera di Beneficenza dell'ospizio Stimatine e del patronato Artigianelli', 1902; 'Inaugurazione dell'acquedotto di Pontelagoscuro', 1902; 'Associazione mandamentale per il risveglio Copparese', 1903; 'Banda Ariosto – Ricordo della gara musicale', 1903; 'Arrivo del primo treno a Copparo', 1903; 'Ricordo della inaugurazione della Ferrovia Ferrara-Copparo', 1903; '50° anniversario della morte dei tre martiri', 1903; '50° anniversario della fucilazione di Succi, Malaguti, Parmeggiani', 1903; 'Società di Mutuo Soccorso fra Camerieri, Cuochi ed affini', 1903; 'A Gugliemo Morandi Migliarino', 1903; 'Festeggiamenti in occasione del XVI Centenario di S. Giorgio che uccide il drago', 1903; series of 3 p. 'Festeggiamenti in onore di S. Giorgio', 1903; 'Comizio Agrario', 1904; 'Unione Ciclistica Ferrarese, Veloce Club Trentino', 1904; 'Disastro ferro-

viario', 1904; 'Feste di Maggio', 1905; 'Società Enigmofila', 1905; 'Società Enigmofila gruppo gynasium inaugurazione della bandiera sociale', 1905; series of 6 p. 'XXV anniversario della fondazione palestra ginnastiea di Ferrara', 1905; 'Esposizione nazionale artisticaumoristica', 1905; 'Ricordo 20 settembre', 1906; 'Ricordo festa per separazione delle ville di Ruina, Ro, Guarda, Cologna, Berra, Serravalle da Copparo', 1906; 'Inaugurazione della Casa del Popolo di Ferrara', 1906; 'Inaugurazione del ponte fra Stellata e Ficarolo', 1906; 'Ricordo dell'inaugurazione dell'edificio scolastico di Copparo', 1906; series of 36 p. 'Mutua assistenza fra le masse corali', 1907; 'Nel regno delle bambole', 1908; 'Navigazione fluviale Ferrara-Magnavacca', 1908; 'XXX Anniversario di fondazione della società di mutuo soccorso fra barbieri e parrucchieri', 1909; 'Inaugurazione della ferrovia Ferrara-Cento', 1909; 'Croce Rossa Italiana comitato di Ferrara', 1917; publicity for Il Fanale Aquilas, 'Si sa come si parte, ma come si arriva?', 1917; humorous p. about the war, 1918; 'Un saluto da Ferrara'; 'VII Congresso Internazionale di Agricoltura', 4 versions with different impressions; series of 5 p. 'Il melologo di Parisina al castello estense'; 'A ricordo del 50° anniversario della partenza degli Austriaci'; humorous 'Concorrenza ai bombardamenti nel conflitto Europeo'; 'Comitato provinciale per un ricordo ai martiri Ferraresi'; 'Consociazione Mutua fra gli Operai Ferraresi pro Sicilia e Calabria'; 'Convegno Turistico Nazionale'; 'Omaggio a Vittorio Emanuele'; 'Ricordo di Argenta-Inaugurazione di una lapide a Gustavo Bianchi'; 'Ricordo del Conte di Torino'; 'Ricordo della XXIV legislatura . . .'; 'Fratelli Bonnet di Comacchio – L'Assalto al casino dei Quattro Venti'.

Bibl.: L. Scardino-A. Fabbri, *Edmondo Fontana. Un grafico ferrarese 1861-1929*, Ferrara s.d; V. Pederzani-R. Zaramella, '*Edmondo Fontana*', in *Emilia-Romagna*, supplement to *La Cartolina*, n. 4, 1982; Arrasich 1984.

Jean-Louis FORAIN
Reims, 23.10.1852 – Paris, 11.7.1931
Engraver, painter, commercial artist, illustrator.
He completed a period of study with the history painter J. de la Chevreuse and attended the Ecole des Beaux-Arts in Paris, where he was the pupil of J.-L. Gérôme and the sculptor J.-B. Carpeaux. In 1879 and 1880 he took part in impressionist exhibitions. From 1876 he worked as an illustrator for the papers *Scapin, La Cravache Parisienne, L'Avant-Scène*. He worked on several other magazines: *Courrier Français, Echo de Paris, L'Album* (1900) *Le Figaro, Journal amusant, Monde Parisien, Revue Illustrée, Le Rire, La Vie Parisienne*. In 1889 he founded the weekly magazine *Le Fifre* and in 1898 with Caran d'Ache, the newspaper *Psst!* the organ of nationalistic reaction against the Dreyfus party. He was the author of the albums: *La Comédie Parisienne* (1892); *Nous, vous, eux* (1893); *Les Temps difficiles* (1893); *Album Forain* (1896); *Doux Pays* (1897); *La Vie*. He illustrated with others, the books *Croquis Parisiens* by Huysmans (1879, with Ibels); *La Vraie tentation du grand Saint Antoine* by P. Arène (1880); *Chansons fin de siècle* by J. Oudot (1891); *Rires & Grimaces* (1892). He was the author of several etchings, lithographic prints and posters. During the war he made a series of engravings *De le Marne au Rhin*.

Postcards: several showing episodes in the war 1914-18.
Bibl.: Zeyons 1979.

Carlo FORNARA
Prestinone, Novara, 21.10.1871 – Prestinone, 15.9.1968
Painter.
He attended the school at S. Maria Maggiore in Val Vigezzo and completed his studies of painting at Lyon under the guidance of Guichard. In 1891 he exhibited at the Milan Triennale at the Brera. Between 1894 and 1895 he lived in Paris. He collaborated with G. Segantini on the monumental 'Engadina' at the Exposition Universelle 1900 in Paris. In 1901 he exhibited at the Biennale in Venice. As one of the leading divisionist painters he exhibited at many national and international exhibitions: Quadriennale in Turin (1902); Munich (1905); the exhibition of Italian divisionists in Paris (1907); the Anglo-Latin exhibition in London (1912); Venice Biennale (1914). In 1910 he held one-man shows in Belgium and Holland.
Postcards: 'Cartolina commemorativa dell'inaugurazione Traforo del Sempione', publ. A. Grubicy, Milan 1906.
Bibl.: Mordente 1982.

Roberto FRANZONI
Bologna, 29.4.1882 – Bologna, 1960
Painter, decorator, commercial artist, tapestry designer, graphic designer (commercial and publicity graphics and stamps).
He was educated at the Accademia di Belle Arti in Bologna, in the realist school of E. Barbieri and D. Ferri. From 1899 his pictorial and graphic production returned to Liberty themes and showed a personal re-elaboration of formal devices deriving from Mucha and Larsson.
Postcards: publicity p. for *L'Avvenire d'Italia*, the Bologna daily newspaper, 1902; 'Feste di Maggio, Bologna 1902', Lith. Casanova, Bologna; 'Ricordo della Gara Regionale Bandistica, Bologna 1902', Lith. Casanova, Bologna; 'Ricordo dei grandi concerti musicali diretti dal M° Mascagni, Bologna, maggio 1902', publ. C. A. Pini, Bologna; 'Feste di maggio, Bologna 1904', publ. C. A. Pini, Bologna; 'Teatro Comunale, Gran Veglione di Beneficenza, Bologna 20 febbraio 1904'; Lith. Sordomuti, Bologna; 'Città di Bologna, Feste di Primavera 1905', Lith. Sordomuti, Bologna; 'III Centenario della nascita di Evangelista Torricelli faentino 1608-1908', S.A.I.C.A. Armanino, Genova, series of 'donnine'.
Bibl.: Bartoli-Mataloni 1979; Mordente 1982; Arrasich 1984.

Mitzi FRIEDMANN-OTTEN
Vienna, 28.11.1884 – New York, 5.5.1955
Graphic designer (ex libris, publicity and commercial graphics, commercial designer, illustrator, designer of fabrics, fashions, objects of daily use, metalwork, jewellery, enamel.
She attended the Kunstschule für Frauen und Mädchen and the Kunstgewerbeschule O. Strnad). She worked with the Wiener Werkstätte in several fields, and also on the magazines *Hohe Warte, Erdgeist, Die Aktion*.
Exhibitions: The Kunstschau Vienna 1908.
Postcards: 6 p. in the series of the Wiener Werkstätte, 5 decorative (nos. 543-545, 785, 786), a greetings p. (n. 800); p. in the special series of the Wiener Werkstätte of fabric designs, Brüder Kohn, Vienna.
Bibl.: Dichand-Martischnig 1978; Baudet

1980; Drago 1981; Hansen 1982.

Lotte FRÖMMEL-FOCHLER
Vienna, 1.5.1884 – ?
Fabric designer, designer of fashion accessories, of embroidery, ceramist.
She attended the Fachschule für Kunststickerei and from 1904 to 1908 the Kunstgewerbeschule in Vienna (J. Hoffmann).
Postcards: p. in the special series of the Wiener Werkstätte of fabric designs, Brüder Kohn, Vienna.

G

Akseli Waldemar GALLEN-KALLELA
Björneborg, 26.5.1865 – Stockholm, 7.3.1931
Painter, illustrator, engraver, woodcut artist, commercial artist, designer of furniture, tapestries, carpets, furnishing.
He completed his early studies at the art school in Helsinki and, privately, in the studios of S. A. Keinänen and A. v. Becker. Then he attended the Académie Julian in Paris where he was the student of A. Bougereau and T. Robert-Fleury, and in the studio of Cormon. In Paris he frequented the Nabis group and Bastien Lepage and became an admirer of Puvis de Chavannes. He made study trips to Africa and North America. His fresco cycle in the Finnish pavilion at the Exposition Universelle 1900 in Paris gained him recognition on an international level and made him the most important Finnish symbolist painter. In his own country he was given important public commissions like the frescoes for the vault in the Hall of the National Museum in Helsinki, designed by H. Gesellius, A. Lindgren and E. Saarinen. As well as painting, he worked in the fields of decorative arts and illustration: he illustrated among others the books: *Kalevala, epopea finnica* and *Sette Fratelli* by A. Kivi (1908).
Postcards: most of them reproduce his paintings, but it seems that some of his designs were executed for postcards.

Arthur Joseph GASKIN
Birmingham, 1862 – Birmingham, 4.6.1928
Painter, graphic designer, illustrator, jewellery designer.
He attended the School of Art in Birmingham, where he later became a teacher. His work places him in the Arts and Crafts movement of W. Morris, with whom he collaborated in the production of the Kelmscott Press.
Postcards: several decorative p.
Bibl.: Rostenne 1979

Georges GAUDY
St. Josse-ten-Noode, Belgium, 6.10.1872 – ?
Illustrator, commercial artist, painter.
A well known racing cyclist, he worked on several sporting magazines (*Cycliste Belge illustré, Veloce, Foyer, Flirt*). His posters from the first one in 1893 have sport as their subject. They are 'Vélodrome de Bruxelles', 'Ligue Vélocipédique Belge' (1896), for the 'Automobile Club de Belgique' (1898), for the 'Usines Delin', (1898), for the 'Syndicat Coureurs' and for several kinds of bicycles.
Postcards: series of publicity p. for the paper *Le Sportsman*.

Albert GEBHARD
Toholampi, 29.4.1869 – Helsinki, 15.5.1937

Painter, caricaturist, illustrator.
He completed his studies in Helsinki, then in Paris, where he attended the studio of Cormon (1890-91) and the Académie Julian (1898), and in Florence (1897-98). He made decorative panels for the Finnish pavilion at the Exposition Universelle 1900 in Paris, where he was honoured with a silver medal. For many years he taught at the Academy in Helsinki.
Postcards: several from the period 1910-30, amongst them there is a series inspired by Kalevala.
Bibl.: Johanson-Termonen 1983.

Henri GERBAULT
Châtenay, Hauts-de-Seine, 1863 – Roscoff, 1930
Illustrator, commercial artist, cartoonist, watercolourist, graphic designer (song scores, programmes).
A nephew of the poet Sully-Prudhomme. He was a student of P. Colin, P. Dubois and H. Gervex. He worked on the magazines: *L'art et la mode*, *Le Courrier Français* (1886-90), *Gil Blas illustré*, *Lectures pour tous*, *Monde illustré*, *Revue Mame*, *Le Rire*, *Sourire*, *Vie moderne*, *La vie parisienne* (1888-90), *Les premières illustrées*. He was the author of the albums: *Les éréintés de la vie* and *Etoiles* by F. Champsaur (1888); *Paris, voici Paris* by H. Seigneur (1889); *Chansons due Chat Noir* (1890) and *Nouvelles Chansons . . .* (1892) by Mac Nab; *Lettres de femmes* by Prévost (1895); *Le Cirque et les forains* by H. Frichet (1897); *L'Ami des enfants* by Berquin (1898); *Les Gosses de Paris* by J. Lévy (1898); *Chansons du vieux temps* by J. Tiersot (1904). In collaboration with others he illustrated *Entrées de clowns* (1885), *Lulu* (1888, 1901), *La gomme* (1889) by F. Champsaur; *Contes* by Perrault (1897).
Postcards: 1 p. in the 'Collection des Cent', publ. Gréningaire, Paris, c.1901; 1 p. in the series 'Les Affiches Celebres', publ. Tuck, London; 1 p. in the series 'Les Voeux de la France, Rire Rouge', 1 p. in the series 'Les Chansons de France de M. Boukay', 1915 ca.; several erotic subjects.
Bibl.: Baudet 1978.

Remigius GEYLING
Vienna, 29.6.1878 – Vienna, 4.3.1974
Graphic designer (calendars, commercial graphics), commercial artist, designer of fabrics, fashion accessories, of jewellery, of glass windows, scenographer and theatrical costumier and cinematographer.
He was the son of the glass window manufacturer Rudolf. He attended the Kunstgewerbeschule in Vienna and from 1902 to 1904 the Academy in Munich (L. Herterich, F. V. Stuck, W. Thöny). From 1928 to 1946 he taught at the Kunstgewerbeschule. In 1908 he was one of the main organisers of the festivities for the Jubilee of the Kaiser (600 drawings of costumes). He worked on the newspaper *Die Muskete*.
Exhibitions: Exposition Universelle in Paris 1900; Kunstschau, Vienna 1908.
Postcards: 13 p. in the series of the Wiener Werkstätte, 8 p. for the Kaiser's Jubilee in 1908 (nos. 164-167, 177, 181, 185, 186). 5 p. of fashion (nos. 283-287).
Bibl.: Cat. Wien 1964; Mrazek 1977; Baudet 1980; Hansen 1982; Schweiger 1982.

Charles Dana GIBSON
Roxbury, Massachusetts, 14.9.1867 – New York, 23.12.1944
Painter, commercial artist, illustrator.
He attended the Arts Students League in New York and the Académie Julian in Paris from 1884 to 1885. His designs for several American magazines, first of all for *Life*, had enormous success and launched a fashion. He created a feminine type the 'Gibson Girl' – volatile, sporty, proud, carefree – known worldwide as the paradigm of American beauty, and emulated by many other American and even European designers, but unsurpassed in the psychological and formality qualities of their design. The models of the 'Gibson Girl' influenced fashion, recreation and hairstyles of the period. He illustrated many books and also wrote some of their texts. He was president of the Society of Illustrators. He worked on several magazines: *Collier's Weekly*, *Cosmopolitan*, *Life* (which he edited from 1920), *McClure's*, *Lectures pour Tous*, *Scribner's*, *Harper's*, *The Century*.
Postcards: several series, all with the glamour theme of the 'Gibson Girl', mostly published by James Henderson & Sons, London, often reproducing illustrations from the magazine *Snap-Shots*, but the same publisher. They are published in 'sepia collogravure' or in photochalcography. At the end of 1903 the series 'C. D. Gibson's Drawings' (4 series of 6 p.), 'The Education of Mr. Pipp' (4 series of 9 p.) existed. Many other series followed of 6 p. Some p. were reproduced by A. Schweizer Kunstverlag, Hamburg ('Gibson Karten').
Bibl: Lyons·1975; Holt 1980, 1983.

Charles Allan GILBERT
Hartford, Connecticut, 1873-?
Illustrator, painter.
His biographical details are unknown. He studied in New York and in Paris.
Postcards: several series above all in the glamour genre, in which he proposed a variant on the 'Gibson Girl'; in the series 'Pictorial Comedy', J. Henderson & Son, London.
Bibl.: Holt 1980, 1983.

Adolphe-Paul GIRALDON
Marseille, 4.5.1855 – Paris, 1933
Painter, engraver, illustrator, commercial artist, graphic designer (books, ex libris, song scores, lettering), designer of furniture, fabrics, tapestries, jewellery, metalwork, ceramics, interior designer.
He was a pupil of the landscape painter F.-L. Français, of the sculptor A. Lequien and the painter and illustrator L.-O. Merson. From 1879 he exhibited at the Salon (from 1897 to 1913 in that of the Société Nationale des Beaux-Arts). He illustrated the books: *Tolla* by E. About (1889), *Missel de Jeanne d'Arc* (1895); *Aspasie* (1898); *Bartet* (1903); *Le Chansonnier Normand* (1905); *Les Eglogues de Virgile* (1906); *Les Nuits* by A. Musset (1911); *La Vie des abeilles* by M. Maeterlinck (1918). In 1897 he designed the initials for O. Uzanne's magazine *Le Livre*. In 1906 (for the Deberny foundry) he designed the typeface 'Giraldon-Antiqua' which was used for books for bibliophiles and was almost as successful as the 'Grasset' and 'Auriol' typefaces. From 1907 he designed almost 400 book-bindings. He worked on the magazines *Revue Illustrée* (for which he illustrated, in collaboration with others, the 1888 supplement *Roses et Noël* and *L'Estampe moderne*). He was asked to teach at Glasgow School of Art because of his competence in book design.

Postcards: 1 p. in the 'Collection des Cent', publ. Gréningaire, Paris, c.1901; 1 p. in the series 'Byrrh', 1906; 1 p. in the series 'Album Mariani', c.1910.
Bibl.: Baudet 1978; Neudin 1983.

Louis-Auguste GIRARDOT
Loulans-les-Forges, Haute-Saône, 1858 – Paris 1933
Painter, lithographer, commercial artist.
He was a pupil of J.-L. Gérôme and P. Dubois. He exhibited from 1881 to 1889 at the Salon of the Société des Artistes Français and from 1890 at the Salon of the Société Nationale des Beaux-Arts. He was a member of the Société des Peintres Orientalistes.
Postcards: 1 p. in the 'Collection des Cent', publ. Gréningaire, c.1901; 1 p. in the series 'Album Mariani', c.1910; series of women in African costume (included in the series is the p. which was in the 'Collection des Cent').
Bibl.: Baudet 1978; Neudin 1979.

GOLIA, pseudonym for Eugenio COLMO
Turin, 29.10.1885 – Turin, 15.9.1967
Caricaturist, illustrator, fashion designer, ceramicist, commercial artist, graphic designer (publicity graphics), painter.
He was at school with Guido Gozzano, who coined his nickname Golia, on account of his tallness. He began to study law, but abandoned it to devote himself to caricature for several humorous magazines. In 1911 he organized with G. Manca the international Salon of humour 'Frigidarium' in the castle at Rivoli and he began work on the magazine *La Donna*. In 1914 he began working intensively as an illustrator for children's books (he wrote the text of some of them), and he founded the satirical magazine *Numero* (published until 1922), which was involved in a fervid interventionist campaign in support of the war. After the first world war he was also active as a painter, ceramicist, commercial artist and graphic designer.
Postcards: 'Omaggio della stampa sportiva ai visitatori della IV esposozione internazionale del-l'automobilismo, Torino 1907'; 'Al Verde, 1908, Veglione Studenti Sartine'; Velgione Dantesco Torino 1910; 'Pro Bibliotechine Rurali Zia Mariu, 1910'; 'Festa delle Fragole', 1913; several for the national loan, c. 1915; several satirical p. of war progaganda, 1915-18; series of 'donnine', 1915-18.
Bibl.: Bartoli-Mataloni 1979; Gaibazzi 1979; Mordente 1982; Arrasich 1984.

Auguste François GORGUET
Paris 27.9.1862 – Paris, 1927
Painter, illustrator, commercial artist, tapestry designer, lithographer, graphic designer (menus, theatre programmes).
He was a pupil of G. Boulanger, J.-L. Gérôme and L. Bonnat. From 1883 he exhibited at the Salon. In 1899 he exhibited paintings at the Exposition Universelle in Paris. With the support of a grant he made study trips to Spain, where he studied early tapestries, and to Italy, where he broadened his knowledge of the frescoes of the XIV and XV centuries in Siena, Padua and Pisa. Echoes of these studies are evident in the fresco showing king Jean Le Bon, in the Gothic room in the town hall in Douai and in the Gobelins made for the Rennes Parliament. He was above all well-known as a fresco painter and Gobelins designer, he also illustrated books and worked on the magazines: *Le Chat Noir*, *Figaro illustré*, *Paris*

illustré, La Vie moderne, Lectures pour Tous.
He illustrated the books *Gauche célèbre* by
Gyp (1886); *Reine Janvier* by H. Lavedan
(1886); *Pierrot et sa conscience* by F. Champsaur (1896); *Sapho* by A. Daudet (1897); *Le
Procurateur de Judeée* (1902) and *Le Lys rouge*
(1903) by A. France; *Capitaines courageux* by
R. Kipling (1903); *El Cid* by Corneille (1909);
Bains de Phalère by L. Bertrant (1910); *La
Princesse lointaine* (1910) and *Musardises*
(1911) by E. Rostand. In collaboration with
others he illustrated: *La Feuille à l'envers* by E.
Montagne (1885, with Fau); *Entrée de clowns*
by F. Champsaur (1885); *Contes à la paresseuse* by Dubut de Laforest (1885); *Amour
suprême* by Villiers de l'Ilse Adam (1886); *Nos
Ancêtres* by A. Rolland (1889). He collaborated on L'Estampe moderne.
Postcards: 1 p. in the 'Collection des Cent',
publ. Gréningaire, c. 1901.
Bibl.: Baudet 1978; Neudin 1983.

Xavier GOSÉ
Alcalá de Henares, 2.7.1876 – Lérida,
16.3.1915
Illustrator, commercial artist, painter, designer, graphic designer (musical scores).
He studied at the School of Fine Arts in
Barcelona and he then worked in the studio of
Josep Lluis Pellicer. From 1910 to 1914 he
lived in Paris, where he exhibited at the Salon
of the Société Nationale des Beaux-Arts (1903)
and he worked on the newspapers *Le Rire* and
L'Assette au Beurre. A series of his drawings of
Paris were exhibited in 1911 in Barcelona. He
also worked for *Jugend, Simplicissimus* and
several Catalan magazines: *(El Gato Negro,
Hispania, Ilustració Catalana, La Ilustració
Llevantina, Catalunya Artistica, Quartre Gats,
Pèl & Ploma)*.
Postcards: 1 p. in the 'Collection des Cent',
publ. Gréningaire, Paris, c. 1901; 1 p. for
'Byrrh', 1906; New Year p. for Ribalta
champagne.
Bibl.: Trenc Ballester 1977; Baudet 1978.

Fernand Louis GOTTLOB
Paris, 1873 – Paris, 1935
Painter, lithographer, caricaturist, commercial
artist, illustrator, graphic designer (song
scores).
He was a student of the painter-decorator F.-
A.-M. Jobbé-Dival sen. From 1891 he exhibited lithographic prints inspired by E. Carrière
at the Salon des Artistes Français. From c.
1897 he was active as a caricaturist and illustrator for magazines like *Le Rire, L'Assiette au
Beurre, Gil Blas illustré, Le Sourire*. He illustrated the books: *Interieurs d'officiers* by M.
Corday (1894), *Boubouroche* by G. Courteline
(1907), *Trop jolie* by R. Maizeroy (1912). He
made several posters, above all for opera.
Postcards: series 'Les trottins de Paris'.

Otto GRÄBER
Eberbach am Neckar, 12.2.1885 – Karlsruhe,
17.3.1952
Painter, etcher, graphic designer.
He attended from 1900 to 1904 the
Kunstgewerbeschule and from 1904 to 1912 the
Academy in Karlsruhe. From 1908 to 1912 he
was the pupil of W. Trübner.
Postcards: 'Gruss vom Schlusskommers der
Kunstgewerbeschüler in Karlsruhe'.

Oskar GRAF
Freiburg, 26.12.1873 – Göppingen, 22.2.1958
Painter, commercial artist, graphic designer.

He attended the Academy in Munich (with H.
Knirr, Schmid-Reutte, Hölzel). Around 1900
he is recorded as active in Dachau and from
1901 in Munich. From 1919 he taught at the
Technische Hochschule in Munich.
Postcards: 'Ausstellung Büro u. Geschäftshaus. Munchen. 1913', a reproduction of the
poster.

Eugène GRASSET
Lausanne, 25.5.1841 (or 1843, 1844, 1845) –
Sceaux, 23.10.1917
Lithographer, commercial artist, illustrator,
graphic designer (musical scores, calendars,
lettering, books, stamps), painter, interior designer, designer of furniture, of glass windows,
of ceramics, of fabrics, of wallpaper, of mosaics, of jewellery, of wrought iron, art theorist.
He was the son of a cabinet-maker, he attended courses in architecture for two years at the
Polytechnic in Zurich, and he worked in a
studio in Lausanne. In 1866 he made a journey
to Egypt. In 1871 he settled in Paris, where he
earned his living making fabric and wallpaper
designs, and he taught himself art, having
particular interest in the works of Viollet-le-
Duc and Japanese graphic art. Between 1877
and 1878 he completed his first experiments in
photo-engraving patented by Charles Gillot,
which he used to make the illustrations for the
children's story by Saint-Juirs *Le Petit Nab* and
which he then used for other books (e.g. the
book *Histoire des quatre Fils Aymon* (1883).
Between 1880 and 1881 he designed some
furniture for Ch. Gillot's house, which was still
medievalist in style. From the '80s he was
active as a commercial artist and designer of
the covers and illustrations for several magazines: *Courrier français, Figaro illustré, Paris
illustré* (1888), *Revue illustrée*, Frank Leslie's
Illustrated Newspaper (1882), *Harper's Bazaar*
(1889, 1891, 1892), *La Grande Dame* (1893).
In collaboration with others he illustrated the
books: *Clair de lune* by Maupassant (1884),
Les Échos du Nord by R. Ponsard (1884),
Scènes et episodes de l'Histoire nationale by Ch.
Seignobos (1891). In the last decade of the
century he extended his activities to other
areas: he made mosaic decorations for the
church of St-Étienne in Briare (1895-97); ceramics for the Müller company in Ivry (1895);
the famous typeface which bears his name for
the Peignot printing works (1897); windows for
churches and secular buildings in France and
the United States (amongst these the series 'La
Vie de Jeanne d'Arc' for the Cathedral in
Orleans 1893 and the windows for the Chamber of Commerce in Paris 1900, are outstanding). In 1894 he held a one-man show at the
offices of the magazine *La Plume*, which
honoured him as one of the foremost artists of
Art Nouveau in France. In this period he was
also teaching decorative composition at the
École Guérin. The result of his didactic efforts
were the volumes *La Plante et ses applications
ornementales* (1896-98) and *La Méthode de
Composition ornementale* (1905).
Postcards: 2 p. in the series 'Cinos', 1898,
reproducing the posters 'Napoléon-The Century Magazine' 'The June Century-Napoleon in
Egypt'; 1 p. in the 'Collection des Cent', publ.
Gréningaire, Paris, 1901, reproducing the
poster for the Salon des Cent 1894; 1 p. in the
series 'Les Affiches Célèbres', publ. Tuck,
London, reproducing the poster 'A la Place
Clichy' c. 1891.
Bibl.: Baudet 1978, 1980; *La Cartolina*, n. 12,
1983; Arrasich 1984.

Vittorio GRASSI
Rome, 14.7.1878 – Rome, 1958
Painter, engraver, interior designer, scenographer and theatrical costumier, illustrator,
commercial artist, designer of furniture, fashion, ceramics, windows, graphic designer,
(stamps, publicity and commercial graphics, ex
libris).
He was self-taught. From 1903 he took part in
the Roman exhibitions of the Amatori e Cultori and in 1905 he joined the group 'IXXV
della Campagna Romana'. From 1908 he published furnishing designs in the magazine *La
Casa*. He worked on the magazines *Novissima*
(1910), *Roma* (1911), *Harmonia* (1913), *Noi e
il Mondo* (1913), *Il Primato Artistico* (1918-
19). He took part in the exhibitions of the
Roman Secession (1913, 1914, 1915) for which
he decorated some rooms and designed posters
and catalogue covers. From 1913 to 1949 he
was professor of ornament, engraving and
scenography at the Accademia di Belle Arti in
Rome. In 1915 he installed the Italian pavilion
at the exhibition in San Francisco. He illustrated *Vita Nova* by Dante (1917-21). From 1921
he taught furnishing and interior design at the
new Sculoa Superiore di Architettura in
Rome. From 1921 he edited the magazine
Architettura e Arti Decorative, for which he
designed the cover.
Postcards: 1 p. in the publicity series for the
newspaper *Travaso delle idee* ('Il Travaso ne
paese delle freddure'), c. 1910; several war
propaganda and regimental p., 1915-18.
Bibl.: Mordente 1982; *La Carolina*, III (1983,
n. 10), pp. 20-21; Arrasich 1984.

Guillem de GRAU
Barcelona, 1875 – Barcelona, 1944
Painter, illustrator.
He took part in several group exhibitions in
Barcelona showing landscapes and portraits.
Postcards: series of 5 publicity p. for the wines
'Jaume Serra'.
Bibl.: Trenc Ballester 1977.

Kate (Catherine) GREENAWAY
London, 17.3.1846 – Hampstead, 7.11.1901
Watercolourist, illustrator
She was the daughter of a wood engraver. She
attended the National Art Training School in
South Kensington, the Heatherley School of
Fine Art and the Slade School of Fine Art (A.
Legros) in London. From 1877 she attended
the Royal Academy and started to work for the
publisher E. Evans.
She was the author of many illustrated
children's books, which were very successful
and influential, including *Under the Window*
(1878), *Kate Greenaway's Birthday Book for
Children* (1880), *London Lyrics* (1881), *Almanacks* (1884), *Language of Flowers* (1884).
She worked on the magazines: *People's Magazine, Little Folks, The Illustrated London
News, Cassel's Magazine*, etc. She designed
greetings cards for the publisher Marcus Ward
& Co, from the first years of the '80s.
Postcards: Some series were published after
her death in the period 1902-1914, and reproduced her drawings and illustrations.
Bibl.: White 1894; Neudin 1978.

H. B. GRIGGS
His biographical details are unknown. An
American author of many decorative postcards
(greetings, Valentine etc.), signed H.B.G.
Only part of his work can be directly related to
Art Nouveau.

Bibl.: E. Austin, *Checklist of H. B. Griggs signed Postcards*, Pawcatuck, Conn., 1972.

Jules Alexandre GRÜN
Paris, 25.5.1868 – Paris, 15.2.1934
Illustrator, commercial artist, painter.
He was a student of Lavastre and A. Guillemet. From 1887 he exhibited at the Salon of the Société des Artistes Français. With Faivre, Léandre, Steinlen and Willette, he was a member of the group 'Taverne de Paris'. He designed silhouettes for shadow shows for several Montmartre theatres and cabarets, for which he also made several posters. As an illustrator he collaborated with the magazines: *La Caricature*, *Fin de Siècle*, *Courrier français*, *L'Assiette au Beurre*, *Le Rire*, *Le Sourire*, À la Baïonnette.

He designed the illustrations for *Chansons sans gêne* by Xanrof and he collaborated with Bofa, Brunelleschi, Cappiello, Faivre and Sem, on the *Album de Luxe* published in 1912 by the Société des Artistes Humoristes.
Postcards: 1 p. in the 'Collection des Cent', publ. Gréningaire, Paris, c. 1901; p. in the series 'Affiches Gérin', c. 1901; p. in the series 'Gala Henry Monnier', 1904; 1 p. in the series 'Album Mariani', c. 1910; p. in the series 'Affiches des Chemins de fer'; p. in the series 'Les Affiches célèbres' ('Moulin Rouge'), publ. Tuck, London.
Bibl.: Weill 1977; Baudet 1978, 1980; Forissier 1978.

Giovanni GUERRINI
Imola, 28.5.1887 – Rome, 1972
Painter, engraver, lithographer, commercial artist, illustrator, graphic artist (books, ex libris), designer of furniture and wrought iron.
After his early artistic studies in Faenza with A. Berti, he attended the Academy in Bologna and the Art Institute in Florence. He was in touch with the circle of D. Baccarini and worked initially in engraving, with a preference for lithography. He executed decorative frescoes in several buildings in Faenza, amongst them those in the Albergo Vittoria (1909). In 1919 he began a fresco cycle in the great room in the Palazzo Byron in Ravenna, which was entirely destroyed when fire devastated the palace. He was also intensely active in applied arts: he designed covers, book illustrations, posters (in 1923 he won a prize in the competition for the exhibition on Monza), wrought iron lamps manufactured by Matteucci in Faenza, furniture made by the cabinet maker Casalini in Faenza. He exhibited at the Biennale in Venice in 1912, 1914 and 1920. In 1924 he became the director of the Academy in Perugia and he was also a professor at the Accademia di Belle Arti in Ravenna.
Postcards: 'Esposizione di Faenza. III centenario della nascita di Evangelista Torricelli', 1908.
Bibl.: Mordente 1982; Arrasich 1984.

Albert-André GUILLAUME
Paris, 14.2.1873 – Faux, Dordogne, 1942
Caricaturist, illustrator, commercial artist, painter, watercolourist, graphic designer (menus, programmes).
Son of the architect Edmond G., a professor at the École des Beaux-Arts in Paris. In 1891 he attended the studio of J.-L. Gérôme at the École des Beaux-Artsé, but he was self-taught. Already in 1890 he published the album *Les Bonshommes* (II vol., 1892), followed by: *Petites femmes* (1891); *Les Mémoires d'unne*

glace (1893); *Faut voir* (1894); *Mes Campagnes* (1895); *Etoile de mer* (1895); *Y a des dames* (1896); *Madame est servie* (1897); *Pour vos beaux yeux* (1899); *Revue de fin d'année* (1900); *Mon sursis* (1901). In collaboration with Caran d'Ache, he illustrated À la decouverte de la Russie. He illustrated the children's albums *Le repas à travers les âges* (1890); *Le Tennis à travers le âges* (1890); *Monsieur Strong* (1890); and the books: *En se cherchant* by H. Gautier (1890); *Manuel des exercises physiques* by Strehly (1890); *L'Année fantaisiste* by Willy (1891; in coll. with Christophe); *Armour et la vie* by Xanrof (1894); *Théâtreuses* by A. Germain (1895); *Train de 8h47* by G. Courteline (1896). He worked on the magazines: *L'Assiette au Beurre*; *La Caricature*; *Le Courrier français*; *Figaro illustré*; *Franc-Gascon*; *Gaulois*; *Gil Blas illustré*; *The Graphic*; *Le Journal*; *Le Matin*; *Monde illustré*; *Le Rire*; *Tatler*. In 1899 he exhibited at the Salon of the Société Nationale des Beaux-Arts the pictorial frieze for the Théâtre des Bonshommes.
Postcards: 1 p. in the series 'Cinos', 1898, reproducing 'Le Pole Nord'; 1 p. in the 'Collection des Cent', publ. Gréningaire, Paris, c. 1901; 1 p. in the series 'Les Voeux de la France, Rire Rouge', 1914; 1 p. in the series 'Les Chansons de France de M. Boukay', c. 1915; series 'Anti-paludéenne'; series 'La Valse', Imp. Camis, Paris; publicity series for Chocolat Louit of c. 70 p. with scenes of military life; publicity p. 'Soldat: prends chaque jour ta quinine'; publicity p. 'Service de Santé Psépia'; several publicity cards for humorous albums (Contre le Spleen, etc); several reproducing plates from albums; series 'Nos Humoristes'.
Bibl.: Baudet 1978, 1980; Neudin 1983.

H

Wenzel August HABLIK
Brüx, Bohemia (Most, Czechoslovakia), 4.8.1881 –
Itzehoe, Hamburg, 24.3.1934
Painter, etcher, graphic designer, (ex libris, paper money, publicity graphics), architect, designer of fabrics, wallpaper, furniture, fashion, jewellery, ceramist.
He worked as a carpenter in his father's workshop. He attended from 1898 the Fachschule in Teplitz, from 1902 the Kunstgewerbeschule in Vienna (F. V. Myrbach, R. V. Larish, C. O. Czeschka) and in 1905 the Prague Academy (F. Thiele). In 1907 he opened an art school in Königsberg with his friend O. Ewel. He worked on the magazine *Kunstwart*. In 1907 the wood merchant R. Biel asked him to redesign his house in Itzehoe, where Hablik decided to settle and where he remained for the rest of his life. IN 1909 he made the series of etchings 'Schaffende Kräfte', he exhibited at the Berlin Secession in 1908 and at the third exhibition of the group 'Sturm' (Berlin, 1912). In 1915 he finished a cycle of engravings: 'Das Meer'. Between 1909 and 1924 he painted and designed several architectural pieces which made him one of the most interesting figures of German Expressionism. In 1919 he was a member of the Arbeitsrat für Kunst in Berlin and he took part in the exhibition 'Unbekannte Architekten'. In 1917 he opened in Itzehoe with his wife Lisbeth Lindemann the 'Hablik-Lindemann handweberei', which long continued to produce fabrics.

Postcards: 'Ortsgruppe Brüx des deutschen Schulvereines', 1902; Several with views of modern architecture in Hamburg.

Artur Lajos HALMI
Budapest, 8.12.1866 – Budapest, 1939
Painter, illustrator.
He attended the Academy in Munich (L. v. Löfftz). He was active in Munich and in Berlin. He worked on the magazines *Meggendorfer Blätter* and *Jugend* from 1896.
Postcards: in the first three series of 'Künstler-Postkarten' for Jugend, G. Hirth, Munich, 1998-99.
Bibl.: Baudet 1980.

Elsa HAMMAR MOESCHLIN
Stockholm, 9.1.1879 – Brissago, Switzerland, 16.8.1950
Painter, woodcut artist, graphic designer (commercial and publicity graphics).
She was trained at the Technical School in Stockholm. She made study trips to Paris (1903-06), Italy, Holland (1906) and to Munich (1908). Between 1907 to 1914 she was active in Switzerland. In 1909 she married the writer Felix Moeschlin from Basel. She exhibited in the exhibitions in Stockholm (1911), Lund (1912) in Malmö (1914). As an illustrator she was mainly active in the field of children's books.
Postcards: several greetings.

Walter Sigmund HAMPEL
Vienna, 17.7.1868 – Nussdorf am Attersee, 17.1.1949
Painter, watercolourist, graphic artist (books), designer of painting on glass, of decorations, inventor of decalcomania.
He attended the Staatsgewerbeschule of the IV Bezirk in Vienna and from 1885 to 1888 the Academy (A. Eisenmerger, H. v. Angeli, S. L'Allemand), from which he was expelled for his opposition to conservative teaching methods. He was a member of the group of artists who gravitated towards the 'Siebener Club'. From 1910 to 1911 he was a member of the Hagenbund.
Postcards: series 'Wiener Künstler-Postkarten', Philipp & Kramer, Vienna, 1898-1901: VI (cyclists), VII (cyclists), XI (beach scenes), XIII, XVII (Carnivals), XXX (singing cafés); XLII, LXII; P. publ. Gerlach & Schenk, Vienna; P. in the series II 'Künstler-Postkarten' for Jugend, G. Hirth, Munich, 1898.
Bibl.: Neudin 1978, 1980; Gaibazzi 1979; Drago 1981; Holt 1981, 1983.

Hansi, pseudonym of J. J. WALTZ
Colmar, Haut-Rhin, 23.2.1873 – Colmar, 10.6.1951
Engraver, illustrator, cartoonist.
The son of an Alsatian engraver and curator in the museum in Colmar, he studied industrial design at Lyon. He was famous for a series of albums, prints and popular images which have as their subject the Alsatian protest against German oppression and the return of Alsace to France. Condemned to imprisonment by the tribunal in Leipzig, he returned to France at the beginning of the first world war, where he made anti-German propaganda. Between 1914 and 1918 he published a series of prints 'Images de petits soldats'. He illustrated the books: *Le Professeur Knatsche* (1896); *Histoire de Alsace* (1913); *Mon village* (1913 or 1920); *Le paradis bicolore* (1918); *L'Alsace heureuse* (1919); *Colmar en France* (1923); À travers les lignes

ennemies; *La Merveilleuse histoire de Saint-Florentin; Tours et portes d'Alsace; Histoire de l'Alsace racontée aux petits enfants; Die Hochkönigsburg.*
Postcards: 1p. in the series 'Album Mariani', c. 1910; several reproducing his book illustrations, several of anti-German propagandas about the annexation of Alsace to France; several of war propagandas.
Bibl.: Baudet 1978; M. Thomasin and Lajournade, *'Hansi', Le Collectionneur Francais,* maggio-giugno 1978; Zeyons 1979; Holt 1981.

Dudley HARDY
Sheffield, Yorkshire, 15.1.1867 – London, 11.8.1922
Painter, commercial artist, illustrator.
He was the son of the painter Thomas Busch Hardy. He studied at the Academy in Düsseldorf, with M.C. Verlat in Antwerp, and from 1888 to 1889 with R. Collin and P. -A. -J. Dagnan-Bouveret in Paris. From 1886 he made drawings for several London newspapers and magazines, including *The Pictorial World, The Lady's Pictorial, The Graphic, The Illustrated London News, Punch, Black and White,* etc. From 1890 he regularly took part in the exhibitions of the Royal Academy and of the Society of British Artists. His 1894 poster for the musical 'A Gaiety Girl', an original interpretation of Chéret's posters, made him enormously famous.
Postcards: several in the series 1502, 'Celebrated Posters', R. Tuck, London, 1903 ('The Pearl Girl', 'Egyptian Mail Steamship Co.', 'Royal Naval Tournament', etc): 'Dancing Maiden', H. J. Smith, 1902; series of sporting ladies, F. Hartmann, London, 1903; several humorous p. R. Tuck, London.
Bibl.: Holt 1980, 1983.

Florence HARDY
Her biographical details are unknown.
Postcards: several series with children and couples in costumes, produced by publishers in several countries including B. Dondorf (Frankfurt a.M.), M. Munk (Vienna) and above all C. W. Faulkner (London; in the first decade of the century).
Bibl.: Cope 1978; Holt 1980, 1983.

John HASSAL
Walmer, Kent, 1868 – London, 8.3.1948
Painter, xylographer, watercolourist, commercial artist, illustrator.
He attended the Academy in Antwerp (V. Havermaet) and l'Académie Julian in Paris (A. Bouguereau). A member of the London Sketch Club, he became its president in 1913. He was involved in many sectors of applied graphic arts, particularly in posters (c. 600) and in illustrated books. He worked on the magazines *Daily Graphic, Punch, The Graphic Illustrated London News, Moonshine, Pick-Me-Up, Sketch,* etc.
Postcards: 'Celebrated Posters', R. Tuck, London 1903, series 1500 ('Colman's Mustard'), 1501 ('A Country Girl'), 1507 ('Shredded Wheat'); several publicity p. 'Blackpool Herald', 'Everybody's', 'Nestles Milk', 'Sternol Oil', 'Sunlight Soap', 'Tantalum Lamps', etc.; several publicity p. for theatrical shows for the publisher David Allen, London, and other publishers; at least 20 series of humorous p. for Davidson Bros., London, often reproducing book illustrations; several humorous series for different publishers; series of greetings p. for R. Tuck, London.

Bibl.: Cope 1978; Holt 1980, 1983.

Paul HAUSTEIN
Chemnitz, 17.5.1880 – Stuttgart, 6.9.1944
Painter, graphic designer, illustrator, commercial artist, metalwork designer, jeweller, ceramics.
He attended from 1896 to 1897 the Kunstgewerbeschule in Dresden; from 1897 to 1898 the Kunstgewerbeschule in Munich; from 1898 to 1899 the Academy in Munich (J. Herterich). From 1903 to 1904 he was a member of the Künstlerkolonie in Darmstadt. He collaborated on the magazine *Jugend* (from 1897). He published with R. Rochga the album *Étoffes Modernes,* Paris, s.d. (c. 1900).
Postcards: series of p. for the 'Ausstellung der Darmstädter Künstlerkolonie in Darmstadt 1904'
Bibl.: cat. Darmstadt 1977.

Ernst HEILEMANN
Berlin, 8.8.1870 – ?
Painter, graphic designer, illustrator.
He attended the Academy in Berlin, then he studied on his own by travelling in Europe and in America. He worked on the magazines *Die Lustige Blätter, Simplicissimus, Jugend.*
Postcards: in the series for *Die Lustige Blätter,* with scenes of fashionable Berlin life.

Thomas Theodor HEINE
Leipzig, 28.2.1867 – Stockholm, 26.1.1948
Painter, commercial artist, illustrator.
He attended from 1883 to 1887 the Academy in Düsseldorf. From 1889 he was in Munich. In 1933 he moved to Prague, then to Oslo and Stockholm. He collaborated on *Jugend, Fliegende Blätter, Simplicissimus,* and other magazines.
Postcards: 'Berliner Secession', reproducing the poster M. Fischer Kunstverlag, Berlin, 1901; p. in the series for *Simplicissimus;* publicity for the cabaret 'Die elf Scharfrichter'; publicity p. 'Künstler Kneipe Simplicissimus', Verlag Hans Pernat, Spezialhaus für Ansichtskarten, Munich.
Bibl.: cat. Altonaer Museum, Hamburg 1970; Lebeck 1978; Weiss 1985 (II).

Paul César François HELLEU
Vannes, Morbihan, 17.12.1859 – Paris, 23.3.1927.
Engraver, painter, commercial.
From 1874 to 1876 he studied with J. -L. Gérôme at the Ecole des Beaux-Arts in Paris. Then he worked in the workshop of the ceramist J. Th. Deck. From 1885 he was involved in engraving. He exhibited at the Society of Painters and Etchers in London. He worked on the magazines *The Graphic* (1901) and *Jugend.*
Postcards: several, mainly black and white, with Parisian women as their subject.
Bibl.: Weill 1977.

Joseph HÉMARD
Murreaux (Yvelines), 2.8.1880 – Paris, 9.8.1961
Cartoonist, illustrator, scenographer
He worked on the newspapers *L'Assiette au Beurre, Fantasio, Journal amusant, Lectures pour tous, Pêle-Mêle* (1899). *Le Rire, Le Sourire, La Vie Parisienne.* He illustrated the book *L'Infortune Plumard* by R. Bringer (1908). After the first world war he became intensely involved in book illustration.
Postcards: 1 p. in the series 'Byrrh', 1906.

Bibl.: Baudet 1978.

Edwin Hermann Richard HENEL
Breslau (Wroclaw, Poland), 21.11.1883 – Garmisch-Partenkirchen, 7.3.1953
Painter, commercial artist, graphic designer.
He attended the Academy in Breslau from 1908-1910.
Postcards: for air shows, reproducing the posters without text, Edwin Henel, Munich, 1913.

Arsene HERBINIER
Paris, 14.5.1869 – ?
Lithographer, painter.
He was a pupil of L. O. Merson, E. Grasset and Broquelet. From 1909 he was a member of the Société des Artistes Français.
Postcards: 1 p. in the 'Collection des Cent', publ. Gréningaire, Paris, c. 1901; 1 p. in the series 'Byrrh', 1906.
Bibl.: Baudet 1978.

René Georges HERMANN-PAUL
Paris, 27.12.1864 (or 1874) – Les Saintes Maries-de-lar-Mer, July 1940.
Illustrator, caricaturist, commercial artist, painter, lithographer, woodcut artist.
He studied at the Ecole des Arts décoratifs in Paris and at the Académie Julian. He was a student of H. Lerolle and G. Colin. His first works were the lithographic prints which show the influence of Toulouse-Lautrec, Bonnard and Vallotton, his companions at the Acedémie Julian. From 1892 he was intensely active as a caricaturist and illustrator, working on the magazines: *L'Album* (1902), *L'Assiette au Beurre, Le Canard Sauvage, Candide, Le Courrier Européen, Le Courrier Français, Le Cri de Paris, L'Écho de Paris, Les Droits de l'Homme, La Feuille, Frou-Frou, Gil Blas illustré, L'Escarmouche, L'Homme Libre, Le Journal, Le Petit Bleu, Le Rire, Les Temps Nouveaux, La Vie Parisienne.* In 1899 he published in *Figaro* vignettes in favour of the Dreyfus cause. During the war he contributed patriotic propaganda designs to the newspapers *La Guèrre Sociale, L'Opinion, La Victoire.* He was the author of the albums: *La vie di M. Quelconque* (1895); *La L'Alphabet pour les grands enfants* (1897). He illustrated the books *Transatlantiques* by A. Hermant (1904), and *Le Veau Gras* (1904). From 1915 he worked in xylography, which he used in the *Calendrier de guèrre* (1915, 1916) and in the album *Danse macabre* (1919) and which he used after the war to illustrate books. He spent the last years of his life in the Camargue, to which he devoted the series of lithographic prints *Heures Carmarguaises* (1931).
Postcards: 1 p. in the 'Collection des Cent', publ. Gréningaire, Paris, c. 1901; 3 p. in the series 'Leur Code', 'Leur Discipline', 'Leur Justice' from the collection 'À bas la justice militaire', 1904; 1 p. in the series 'Pochette de la Paix', 1907; 1 p. in the series 'Album Mariani' c. 1910; 2 p. in the series 'Patriotisme et colonisation' and 'Gravures de Berger' from the collection 'Les Temps Nouveaux'.
Bibl.: Baudet 1978.

Paul HEY
Munich, 19.10.1867 – Munich, 1952.
Painter, etcher, illustrator.
He entered the Academy in Munich (K. Raupp, J. Herterich, L. v. Löfftz). He made study trips to Italy, Greece, Egypt, England, Scotland. From 1906 he made a series of large lithographic plates for schools, with illustra-

tions of fables.
Postcards: 'Volksliederkarten', 1900–1910; series of P. with subjects of *Heimat,* Druck Hubert Köhler, Munich, 1900–1910.
Bibl.: cat. Altonaer Museum, Hamburg 1970; Douliez 1980.

Josef HOFFMANN
Pirnitz, Moravia, 15.12.1870 – Vienna, 7.5.1956
Architect, designer of fabrics, wallpapers, furniture, objects of daily use, furnishing jewellery, toys, glass, metalwork, ceramist, commercial artist, illustrator, graphic designer (books).
From 1892 to 1895 he studied at the academy in Vienna (Architekturklasse of K. Hasenauer and then of O. Wagner). From 1898 he taught at the Kunstgewerbeschule. From c. 1895 he was a member of the 'Siebener Club', and he made friends and collaborated with K. Moser. In the works of applied graphic arts done together, Hoffmann designed the abstract decorations (cornices, etc), and Moser the figurative elements. In July 1897 he was part of the Viennese Secession. In 1903 with Moser he founded the Wiener Werkstätte, with which he was intensely involved on all levels from architectural designs to objects of daily use. In the graphic field he designed the decorations for *Ver Sacrum,* posters for the Wiener Werkstätte, and several books. He was one of the major figures of Austrian architecture of the nineteenth century. He worked on the magazines *Meggendorfer Blätter, Ver Sacrum, Hohe Warte.* Exhibitions: Ausstellung Künstlerischer Reklame, Brno 1905; Internationale Buch-binderkunst-Ausstellung, Frankfurt 1906; Bugra, Leipzig 1914.
Postcards: several p. in the first 5 series of the 'Wiener Künstler-Postkarten', Philipp & Kramer, Vienna, in collaboration with K. Moser or L. Kainradl (I series, n. 4; II series, nos. 1, 9; IV series, nos. 5, 10 etc.), c. 1897; in the series 'Ver Sacrum', published for the I exhibition of the Viennese Secession, Verlag Gerlach & Schenk 1898, in collaboration with K. Moser; 'Officielle Postkarten Jubiläums–Ausstellung 1898 Wien', Philipp & Kramer, 18 p.; 'Stilistisches' series XXXIII of the 'Wiener Künstler-Postkarten', Philipp & Kramer, Vienna, c. 1898; 10 p.; 3 p. in the series of the Wiener Werkstätte: greetings (n. 5), 2 with drawings of the interior of the cabaret 'Fledermaus' (nos. 67, 74); p. in the special series of the Wiener Werkstätte of fabric designs, Brüder Kohn, Vienna.
Bibl.: Baudet 1980; Hansen 1982; Neuwirth 1984.

Adolfo HOHENSTEIN
St. Petersburg 1854 – ?
Commercial artist, lithographer, illustrator.
Born in Russia of a German family, he settled in Milan, where in 1889 he began his collaboration with the Officine Grafiche Ricordi. The poster for Puccini's *Edgar* (1889) is his first known design for the Milanese company, of which he later became artistic director. After his debut as a commerical artist, which was influenced by the formulae of Chevret, he adopted stylistic formulae closer to Jugendstil. He designed covers for musical scores, for books and magazines and as an illustrator he worked on *Emporium.* After the world war there is no record of him.
Postcards: 'Club Alpino Italiano sez. di Milano 25° anniversario 11.12.1898', publ. Ricordi,

Milan; 6 p. of the series of 12 p. 'Iris' by Mascagni, publ. Ricordi, Milan, 1899; 'Esposizione Elettricità e Industria serica, Como 1899'; 'Onoranze a Volta nel centenario della Pila', publ. Ricordi, Milan, 1899; 'Esposizione de igiene di Napoli', publ. Ricordi, Milan, 1900; series of 6 p. 'Esposizione Internazionale de Milano-Giardini Pubblici-Maggio 1901', without a publisher's name; series of 6 p. 'Esposizione Internazionale allevamento e sport, Milano', publ. Armanino, Genoa, 1901, there is also a monochrome version of the series publ. G. Boccolari; series 'Venustas Amor Charitas, Rome 1901'; 'Sempione 1906', Arti Grafiche T. Termali, Milan, typ. Ronchi & Roncoroni; several 'Esposizione de Faenza 1908, onoranze a Torricelli'; 'Veglia di Beneficenza, Bologna 1908', Wenk e figli, Bologna; 'Grosse Kunstausstellung Düsseldorf 1911'; 'Veglia di Beneficenza, Bologna 1913', Lith. R. Roveri & C., Bologna; 'Veglia di Beneficenza, Bologna 1915', Lith. R. Roveri & C., Bologna; series 'Lega Navale de La Spezia'; 'Cassa Nazionale Mutua Cooperative per le Pensioni'; publicity for electrical suppliers Cesare Urtis, Turin; publicity 'Vermouth Cinzano'; publicity 'Bertieri, Torino'.
Bibl.: Bobba 1979; Gaibazzi 1979; *La Cartolina,* I. n. 4, 1982; Mordente 1982; Arrasich 1984.

Ludwig HOHLWEIN
Wiesbaden, 27.7.1874 – Berchtesgaden, 15.9.1949.
Painter, commercial artist, illustrator, graphic designer (commercial and publicity graphics, ex libris, etc.), interior designer.
He attended the Technische Hochschule in Munich (F. v. Thiersch). He made study trips to Paris and London. He was assistant to P. Wallot in Dresden. From 1906 he was in Munich. His important work as a commercial artist, which began in 1898 and continued until 1940, had a wide influence in Germany in the change from Jugendstil to Art Déco. He worked on the magazines *Meggendorfer Blätter, Das Plakat.*
Postcards: p. from the series 'Ausstellung München 1908', Druck H. Köhler, Munich; 'Bayerischen Blumentag Offizielle Postkarte, 1911', Druck und Ausführung O. Consée, Munich; publicity greetings 'Velhagen & Klasings Monatshefte', series of publicity p. for Hülsmann Beer, c. 1915; 'Zur Elinnerung an die Volksspende für die deutschen Kriegs-und Zivilgefangenen', 1916; series for the military post (Feldpostkarten) by the Keks-Fabrik H. Bahlsen, Hannover; several p. with soldiers of the first world war 'Offizielle Postkarte des Wohlfahrtsausschusses', C. Wolf GmbH, Munich.
Bibl.: cat. Altonaer Museum, Hamburg 1970; Lebeck 1978; Till 1983; Weiss 1985 (II).

Thorolf HOLMBOE
Vefsen, 10.5.1866 – Oslo, 8.3.1935.
Painter, illustrator, designer of fabrics, ceramics, graphic designer (books, ex libris).
He was a student of the sculptor Julius Olavus Middelthun at the School of Art and Handicrafts in Kristiania (now Oslo), of Hans Fredrik Gude in Berlin (1886-87) and of Fernand Cormon in Paris (1889-90). During his stay in Paris he made a profound study of Japanese prints, which had a determining influence on his graphic work. He made several study trips to Italy (1891-93), to Copenhagen, Stockholm, Spitsbergen (1908) and New York. He exhibit-

ed paintings, graphic work and applied arts at important international exhibitions, Munich (Glaspalast), 1891, 1901, 1913; Berlin, International Ausstellung 1897; Stockholm (Scandinavian exhibition), 1897; Venice, 1897, 1907, 1914; Paris (Exposition Universelle) 1900; Düsseldorf, 1904; Rome 1911, 1913 (Roman Secession); Vienna (Hagenbund), 1912; San Francisco, 1915. He did the decoration for the Norwegian section of the Jagdausstellung in Vienna in 1910. His fame is attached above all to the illustration of books like *Nordlands Trompet* (1892), *Norske Digte* (1894) and *Sjʒ⁄₈sfgl* (1896), which are among the most important works of Art Nouveau in Norway.
Postcards: several with scenes of bourgeois life, and with the mountainous woodland landscapes of the Norwegian fjords.

Emil HOPPE
Vienna, 2.4.1876 – Salzburg, 14.8.1957.
Architect, designer of fabrics, glass, graphic designer.
He attended the Academy in Vienna from 1898 to 1901 (Architekturklasse of O. Wagner). He opened a studio with Otto Schönthal and Marcel Kammerer.
Exhibitions: Kunstschau, Vienna 1908.
Postcards: II p. in the series of the Wiener Werkstätte 4 with views of the Kunstschau 1908 (nos. 1-4), 7 with views of Vienna and other places (nos. 22-26, 46-47).
Bibl.: Mrazek 1977; Neudin 1977; Dichand-Martischnig 1978; Trost-Martischnig 1978; Baudet 1980; Hansen 1982; Schweiger 1982.

Theodor van HOYTEMA
The Hague, 18.12.1863 – The Hague 28.8.1917.
Painter, lithographer, illustrator, graphic designer (books, calendars, ex libris, menus, programmes, publicity graphics), commercial artist.
He went to the Art Academy in The Hague (1887-92), where he was a student of F. Jansen. From the beginning he was interested in animals, which he studied in the zoos in Leiden (where he worked as a draughtsman from 1888) and in Amsterdam. From 1892 he published a series of books for children printed entirely lithographically, which have animals as protagonists: *Hoe de Vogels aan een Koning Kwamen* (1892); *Het leelijke jonge Eendje* (1893); *The Ugly Duckling* (1894); *Uilengeluk* (1895); *The Happy Owls* (1896); *Twee Hanen* (1898); *Voglvreugd* (1904). In 1898 he published a collection of six lithographic prints with animal subjects, and in 1905 a collection of four lithographic prints of flowers. From 1902 to 1918 he published calendars with 12 lithographic plates, drawn directly on to the stone, which have animals as their subjects. A member of the Haagse Kunstkring (from 1892) and the association of 'Arti et Amicitiae' in Amsterdam (from 1893), he took part in important international exhibitions: Munich (Secession), 1895, 1913; Brussels (Libre Esthétique), 1895, 1898, 1900; Venice, 1897, 1907, 1914; Paris (Salon de la Soc. Nationale des Beaux-Arts), 1900; San Francisco, 1915.
Postcards: series of 6 publicity p. of animal designs, for the company Van Houlen; publicity p. for the book *Hoe de Vogels aan een Koning Kwamen,* 1892; publicity p. for the book *Uilengeluk,* 1895; publicity p. for calendars 1903, 1904, 1905, 1908, 1909.
Bibl.: *De Grafiek van Theo van Hoytema,* 1863-1917, cat. of the exhibition Rijksprenten-

kabinet, Rijksmuseum Amsterdam 1977.

Henry HUTT
Chicago, Illinois, 1875-??.
Biographical facts are unknown.
Postcards: series for Detroit Publ. and for other publishers, with the *glamour* theme, close to the fashion started by C. D. Gibson.

I

Henri Gabriel IBELS
Paris, 30.11.1867 – Paris, February 1936
Illustrator, painter, commercial artist, caricaturist, scenographer and theatrical costumier, graphic designer (theatre programmes, song scores), designer of glass windows.
He attended the Académie Julian in Paris and came into contact with the Nabis. In 1891 and 1892 he exhibited at the Salon des Indépendants; in 1892 he took part with Toulouse-Lautrec and the Nabies in an exhibition at the gallery 'Le Barc de Boutteville'. In 1893 he executed in collaboration with Toulouse-Lautrec the collection of lithographic prints *Le Café Concert*. He designed programmes and posters for the Théâtre Libre and the Théâtre de l'Art. In 1894 he had a one-man show at the gallery 'La Bodinière'. He designed windows for Tiffany, which were exhibited in 1895 in S. Bing's gallery 'L'Art Nouveau'. From 1900 he worked mostly as a scenographer and theatrical costumier. In 1906 he became the artistic secretary to the Théâtre de l'Odéon, where he worked with André Antoine. He made humorous drawings for several magazines: *L'Escarmouche, Le Cri de Paris, Le Rire, Le Sourire, La Revue Blanche, L'Assiette au Beurre L'Echo de Paris, Action, Café Concert, Messager français, Les Hommes d'aujourd'hui, Le Journal, La baïonnette, La Victoire*. He worked on behalf of the Dreyfus cause by designing a series of satirical vignettes published by the newspaper *Le Sifflet*. He was the author of a series of antimilitarist caricatures with the title *Allons-y* (1898) and of the album *L'Art et la manière de former un ministère*. He illustrated the books: *La Terre* by Zola (1897); *Sébastien Roch* by O. Mirbeau (1906); *La Fille Elisa* by J. and E. de Goncourt (1908).
Postcards: 1p. in the 'Collection des Cent', publ. Gréningaire, Paris, 1901; 1p. in the series 'Leur Code' 'À bas la justice militaire', 1904; several p. in favour of Dreyfus; satirical p. showing the Kaiser dressed as the bandit Bonnot; several war propaganda p.
Bibl.: Baudet 1978; Rostenne 1979.

J

Greta-Lisa JÄDERHOLM SNELLMAN
Helsinki, 22.5.1894—Helsinki, 9.2.1973
Ceramist, illustrator.
She attended the School of Industrial Art in Helsinki and then made study trips to Sweden, England and France. From 1914 to 1919 and from 1920 to 1921 she was in Paris to perfect her painting on ceramics. In France she worked at the Sèvres factory (1937-39) and in Finland for the 'Arabia' company and 'Riihimäen Lasitehdas', a well known glass factory.
Postcards: several greetings and humorous p. in the period 1910-30.
Bibl.: Johanson-Termonen 1983.

Angelo JANK
Munich 30.10.1868—Munich, 9.10.1940
Painter, commercial artist, illustrator.
He attended from 1891 to 1896 the academy in Munich (S. Hollosy, L. V. Löfftz, P. Höcker). From 1899 to 1907 he taught at the Damenakademie, then at the Academy in Munich. In 1895 he was a member of the 'Scholle' group in Munich. He worked on the magazines *Jugend* (from 1896) and *Simplicissimus*.
Postcards: p. in the first series of the 'Künstler-Postkarten' for Jugend, G. Hirth, München, 1898; p. in the series 'Jugend—Reisenpostkarten', G. Hirth, 1898; 'Hundertjahrfeier d. Landw. Vereins i/B. Landw. Ausstellungen', Munich 1910, reproducing the poster.
Bibl.: Baudet 1980.

Urban JANKE
Blottendorf, Bohemia, 12.2.1887-1914 (lost on the Eastern front)
Graphic designer, commercial artist, designer of glass decoration.
He attended from 1903 to 1908 the Kunstgewerbeschule in Vienna (B. Löffler). From 1908 he taught at the Kunstgewerbeschule in Magdeburg. He worked on the magazine *Erdgeist*. Exhibitions: Kunstschau, Vienna 1908; Bugra, Leipzig 1914.
Postcards: c. 18 p. in the series of the Wiener Werkstätte: 9 with views of Vienna (nos. 133-140, 291), 6 of fashions (nos. 126-128, 130?, 131, 132?), a greetings p. (n. 145), a decorative p. (n. 18), and a p. without a number with a view of the Hofzuckerbäckerei Demel, which was also used on the shop's boxes.
Bibl.: Dichand-Martischnig 1978; Trost-Martischnig 1978; Baudet 1980; Hansen 1982.

JAPHET, pseudonym of Alexandre Jean Louis JAZET
Paris, 10.5.1814—?
Painter, engraver, commercial artist, illustrator.
He was a student of his father J.-P.-M. Jazet, and of L. Cogniet. From 1839 to 1864 he exhibited at the Salon. He made engravings of the paintings of Horace Vernet. With his pseudonym A. Japhet he worked on the magazines *Mon Village, Gil Blas Illustré*. He was the author of posters which show the permanence of nineteenth-century taste, tempered by the lessons of Chéret.
Postcards: 1 p. in the series 'Cinos', reproducing the poster, 1898; series 'Palais du costume—Projet Felix', 1900.
Bibl.: Baudet 1980.

Hilda JESSER-SCHMIDT
Marburg, 21.5.1894—?
Graphic designer (commercial and publicity graphics), designer of fashion, furnishings, objects of daily use, glass, jewellery.
She attended the Kunstschule für Frauen und Mädchen and from 1912 to 1917 at the Kunstgewerbeschule in Vienna.
Postcards: 3 p. in the series of the Wiener Werkstätte, all of fashions (nos. 1007, 1008, 1011).
Bibl.: Baudet 1980; Hansen 1982.

Wilhelm JONASCH
Vienna, 12.5.1892—?
Graphic designer, designer of objects of applied arts.
He attended the Fashschule für Tischlerei (carpentry) and from 1910 the Kunstgewerbeschule (O. Strnad, J. Hoffmann). He collabo-

rated with the Wiener Werkstätte on fabric designs.
Postcards: p. in the special series for the Wiener Werkstätte of fabric designs, Brüder Kohn, Vienna.

Gustave-Henri JOSSOT
Dijon, 16.4.1866—Tunis, 7.4.1951.
Illustrator, caricaturist, commercial artist, graphic designer (menus, playing cards, song scores, ex libris, publicity graphics), painter, watercolourist.
He was a pupil of J. P. Laurens and of E. Carrière. From 1886 he began working as an illustrator on several humorous newspapers. He worked on the magazines: *Le Sans-Souci* (1886), *La Butte* (1892), *Paris-Joyeux* (1893), *La Caricature* (1893-94), *La Vie drôle* (1893-94), *Le Cycle* (1894-95), *La Plume* (1894-97), *Le Rire* (1894-97), *L'Ymagier* (1895), *Le Jaquemart* (1895), *La Revue artistique* (1895); *La Critique* (1895-1901), *Au Quartier Latin* (1896), *L'Eclair* (1896), *Le Pêle-Mêle* (1896), *Jugend* (1896-1911), *Almanach Georges Bans* (1897), *L'Omnibus de Corinthe* (1897), *L'Estampe et l'Affiche* (1897-98), *L'Art Décoratif* (1899), *Le Cried Paris* (1899-1900), *Almanach universal* (1900 ?), *Cocorico* (1901), *Die Insel* (1901), *L'Assiette au Beurre* (1901-07), *La raison* (1905-05), *Le Diable* (1903), *L'Action* (1903-04), *Bulletin officiel de la Ligue internationale pour la défense du Soldat* (1904), *Catalogue de l'exposition de la caricature judiciarire d'Anvers* (1904), *L'Oeuvre* (1904), *Le Figaro-supplement illustré* (1904), *Les temps Nouveaux* (1905-07), *Internacia Sociarevuo* (1905-07), *Maj* (1908), *Le Journal* (1912), *Le Scorpion* (1912). To this vast anarchically inspired production of satirical designs, with bourgeois family life, the army, the clergy, the magistracy as its targets, and done for papers, one should add those collected in albums: *Artistes et Bourgeois* (1894); *Mince de Trognes* (1897), *Femelles* (1901). He also illustrated books (*Les Rats* by H. Heine, 1895; *Album publié par les etudiants de Lyon a l'occasion de leur tournoi international d'esrime*, 1898) and he designed between 1894 and 1917 about 20 posters (some for the Grand Guignol). From 1908 he interrupted his activity as a satirical draughtsman. In 1911 he settled in Tunisia, where he worked on painting. In February of 1913 he converted to Islam and took the name Abdoul-Karim Jossot.
Postcards: 'Les Rats' (publicity for Heine's poem illustrated by him), c. 1895; 'La Critique' (publicity for the paper), 1895-1901 (?); 3 p. in the I, II and IV series of 'les Maîtres de la Carte Postale' (Pianiste; 'Pussy'; 'Tenor'), 1898-1900; 1 p. in the 'Collection des Cent' ('Salut et cigare') publ. Gréningaire, Paris, c. 1901; 'Tournées Ch. Baret' (publicity), 1903; 'Tailleur Lejeune' (publicity), 1903; 'L'Action' (publicity for the paper), 1903 or 1904; 3 p. in the series 'A bas la justice militaire' ('Leur code'; 'Leur discipline'; 'Leur justice'); 1 p. in the series 'Pochette de la Paix' ('Pour le désarmement'), 1907; 1 p. in the series 'Les Affiches Célèbres'; 1 p. in the series 'Cartes de l'I.P.C.C.' ('Le crâne'); 2 p. in favour of Dreyfus ('Sabre et goupillon'; 'L'éteignoir'; 'Office de photographie de Neufchâtel' (publicity); 'Le Capital est en danger'; 'A as les Calottes'.
Bibl.: *La Carte postale illustrée*, 1899-1903; *La lettre ouverte*, n. 12, 17.11.1977; Baudet 1978, 1980; Neudin 1978, 1980, 1983; Fildier 1979; Zeyons 1979; Holt 1981; M. Dixmier, *Jossot*,

Paris, *Cahier de l'art mineur* n. 23, s.d.

Carl (Karoly) JÓZSA
Szegedin (Szeged), Hungary 16.12.1872—?, 1929
Painter, woodcut artist, commercial artist, illustrator.
He attended the Academy in Vienna (C. Griepenkerl), the Academy in Munich (A. Azbé) and the Académie Julian in Paris. He made study trips to London, Holland, Belgium and Denmark. He worked in Munich and then in Budapest. His postcards are strongly influenced by R. Kirchner.
Postcards: series 'Sirenen und Circen', series VII, A. Sockl, Vienna, c. 1899; series 'Sirenen', E.S.D.-B., c. 1900; series 'Elfen'; series 'Secession'; series 'Rauchringe'; several greetings and decorative p.
Bibl.: Baudet 1978, 1980; Fildier 1979; Gaibazzi 1979; Baudet 1980; Holt 1980, 1983; Lebeck 1980; Neudin 1980; Drago 1981.

Moriz JUNG
Nikolsburg (Mikulov), Moravia, 22.10.1885—11.3.1915 (he fell in the First World War)
Graphic designer (commercial graphics, calendars, decorative prints), commercial artist, glass designer.
From 1901 to 1908 he attended the Kunstgewerbeschule in Vienna (A. Roller, F. V. Myrback, C. O. Czeschka, B. Löffler). He made designs for Wiener Werkstätte postcards, posters, programme n. 2. for the cabaret 'Fledermaus', illustrations for the 1911 almanac and illustrated sheets. He worked on the magazines *Ver Sacrum, Erdgeist, Der Ruf,* and on the sports supplement to the *Wiener Fremden-Blatt* and the *Witzblatt Glühlichter.* Exhibitions: Viennese Secession; Kunstschau, Vienna 1908; Bugra, Leipzig 1914.
Postcards: circa 70 p. in the series of the Wiener Werkstätte: a greeting p. (no. 28), 44 p. humorous and caricatural (nos. 52, 54?, 58?, 62, 66?, 339-344, 358-361?, 383?, 406?, 407, 503-512, 513-516?, 529-534, 727-732?), 12 relative to the cabaret 'Fledermaus' (nos. 486, 597-601, 658-663?, 802).
Bibl.: Mrazek 1977; Dichand, Martischnig 1978; Trost-Martischnig 1978; Baudet 1980; Drago 1981; Neudin 1981; Hansen 1982; Schweiger 1982.

Ludwig Heinrich JUNGNICKEL
Wunsiedel, Franconia, 22.7.1881—Vienna 14.2.1965
Painter, author of prints using stencils, designer of fabrics, tapestries, glass.
He studied at the Kunstgewerbeschule in Munich, in 1899 at the Academy in Vienna (C. Griepenkerl), from 1902 to 1903 at the Kunstgewerbeschule in Vienna (A. Roller); in 1905 at the Academy in Munich, from 1906 to 1907 at the Academy in Vienna (W. Unger). From 1911 he taught at the Kunstgewerbeschule in Frankfurt. In 1938 he settled in Split, then in Abbazia; in 1952 he returned to Austria. His original method of printing in several colours using stencils is illustrated in *The Studio* in 1907. Exhibitions Kunstschau, Vienna 1908; The International Schwarz-Weiss-Ausstellung 1913; Bugra, Leipzig 1914.
Postcards: 11 p. in the series of the Wiener Werkstätte all with humorous subjects (nos. 328-333, 376-380), probably from the period 1910-11.
Bibl.: Mrazek 1977; Fildier 1979; Baudet 1980; Hansen 1982; Schweiger 1982.

Sebastiá JUNYENT
Barcelona, 27.9.1865—Barcelona, 1915
Painter, illustrator, graphic designer (musical scores, publicity and commercial graphics, invitation cards), art critic.
He was educated at the School of Fine Art in Barcelona. As an illustrator he worked on the magazine *Garba* and as a art critic on *Joventut.* He made illustrations for the book by J. Maragall *Les disperses* (1904).
Postcards: series of 8 p. illustrating the anthem *Els Segadors*; 'Sant Jordi', p. dedicated to the patron saint of Catalonia; his single-copy postcards in watercolour are also well known.
Bibl.: Trenc Ballester 1977.

K

Leo KAINRADL
Klagenfurt, 30.4.1872 – Munich, 26.5.1943
Painter, graphic designer, illustrator.
He studied at the Academy in Vienna (C. Griepenkerl). He was a member of the 'Siebener Club'. In autumn of 1896 he moved to Munich, where he became the chief editor of the magazine *Fliegende Blätter*, and remained until 1914. He collaborated also with the magazine *Meggendorfer Blätter* (1895-1914).
Postcards: 10 p. in single copy (pen and colours) drawn for the correspondence between the artists of the 'Siebener Club', from 1895-97 addressed to the writer H. Fraungruber, conserved in the Historisches Museum der Stadt Wien; p. in the series 'Künstler-Postkarten der Meggendorfer Blätter', Verlag J. F. Schreiber, Esslingen; several in the first five series of the 'Wiener Künstler-Postkarten', Philipp & Kramer, Vienna, 1897, some in collaboration with friends from the 'Siebener Club' K. Moser, J. Hoffmann, R. Konopa (series I: 1, 8; series II: 1 (with J. Hoffmann), 4, 8; (with K. Moser), 3, 8, 9, 10; series IV: 2 (with R. Konopa), 3, 4, 10 (with J. Hoffmann); series V: 6, 8, 9, etc.).
Bibl: cat Wien 1979; Gaibazzi 1979; Baudet 1980; Arrisich 1984.

Gustav KALHAMMER
Vienna, 16.6.1886 – declared missing at the end of the First World War.
Graphic designer (commercial graphics), designer of fabrics, jewellery, decoration on porcelain.
He attended from 1905 to 1910 the Kunstgewerbeschule in Vienna (K. Moser). His works, above all in commercial graphics, are published in *Jung Wien* (1906), *The Studio* (1908), *Deutsch Kunst und Dekoration* (1911-14). Exhibitions: Kunstschau, Vienna 1908.
Postcards: 15 p. in the series of the Wiener Werkstätte; 6 with views of Vienna (nos. 408-412, 489, 490), 5 with views of Berlin (nos. 431, 434-436, 438); 3 decorative (nos. 17?, 51, 65).
Bibl.: Dichand-Martischnig 1978; Trost-Martischnig 1978; Baudet 1980; Fanelli 1981, 1983; Hansen 1982.

Friedrich KALLMORGEN
Altona, 15.11.1856 – Grötzingen, near to Karlsruhe, 4.6.1924
Painter, lithographer, etcher.
He attended the Kunstgewerbeschule in Altona; then from 1875 to 1877, the Academy in Düsseldorf (A. Muller, Deger) and, in 1877, the Kunstschule of Karlsruhe (H. F. Gude). In Karlsruhe he was in contact with Schönleber

and H. Baisch. From 1891 he was professor at Karlsruhe Academy.
Postcards: series of p. reproducing lithographic prints by the artist, Verlag der Kunstdruckerei Künstlerbund Karlsruhe, 1897 and series; 'Kinderhilfstag, Altona 1911'.
Bibl.: Lehrs 1898; cat. Altona 1970.

Hans KALMSTEINER
1886 – he fell in the First World War
Graphic designer, designer of decorations on porcelain.
His biographical details are unknown. Exhibitions: Kunstschau Vienna 1908, 1909.
Postcards: 7 p. in a series of the Wiener Werkstätte, with subjects from childhood and fables (nos. 30, 31, 34, 35, 38, 42, 382); p. for the restaurant 'Zum Weingart', Druck A. Berger, Vienna; p. for the 'Öst. Adria Ausstellung', Vienna, 1913.
Bibl.: cat. Wien 1964; Mrazek 1977; Baudet 1980; Hansen 1982.

Rudolf KALVACH
Vienna, 22.12.1883 – Kosmanos, Czechoslovakia, 13.3.1932
Painter, woodcut artist, graphic designer.
He attended from 1900 the Kunstgewerbeschule in Vienna (A. Roller, F. V. Myrbach, C. O. Czeschka, B. Löffler, A. v. Stark). His graphic works appear in *Die Fläche*, (vol. 1, 1902), *Erdgeist* (1908), *The Studio* (1910), *Kunst und Kunsthandwerk.*
Exhibitions: Kunstschau, Vienna 1908, 1909; Bugra, Leipzig 1914.
Postcards: 23 p. in the series of the Wiener Werkstätte: 17 humorous and caricatural (nos. 33, 49, 59, 84, 85, 89, 90, 94, 95, 99, 103?, 105-109, 149), 4 greetings (nos. 15, 16, 27, 29).
Bibl.: Mrazek 1977; Baudet 1980; Lebeck 1980; Neudin 1980; Hansen 1982; Schweiger 1982.

Gustav KAMPMANN
Boppard a. Rh., 30.9.1859 – Godesberg a. Rh., 12.8.1917
Painter, etcher, lithographer.
He attended from 1879 to 1881 the Kunstschule in Karlsruhe, there he was the student of G. Schönleber (1881-82) and of H. Baisch (1882-84). He was active in Munich from 1884 and then in Lübeck and Schleissheim. He took part in the Karlsruhe Künstlerbund. He worked on the magazine *Pan*. His works were published in *The Studio*. He took part in the Exposition Universelle 1900 in Paris and at the Munich Secession (1893-96, 1907).
Postcards: 'Deutsche Graphiker', series n. 8, reproducing lithographic plates, Verlag der Kunstdruckerei Künstlerbund Karlsruhe, c. 1900.

Gottlieb Theodor KEMPF-HARTENKAMPF
Vienna, 23.6.1871 – Kutzbühel, 17.3.1964
Painter, etcher, illustrator.
From 1888 to 1896 he attended the Academy in Vienna (J. V. Berger, L. C. Müller, J. M. Trenkwald, A. Eisenmenger). He belonged to the group the 'Siebener Club'. From 1902 he was a member of the Wiener Künstlerhaus. He worked on the albums *Allegorien, Neue Folge* (1895-97), on the magazine *Meggendorfer Blätter* etc.
Postcards: series XLVIII of the 'Wiener Künstler-Postkarten', Philipp & Kramer, Vienna, c. 1899; series of 10 p. with symbolist subjects, no publisher's name, 'Series 165', c. 1900.

Giorgio KIENERK
Florence, 5.5.1869 – Fauglia, 15.2.1948
Painter, engraver, sculptor, illustrator.
His artistic formation took place with the macchiatoli, under the guidance of A. Cecioni and T. Signorini. In the last decade of the nineteenth century he turned to divisionism. In 1888 he exhibited for the first time at the Promotrice di Bella Arti in Florence. In 1892 he won the Baruzzi prize for sculpture in Bologna. From 1899 he exhibited at the Biennale in Venice. About 1900 he was intensely active as an illustrator on Italian and foreign magazines: *Gil Blas illustré, Cocorico, La Rivera Ligure, Fiammetta, Italia ride, La Domenica dell'Avanti, Numero, Novissima*. In 1905 he was nominated director of the civic school of painting and design in Pavia, where he taught until 1934.
Postcards: 1 p. in the series 'Cocorico', c. 1899-1900; publicity p. for the magazine *Italia ride*, c. 1900; publicity p. for the magazine *Italia ride*, c. 1900; 'Pro Sicilia, Firenze 1902'; 1 p. in the series 'Byrrh', c. 1906; in the series 'Divina Commedia', publ. Alterocca, Terni.
Bibl.: Baudet 1978; Bartoli-Mataloni 1979; Mordente 1982; Arrasich 1984.

Jessie Marion KING
Scotland 1876 – ?, 1949
Painter, illustrator, commercial artist, graphic designer (menus, ex libris), designer of fabrics, embroidery, mosaics, ceramics.
She attended the Glasgow School of Art and then the school in South Kensington. From 1902 she taught at the Glasgow School of Art and was a member of the 'Glasgow School' with C. R. Mackintosh and M. Macdonald Mackintosh. She participated in the Esposizione di Arti Decorative e Industriali in Turin in 1902, where she received a prize for her designs and watercolours. In 1911 she moved with her husband, the artist E. A. Taylor, to Paris where she was inspired by the Ballets Russes. In 1913 she returned to Scotland.
Postcards: 'The National Series 122', Millar & Lang, Glasgow.
Bibl.: Cope 1978.

Raphael KIRCHNER
Vienna, 1876 – New York, 2.8.1917
Portrait painter, illustrator, graphic designer (menus, publicity), engraver, scenographer.
He attended the Akademie der bildenden Künste in Vienna. He started work as a portrait painter of women from the high and middle bourgeoisie in Vienna, and as a book illustrator (Radlerei, 1897). Between 1900 and 1901 he settled in Paris. After the outbreak of war he moved to the United States where he was active as a portrait painter and illustrator. The 'Kirchner-woman' could be seen as one of the first pin-ups. He worked for the magazines *La Vie Parisienne, L'Assiette au Beurre, The Sketch*. He illustrated several books for parisian publishers including *L'Arriviste* and *Le Bandeau* (1916) by F. Champsaur. In 1903 he designed the membership card for the 'Union Cartophile Universelle de la Revue Française de la Carte Postale Artistique'. His first series of postcards were probably 'Wiener Typen' (unsigned) and the one for the 'Wiener Künstler-Postkarten' Philipp & Kramer c. 1898. His work for postcards was immediately successful. According to a witness he made about a thousand different designs for Austrian, German, French, English and American publishers. According to the artist the series

'Geisha' with four successive reprints reached 40,000 copies. His production can be divided into three distinct periods: I) before 1900: postcards published above all by the publishers Philipp & Kramer, Vienna; Reifler's Söhne, Vienna; 'Kosmos', Munich – Budapest – Graz; II) 1900-1903 chromolithographically printed series by publishers in many countries; III) after 1903: series often printed in typography, in which Art Nouveau taste is more pronounced.
Postcards: the list is based on the one published by Neudin (1980 pp 176-179), which lists c. 630 postcards, of which 510 are signed and 120 attributed. a) Series of single c., Signed and with titles (in alphabetical order of the titles); 1. 'Aus Arkadien', 6 p., series 1040 publ. Back & Schmitt, Vienna; 2. 'Concours Byrrh', 1 p., 1906; 3. 'China', 10 p. publ. A. Sockl (?), Vienna, 1900; 4. 'Les cigarettes du monde', 6 p. ('Miss Edith', 'A'Ala', 'Zaziza', 'Estramadura', 'Khédive', 'Musette'), publ. E. Storch, Vienna, 1900; 5. 'Continental', number of p. unknown, series 1190 publ. R. Tuck, London; 6. 'Demi Vierge', 6 p., series 927 publ. a. Sockl, Vienna; 7. 'Eisblumen', 10 p. Kunstantalt 'Kosmos', Munich-Budapest-Graz, c. 1899. (The series also exists with the titles 'Fleurs d'Hiver' and 'Jegviragok'); 8. 'Enfants de la mer', 10 p., publ. Reifler's Söhne, Vienna and A. Sockl, Vienna; 9. 'Les Éphémères', 5 p., Series 375 publ. R. Tuck, London; 10. 'Erika', series of 6 p. nos 1119-1124, no publisher's mark, head of a woman against a background of flowers (1119: tulips; 1123: pansies; 1124: chrysanthemums, etc.); 11. 'Fables', 6 p. no publisher's mark but probably H. Moss & Co. London, series 20, medallions against a woven ground containing images of a woman with a book, with a pelican, with a snail, with a tortoise, with a viper, with a ram; 12. 'Les farfadets', 6 p., series 286 publ. R. Tuck, London; 13. 'La favorite', 6 p., publ. E. Storch, Vienna, 1900; 14. 'Fleurs d'amour', 6 p. on 12 p. I'H., Paris, before 1901; 15. 'Fleurs de Chemins', 6 p., series 1030 publ. Back & Schmitt, Vienna, at least 3 editions after 1898; 16. 'Flussnixe', 6 c. (?), J. Gerson, Paris, before 1901; 17. 'Fruits doux', 6 c. publ. E. Storch, Vienna; 18. 'Geisha', 10 c. publ. E. Storch, Vienna Reifler's Söhne, Vienna (these exist also unsigned and unnumbered, with different colours); 19. 'All Heil', 10 p., publ. A. Sockl (?), Vienna; 20. 'Hinter den Coulissen', 10 c. publ. E. Arenz, Vienna, c. 1899 (the series is also entitled 'Derrière la coulisse'); 21. 'Legendes', 6 p. series 311 publ. Théo Stroefer, Nürnberg, and E. Storch, Vienna, and no publisher's mark; 22. 'Marionnettes', 6 p. publ. E. Storch, Vienna Pascalis & Moss (series 4140), London; 23. 'Mikado', 6 p. publ. E. Storch, Vienna 1900; 24. 'Moderne Mädchen', series 1129 Meissner & Buch, Leipzig; 25. 'Les parfums', 6 p. publ. A. Sockl (?), Vienna, 1900; 26. 'Les Péchés capitaux'. 7 c. publ. Librairie de l'Estampe, Paris, second period; 27. 'Pour le droit et la Liberté', publ. Librairie de l'Estampe, Paris, 1914; 28. 'A quatre feuilles', 6 p. no publisher's mark, c. 1899; 29. 'Radlerei', 6 p. series 1044 publ. Back & Schmitt, Vienna; 30. 'Rêveries', 4 p., publ. R. Tuck, London, 1903; 31. 'Roma', 10 p. publ. Théo Stroefer, Nürnberg, series 220 or unnumbered before 1903; 32. 'Salomé', 6 p. publ. R. Tuck, London, 1903; 33. 'Salon de 1904', no publisher's mark; 34. 'Santoy', 6 p. publ. A. Arenz, Vienna, or no publisher's mark, before 1904; 35. 'Au serail', 6 p. A.

Sockl (?), Vienna, or no publisher's mark c. 1900; 36. 'Auf Sommerfreische', 10 p. series XVIII for the 'Wiener Künstler-Postkarten' publ. Philipp & Kramer, Vienna, 1898; 37. 'Les Sylphides', 6 p. series 285 publ. R. Tuck, London, 1903; 38. 'Um die Liebe', number of p. unknown, series 1040 publ. Back & Schmitt, Vienna; 39. 'Vieux Temps', 6 p. no publisher's mark, before 1901; 40. 'Wiener Blut', 6 p. series 1042 publ. Back & Schmitt, Vienna, before 1900; 41. Series of 6 p. ('Altweibersommer', 'Elfentanz', 'Flirt', 'Libellen', 'Troika', etc.), series 1031 publ. Back & Schmitt, Vienna, or J. Gerson, Paris; 42. Series publ. Librairie de l'Estampe and printed by A. Leroy and R. Crémieu, Paris, with some p. reproducing variants on K's illustrations for *Le Bandeau* by F. Champsaur (1916), n. 9 'Glaneuse', n. 10 'La première voilette', n. 11 'Dans les petits cheveux du cou', n. 12 'Le coup de la jarretelle', n. 13 'Princesse Riquette', n. 14 'Peinte par elle même', n. 15 'Le masque impassible', n. 16 'Le manchon de gui', n. 17 'Le modèle irrévérencieux', n. 18 'Une grande Dame', n. 19 'La baigneuse', n. 20 'Riquette et son chien', n. 21 'La mer fleurie', n. 22 'Le gui de Paris', n. 31 'Ondine', n. 35 'Les Zeppelins a Paris', n. 44 'Oui je t'attends', n. 45 'Rose respirant une femme', n. 46 'Le petit indiscret', n. 47 'La lettre de l'aimé', n. 48 'Salomé Montmartroise', n. 49 'Lulu', n. 50 'La jolie Maud', n. 70 'L'arpéte Montmartroise', n. 71 'Silhouette de Montmartre', n. 72 'Danseuses de Montmartre', n. 73 'Lélie fumêûse d'opium', n. 83 'Maude cambrioleuse', n. 163 'Maude demme du monde cambrioleuse', n. 304 'L'escarpolette', n. 305 'Poinsson d'avril', n. 311 'la chemise transparente'; 43. At least 36 p. publ. 'Bruton Galleries', London, printed by Alphalsa Publishing Co., London ('Bubbles', 'Entente cordiale', 'Feather in her Cap', 'Frovolerie', 'Medallion', 'Stop', 'Sunshine', 'Sweetmeats', 'The Call', 'The Chinese Lantern', 'The Rendezvous', 'The Vision') or by Delta Fine Art Co., London ('Cupid's Captive', 'A Duck's Egg', 'The Fan', 'Faunesse', 'The glad Eye', 'Goddess in a Car', 'Harlequinade', 'Hatched!', 'The little Sister', 'Lizzie', 'Lolotte', 'Mar Marraine', 'Mélisande', 'Merci', 'Miss Red-Cap', 'A Peep', 'Reflections', 'Rosalba', 'The Scout', 'Singed Wings', 'The Skating Girl', 'The Swing', 'Souvenir', 'Two in a Car'), some reproducing illustrations from two albums *The Sketch*, c. 1916-17; 44. Series of 10 p. nos. 990-999, publ. Reinthal & Newman, New York (n. 990 'Covetousness', n. 991 'Pride', n. 992 'Temptation', n. 993 'Anger', n. 994 'Sloth', n. 995 'The Dream', n. 996 'Expiation', n. 997 'Luxury', n. 998 'Gluttony', n. 999 'Envy'), probably reproducing designs for the decorative panels by K for the Century Theater in New York. Series of single p., signed, untitled (in alphabetical order of publisher or printer): 1. E. Arenz, Vienna and Christopher Reisser's Sohne, Vienna, 6 p. showing a couple in an oval frame set in the vertical margins of the p.; 2. Back d Schmitt, Vienna series 538, 6 p. with a geometric motif on a gold ground; 3. Back and Schmitt, Vienna, series 539 6 p. with geometrical floral motifs on a gold ground; J. Gerson, Paris, 6 p. cream ground with red, pigs (3.c.), the hours (2.c.), the snowman (1.c.); 5. Druck Max Herzig & Co., Vienna, 6 p. gold, grey brown with two lateral grey/brown bands, figures a woman with a gold striped dress; one traces the shape of hearts on a wall, one holds a shawl, one with a mirror, one looks at the sea, one in profile with her hair blowing in the wind, one reading; 6. Brüder Kohn, Vienna series 2049, 10 p. (some exist with the printed message 'Heureux Noël'); 7. H. Moss & Co., London, series 123, number of p. not known, designs with geometrical motifs on a gold ground from series B2 and B3; 8. M. Munk, Vienna, series of 12 p. flowers at the feet (title Neudin 1980), 5 or 6 p. designed with a technique close to that used for glass window cartoons; 10. Théo Stroefer, Nürnberg, series 71, 16 p. female figures; 11. Théo Stroefer, Nürnberg, and Druck Meissner & Buch, Leipzig, series 99, then also Terry Columbus series of 12 p., women with flowers, with musical instruments etc., 1900; 12. Théo Stroeffer, Nürnberg, series 197, 6 p. Christmas greetings; 13. Théo Shoeffer, Nürnberg, series 222, 12 p. with grapes before 1903; 14. Théo Stroeffer, Nürnberg, series 235, then also L. J. 10 p. good luck p. showing women with horse shoes, with clover etc. (some exist with the printed message 'Prosit Neujahr'). 15. Théo Stroefer, Nurnberg, series 427, unknown number of p., Surrealist genre with rock-woman. 16. Théo Stroefer, Nurnberg series 622, 6 c. women with grapes; 17. Tournier Clément, Geneva, series 702, unknown number of P., before 1902; 18. R. Tuck, London, series 241, at least 4 p. with female profiles; 19. R. Tuck, London, series 598. 6 p. with automobiles before 1904; 20. R. Tuck, London, series 2571, unknown number of p. of women and hearts. c. series of single p. signed, without publisher's mark and untitled: 1. At least 4 p. pierced to be seen in transparency; 2. Series of 6 p. numbered 249-254 showing heads of women in a tondo over chords of musical instruments, clover, hearts; 3. At least 5 p. in red and white with little shields with carnival subjects; 4. series of 6 p. heads of women with green bands on the right (there are p. with white bands on left and right and other variants). c. 1901; 5. series of 12 p. women smoking; 6. Series of 6 p. busts of women with a grey band on the right; 7. At least 5 p. series n. 184, Christmas themes: children in the snow with furs, a woman who descends from the sky, an angel, two musical angels etc. d. Unsigned postcards: 1. series known as the 'Wiener Typen', c. 1897-98; 2. series of 6 p. with women's heads against a sunray ground (printed in gold) publ. Arenz Verlag, Vienna, later also by S. Hildesheimer & Co., London (with the variant without sunrays); 3. series of 10 p. of Leda and the Swan, E. Arenz, Vienna (?); 4. series of at least 5 p. of women with pigs B. R. W. Vienna, series 362, 5. 'Postkarten der Modernen', series of 10 p. nos 5525-5534, publ. Théo Stroefer, Nürnberg (they also exist with the title 'Coeur Dame'); 6. Series of 10 p., ed. PMM with women's faces in relief on a beige and smoky green ground with a Greek inscription; 7. series publ. M. Munk, Vienna, of at least 9 p., 8 of which are vertical in black or in colour showing a woman looking at herself in a mirror, with incense, with a flute, with a harp, with an iris in her right hand (etc. Neudin: D3); 8. series of 20 p. publ. M. Munk, Vienna, showing a woman against a violet or greenish brown ground in a geometric frame. (Neudin: D.S.).

Bibl.: F. Steno, 'Trefles porte bonheur', *Il Raccoglitore di cartoline illustrate*, I. (1899, n. 11), pp. 128-129; H. Harvey, 'Raphael Kirchner and his art', *Cartoons Magazine*, vol. II 1917, pp. 614-626; Eluard 1933; J. and G. Neudin, 'Kirchner: le Raphael de la carte

postale', *Le Collectionneur français*, XIII, 1977, n. 140, pp. 14-15; Baudet 1978, 1980; Bartoli-Mataloni 1979; Gaibazzi 1979; Holt 1980, 1983; Lebeck 1980; Neudin 1980; Drago 1981; Fanelli 1981, 1983; Till 1981; Mordente 1982; R. G. Woodall, 'Presenting Kirchner', *Picture Postcard Monthly*, 1983, n. 56, p. 26; 1984, n. 62, pp. 32, 33; n. 68, pp. 10-12; A. and P. Dell'Aquila, 'Kirchner, l'illustratore della femminilità', *La Cartolina*, 1984, n. 15, pp. 15-17; Arrasich 1984.

Fritz KLEE
Würzburg, 1876 – ?
Architect, illustrator, graphic designer.
He studied architecture at the Technische Hochschulle in Munich. He worked as an architect in Munich and in Dresden. From 1908 he was the director of the Staatl Fachschule für Porzellanindustrie in Dresden.
Postcards: 'Ausstellung München 1908', commemorative 'Johanni Dult', Druck Allgemeine Zeitung, Munich.
Bibl.: Till 1983.

Friedrich Wilhelm KLEUKENS
Achim, Bremen, 7.5.1878 – Nürtingen, 22.8.1956
Painter, commercial artist, illustrator, designer in applied arts.
After working as a designer in a silver factory near to Bremen, he attended the Kunstgewerbeschule in Berlin (E. Döpler jr.). In 1900 he founded with F. H. Emcke and G. Belwe the 'Steglitzer Werkstatt', which promoted an important development in applied arts. From 1903 to 1906 he taught at the Akademie für Graphische Künste and Buchgewerbe in Leipzig. In 1906 he was invited to the Könstlerkolonie, where in 1907 he directed the Ernst Ludwig Presse.
Postcards: series of the 'Steglitzer Werkstatt', publicised by a poster designed by him; 'Hessische-Landes-Ausstellung für freie u. angewandte Kunst. Darmstadt 1908', 'Der Mensch Ausstellung', Darmstadt 1912; 'Darmstädter Kunstjahr 1914;, FWK.
Bibl.: cat. Darmstadt 1977.

Julius KLINGER
Vienna, 22.5.1876 – Vienna, 1950
Painter, commercial artist, graphic designer.
He attended the Technologisches Gewerbemuseum in Vienna for three years. In 1895 he entered the workshop of the designers *Wiener Mode*, where he met K. Moser and he was introduced by him to the *Meggendorfer Blätter*. In 1896 he moved to Munich and in 1897 to Berlin, where he was active until 1915. His work in the field of applied graphics and in particular his posters had wide influence in Germany. After the first world war he opened a Werbeatelier in Vienna; he quarrelled with the Wiener Werkstätte. He worked on the magazines: *Wiener Mode, Meggendorfer Blätter, Die Lustigen Blätter, Das kleine Witzblatt*. He was the author of *Das Weib im modernen Ornament. Ein Vorlagewerk für alle Gebiete des Kunstgewerbes*, Berlin s.d. c. 1902, and of a collection of decorative plates in collaboration with H. Anker; *Die Grotepsklinie und ihre Spiegelvariation im modernen Ornament und in der Dekorationsmalerei*, Berlin-Cologne s.d. c. 1905.
Postcards: p. in the series 'Künstler-Postkarten der Meggendorfer Blätter', Verlag J. F. Schreiber, Munich; several reproducing his posters, eg. 'Grosse Berliner Kunst-Ausstel-

lung 1909', Kunstanstalt A. Weylandt, Berlin S.O.

Max KLINGER
Plagwitz, Leipzig, 18.2.1857 – Grossjena, Naumburg, 4.7.1920
Painter, sculptor, engraver, graphic designer (ex libris).
He attended the art school at Karlsruhe (K. Gussow), in Berlin, Brussels, and Munich. He lived in Paris from 1885 to 1886 and from 1888 to 1892 in Rome. From 1897 he taught at the Akademie der Graphischen Künste in Leipzig. He participated in the Berlin Secession when in 1892, and he was a member of the Vienna Secession when in 1902 it devoted an important exhibition to him. He founded the Villa Romana in Florence, and the Deutsche Künstlerbund for young German artists. He was one of the major *fin de siècle* figures in Germany.
Postcards: 'Margueritentag, Leipzig II februar 1911' Druck Meissner & Buch, Leipzig; several p. reproducing his paintings.
Bibl.: Lebeck 1980; Drago 1981.

Mela (Melanie Leopoldina) KÖHLER-BROMAN
Vienna, 18.11.1885 – Stockholm, 15.12.1960
Graphic designer (postcards, illustrated sheets, commercial and publicity graphics), illustrator, designer of fabrics and ceramics.
She attended the Malschule Hohenberger, then (1905-10) the Kunstgewerbeschule in Vienna (K. Moser, B. Löffler). She worked with the Wiener Werkstätte. She worked for several Austrian publishers in graphic arts. Her works are published in the *The Studio* (1904), *Jung Wien, Ergebnisse der Wiener Kunstgewerbeschule* (1907). She worked for the magazine *Wiener Mode*. Exhibitions: of the Kunstgewerbeschule, London 1908; Kunstschau, Vienna 1909.
Postcards: c. 150 p. in the series of the Wiener Werkstätte, which have fashion plates as subjects (nos. 269-276, 310-315, 321-326, 345-352, 364, 367?, 368-375, 413-418, 420-429, 470-475, 518-523, 569-575, 579-596, 603-608, 638-643, 648, 649, 758) also greetings p. (nos. 476-485, 524-528, 551-556, 735-740) or about childhood and fable (nos. 8-10, 110-115, 306, 307); p. in the special series of the Wiener Werkstätte with fabric designs, Brüder Kohn Wien; several series for different publ. incl. M. Munk, Wien (series nos. 131, 178, 188, 418, 481, 620, 641, 843, 3142, etc.) or Brüder Kohn (series nos. 1132, 1118, 1187 etc.).
Bibl.: Mrazek 1977; Baudet 1978, 1980; Neudin 1978; Dichand-Martischnig 1978; Gaibazzi 1979; Drago 1981; Hansen 1982; Schweiger 1982; cat. Wien 1984; Neuwirth 1984.

Oskar KOKOSCHKA
Pöchlarn, Austria, 1.3.1886 – Montreux, Switzerland, 22.2.1980
Painter, xylographer, illustrator, commercial artist, graphic designer.
From 1906 to 1909 he attended the Kunstgewerbeschule (A. Kenner, C. O. Czeschka, B. Löffler). He worked with the Wiener Werkstätte from 1907 to 1909: in 1908 he designed a series of eight colour lithographies *Die Träumenden Knaben* and the almanac in 1911.
Postcards: 19 p. in the series of the Wiener Werkstätte, 8 greetings (nos. 21, 116, 143, 144, 147, 151, 155, 157), 11 decorative p. of fables (nos. 55, 64, 72, 73, 76-80, 117, 152). There is a project in a private collection which has a

'Töpelspiel' 1907 as a subject, and which has recently been printed by Verlag Weiz Salzbury.
Bibl.: cat. Altonaer Museum, Hamburg 1970; Mrazek 1977; Baudet 1978, 1980; Neudin 1978, 1979, 1981; Dichand-Martischnig 1978; Hansen 1982; Schweiger 1982; *Der junge Kokoschka*. Kunstgewerbeschule, Wiener Werkstätte, *Cabaret Fledermaus, Kunstchau* 1908, Vienna 1983, cat. of the exhibition edited by W. J. Schweiger.

Leopoldine KOLBE
Vienna, 2.10.1870 – ?
Graphic designer.
She attended from 1901 the Kunstgewerbeschule in Vienna (K. Moser). Exhibition: of the Kunstgewerbeschule, London 1908.
Postcards: 6 decorative p. in the series of Wiener Werkstätte (nos. 32, 36, 39, 40, 43, 44).
Bibl. : Baudet 1980; Hansen 1982.

Rudolf KONOPA
Vienna, 2.2.1864 – ivi, 6.10.1936
Painter, graphic designer.
He attended the academy in Vienna from 1881 (Huber, J. H. Trenkwald). A founder member of the Hagenbund (1900-1906).
Postcards: series 'Wiener Künstler-Postkarten', Philipp & Kramer, Vienna, 1898-99; XIII (Charivari); XX (Vienna); XLVI (smokers).
Bibl.: Neudin 1979.

Ernst Konrad Theophil KREIDOLF
Bern, 9.2.1863 – Bern, 12.8.1956
Illustrator, engraver, painter, graphic designer (ex libris, greetings notes), watercolourist.
From 1883 he studied at the Kunstgewerbeschule and from 1886 at the Academy in Munich, where he was a student of G. Hackl and L. V. Löfftz. From 1889 to 1895 he lived in Partenkirken, where he taught the Princess von Schaumburg-Lippe. From 1898 he was intensely active as a book illustrator, especially for children's books. He wrote the text of some of them: *Blumenmärchen* (Munich 1898); *Schlafende Baüme* (1901); *Wiesenzwerge* (1902); *Schwätzchen* (1903); *Sommervögel* (1908); *Gartentraum* (1911); *Lenzgesind* (1926). He also illustrated: *Bilderbuch ohne Bilder* by Andersen; *Fitzebutze* by Paula and Richard Dehmel (1900); *Traumgestalten* by L. Weber (1900); *Buntscheck* by R. Dehmel; *Alte Kinderreime* (1905); *Sechs deutsche Lieder in Bildern* (1915); *Miss Chindli* by S. Hammerli-Marti (1916); *Kinderland* by O. Volkart (1917); *Aus meinem Sommergarten* by A. Huggenberger (1919). He was a member of the Swiss association of graphic artists 'Die Walze'. In the winter of 1913-14 he took part in the Munich Secession.
Postcards: some series for the publisher G. D. W. Callwey, Munich, which probably reproduced illustrations from children's books; a series of military subjects ('Ich hatt' einen Kameraden . . .', 'Drei Lilien, Drei Lilien', 'Steh Ich in Finstrer Mitternacht' etc.), publ. O. Gmelin, Munich, c. 1915.

Carl KRENEK
Vienna, 7.9.1880 – Vienna, 15.12.1948
Woodcut artist, etcher, painter, illustrator, graphic designer (book design, calendars, ex libris), commercial artist, ceramist.
From 1896 to 1898 he attended the Manufakturzeichenschule of the k. k. Lehranstalt für Textil-Industrie; from 1898 to 1906 the

Kunstgewerbeschule (A. Roller, F. V. Myrbach, K. Moser, C. O. Czeschka, R. V. Larisch); from 1907 to 1908 the Academy in Vienna (H. Lefler). By 1906 he hand completed his own series of woodcuts *Die vier Jahreszeiten* and for Zeitler Verlag in Leipzig *Kleine Szenen. Original Farbholzschnitte.* Exhibitions: Kunstschau, Vienna 1909; Vienna Secession, 1912; Bugra, Leipzig 1914.
Postcards: 12 p. in the series for the Wiener Werkstätte; two greetings (nos. 193, 629), 10 with fairytale landscapes (nos. 253-258, 761, 762, 908, 909).
Bibl.: Mrazek 1977; Trast-Martischnig 1978; Bartoloni-Mataloni 1979; Badet 1980; Hansen 1982; Schweiger 1982.

Ferdinand KRUIS
Pisek, Bohemia, 25.4.1869 – Innsbruck, 17.1.1944
Painter, lithographer, illustrator.
He attended the Academy in Vienna (Rumpler, S. L'Allemand, A. Eisenmenger). He worked on several Viennese magazines (*Die Bombe* etc.), under the pseudonym Lorenze.
In 1898 he joined the Viennese Secession.
Postcards: several in the series 'Künstlerpostkarten' publ. F. A. Ackermann, Munich.

Franz KUHN
Mistelbach, Austria, 7.5.1889 – Vienna, 9.5.1952
Architect, graphic designer, fabric designer.
He studied design privately; from 1910 he attended the Kunstgewerbeschule (R. V. Larisch, O. Strnad, H. Tessenow). He worked with the Wiener Werkstätte designing postcards and fabrics. As an architect he worked with O. Prutscher and built houses in Vienna, Bohemia and Moravia.
Postcards: 36 p. in the series for the Wiener Werkstätte c. 1911-12, with views of Berlin (nos. 430, 432, 436 439-441, 443-449), of Budapest (nos. 450-469) or greetings p. (nos. 815-817).
Bibl.: Dichand-Martischnig 1978; Trost-Martischnig 1978; Baudet 1980; Hensen 1982.

Joseph KUHN-REGNIER
Paris, 10.12.1873 – ?
Illustrator, painter.
He exhibited at the Salon d'Automne. He worked on the magazines: *La Vie Parisienne, Fantasio* and *Fliegende Blätter* (from 1898 to 1914). In 1932 he illustrated the complete work of Hippocrates.
Postcards: serveral greetings in the series 10 for the 'Künstlerkarten', publ. Stengel & Co., Dresden-Berlin, c. 1899.
Bibl.: Baudet 1978.

Stanislav KULHÁNEK
Kladně, Bohemia, 28.5.1885 – ?
Painter, graphic designer.
He studied at the school of decorative arts in Prague (J. Schikanedra).
Postcards: 'Veselé svatky velikonoční', Kladně.

Carl KUNST
Fürstenfeldbruck, 27.2.1884 – Munich, 3.11.1912
Painter, commercial artist, graphic designer, designer in the applied arts.
He attended the architecture department of the Kunstgewerbeschule in Munich (M. Dasio, L. v. Langenmantel, T. Spiess) and at the Academy in Munich (P. Halm, F. v. Stuck).

He was very active as a commercial artist.
Postcards: 'Jugendblätter', c. 1905; 'Ausstellung Münchem 1908'; series of views of Munich; publicity postcard 'Bilgeri-Ski-Ausrüstung'; 'Dr Dessauers Touring-Apotheke', Druck Bickel Söhne, Munich, c. 1910.
Bibl.: Lebeck 1978; Till 1983.

František KUPKA
Opočno, eastern Bohemia, 23.9.1871 – Puteaux, 21.6.1957
Painter, illustrator, engraver.
He attended from 1887 to 1891 the Academy in Prague (F. Sequens), from 1891 to 1892 the Academy in Vienna (A. Eisenmenger). From 1895 he lived in Paris and worked as a fashion designer. From 1902 he made satirical and decorative drawings for several magazines and newspapers: *La Plume, Cocorico, L'Assiette au Beurre, Le Rire, Les Temps Nouveaux, Der Tag*, etc.
Postcards: p. in the series 'Cocorico', c. 1899; 2 p. in the II and III series 'À bas la justice militaire', 1904; several of political satire, published in France.
Bibl.: Baudet 1978; Rostenne 1979.

Max (Maximilian) KURZWEIL
Bisenz, Moravia, 13.10.1867 – Vienna, 10.5.1916
Painter, commercial artist, engraver, graphic designer.
He attended from 1886 to 1892 the Academy in Vienna (C. Griepenkerl, L. C. Müller, K. Pochwalski), from 1892 to 1894 the Académie Julian in Paris. From 1895 he was a member of the 'Siebener Club'. A founder member of the Vienna Secession, which he left in 1905 with the Klimt group. He worked on *Ver Sacrum*. He took part in the Secession exhibitions.
Postcards: several in the first 5 series of the 'Wiener Künstler-Postkarten', Philipp & Kramer, Vienna 1897, in collaboration with his friends in the 'Siebener Club'.
Bibl.: Baudet 1980.

František KYSELA
Koůrim, 4.9.1881 – Prague, 20.2.1941
Painter, commercial artist, graphic designer (books, ex libris), decorator.
From 1900 to 1908 he attended the School of Applied Arts, from 1904 to 1906 the Academy (H. Schwaiger) in Prague. He was an important Art Nouveau commercial artist in Czechoslovakia.
Postcards: 'Všestudentská slavnost', reproducing the poster of 1905.

L

Lluis LABARTA I GRAÑÉ
Barcelona, 4.4.1852 – Barcelona, 1924
Commercial artist, illustrator, scenographer, theatrical costumier, painter, graphic designer (theatre programmes, invitation cards, ball carnets, colour lithographies), designer of wrought iron.
He was a student of E. Planas at the Academy of Fine Art in Barcelona. A member of the *Institute Català de les Arts del Llibro*, he worked as an illustrator on several magazines. Two hundred designs for wrought-iron are collected in an album. His poster designs for bull fights and carnivals are especially famous. He received a mention in the competition for the 'Anis del Mono' poster (1898).
Postcards: 1 p. in the series reproducing the

eight sketches for the prize-winning posters in the 'Anis del Mono-Vicente Bosch, Badalona' competition, held in 1898; series of 12 p., of the months, Lith M. Pujadas, Barcelona, C. 1903.
Bibl.: Fidier 1977; Trenc Ballester 1977

Carl LARSSON
Stockholm, 28.5.1853 – Sundborn, near Falun, 22.1.1919
Painter, watercolourist, illustrator, engraver.
He was a student of G. von Rosen at the Academy in Stockholm. From 1876 to 1878 he was in Paris, where he returned in 1880. From 1886 to 1891 he lived in Gothenburg, where he was the director of the school of design and painting at the local museum. In 1888-89 he painted the triptych, 'Renaissance', 'Rococo', 'Art of the present', in P. Furstenberg's gallery. In 1889 and in 1890 he won two gold medals at the Expositions Universelles in Paris; in 1891 the first prize in the competition for the cartoons for the murals in the National Museum in Stockholm. In 1891 he painted the murals on the staircase of a girls' school in Gothenberg. In 1894 he went to Italy to study fresco technique and in 1896 he began a cycle of 6 fresco paintings on the walls of the great staircase in the National Museum in Stockholm. He did other monumental cycles in the foyer of the Opera (1898) and in a gymnasium in Stockholm (1901) and in the Gymnasium in Gothenburg (1903). From 1901 he withdrew to live on his farm at Sundborn near Falun. He illustrated several books: *Svenska folksagor* by Hyltén-Cavallius (1875); *Sagor och berättelser* by H. C. Andersen (1877); *Sagor* by A. Segerstedt (1972); *Karin Mänsdotter saga* by O. M. Reuter (1880); *Dödens Engel* by J. O. Wallin (1880); *Svenska folket i helg och söcken* by A. Strindberg (1881-82); *Nya Sagor* by A. Segerstedt (1883); *L'espion des écoles* by L. Ulbach (1883); *Kabale und Liebe* by F. v. Schiller (1892); *Singoalla* by V. Rydberg (1894); *Sagan om rosen* by C. Wahlund (1899); *Läsning för barn* by Z. Tofelius (1902-03). He wrote the text and did the illustrations for some albums: *De Mina* (1895); *Ett Hem* (1899); *Spad-arfvet mit lilla landtbruk* (1906); *Svenska kvinnan genom seklen* (1909); *At Solsidan* (1910); *Andras barn* (1913). He worked as an illustrator on the magazines *Ny Illustrerad Tidning*, *Saint-Nicolas*, *Illustrated London News*.
Postcards: several reproducing the plates from his albums; p. for charity '*I Majblommans Jubileums-Brevkort* 1908-1912'.

Franz (François) LASKOFF (LASKOWSKI)
Bromberg (Bydgoszcz), Poland, 18.6.1869 – 1919 (or 1921)
Painter, commercial artist, graphic designer.
His biographical details are unknown. He studied at the Kunstgewerbeschule in Strasbourg (he is recorded there between 1895 and 1897) and in Paris. A poster by him for the retrospective exhibitions of Alsace and Lorraine in Strasbourg 1895 was directly influenced by the poster by E. Grasset for *La Plume*. In 1898 he moved to Italy, then to Great Britain. He worked for the Officine Grafiche Ricordi, Milan, from 1900 to 1906. He worked on *Jugend* (1898), *Italia Ride* (1900), *Musica e Musicisti*, *La Riviera Ligure* (1901).
Postcards: in the publicity series for the magazine *Musica e Musicisti*, publ. Ricordi, Milan 1900; series of 12 p., 'Les mois', publ. Ricordi,

Milan 1901; 'Esposizione Canina Internazionale, Milano 1901'; p. in the series 'Chocolat Talmone', publ. Ricordi, Milan 1900; p. with studies of women, Ricordi & C., for France; series of sport; several commemorative and publicity.
Bibl.: Bartoli-Mataloni 1979; Gaibazzi 1979; Baudet 1980; Mordente 1982; *La Cartolina*, n. 4, 1982; Arrasich 1984.

Richard LAUDA
Jistebnice, 3.1.1873 – Tabor, 24.7.1929
Painter, engraver, illustrator.
He studied at the Academy in Prague (1894-1901), Munich (1904) and then Prague with T. F. Simon (graphic arts). In 1909 he was in Germany, in 1911 in Paris.
Postcards: several decorative p. with female figures and other subjects.

Charles Lucien LÉANDRE
Champsecret, 23.7.1862 – Paris, 1930 (or 1934)
Painter, caricaturist, illustrator, commercial artist, graphic designer (theatre programmes, menus, books), sculptor.
From 1878 he attended the school of design of Emile Blin in Paris, and then he studied (from c. 1885) with A. Cabanel. From 1883 he exhibited at the Salon of the Société des Artistes Français. He produced caricatures and vignettes of political satire for the magazines: *Le Rire*, *Gil Blas illustré*, *Le Chat Noir*, *La Vie moderne*, *Journal amusant*, *L'Assiette au Beurre*, *Le Figaro*, *Gaulois*, *Grosse Caisse*, *L'Illustration*. He was the author of the albums: *Musée des souverains; Nocturnes; Paris et la Province*. He illustrated the books: *La Légende de l'Aven* by P. Arène (1892); *La Famille Cardinal* by L. Halévy (1893); *Nos chers Souverains* by P. Bosq (1898); *Nuits de quinze ans* by F. de Croisset (1898); *L'Avenir d'Aline* by H. Greville (1899); *Folle Chanson* by G. Montoya (1899); *Facino Cane* by H. Balzac (1910). He made posters for singers' performances, for cabarets and theatres in Montmarte.
Postcards: 1 p. in the 'Collection des Cent', publ. Gréningaire, Paris, c. 1901; 1 p. in the series 'Cocorico'; p. in the series 'Le Musée des Sires' and 'Le Musée des Souverains', published by the paper *Le Rire*, reproducing designs used for covers of the paper; 1 p. in the series 'Album mariani', c. 1910; 1 p. in the 'Collection Job', series of 1911, 1912; 2 p. of the series 'les Voeux de la France, Rire Rouge', 1914; 1 p. in the series 'Journée du Secours National'; several p. reproducing posters; several p. of war propaganda.
Bibl.: Forissier 1976; Weill 1977; Baudet 1978.

Léon G. LEBÈGUE
Orléans, 1863 – c.-1944
Engraver, illustrator, commercial designer, painter.
He was a student of J. L. Gérôme in Paris. From 1907 he exhibited at the Salon of the Société des Artistes Français. He worked on the papers: *Le Courrier français*, *Le Rire*, *Gil Blas illustré*, *La Plume*. He illustrated the books: *Les Contes aux Étoiles* by Ponsard (1888); *Les Bals travestis* by P. de Lano (1893); *La Leçon bien apprise* by A. France (1898); *Pervenche* by M. Bouchor (1900); *La Mye du Roy* by H. Balzac (1902); *Histoire de Dona Maria . . .* by A. France (1902); *La Fiancée* by Boccaccio (1903); *Les Contes de jacques Tournebroche* by A. France (1908); *Les Trois Roses de Marie-Anne* by P. Louys (1909); *Roi Dago-*

bert by E. Gebhart (1911); *La Caution* by A. France (1912); *Rola e Nuits* by A. de Musset (1912); *Fêtes galantes* by P. Verlaine (1913); *La Bièvre* by Huysmans (1914); *La Passion de notre frère le Poilu* by M. Leclerc (1918).
Postcards: 1 p. in the first series of the collection 'Les Maîtres de la Carte Postale', 1898; 1 p. in the second series of the collection 'Les maîtres de la Carte Postale', c. 1899; 2 p. in the 'Collection des Cent', publ. Gréningaire, Paris, c. 1901.
Bibl.: Baudet 1978; Neudin 1983.

Franz LEBISCH
Vienna, 2.11.1881 – Merkendorf, 23.12.1965
Architect.
He attended from 1903 to 1907 the Kungstgewerbeschule in Vienna (J. Hoffman). As an architect he was above all famous for his garden projects published in *Hohe Warte* (1905-07). He designed the open air theatre of the Kunstschau in Vienna, 1908 and 1909.
Postcards: 11 p. in the series of the Wiener Werkstätte: 2 p. with decorative landscapes (nos. 11, 13?), 1 greetings p. (n. 14?), 6 decorative p. (nos. 118-122, 124), 2 with garden designs (nos. 12, 123).
Bibl.: Baudet 1908; Hansen 1982; Schweiger 1982.

Michel Maximilien LEENHARDT
Montpellier, 2.4.1853 – ?
Painter, sculptor.
He was a student of E. B. Michel and A. Cabanel. From 1878 he exhibited at the Salon of the Société des Artistes Français, where he received an honorary citation in 1882, a third-class medal in 1884 and a bronze medal in 1889.
Postcards: 1 p. in the series 'Byrrh', 1906.
Bibl.: Baudet 1978; Arrasich 1984.

Léo (Léopold) LELÉE
Chemazé, Mayenne, 13.12.1872 – Arles 26.6.1947
Watercolourist, painter, lithographer, illustrator, commercial artist, furniture designer.
He was a student of E. Lechevallier-Chevignard and Ch. Genuys. About 1902 he settled in Arles, where he became famous as the 'peintre des Arlésiennes', whom he painted in traditional costumes. He illustrated the books: *Douze contes de Paris et de Provence* and *Contes et nouvelles de Provence* by Paul Arène; *Sang de Camargue* by René Barbier; several works by Provençal writers (Mistral, J. d'Arbaud). He was one of the principal craftsmen in Daudet's Mill at Fontvieille and a small mill adjacent to it. There are rooms dedicated to his work in the Musée Arlesien in Arles and in the Musée La Perrine in Laval.
Postcards: 1 p. in the series 'Collection des Cent', publ. Gréningaire, Paris, c. 1901; series of 10 p. with women's faces, c. 1901; series of scenes of life in ancient Egypt ('Sur le Nil', 'Cueillette des Nymphées', 'Le Retour', 'Sur la Terrasse', etc.); series 'Midi, Minuit'.
Bibl.: Baudet 1978, 1980; Gaibazzi 1979; Holt 1983.

Otto LENDECKE
Lemberg (Lwów, Poland; now in USSR), 4.5.1886 – Vienna, 17.10.1918
Graphic designer (commercial graphics, books), commercial artist, fashion designer, scenographer and theatrical costumier.
After a period at the military academy, he continued his education alone. In Paris he

worked for a short time with Paul Poiret. From 1911 he collaborated with the Wiener Werkstätte where he made notable contributions to the formulation of their fashions. In 1917 he published the magazine *Die Damenwelt*; he worked on the magazines: *Wiener Mode, Licht und Schatten, Die Dame, Wieland, Fantasio, Muskete, Meggendorfer Blätter, Jugend, Simplicissimus*.
Postcards: 14 p. circa in the series of the Wiener Werkstätte; 2 greetings (nos. 156?, 159?), 12 of fashion (nos. 848-859).
Bibl.: Baudet 1980; Hansen 1982; Neuwirth 1984; cat. Wien 1984.

Maximilian LENZ
Vienna, 4.10.1860 – Vienna 18.5.1948
Painter, commercial artist, illustrator, graphic designer (commercial graphics, calendars, paper money).
He attended from 1874 to 1877 the Kunstgewerbeschule (M. Rieser, F. Laufenberger) and the Academy (C. Wurzinger, C. Griepenkerl, A. Eisenmenger) in Vienna. In 1903 he made a journey to Italy with G. Klimt. He was a founder member of the Vienna Secession (1897). He worked on the magazine *Ver Sacrum*.
Postcards: series of the 'Wiener Künstler-Postkarten', Philipp & Kramer, Vienna, 1898; X (skaters), XVI (acrobats); p. for the war loan 'Wiener Bank-Verein', Lith. A. Berger, Vienna, 1917.

Ernest Louis LESSIEUSX
La Rochele, 3.8.1848 – Menton, 4.1.1925
Painter, watercolourist, commercial artist, graphic designer (calendars, commercial and publicity graphics).
He was professor of design at the High School in Rochefort. From 1878 he exhibited watercolours of Spanish landscapes and marine scenes at the Salon. His land- and seascapes are reproduced in chromolithography, in calendars for the Post Office and for local tourist bars.
Postcards: series (?) 'Moderne', 1900 (date of the design); series 'Bathing through the Centuries' 1900 c; series of 'Mythological Deities' ('Bacchus', 'Venus', 'Mercury', etc.) series 137 Théo Stroefer Kunstverlag, Nürnberg, c. 1900; series devoted to heroines from literature 'Salamoo', 'Thais', 'Sapho', 'Mireille'), 1900 (date of the designs); series 'Precious Stones' ('L'opale', 'La Topaze', 'Le Saphir', 'La Perle', 'L'Emeraude', 'Le Diamant', 'L'Agate', 'La Turquoise', 'Le Rubis', etc.), c. 1901; female figure with a peacock skirt 1902; series on crafts ('La Gravure', 'L'Orfevrerie', etc.).
Bibl.: Baudet 1978, 1980; Bartoli-Mataloni 1979; Gaibazzi 1979.

Alois LEUPOLD VON LÖWENTHAL
Vienna 1888 – died during the Second World War.
Graphic designer (commercial graphics), enamel designer.
He attended the Kunstgewerbeschule in Vienna (B. Löffler). He worked on *Die Fläche* (vol. II, 1909).
Postcards: 2 p. in the series of the Wiener Werkstätte, one with a view of Karlsbad (n. 212), the other with a view of the villa Hochsetter, in the Steinfeldgasse, in Vienna, designed by J. Hoffmann.
Bibl.: Baudet 1980; Hansen 1982.

Kurt LIBESNY

Vienna, 24.10.1982 – ?
Painter, commercial artist, graphic designer.
He attended the Academy in Vienna (S. L Ailemand, R. Bacher, F. Schmutzer). He was president of the Bundes Öst. Gebrauchsgraphiker.
Postcards: 'Öst. Adria Austellung 1913'.
Bibl.: Baudet 1980.

Ernst LIEBERMANN
Langemüss, Meiningen, 9.5.1869 – ?
Painter, lithographer, illustrator, graphic designer.
From 1890 to 1893 he attended the Academy in Berlin (J. Scheurenberg). He travelled in France (Paris), in Italy, in Germany. From 1897 he was active in Munich. He illustrated several books in the series 'Der deutsche Spielmann'.
Postcards: series of landscapes, Druck H. Köhler, Munich; series of landscapes, Druck und Verlag H. Hohmann, Darmstadt.

Maria LIKARZ-STRAUSS
Przemysl, 28.3.1893 – ?
Graphic designer (commercial graphics), designer of fabrics, fashion, embroidery, glass, decorations on glass, boxes, leatherware, ceramist.
From 1908 to 1910 she attended the Kunstschule für Frauen und Mädchen (O. Friedrich) and from 1911 to 1915 the Kunstgewerbeschule in Vienna (A. v. Kenner, J. Hoffmann). She worked with the Wiener Werkstätte, from 1912 to 1914 and from 1920 to 1931 above all in the fields of graphic arts and later in fashion. In 1928 she moved to Rome, where she was a ceramist until the fifties.
Postcards: c. 80 p. in the series of the Wiener Werkstätte; p. 67. have fashion as their subject (nos. 557-566, 612-616, 682-693, 710-714, 765-781, 829-836, 840?, 843?, 880-885?), p. 9 greetings p. (742-744, 746-748, 797-888?, 889?), one decorative (n. 750).
Bibl.: Mrazek 1977; Baudet 1978; Dichand-Martischnig 1978; Baudet 1980; Lebeck 1980; Drago 1981; hansen 1982; Schweiger 1982; Arrasich 1984.

Ephraim Moses LILIEN
Drohóbycz (Drogobytsch, USSR), near to Lemberg (Lwéw) Galizia, 23.5.1874 – Badenweiler, 1925
Painter, illustrator, graphic designer (ex libris) commercial artist.
He attended for a short time the art school in Cracov (J. Matejko), but he was substantially self-taught. In 1894 he moved to Munich, where he worked on socialist newspapers, and in 1908 to Berlin. He was intensely active in Jewish art and in 1902 he founded the Jüdischer Verlag in Berlin. He worked on the magazines *Pan, Jugend, Berliner Tageblatt, Leipziger Volkszeitung, Süddeutscher Postillon*.
Postcards: p. in the series III of the 'Künstler-Postkarten' for *Jugend*, G. Hirth, Munich, 1899; several p. reproducing his book illustrations, like *Juda* (1900), *Lieder des Ghetto* (1902) etc.

Maj (Mary) LINDMAN JAN
Örebro, Sweden, 17.8.1886 – ?
Painter, designer, illustrator, sculptress.
She was above all famous for her work as an illustrator of children's books. In 1907 she married the painter Gustaf Jan.
Postcards: several greetings p. published by

Axel Eliassons Konstförlag, Stockholm.

Friedrich LISSMANN
Bremen, 4.10.1880 – he fell in the First World War.
Painter, woodcut artist, graphic designer.
He went to the Academy in Karlsruhe (E. Schurth, V. Weishaupt, H. W. Trübner). From 1906 he worked in Hamburg.
Postcards: series 'Deutscher Graphiker', Berlag der Kunstdruckerei Künstlerbund Karlsruhe', c. 1900, reproducing the artist's lithographic plates.

Privat LIVEMONT
Schaerbeek, 9.10.1861 – Schaerbeek, 4.10.1936
Illustrator, commercial artist, lithographer, decorative painter, designer of ceramics, of fabrics, graphic designers (publicity graphics, ex libris).
He studied at the Ecole des Arts Décoratifs at Saint-Josse-ten-Noode where he was the pupil of L. Hendrickxs, A. Bourson (design) and G. Kesten (decorative arts). From 1883 to 1889 he lived, thanks to a grant, in Paris, where he worked with Ph. –J. –H. Lemaire on the decoration of the Hôtel de la Ville. He worked for two years with J. B. Lavastre, the scenographer, at the Paris Opera, under whose guidance he helped with the production of Hamlet at the Théâtre Français. He also worked in the studio of the Comédie Française's scenographer. In Paris he attended the Etienne-Marrel school of design. In 1889 he returned to Schaerbeek, where he opened, in 1890, a decorative art studio. From 1890 he participated in the activities of the Cercle Artistique in Schaerbeek, for which he designed posters. His work as a decorative artist is recalled in the interior decorations of the provincial government building at Hasselt (in coll. with the architect P. Saintenoy); the decoration of the dome in the house of Mors the engineer in Passy (Paris), the large decorative panel 'La Marche à l'Etoile' for the Héle house in Brussels; the ceramic allegorical figures for the 'Maison de Blanc' in Brussels. He was the author of more than 50 posters, some of these were reproduced as postcards.
Postcards: 2 p. 'Automobile Club de France-6ᵐᶜ Exposition Internationale de l'Automobile et des Sports au Grand Palais du 10 au 25 décembre 1903', 1903 (of one of the two there is a variant with a mirror image of the design); publicity p. 'Phototypogravure en 3 couleurs'; p. with drawn female figure (?). Bibl.: forissier 1978; Fildier 1979; Rostenne 1979; Baudet 1980.

Berthold LÖFFLER
Nieder-Rosenthal, near Reichenberg (Liberc), Bohemia, 28.9.1874 – Vienna, 23.3.1960.
Painter, commercial artist, graphic designer, (books, commercial graphics, calendars, ex libris, programmes) designer of glass and ceramics.
He was the son of a fabric designer and manufacturer. He studied at the Zeichenschule of the Nordóhmisches Gewerbemuseum in Reichenberg; from 1890 to 1900 at the Kunstgewerbeschule in Vienna (F. Matsch, C. O. Czeschka). From 1904 to 1909 he taught at the Kunststickereischule where he succeeded Czeschka. He worked with the Wiener Werkstätte making designs for commercial graphics, calendars, almanacs, costumes and posters for the cabaret 'Fledermaus', and jewellery. He

worked on the furnishing of the cabaret 'Fledermaus' and of the Palais Stoclet by J. Hoffmann in Brussels. He worked on the collection *Allegorien, neue Folge*, Gerlach Verlag (1899) and on the magazines *Meggendorfer Blätter, Ver Sacrum, Der liebe Augustin, Donauland*. Exhibitions: The world of childhood, St. Petersburg 1903-04; Kumstschau Vienna 1908, 1909; Bugra, Leipzig 1914. Postcards: c. 23 p. in the series of the Wiener Werkstätte: 8 decorative, with putti etc. Nos 48, 617-621, 623-628), 4 for the Kaiser's Jubilee in 1908 (nos. 172, 175, 179, 187), 10 with reproductions of the designs for the frescoes in the Salzburg Volkskeller (nos. 911-920); 1 reproducing the poster for the cabaret 'Fledermaus' (n. 71); series of 6 p. 'Adria Ausstellung, Wien 1913' Druck & Berger.
Bibl.: cat. Wien 1964; Mrazek 1977; Baudet 1978, 1980; Lebeck 1980; Neudin 1980; Drago 1981; Hansen 1982; Schweiger 1982.

Ramiro LORENZALE i ROGENT
Barcelona, 1859 – Barcelona, 1917
Painter, graphic designer (commercial and publicity graphics).
He was a student of his father, the painter Claudi. He attended the school of fine arts at Lonja and he went to Paris to perfect his studies. He did the decorative panels for the Liceu theatre in Barcelona.
Postcards: publicity for the 'Mitjans i Pala' house, 1 p. in the series 'Papeles Roca para fumar', typ. Thomas, Barcelona.
Bibl.: Trenc Ballester 1977.

Maurice LORDEY, Pseudonym of Maurice LE-FÈBVRE-LOURDET
Paris, 8.4.1860 – ivi, 1934
Painter, cartoonist, commercial artist, scenographer, illustrator.
He exhibited at the Salon of the Société des Artistes Français (1885-92) and at the Salon des Humoristes (1907-15). He worked on the newspapers *Le Courrier Français, Gil Blas illustré, Le Journal, Le Rire, Le Sourire*. He illustrated the books *Paris qui m'amuse* by Xanrof and *De l'Autel a l'hôtel* (1902). He designed several posters, above all for the Théâtre Marigny.
Postcards: 2 p. in the series 'Gala H. Monnier', 1904; 1 p. in the series 'Album Mariani' c. 1900.

Fritzi (Friederike) LÖW-LAZAR
Vienna 23.10.1891 – ivi, 19.9.1975
Illustrator, graphic designer (books), designer of fabrics, fashion accessories, jewellery, toys, glass, glass decorations, ceramist.
From 1907 to 1910 she attended the Kunstschule für Frauen und Mädchen (A. Böhm); from 1910 to 1918 the Kunstgewerbeschule in Vienna (J. Hoffmann, O. Strnad, A. Roller, M. Powolny). She worked with the Wiener Werkstätte in several areas of applied arts and in fashion. From 1917 to 1925 she illustrated collectors' books for Anton Schroll Verlag. In 1938 she moved to Brazil. She returned to Vienna in 1955. Postcards: 43 p. in the series of the Wiener Werkstätte 18 of fashion (nos. 701-709, 871-873, 1000-1005), 11 calendar designs (nos. 818-828); 5 greetings (nos. 871, 808, 809, 812, 839), 3 with different subjects (nos. 695, 702, 703).
Bibl.: Mrazek 1977; Dichand-Martischnig 1978; Baudet 1980; Hansen 1982; Schweiger 1982.

Fritz LÖWENSOHN
Vienna, 12.12.1893 – ?
Graphic designer.
Biographical details are not known. From 1918 he attended the Kunstgewerbeschule (K. Moser, A. Böhm). Postcards: there is only one known postcard, a greetings p. in the series of the Wiener Werkstätte.
Bibl.: Hansen 1982.

Amédée Ernest LYNEN
Saint-Josse-ten-Noode, Belgium, 30.6.1852 – Brussels, 1938
Painter, illustrator, watercolourist, etcher, commercial artist, writer, graphic designer (publicity graphics, ex libris).
He was a student at the Academy of Fine Art in Brussels of P. Lauters and J. Stallaert. From 1880 to 1890 he actively took part in the activities of the group 'L'Essor' and in 1892 he was one of the founder members of the group 'Pour L'Art'. He was the founder and leading spirit in the cabaret 'Diable au Corps' in Brussels. He worked on several magazines (*L'Artiste, Pourquoi pas*, and others). He made many book illustrations, his most famous work in this field are for; *Les 36 renocontres de Jean Dugauguet* and *Le Poirier misère* by Charles Deulin, *Les Frères de la bonne Trogne* by Charles Decoster (1884), *La Lègende et les aventures . . d'Ulenspiegel* (1886), *La Cité ardemte e Les vertus* bourgeoises by Carton de Wiart, *La Belgique* by Camille Lemonnier (1888). He also illustrated with watercolours works by Ch. Deulin, Th. Hannon and E. Verhaeren. He was the author of engravings (*Kermesses*, 1889) and of lithographs which depict scenes of Brussels life.
Postcards: series of p. with surrealist interiors, publ. Malvauz; series of landscapes; publicity p. 'Vitello' and 'Sodex'; series of 201 p. 'De-ci, de-la, à Bruxelles et en Brabant', c. 1905.
Bibl.: Philippen 1977; Baudet 1978, 1980; Rostenne 1979; Holt 1983.

Ernst Arnold LYONGRÜN
Domnau, East Prussia, 2.10.1871 – ?
He studied with J. Lefebvre and T. Robert-Fleury. He was the author of the collections *Stifformen entwickelt aus Naturformen*, Dresden s.d., *Moderne vorbilder für Decken- u. Wandmalerei*; *Neue Ideen*, s.d. (1901) Postcards: p. in the series 'Les mâitres de la Carte Postale', 1° group 2nd series, 1898-1900; publicity p. for I.P.C.C.; several decorative p.
Bibl.: Baudet 1980.

Jaume LLONGUERAS i BADIA
Barcelona, 1883-Barcelona – (?), 1955
Painter, decorator, designer of glass windows, graphic designer (ex libris, books, commercial and publicity graphics).
He was trained at the School of Fine Arts in Barcelona, under the guidance of J. Pascó. He studied engraving with A. de Riquer. He completed his artistic training in Paris and Madrid. In 1907 and 1908 he worked in the construction yard of the Sagrada Familia, where on the invitation of Gaudí he began to design glass windows. His main field of activity was interior decoration.
Postcards: 'Visca la Solidaritat Catalana 1906', typ. J. Horta, Barcelona.
Bibl.: Trenc Ballester 1977; Neudin 1983.

Joan LLIMONA i BRUGUERA
Barcelona, 20.6.1860 – Barcelona, 3.2.1926
Painter, illustrator, commercial artist, carica-turist, graphic artist (musical scores).
He began his studies in architecture, which he abandoned for painting. He was a pupil of R. Marti i Alsina and A. Fabrés in Rome, where he lived with his brother, the sculptor Josep, from 1880 to 1883. A member of the 'Cercele de Sant Lluc', he executed several frescoes in the churches in Barcelona and in Montserrat and in the Palace of Justice in Barcelona. He was the artistic director of the monthly *Empori* (1907-08), he worked on several Catalan magazines: *La Ilustració Catalana, La Ilustración Artistica, Hispania, Calendari del Cu-Cut, La Ilustració Llevantina, Garba, Forma*. He was the author of several posters for exhibitions and religious ceremonies, in 1911 he won the first prize in the competition for the Industrial Exhibition of the Electrical Industries in Barcelona. Postcards: Series of 10 p. 'Ave Maria Purissima', publ. Ll Bartrina, Typ. Thomas, Barcelona; 'Ajuntamento de Barcelona V. Exposicio Internazional d'Art-Abril de 1907', reproducing the poster; p. in the series for the artistic circle of Sant Lluc.
Bibl.: Trenc Ballester 1977.

M

A. K. MACDONALD
The biographical details are unknown. Postcards: several decorative p. and p. with female figures, for several publishers, including J. Henderson, London; series for the 'Franco – British Exhibition', London, 1908; series for the 'Japanese – British Exhibition', London 1910, Valentine & Sons, London.
Bibl.: Holt 1980, 1983.

Adolfo MAGRINI
Ferrara, 10.7.1876 (or 1874) – Milan 1957.
Painter, engraver, scenographer, illustrator, commercial artist.
He completed his early artistic studies in Ferrara with A. Longanesi, Ravagnani, and C. Legnani. Then he attended the Academy of Fine Art in Naples, where he was the student of D. Morelli. He exhibited in the major Italian cities as well as in Munich, Monte Carlo, Berlin and Paris. In 1906 he was awarded two Grand Prix and a silver medal and the 'Espozione del Sempione' in Milan.
Postcards: series of ballerinas, 1902; 'Mostra Segantini – Milan 1906', reproducing the poster; 'Citta di Parma – Settembre 1907', reproducing the poster; 'Circuito di Bologna – Coppa Florio 1908'; 'Mostra delle Bonifiche – Ferrara 1910'; 'Mostra Antica Arte Senese – Siena 1914'; p. in the series of the 'Divina Commedia', publ. Alterocca, Terni; several Liberty 'donnine'.
Bibl.: Bobbaf 1979; Mordente 1982; Arrasich 1984.

Augusto MAJANI, known also under the pseudonym NASICA.
Burdrio, 30.1.1867 – Buttrio. prov. of Udine, 1959 (or 1958).
Caricaturist, cartoonist, illustrator, commercial artist, painter.
He attended the Academy of Fine Art in Rome from 1889 to 1898 and the one in Bologna, where he later taught from 1905 to 1937. He took part in several international exhibitions in Florence (1896), in Venice (1897), in Turin (1898) and in Milan (Sempione exhibition, 1906). As an illustrator he worked on the

magazines *Bologna che dorme* (1898), *Italia ride* (1900), *Varietas*, *Novissima*, etc. His caricatures were frequently published in the Bolognese daily paper *Il Resto di Carlino*. He designed covers and book illustrations (covers for *Levia Gravia* by Carducci and for *I sette peccati* by Giovannetti, 1908, and illustrations for the *Divina commedia*, 1912). He made several posters and cards for the 'Partito Socialista' and for the 'Camera del Lavoro'.
Postcards: 'Festa delle Matricole, Bologna, 1899', Lith. Sauer e Barigazzi, Bologna; 'La Virtus commora Re Umberto, Bologna 1900', Stab. Zamorani e Albertazzi, Bologna; 'Festa Fossalta, Bologna 1901'; 'Il Resto del Carlino augura ai suoi abbonati buon-anno e buon secolo', Stab. Zamorani e Albertazzi, Bologna 1901; '7° Congresso Socialista Italiano, Imola, 1902'; 'Il Resto de Carlino-Veglione della stampa, 1904', 'Cartolina d'allerme-Ass. XX Settembre', Bologna 1905; 'Circuito di Bologna-Coppa Florio 1908'; 'Festa Mutino-Bononiense alla Fossalta, 1908', Lith. A. Dal Re, Modena; series of 6 c. '50° Anniv. Soc. Mutuo Soccorso tratipografi', 1908; 'Associazione della stampa emiliana', 1910; 'Bologna a G. Verdi, 1913'; 'Feste di beneficenza, 1914'; several war propaganda p., 1915-18; series of 12 p. 'Le maschere di Mascagni', publ. Menolia, Bologna; several cards caricaturing famous men (Mascagni, Fogazzaro, Panzacchi, Stecchetti, etc.); several propaganda p. for the Partito Socialista; several anticlerical p.; '5° Centenario dell 'invenzione della tagliatella'; 'L'Aerotravaso'; commemorative p. of Testonie; 'Esposizione della guerra, Bologna'; 'I cuccoli burattinai, Bologna'; 'Albero di Natale della Stampa Emiliana'; publicity p. 'Spumante Gagliardi'; series dedicated to the poems by Trilussa; '1860 Garibaldi a Napoli' from the series 'Unità d'Italia'.
Bibl.: Gaibazzi 1979; Mordente 1982; Arrasich 1984.

Elena MAKOWSKY (MAKOWSKAJA, MAKOWSKA) – LUKSCH
St. Petersburg, 14.11.1878 – Hamburg 15.9.1967.
Illustrator, designer of screens, of painted boxes, of panels, of embossed metal and silver, of furnishing.
She was the daughter of a painter. She attended the Academy in St. Petersburg (I. E. Répin) and in Munich (A. Azbé), where she met the Viennese sculptor Richard Luksch, whom she married in 1900. She worked with the Wiener Werkstätte on the furnishing for the Wittgenstein hunting lodge at Hochreith. She worked on the magazines *Ver Sacrum*, *der liebe Augustin*. Exhibitions: Vienna Secession; Kunstschañ, Vienna 1908.
Postcards: 14 p. in the series of the Wiener Werkstätte, all illustrating Russian proverbs (nos. 384-395, 411, 412).
Bibl.: Baudet 1980; Bichand-Martischnig 1978; Hansen 1982.

Louis-Jules MALTESTE
Chârtres, ?-?.
Illustrator, lithographer, commercial artist.
In 1897 he exhibited at the Salon des Cent; in 1898 and in 1902 at the Salon of the Société Nationale des Beaux-Arts. He worked on the collection *L'Estampe Moderne* and on the magazine *L'Assiette au Beurre*.
Postcards: 1 p. in the 'Collection des Cent', publ. Gréningaire, Paris, c. 1901; 1 p. in the series 'Affiches Gérin', c. 1901.

Bibl.: Baudet 1978; Neudin 1979.

Burkhard MANGOLD
Basel, 10.9.1873 – Basel 17.10.1950.
Painter, engraver, lithographer, graphic designer (books, ex libris), commercial artist, illustrator.
He completed his early studies at the Kunstgewerbeschule in Basel and then he attended the private academies in Paris (1894) and Munich (1894-1900). He executed several monumental frescoes in several buildings – Basel Town Hall, Gasthof 'Zum Bären', Gotthilf-Schulhaus, Hauptpost, Volksbank, Schalterhalle). He illustrated books by E. Zahn, E. Stückelberger, C. F. Meyer (*J. Jenatsch*), and others.
Postcards: in the series Gordon Bennett-Wettfliegen 30. Sept. – 3. Okt., Zürich, 1909', Graph. Anstalt J. E. Wolfensberger, Zurich; p. for the national holiday 1. August 1912; 'Offizielle Künstlerpostkarten der Schweiz. Landes-Ausstellung in Bern, 1914', Graph. Anstalt W. Wasserman, Basel; '1315 – Unpour-Tous pour-un – 1915 – Fête anniversaire de la Bataille de Mortgarten en Faveur d'Uri', Graph. Anstalt J. E. Wolfensberger, Zurich.

Amanuel Josef MARGOLD
Vienna, 4.5.1888 – Bratislava, 2.5.1962.
Architect, commercial artist, graphic designer (commercial graphics), designer of fabrics, furniture, furnishings, decorations, glass, metalwork, jewellery.
He attended the Kunstgewerbeschule in Mainz, the Fachschule für Holzbearbeitung in Königsberg and from 1906 the Kunstgewerbeschule in Vienna. (J. Hoffmann). As J. Hoffmann's assistant he taught at the Kunstgewerbeschule. He worked with the Wiener Werkstätte. In 1911 he was invited to join the Künstlerkolonie in Darmstadt. In 1929 he moved to Berlin. Exhibitions: Kunstschau, Vienna 1908, 1909.
Postcards: 2 projects for p. for the cabaret 'Fledermaus' in Vienna, illustrated in *Deutsche Kunst und Dekoration* XXVI (1910), p.68. Whether they were carried out is uncertain.
Bibl.: Hansen 1982.

Gustav MARISCH
Vienna, 17.7.1887 – ?.
Graphic designer (books), glass designer.
He attended the Graphische – Lehr-und Versuchsanstalt, and from 1905 to 1908 the Kunstgewerbeschule in Vienna (B. Loffler). He worked on *Die Fläche*.
Postcards: 8 decorative p. in the series of the Wiener Werkstätte (nos. 546, 547, 609-611, 782-784); series with birds in clothes, Brüder Kohn, Vienna.
Bibl.: Baudet 1980; Hansen 1982.

MARS, pseudonym of Maurice Bonvoisin.
Verviers, province of Liège, 26.5.1849 – Paris, April 1912.
Illustrator, watercolourist, cartoonist.
From the 70's he was very active as an illustrator on many French and English magazines, to which he contributed drawings of fashionable places (race courses, fashionable beach resorts, exhibitions, etc), which he made while on his frequent travels in Europe. He worked on the magazines: *The Graphic*, *The Illustrated London News*, *The Sketch Illustrated Bits*, *The Daily Graphic*, *Chiarivari*, *Illustration*, *Journal amusant*, *Revue illustrée*, *Vie moderne*, *Vie elegante*, *Monde illustré*, *Petit Journal pour*

rire. (He was the author of the albums *Aux bains de mer d'Ostende*, *Aux Rives d'or*, *Paris brilliant*, *La vie de Londres*, *L'escrime à l'Elysée Les plages de Bretagne et de Jersey*, *Sable et Galets*, *Croquis de plage*, *Nos cheris à la ville, à la mer, chez eux, à la campagne, dans le monde* (1886), *Joies d'enfants*, *A travers le Havre* (1887), *Anvers exposition*, *Bruxelles exposition*, *Boulogne-sur-Mer*, *Schéveningue et Le Haye*, *La reine bicyclette*, *Mesdames les cyclistes*, *Le carnaval niçois*, *Nice en fête*. He illustrated the book *Trop grande* by Hervilly.
Postcards: several p. reproducing his book illustrations (beach scenes, fashionable places, etc.), dateable c. 1899-1900; 1 p. in the series 'Album Mariani' c. 1900.

Alberto MARTINI
Oderzo, 24.11.1876 – Milan, 8.11.1954.
Painter, engraver, lithographer, illustrator, graphic designer (ex libris, visiting cards).
He trained in drawing and painting under the guidance of his father Giorgio, who copied old masters and who was professor of drawing at the Istituto Tecnico in Treviso. From 1895 he made the cycle of illustrations for Morgante Maggiore by Pulci and for the *Secchiarapita* by Tassoni. In 1897 he exhibited for the first time at the Venice Biennale with the cycle of drawings 'La corte dei miracoli' inspired by *Notre-Dame de Paris* by V. Hugo. In 1898 he stayed in Munich and had the opportunity to work on the magazines *Jugend* and *Dekorative Kunst*. In 1901 he was in touch with the Florentine publisher Vittorio Alinari for the illustrated edition of the Divina Commedia, and he exhibited at the Biennale in Venice the first part of his drawings inspired by *Secchia rapita*, which he completed in 1903 and exhibited them in Venice in that year. In 1904 he began a cycle of erotic drawings, 'Parabola dei celebi' and he illustrated *l Canti delle Stagioni* by L. Orsini: this book was followed by Le Commedie by Terence (1905), *Per la Rinascita* by L. Coletti (1907), *The Life of Edgar Allan Poe* by G. E. Woodberry (1909), *Ill-Castello del Sogno* by E. A. Butti (1910) and *Asse Terrestre* by V. Brjusov (1910). Between 1905 and 1908 he did a series of drawings inspired by the 'Extraordinary Stories' of Poe, which were exhibited at the Biennale, and between 1908 and 1915 cycles based on the plays of Shakespeare's (*Hamlet* and *Macbeth*) and the poetry of Mallarmé, Verlaine and Rimbaud. His production before the first world war also included designs for covers, frontispieces and magazine titles. (*Emporium*, *Poesia*, 1905, *Varietas*, 1905); several ex libris, and some series of lithographies (*Misteri*, 1914-1915; *Donne-farfalle-fiori-animali*, 1915; *Carezze*, 1915-16).
Postcards: series of 12 p. 'Notti serene, notti stellate', Lith. Longo, Treviso, 1899 ('Fine del sogno', 'Notturno', 'Musa silvestre', 'Sinfonia', 'I Fari', 'Ninfa ondivaga', 'Convegno notturno', 'Ore Notturne', 'Notte d'estate', 'Plenilunio', 'Raggio di luna'); Treviso 21 movembre 1899. Inaugurazione 'Borse Agraria', Lith. Longo, Treviso, 1899, issue of 500 copies; 'Beneficenza e divertimento. Treviso Carnevale 1899'. Lith. Longo, Treviso, 1899; 'Cavalchina di Beneficenza, Venezia 1900', Lith. Longo, Treviso 1900; series of 3 c. 'Carnevale olimpico' ('I, Carnevale inebbria il mondo'; "II, Il trionfo della Follia"; 'III, Olimpionico – Fuga finale', Lith. Longo, Treviso 1900 (?); series of 12 p. 'Venetia Antiqua'°, c. 1900; publicity for the opera 'Quo Vadis'°, c. 1900; some p. in the series of the 'Divina

Commedia', publ. Alterocca, Terni; 5 series (The 1st 2nd 3rd and 5th of 12 p. each and the 4th of 6 p.) 'Danza Macabra Europea', Lith. Longo, Treviso, 1915-16; 'Esposizione di alcuni artisti rifiutati alla Biennale veneziana', by Arturo not Alberto, is often wrongly included in the catalogue of p. by Alberto.
Bibl.: Joletta, 'Le Cartoline del sogno', *Il Raccoglitore de cartoline illustrate*, I (in 6, 5.10.1899), pp.67-68; F. Meloni, *L'opera grafica di Alberto Martini* Milano 1975; M. Lorandi, 'Una serie inedita di Alberto Martini', *Il Conoscitore de Stampe*, 1976, 30, pp. 53-60; Baudet 1978, 1980; M. Lorandi, *Alberto Martini simbolista*, Milano 1978; Bobba 1979; Bartoli-Mataloni 1979; Gaibazzi 1979; Mordente 1982; Arrasich 1984.

Alfred MARXER
Turbenthal, Canton Zurich 28.6.1876 – ????
Painter, woodcut artist.
He attended the Kunstgewerbeschule in Winterthur and in Munich. He made several study trips to Vienna and Budapest. From 1897 to 1900 he studied at the Academy of Fine Art in Munich. He executed several mural paintings in churches and public buildings in Switzerland.
Postcards: p. in the series 'Gordon Bennett – Wettfliegen, 30 Sept. – 30 Okt., Zürich 909, Graph. Anstalt J. E. Wolfensberger, Zurich.

Lluis MASRIERA i ROSÉS
Barcelona, 1872 – ????
Painter, designer of enamels, jewellery, scenographer, playwright.
He was the son and student of the painter José Masriera i Manovens. He perfected his studies in enamelling and goldsmithing in Paris, London and Geneva (with Lossier). He took part in several Spanish painting competitions and exhibited in France at the Salon des Artistes Français. He was the scenographer and director of the theatrical company 'Belluguet'. He was vice-president of the artistic circle of Sant Lluc.
Postcards: p. in a single copy in watercolour with the imprint of the Circulo Artistico of Barcelona, 1902.
Bibl.: Fanelli 1983[2].

Giovanni Mario MATALONIE
Rome, 1869 – Rome 1944.
Commercial artist, illustrator, graphic designer (musical scores, calendars).
Born in Rome to a family from the Marche, he settled in Milan, where he worked with the Officine Grafiche Ricordi, first as a typographer, then as a commercial artist. He designed publicity posters for Chappis's the Bolognese publisher. He worked as an illustrator on several magazines: *La Tribuna, Ora di Palermo, Emporium, Novissima*. He designed several covers for musical scores and opera libretti.
Postcards: 6 p. of the series of 12 of 'Iris' by Mascagni, publ. Ricordi, Milan, 1898; 'Distillerie Gio. Buton & C., Bologna, 1900' reproducing the poster of 1895; 'Prima Esposizione Internazionale di Bianco e nero, Rome 1902'; 'Ricordo 1 Maggio 1904', there are also p. with the inscription 'VIII Congresso Nazionale Socialista'; publicity p. for l'Hôtel de Londres in Naples, 1910; 'La vita in fondo al mare', p. n. 6 in the series for Travaso delle Idee, c. 1910; 'XV Congresso Internazional Associazione stampa, Roma 1911'; several p. for the national loan, 1915-1918; 'Roma Victrix', series Un-

ità d'Italia; p. of war propaganda; p. in the series of the 'Divina Commedia', publ. Alterocca, Terni.
Bibl.: Gaibazzi 1979; *La Cartolina*, n. 4, 1982 e. n. 10, 1983; Mordente 1982; Arrasich 1984.

Luciano Achille MAUZAN
Gap, Hautes-Alpes, 15.10.1883 – Gap (?), 15.1.1952.
Commercial artist, graphic designer (ex libris, lettering publicity and commercai graphics), illustrator, engraver, painter, sculptor.
He got his diploma with a gold medal in 1905 from the Ecole des Beaux-Arts in Lyon, and he travelled in Italy and decided to settle in Milan, where he took on work as a graphic designer, designing among other things a monogram for the engraver Soresina, an alphabet of capitals for the typographer Allegretti and a series of ex libris. From 1909 he began working as a commercial artist, he rapidly became one of the most appreciated designers of cinema posters. From 1912 to 1917 he designed posters for the Officine Grafiche Ricordi. During the war years he began designing postcards (between 1917 and 1946 it seems that he designed more than one thousand). In 1917 he stopped working for Ficordi and moved to Rome, where from 1921 to 1923 he made several posters for the agency 'Maga'. In 1923 he started a poster publishing business (Affiches Mauzan-Morzenti'). In December 1926 he moved to Buenos Aires, where he lived until 1932, when he returned to France. In his last years he devoted himself to engraving, painting and sculpture.
Postcards: a) War Propaganda, 'Concerti musicali fra artisti delle Nazioni Alleate – A beneficio dilla Croce Rossa', publ. Comitato di propaganda patriottica, 1915; 'Italia e Francia', publ. Comitato di propaganda patriottica, c. 1915; p. for the war loan, publ. Ricordi, Milan, 1915-16; propaganda p. for the Italian women's loan, publ. Chiattone, Milan, 1915-16; propaganda for the war loan 'Fate tutti il vostro dovere!', publ. Modiano, Trieste, 1915-16; 'Aurora di pace', publ. Dell'Anna e Gasparini, Milan 1918. b) 'Donnine'; several series from c. 1915-1918 publ. Ricordi, and for De Anna e Gasparini, Milan. c) Publicity 'la Rinascente', publ. Ricordi, Milan, c. 1917. His other publicity p. are after 1918.
Bibl.: Forissier 1978; Bartoli-Mataloni 1979; Fanelli 1981; *La Cartolina*, n. 4, 1982; Gli illustratori. Lucien Achille Mauzan (1883-1952), *La Cartolina*, II (1982, n. 5), pp. 16-21; Mordente 1982; Arrasich 1984; *Omaggio a Luciano Achille Mauzan*, cat. of the exhibition edited by M. Marchiondo Pacchiola, Pinerolo 1984.

Edgar MAXENCE
Nantes, 17.9.1871 – La Bernerie-en-Retz, Loire Atlantique, 1954.
Painter.
He was a student of G. Moreau and E. Delaunay. He exhibited at the Salon of the Société des Artistes Français, where he received an honourable mention in 1894, a third-class medal in 1895, and a second-class medal in 1897. From 1895 to 1897 he took part in the Salon de la Rose-Croix, he distinguished himself as one of the leading French symbolist painters.
Postcards: 3 p. in the 'Collection Job', series of 1905, 1907, 1911, 1914; 1 p. in the series 'Album Mariani', c. 1910.

Phil (Philip) MAY, pseudonym of Charlie

SUMMERS
New Wortley, near Leeds, 22.4.1864 – London, 5.8.1903
Painter, commercial artist, illustrator.
He was self-taught. He was a versatile caricaturist. He arrived in London in 1883 and he worked for some newspapers. Then he moved to Australia and from there to Rome and to Paris. From 1895 he was active in London, where he was employed by *Punch*. He worked on several English papers and magazines encluding *Saint Stephen's Review, The Pictorial World, The Sydney Bulletin, The Daily Graphic, The Graphic, Black and White, The Sketch*, etc.
Postcards: 'Celebrated Postcards', R. Tuck, London, 1903, series 1506 ('Apollinaris'); several series of humorous p. for Davidson Bros., London ('The Humour of Life'); Landeker & Brown, London; R. Tuck, London; Valentine & Sons, London; E. Wrench, London.
Bibl.: Holt 1980, 1983.

Aldo MAZZA
Milan, 6.7.1880 – Varese, 26.7.1964
Illustrator, caricaturist, commercial artist, lithographer, painter.
He got a diploma in painting at the Academy at the Brera in Milan, where he was a pupil of C. Tallone, V. Bignami and G. Mentessi. From 1904 to 1924 he worked as an illustrator on *Guerin Meschino* and from 1924 to 1926 on *Secolo*. Towards 1908 he began work as a commercial artist for the publishers Ricordi in Milan and Chappuis in Bologna. He illustrated children's books (*Il prode Anselmo* by E. Visconti di Venosta). He made decorative panels with dance subjects for the Teatro Eden in Milan.
Postcards: a) Commemorative; 'Esposizione di Varese, 1901'; 'Fiera delle Bambole, Milano 1901'; 'V Congresso Commercianti esercenti e industriali italiani, Milano, 1906'; 'Milano Circuito Aereo Internazionale', publ. Ricordi, Milano, 1910; 'Concorsi Aerei di Verona, 1910'; 'Inaugurazione sede Pio Albergo Trivulzio, Milano – Vini d'Italia 1910'; 'Esposizione di Varese 1911'; 'Frigidarium Esposizione Internazionale di Umorismo – Rivoli 1911', publ. Ricordi, Milan. b) Charity: 'Albero di Natale per i fanciulli poveri', c. 1900, issue of 1000 copies 'Patronato della Scuola di S. Orsola, Milano', 1900; 'Esposizione di beneficenza a premio di articoli di vestiario e oggetti artistici (per vittime terremoto 1908)', 1909; 'A beneficio Istituto marchiondi Spagliardi, Milano (Aiutatemi che vi portero fortuna)'; 'Charitas urget nos – Per il patronato della scuola elementare maschile'; 'Comitato Ambrosiano di Beneficenza'. c) Publicity; series of 5 p. 'Olio d'oliva Agnesi & Giaccone Oneglia', 1902; 'Di ricopiar la bicicletta Bianchi . .'; 'Duca d'Alba'; 'Teatro estivo Diana, Milano', d) War propaganda: several about the Italo-Turkish conflict 1911; p. for the national loan 1915-16; series of 6 p. 'La Trincea'; several war propaganda 1915-18. e) 'Donnine' and children: several series, 1915-18.
Bibl.: Bartoli-Mataloni 1979; Bobba 1979; Gaibazzi 1979; *La Cartolina*, n. 4, 1982; Mordente 1982; Arrasich 1984.

Luc-Olivier MERSON
Paris, 21.5.1846 – Paris, 14.11.1920
Painter, illustrator, commercial artist, Gobelins designer.
He was the son of the painter and art critic Charles Olivier. He was the student of Chasse-

vent and of Pils. In 1869 he won the Grand Prix di Rome. From 1867 he exhibited at the Salon, where he won the first-class medal in 1873. He won a gold medal at the Exposition Universelle in Paris 1889 and a Grand Prix at the one 1900. In 1892 he joined the Institut de France and in 1894 was nominated a professor at the Ecole des Beaux-Arts. He illustrated the books: *Chronique du temps qui fut la Jacquerie* by Mayneville (1903); *Les Trophées* by dé Hérédia (1907); *Les Nuits* by dé Musset (1911); *Notre-Dame de Paris* by Hugo; *La Jacquerie* by Mérimée.
Postcards: 1 p. in the 'Collection des Cent', publ. Gréningaire, Paris, 1901; 1 p. in the series 'Album Mariani', c. 1910.
Bibl.: Baudet 1978.

Apel-les MESTRES i OÑÓ
Barcelona, 1854 – Barcelona, 18.7.1936
Illustrator, cartoonist, graphic designer (lettering, books, dance programmes, funeral notices, fashion plates in chromolithography), poet, writer, composer.
He studied in the School of Fine Arts in Barcelona with A. Caba and Ll. Rigalt and he worked in the studios of the painters C. Lorenzale and R. Martí Alsina. In 1872 he began working for the satirical weekly *L'Esquella de la Torratxa* and in 1876 for the magazine *La Campana de Gràcia*. His *Cuentos Vivos*, collected into a volume in 1882, made him one of the most representative Catalan caricaturists. Among the books illustrated by him the most distinguished, other than the many collections of his poetry, are *L'Anima enamorada*, 1884; *Baladas y Idilis*, 1889; *Margaridó*, 1890; *Vobiscum*, 1892; *Odas Serenas*, 1893; *Novas Baladas*, 1893; *Epigramas*, 1894; *Tradicons*, 1895; *Poemas de Terra*, 1906; *Liliana*, 1907; *Don Quijote*, 1897; *La Dama de las Camelias*, 1880; *Cuentos de Andersen*, 1881; *Cantos Modernos*, by R. D. Peres, 1888; *La hija del rey de Egipto*, by Ebers, *El sabor de la tierruca* by Pereda, *El Lazarillo de Tormes*. He worked on the magazines: *L'Avenç*, *El Gato Negro*, *Hojas Selectas*, *Joventut*, *La Ilustració Llevantina*, *Pèl & Ploma*.
Postcards: humorous publicity p. for the 'Pastillas Morelló', 1900; publicity p. for the paper *Joventut*; p. for the festival 'Solaridad Catalan', 1906; series reproducing the costumes for the play 'Er la Vivola d'or', Teatre de Naturalesa, La Garriga, 1914.
Bibl.: Trenc Ballester 1977.

Lucien Marie François MÉTIVET
Paris, 19.1.1863 – Paris, 1932 (or 1930)
Illustrator, commercial artist, painter, graphic designer (song scores).
He studied at the Académie Julian with G. Boulanger and J. J. Lefebvre and then attended the studio of Cormon. From 1889 to 1891 he exhibited at the Salon of the Société des Artistes Français. With Chéret, Grün, Steinlen, Willette and other artists he executed the decorations in the 'Taverne de Paris'. For the Exposition Universelle 1900 in Paris he planned with Faivre, Léandre and Roubille, the theatre 'La Maison du Rire'. He exhibited at the Salon des Humoristes. He worked on the magazines *L'Assiette au Beurre*, *Le Rire*, *Courrier français*, *Figaro illustré*, *Journal amusant*, *Revue Mame*. He illustrated the books *Trains de luxe* by A. Hermand (1908); *Noé dans son arche* and *Les fées en train de plaisir*, by A. Alexandre, *Roi Pausole* by P. Louys, *Cousin de Lavaréde* and *Jean Fanfare* by Ivoi, *Clair de lune* by G. de Maupassant. He designed a lot of son scores for the publisher Enoch & Cie. He designed several posters and in 1895 won first prize in the international competition sponsored by the magazine *The Century* for a poster for the publicity launch of the book *The Life of Napoleon Bonaparte* by W. M. Sloanes.
Postcards: 1p. in the series 'Cinos', 1898 reproducing the poster of Napoleon for *The January Century*; 1 p. in the 'Collection des Cent', publ. Gréningaire, Paris, c. 1901; 1 p. in the series 'Gala Henry Monnier', 1904; 1 p. 'Les Voeux de la France, Rire Rouge', 1914; 1 p. in the series 'Le Rire Rouge', 1915.
Bibl.: Baudet 1980.

Leopoldo METLICOVITZ
Trieste, 1868 – Pontelambro, 19.10.1944
Commercial artist, lithographer, painter, graphic designer (musical scores, publicity graphics).
In 1892 he began working for Officine Grafiche Ricordi, as an assistant lithographic designer employed in the production of posters by Hohenstein, Mataloni and others. From 1896-97 he started to work intensively as a commercial artist for the Milanese firm. He was a landscape painter and portraitist.
Postcards: series of 8 p. 'La Bohème' by Puccini, publ. Ricordi, Milan, 1897; publicity 'Viareggio Bagni', by Ricordi, Milan, 1898; series of 10 p. 'Oratori by Don Lorenzo Perosi', by Ricordi, Milan, 1898-99; series of 12 p. 'Tosca' by Puccini, publ. Ricordi Milan, 1900; several publicity p. for the magazine '*Musica e Musicisti*', publ. Ricordi, Milan, 1900; series of 12 p. 'Verdi a Sant Agat', publ. Ricordi Milan, 1900; series of 5 p. 'Aida' by Verdi, publ. Ricordi, Milan, 1901; series of 5 p. 'Falstaff' by Verdi, Ricordi, Milan, c. 1901; publicity p. for the newspaper *La Sera*, Ricordi, Milan 1902, reproducing the poster; series of 10 p. 'Germania' by Franchetti, Ricordi, Milan 1902; series of 10 p. 'Engadina-St. Moritz', Ricordi, Milan, 1903; series of 12 p. 'Castelli Valdostani', Ricordi, Milan, 1903; series of 12 p. 'Madama Butterfly' by Puccini, Ricordi, Milan, 1904; 'Mostra del ciclo e dell 'automobile', 1905; 'Inaugurazione del Sempione – Esposizione Internazionale Milano', Ricordi, Milan, 1906, reproducing the poster; series of 16 p. 'Il Sempione', Ricordi, Milan, 1906; series of 24 p. '24 pezzi caratteristici per piano forte di A. Longo', Ricordi, Milan, 1907; 'Mostra del ciclo e del 'automobile, 1907'; 'Varo della Regia Nave 'Roma' La Spezia 1907', Ricordi, Milan, reproducing the poster; 'Esposizione Internazionale di Torino 1911', Ricordi, Milan, reproducing the poster 'Feste centenarie di Busseto, 1813-1913', Ricordi, Milan; publicity p. for 'Calzaturificio di Varese', Ricordi (?), Milan, c. 1913; reproducing the poster; 'Spettacoli classici di Firenze, 1914'; 'Agamennone di Eschilo – Teatro greco di Siracusa, 1914', Ricordi, Milan; 'Sempre Avanti!', Ricordi, Milan, c. 1915; series of 6 p. 'Omaggio ai soldati combattenti, dono della Ricordi e di A. Ottolini', Ricordi, Milan 1915-16; series (?) 'Finalmente' (Italia, Trento, Trieste), Ricordi, Milan, 1915-18; several publicity p. for 'Magazzini Mele – Napoli', Ricordi, Milan; publicity for 'Distillerie Italiane, apparecchi a gas o alcool', Ricordi (?), Milan reproducing a poster datable c. 1897.
Bibl.: Lebeck 1978; Bartoli-Mataloni 1979; Bobba 1979; Gaibazzi 1979; *La Cartolina*, I, n. 4, 1982; Mordente 1982; Arrasich 1984.

Georges MEUNIER
Paris, 3.11.1869 – St. Cloud (?), 1934 (or 1942)
Illustrator, commercial artist, painter.
He was a student of H. Bouguerau and T. Robert-Fleury at the Ecole des Beaux-Arts in Paris. He also attended the Ecole des Arts Décoratifs. He exhibited at the Salon of the Société des Artistes Français and from 1909 to 1913 at the Salon des Humoristes. He made several posters for the printing film Chaix which showed the influence of Chéret. He worked on the magazines: *Le Rire and L'Assiette au Beurre*. He illustrated *L'Almanach du Parisien pour 1895*, *Paris-Almanach 1896*, *C'est ça l'amour by R. O. Monroy (1901) and Les Fétards de Paris* by P. Decourcelles (1902).
Postcards: 1 c. in the series 'Cinos' ('Bal Bullier'), 1898; 1 p. in the 'Collection des Cent', publ. Gréningaire, Paris, c. 1901; 1 p. in the series 'Affiches Gérin', c. 1901; series of 8 p. 'Aventure parisienne', 1902; 1 p. in the series 'Byrrh', 1906; 1 p. in the series 'Album Mariani', c. 1910; 1 p. in the 'Collection Job', series of 1911, 1914, reproducing a calendar of 1895; 1 p. in the series 'Les Voeux de lat France, Rire Rouge', 1914; 1 p. in the series 'Gravures de Berger' from the collection 'Les Temps Nouveaux'; several reproducing posters.
Bibl.:Baudet 1978, 1980; Bobba 1979.

Henri MEUNIER
Ixelles, 25.7.1873 – Ixelles 8.9.1922
Lithographer, engraver, commercial artist, illustrator, painter.
He was the son of the engraver Jean-Baptiste, and he completed his early artistic studies under the guidance of this father. He attended the Academy at Ixelles and he was a student of Paris of Blanc-Garin. He first exhibited engravings at the Salon in Mons in 1890. From 1897 he exhibited with the 'Sillon' group. He designed covers and made illustrations for several magazines (*Le Petit Bleu. Le Cottage*, and others). He did much commercial work for the publisher Dietrich in Brussels. During the 1914-18 war he made many drawings at the front.
Postcards: series of 12 p. 'Le Zodiaque', Dietrich & Cie, Brussels, c. 1898; series of 12 p. 'Femmes-fleurs' (Iris-Message', 'Roseau-Musique', 'Laurier-Gloire', 'Eglantier-Inspiration', etc) publ. Dietrich & Cie, Brussels, c. 1898; series 'Chic à Paris'. 1899; series called the 'grandes femmes', 1900; series of the seasons and parts of the day ('Printemps', 'Bonsoir', etc), c. 1900; publicity p. 'Nagant'; 'Appel a la Reine d'Angleterre' (asking her to intervene on behalf of Boer Women and children in camps) 'Rentrée 1587 – Rentrée 1589'; several unsigned publicity p; publicity series 'Biscuits & desserts Victoria Bruxelles-Dordrecht' Chromolitho & Typo F. Wolff, Brussels; p. in series XVII ('Ideal') by Stroefer's Kunstverlag in Munich are attributed to Meunier.
Bibl.: Lehrs 1898; Maggioni 1899; Stoppani 1900; Kyrou 1966; Baudet 1978, 1980; Bartoli-Mataloni 1979; Gaibazzi 1979; Rostenne 1979; Fildier 1980; Lebeck 1980; Neudin 1981.

Victor MIGNOT
Brussels, 20.6.1872 – Paris, 5.3.1944
Commercial artist, illustrator, engraver, painter.
In 1894 he first appeared as an illustrator on the newspaper *Cycliste Belge illustré*; then he worked on several Belgian and French maga-

zines (*Le Petit Bleu*). From 1895 he did much commercial work for sporting associations and events, for the theatre ('le Cénacle') and for artistic groups ('Le Sillon'). He won the first prize in the poster competition for 'Kermesse de Bruxelles'. He illustrated the book *Figures de Paris* (1901). He was a member of the artistic group in Brussels 'Le Sillon'. From 1903 he often worked in Paris.
Postcards: series of 12 p. 'Les Sports', Dietrich & Cie, Brussels, 1899; several publicity p.
Bibl.: Baudet 1978, 1980; Bartoli-Mataloni 1979; Baibazzi 1979; Lebeck 1980, Drago 1981.

MISTI, pseudonym of Ferdinand MIFLIEZ
Paris, 1865 – Neuilly, 1923
Lithographer, commercial artist, graphic designer (song scores).
A student of E. Lechevallier-Chevignard. He exhibited at the Salon of the Société des Artistes Français, where he got an honourable mention in 1907 and at the Salon des Humoristes. In the period 1894 to 1914 he was above all active as a commercial artist: he designed posters for the newspaper *La Critique*, for bicycle races and for several makes of bicycles.
Postcards: 1 p. in the I series (1898) and 1 p. in the IV series (c. 1899) publ. 'Les Maître de la Carte Postale', by the newspaper *La Critique*.
Bibl.: Baudet 1980.

Carlo MONTANI
Saluzzo, 8.11.1868 – Rome, 28.12.1936
Painter, illustrator.
A student of F. Petiti. He was a member of the group 'I XXV della Campagna romana'. He founded the newspaper *Travaso delle idee* and he was the chief editor of the magazines *Don Chisciotte*, *Falchetto*, *Fracassa* and of the *Messaggero*. Mainly active in the first decade of the century in illustration, from the second decade he worked on painting and took part in important art exhibitions.
Postcards: 'Nobile Festino Teatro Argentina – Società contro l'accattonaggio, Roma 1902'; 'Una pagina di storia', p. n. 7 in the series Travaso delle idee', c. 1910.
Bibl.: Arrasich 1984.

Henry MORIN
Strasbourg, 21.1.1873 – Versailles, 4.1.1961
Illustrator, painter, designer of glass windows.
He was educated at the Ecole des Beaux-Arts in Paris. From 1897 to 1925 he was one of the principal illustrators on the magazine *Mon Journal*. He also worked on the magazines *Le Petit Français illustré* and *La Semaine de Suzette*. From 1906 he was mainly active as an illustrator of children's books. Among the books illustrated by him the following are outstanding; *Le Mariage de Minuit* by H. de Régnier (1903); *L'Inconnu* by P. Hervieu (1904); *Renée Mauperin* by E. and J. Goncourt (1905); *Le Bouquet de mauvaises herbes* by E. Belville (1906); *Contes bleus de ma grand-mere* by C. Robert-Dumans (1913); *Petits héros de la Grande Guerre* by J. Jacquin and A. Fabre (1918).
Postcards: publicity p. 'A. Girard graveur-editeur de la Carte Postale'.

Louis MORIN
Paris, 5.8.1855 – Migennes, 1938.
Painter, engraver, illustrator, caricaturist, commercial artist.
He made humorous drawings for the maga-

zines *L'Assiette au Beurre*, *La Caricature* and *Le Chat Noir*. His illustrations were published also in the magazines *Figaro illustré*, *Paris illustré*, *Revue des quatre saisons*, *Revue illustrée*, *Vie parisienne*. He did much work as an illustrator of children's books and special editions for bibliophiles; amongst these the following are outstanding; *Notre ami Pierrot* by J. Doucet (1897); *Confidences d'une aïeule* by A. Hermant (1898); *Trois filles et trois garçons* by M. De Montégut (1899); *Le Roman du Chaperon rouge* by A. Daudet (1902); *Rosette au Paradis* by G. Vicaire (1903); *Baron de Knifhausen* by E. and J. de Concourt (1904); *On ne badine pas avec l'amour* by A. De Musset (1904); *Gargantua et Pantagruel* by Rabelais (1911); *Contes* by Schmid (1912); *Venise. . . Rêve* by E. and J. de Concourt (1913). He was the author of books illustrated by him: *Vieille idylle* (1891); *Carnavals parisiens* (1898); *Monmartre s'en va* (1905); *Joujoux d'Alsace* (1918) and other. For the cabaret 'Chat Noir' he designed *silhouetes* for the Chinese shadow theatre. As a painter decorator his mural decorations for the cupola of the department store 'Au Printemps' (now destroyed) were particularly distinguished. He was a founder member of the Société des Dessinateurs humoristes and he exhibited at the Salon des Humoristes.
Postcards: 2p. in' the 'Collection des Cent' publ. Gréningaire, Paris, c. 1901.
Bibl.: Baudet 1978.

Koloman (Kolo) MOSER
Vienna, 30.3.1868 – Vienna, 18.10.1918
Painter, engraver, commercial artist, illustrator, graphic designer (books, lettering, ex libris, publicity and commercial graphics, calendars, musical scores, paper money, stamps), interior designer, designer of fabrics, wallpaper, furniture, objects of daily use, furnishings, fashion, jewellery, enamels, glass, metalwork, ceramist.
He studied at the Akademie der bildenden Künste (F. Rumpler and C. Griepenkerl) and at the Kunstgewerbeschule (F. V. Matsch) in Vienna. From 1899 to 1918 he taught painting and graphics at the Kunstgewerbeschule. He was one of the founder members of the Viennese Secession in 1897, (he left in 1905 with the Klimt group) and of the Wiener Werkstätte in 1903 (he left it in 1908 to paint). In the forefront of painting and design in the Secession movement, he was particularly active in the graphic arts, particularly in book illustrations (the plates for the album *Allegorien Neue Folge*, 1895-97; 1896 illustrations for books by Bahr, Ewart, Pötzl, etc. The commemorative volume for the state press 1908 as well as for posters, calendars, stamps, stickers, papers. He was a member of the 'Siebener Club', the group (formed c. 1895) by artists who wanted to design objects of the applied arts together. In the group of 7 Moser had a closer relationship as a friend and collaborator with the architect Josef Hoffman; examples of their work designed together are the writing-paper for Hardtmuth, the cover for *Deutsch-Österreichische Literaturgeschichte*, the illustrations for *Meggendorfer Blätter* (1898) the decorations and illustrations for the volume for the Emperor's Jubilee (1898), some postcards in the series 'Ver Sacrum' and 'Wiener Künstler-Poskarten', Philipp & Krammer, Vienna 1897, some in collaborations with his friends from the 'Siebener Club' like J. Hoffmann e/o and/ or L. Kainradle; several in the series 'Ver

Sacrum' publ. for the 1st exhibition of Viennese Seccession Verlag Gerlach & Schenk, Vienna, 1898, in collaborations with J. Hoffmann, J. M. Olbrich o A. Roller; 1p. in ther series 'Les Maîtres de la Carte Postale', publ. by the newpaper *La Critique*, Paris c. 1899; Official p. of the Austrian postal services for the Jubilee of Emperor Franz Josef, 1908, the versions for Austria and for the 'Jubiläumsausstellung Prag'. The Historisches Museum der Stadt in Vienna has 7 postcards in single copy (in pen and colours) designed by Moser for the 'artists' correspondence of the 'Siebener Club' addressed to the writer H. Fraungruber, in 1895.
Bibl.: W. Frenz *Kolo Moser, Internationaler Jugendstil und Wiener Secession*, Salzburg 1978; Baudet 1978, 1980; Neudin 1978, 1979, 1980; *Koloman Moser 1868-1918*, cat. of the exhibition edited by O. Oberhuber and J. Hummel, Hochschule für angewandte Kunst-Österreichisches Museum für angewandte Kunst, Vienna 1979; cat. Wien 1979; Gaibazzi 1979; Baudet 1980; Lebeck 1980; Drago 1981; Fanelli 1981, 1983; Holt 1981; Mordente 1982; *Kolo Moser grafico e designer*, cat. of the exhibition edited by D. Baroni and A. D'Azuria, Padiglione d'arte contemporanea, Milan 1984; W. Fenz, *Koloman Moser, Graphik Kunstgewerbe Malerei*, Salzburg-Vienna 1984; Pabst 1984.

Alphonse MUCHA
Ivancice, Moravia, 24.8.1860 – Prague 14.7.1939
Painter, commercial artist, illustrator, graphic designer (calendars, menus, programmes, decorative prints, commercial and publicity graphics, paper money, stamps), sculptor, architect, decorator, designer of furniture, furnishings, glass windows, objects of daily use, jewellery, scenographer and theatrical costumier.
After he was rejected by the academy in Prague in 1879 he was in Vienna, where he worked as an apprentice theatrical painter at the Ring Theatre. Then he attended the academy in Munich (1885-87), the Académie Julian and L'Académie Colarossi in Paris. He started to work for Parisian magazines as an illustrator. In 1894 his poster 'Gismonda' for Sarah Bernhardt was very successful (8000 copies were issued in the following years). This was the beginning of the fashion 'Style Mucha'. The publisher Champenois had the idea of printing the graphic works of M. in the form of 'panneaux decoratifs' and then as calendars and menus. He began to reproduce the same designs as postcards. Only four of the c. 160 postcards known to be by M. reproduce designs made for postcards. At the end of the '80's he worked on some projects for monumental pavilions at the Exposition Universelle 1900 in Paris. Already in 1900 his style showed a limited use of Art Nouveau devices, and a return to more academic forms. From 1904 to 1912 he was often in the United States, where he taught in New York and Chicago. From 1912 to 1930 he lived mainly in Czechoslovakia and his work celebrated slavonic culture. He designed banknotes and stamps for the new Czechoslovac state. He worked on the following magazines (often designing their covers): *Zlatá Praha*, *Svétozor*, *La Vie Populaire*, *Le Costume au Théâtre*, *Le Petit Français Illustré*, *Le Monda*, *La Plume*, *Au Quartier latin*, *Le Figaro Illustré*, *Les Maîtres de l'Affiche*, *La Revue Mame*, *L'Image*, *Le Courrier Français*, *L'Illustration*, *Paris-Noël*, *Le magasin Pittores-*

que, *L'Estampe Moderne, L'Estampe et l'Affiche, Ver Sacrum, The Magazine of Art, Cocorico, Le Mois Littéraire et Pittoresque, L'Art Photographique, Le Chic, L'Universelle, L'Idée, Noël-Frimas, La Vie Moderne, La Revue du Bien, Paris World, Dvacáty Vek, Vzpomínky, Le Chroniqueur de Paris, Paris Illustré, L'Habitation Pratique, New York Daily News, Le Gaulois du Dimanche, La Parole Republicaine, The Index, Wiener Chic, Everybody's Magazine, The Literary Digest, Hearst's International*, etc. His graphic works are collected in the album *Combinaisons Ornamentales* (1901), *Documents Décoratifs* (1902), *Figures Décoratives* (1905).

Postcards a) Postcards published in France or in the United States: 1. 5 p. for the series 'Editions Cinos' c. 1898, reproducing posters by M. from 1896-97 for Sarah Bernhardt, 'Gismonda', 'La Dame aux Camélias', 'Lorenzaccio', 'La Samaritaine', and for the American company 'Waverley Cycles'. 2. 2 p. in the 'Job papiers à cigarettes' c. 1900, one reproducing a design already used for a calendar, for a poster and for the magazine La Plume, the other reproducing a 1893 poster. 3. 'Moët et Chandon' publ. F. Champenois, 10 p., c. 1900 variants of menus or posters of 1899. 4. 'Cartes postales artistiques' F. Champenois, at least 7 series of 12 p., c. 1900-1903. 4. 1. (The Seasons: *Printemps, Eté, Automne, Hiver*) 4 p. reproducing decorative panlés of c. 1897; (Flowers; *Iris, Oeillet, Lys, Rose*), 4 p. reproducing decorative panesl 1897, (The Ages of Man: *Enfance, Adolescence, Maturity, Vieillese*), 4 p. reproducing the plates for a 1896 calendar for Masson – Chocolat – Mexicain; the four arts: *Danse, Musique, Peinture, Poesie*), 4 p. reproducing decorative panels of 1908; (Byzantine Heads: *Blonde, Brunette*), 2 p. reproducing a decorative panel of c. 1897 (*Rêverie*), 1 p. reproducing a decorative panel of 1896 (Zodiac), 1 p. reproducing a design already used in several mediums; 4. 3. 3 p. with female figures, designed especially for postcards; 4 p. with female figures of the seasons designed for postcards; (*Salomé*), 1 p. variant on the design for *L'Estampe Moderne* of 1897; (*Crespuscule, Aurore, Primevère, La Plume*), 4 p. reproducing decorative panels of 1899; 4. 4. (*Les Mois*), 12 p. variants in colour of designs which first appeared as monochromatic lithographs in *Les Mois Littéraire et Pittoresque* in 1899-1900; each p. has a female figure with a dress and background appropriate to the climate of the month, set in a frame (there are series with the inscription 'Souvenir de la elle Jardinière); 4. 5 (*Sarah Bernhardt*), 1 p. for *La Plume* 1897; 1 p. reproducing a design of 1898 for the Société de la Bienfaisance Austro-Hongroise, 3 p. reproducing the design used for the cover of *Cocorico*. 1 p. reproducing a variant on the menu for Mme de Montholon and M. Monthiers; 4 p. reproducing designs already used for the menu; 1 p. with the design for a screen, from *Documents Décoratifs* (1902); 1 p. reproducing the design for the cover of the catalogue of the Exposition Universelle 1900 in Paris; 4. 6. 1 p. reproducing a design for a calendar or menu; (The times of the day: *Eveil du Matin, Éclat du jour, Rêverie du Soir, Repos de la nuit*), 4. p. reproducing decorative panels of 1899; (*Rêverie, Papeterie, Printemps*), 3 p. reproducing the design for the cover of *L'Estampe Moderne*; (Nénaphar, Fleur de Cerisier), 2 p. reproducing decorative panels of 1898; 4. 7. (Stones: *Améthyste, Émeraude, Rubis, Topaze*), 4. c. reproducing

decorative panels of 1900; (Plants: *Bruyère de falaise, Charden de grèves, Laurier, Lierre*), 4 c. reproducing decorative panels of 1901; (*La fleur, Le fruit*), 2 c. reproducing decorative panels c. 1897; 'Lygie', reproducing a poster of 1901 to publicize objects made by M.; (*Automne*), 1 p. reproducing a decorative panel of c. 1903. 5. 2 p. in the series 'Collection des Cent', publ. Gréningaire, Paris c. 1901, n. 11a (variant of the p. in the series 4.5); reproducing a design of 1907 for the Société de la Bienfaisance Austro-Hongroise; n. 116. seated peasant woman. 6. 'Madame Sarah Bernhardt's Repertoire, ... Farewell American Tour, Season of 1905-06', at least 3 p. reproducing theatre posters for *Gismonda, Lorenzaccio, Hamlet*, in simplified design for monochrome line prints. 7. 'Cognac Bisquit', F. Goosens jr., 1 p. publicity for the Belgian firm. 8. 'Collection Lefèvre Utile', 1. publicity p., a variant on the calendar of 1904 for the same biscuit factory. 9. 1 p. in the series of the Album Mariani, c. 1910. 10. 'Warner's Rust-Proof Corsets', at least 3 publicity p., variants on the poster of 1909 for the American firm. 11. 'Josephine Crane-Slavia, 1909', 1 p. published in the United States, a variant on an oil painting. 12. 'Madame Sarah Bernhardt's Repertoire . . .', at least 2 p. for the tour of Sarah Bernhardt in 1916-17, reproducing the theatre posters for *La Samaritaine, Lorenzaccio*, in simplified designs for monochrome reproduction.

b) Postcards published in Czechoslovakia after 1902: 1. Výstava ve Vyskove', exhibition of agriculture at Vyskov, Jan Hona, Vyskov, 1 p. variant of a poster of 1902. 2. 'Pojistovací banka Slavia' Stenc, Prague, 1909, 1 p. variant of the poster of 1907. 3. series of 7 p., Stenc, Prague, reproducing the illustrations 'The Beatitudes for *Everybody's Magazine* in 1906. 4. 1 p. for the student's day Politika, Prague, 1909. 5. 1 p. Commemorating the City of his birth Ivancice, Navrátil, Ivancice. 6. 15 p. reproducing the frescoes of the mayor's Chamber in Prague, Stenc, Prague, 1912. 7. 1 p. for the Bohemian Charity of the Heart, Politika, Prague 1912. 8. 1 p. 'Krajinská výstava v Ivancicích', Neubert, Prague, c. 1912, 1 p. for an exhibition in Ivancice. 9. 'Jarní slavnosti' (slave days), Neubert, Prague, 1 p. variant of the 1914 poster for the Jubilee of 1928. 10. 1 p. in the defence of national minorities, publ. Prague, 1915. Later during the first world war M. published other p. but only a limited number and less revealing for the history of Art Nouveau.

c) Postcards published in Italy: 1 p. 'Ricordo della Fiera di Beneficenza Bergamo Maggio 1900', Instituto d'Arti grafiche by Bergamo.
Bibl.: J. Mucha, M. Henderson, *The Graphic Work of Alphonse Mucha*, London 1973; J. and G. Neudin, 'Ce cher Mucha', *Le collectionneur français*, XIII (1977, n. 137), pp. 2, 3; Weill 1977; Neudin 1978, 1983; Fildier 1979; Gaibazzi 1979; Klamkin 1979; Baudet 1980; Q. D. Bowers, M. L. Martin, *The Postcards of Alphonse Mucha*, s.l. 1980; *Alphonse Mucha, the complete Graphic Works*, edited by A. Bridges, New York 1980; Drago 1981; Fanelli 1981, 1983; Mordente 1982; A. Weill. *Alphonse Mucha. Toutes les Cartes Postales*, Uppsala 1983.

Wilhelm MÜLLER-HOFMANN
Brünn, 5.4.1885 – ?
Painter, commercial artist, graphic designer.
He attended the Kunstgewerbeschule (M. Da-

sio) and the academy (P. v. Halm, F. v. Stuck, C. v. Marr) in Munich. He worked on the magazine *Jugend*.
Postcards: series 'Ausstellung München 1908'.
Bibl.: cat. Altonaer Museum, Hamburg 1970.

Adolf MÜNZER
Piess, Silesia (Pszczyna, Poland), 5.12.1870 – Landsberg a. Lech, 24.1.1953.
Painter, commercial artist, illustrator.
He attended the academy in Munich (K. Raupp, O. Seitz, P. Höcher). From 1900 to 1902 he was in Paris, from 1903 to 1909 he worked in Munich. From 1909 he was a professor at the Academy in Düsseldorf. He was a member of the group 'Die Scholle' in Munich. He worked on *Jugend*.
Postcards: p. in the first series of the 'Künstler-Postkarten' for Jugend, G. Hirth, Munich, 1898 and in the following series.
Bibl.: cat. Altonaer Museum, Hamburg 1970; Neudin 1983.

Ville MUSTA
Kuopio, 17.1.1886 – Vilppula, 6.3.1932
Painter, decorator.
He was educated at the School of Industrial Design (1902-03) and at the Academy (1903-06) in Helsinki. He was mainly active as a painter decorator.
Postcards: several with scenes of daily life and popular types, dateable around 1920, which still have Jugendstil elements.
Bibl.: Johanson – Termonen 1983.

N

Charles NAILLOD
Paris, 6.6.1876 – ?
Painter, commercial artist.
From 1906 he exhibited at the Salon des Indépendants. From 1920 he was a member of the Société des Artistes Français.
Postcards: 'Bal du Moulin Rouge'; several humorous p. of fashion in the style of Xavier Sager.
Bibl.: Baudet 1978, 1980; Forissier 1978.

Arnold NECHANSKY
Vienna, 17.3.1888 – Kitzbühel, 25.3.1938
Graphic designer, architect, designer of fabrics, tapestries, glass, jewellery, ceramist.
He attended from 1909 to 1913 the Kunstgewerbeschule in Vienna (O. Strnad, A. Böhm, J. Hoffmann). From 1919 to 1933 he taught at the Kunstgewerbeschule in Charlottenburg, Berlin. From 1912 he worked with the Wiener Werkstätte in several departments.
Postcards: 14 p. in the series of the Wiener Werkstätte greetings p. (nos. 792-796, 887, 890-897).
Bibl.: Mrazek 1977; Baudet 1978, 1980; Hansen 1982; Neuwirth 1984.

Ernst NEUMANN
Kassel, 3.9.1871 – Düren, 4.11.1954
Painter, woodcut artist, commercial artist, illustrator, graphic designer (books, publicity graphics).
He was the son of the academic painter Emil. He studied in Kassel, Paris and Munich. He was a member of the German Werkbund from 1912. He worked on the magazine *Jugend* and *Simplicissimus*.
Exhibitions: 'Ernst Neumann und Seine Schüler', Kunstgewerbemuseum, Berlin 1910.

Postcards: p. in the first series of the Künstler-Postkarten of *Jugend*, G. Hirth, Munich, 1898.
Bibl.: Baudet 1980.

William NICHOLSON
Newark-on-Trent, 5.2.1872 – Blewbury, Berkshire, 16.5.1949
Painter, commercial artist, illustrator, graphic designer, scenographer.
Substantially self-taught, except for a short study period at the Académie Julian in Paris (1889-90). He promoted poster design in Great Britain in collaboration with his brother-in-law J. Pryde, under the pseudonym 'The Beggarstaff Brothers', from 1894. He was the author of several albums of lithographs reproducing original colour woodcuts: *The Square Book of Animals* (1896), *An Alphabet* (1898), *An Almanach of Twelve Sports* (1898), *London Types* (1898), *Character of Romance* (1900).
Postcards: see Beggarstaff Brothers.

Ferinand NIGG
Vaduz, Liechtenstein, ? – ?
Painter, commercial artist.
His biographical details are unkown. From 1911 he taught at the Kunstgewerbeschule in Magdeburg and from 1913 in the Kunstgewerbeschule und Handwerkschule in Cologne.
Postcards: p. in the series 10 of the 'Künstlerkarten', Stengel & Co. Dresden a. Berlin; several decorative p.

Emil NOLDE, pseudonym of Emil HANSEN
Nolde, Schleswig, 7.8.1867 – Seebüll, Nordfriesland, 15.4.1956
Painter, engraver, graphic designer.
A woodcarver, in 1890 he moved to Berlin as a furniture maker. From 1892 to 1898 he taught at the Gewerbemuseum in St Gallen. Towards 1895 he drew the famous anthropomorphic Swiss mountains which were reproduced in postcards (1896 and afterwards) by the publishers Fr. A. Prantl, Munich, and F. Killinger, Zurich, and which were enormously successful with the public. They gave him the money to travel and study in Dachau, Munich, Paris, Copenhagen, Berlin. In c. 1905 he became a member of the expressionist group 'Die Brücke', in Dresden.
Bibl.: *Jugend*, I (1896), n. 36, 5 September, p. 585; Lehrs 1898; E. Nolde, *Das eigene Leben. Die Zeit der Jugend* 1867-1902, Cologne 1967[3]; cat. Altonaer Museum, Hamburg 1970; Neudin 1978; Gaibazzi 1979; Holt 1981; Till 1983.

Plinio NOMELLINI
Leghorn, 6.8.1866 – Florence, 8.8.1943
Painter, etcher, illustrator, commercial artist.
He was a student of N. Betti at the School of Design in Leghorn, and of G. Fattori at the Academy of Fine Arts in Florence. His early work was influenced by the Machiaioli, he later moved towards a personal interpretation of divisionism. In the last decade of the century he was in Genoa. From 1902 he settled in Torre del Lago, where he often met Puccini, Pascoli, D'Annunzio, Pizzetti. In 1904 he was nominated professor at the Academy in Florence. He made illustrations for some magazines: *La Riviera Ligure*, *Novissima* (1905), *Il Giornalino della Domenica* (1906) – and for the books: *I Lanzi* by E. Moschino (1908); *Poemi del Risorgimento* by G. Pascoli (1913); *La vita del Pitocco* by De Quevedo (1917). He also designed some posters.
Postcards: 'Municipio de Genova – Inaugura-

zione del Monumento ai Mille – 5 maggio 1915', publ. Ricordi, Milan, reproducing the poster; several war propaganda and a patriotic p., 1915-18.
Bibl.: Bartoli-Mataloni 1979; *La cartolina*, n. 4, 1982; Arrasich 1984.

Isidre NONELL i MONTURIOL
Barcelona, 1873 – Barcelona, 1911
Painter, designer, illustrator.
He was a student at the Mirabent Academy, of M. Altés and at the Escuela de Artes y Aficios Artísticos y Bellas Artes in Barcelona. In 1897 and in 1899 he stayed in Paris, where he had some one-man shows. From 1902 to 1910 he exhibited at the exhibitions of the Société des Artistes Indépendants and at the Brussels exhibition of the Libre Esthétique. He worked on the magazines *La Vanguardia*, *Luz*, *Quatre Gats*, *Pèl & Ploma*, *Papitu*.
Postcards: several in the series 'Pro Patria', publ. Circulo Artistico, Barcelona.
Bibl.: Trenc Ballester 1977.

Francesco NONNI
Faenza, 4.11.1885 – Faenza, September, 1976
Woodcut artist, ceramist, illustrator.
Very young he became an apprentice carver with the craftsmen Ebanisteria Casalini in Faenza. At the same time attended the municipal evening arts and trade school 'Minardi', where he met D. Baccarini and other artists in his circle and where he had Berti, the architect Pritelli and the sculptor Campello as his teachers. From 1902 he made several engravings which showed the influence of A. Baruffi and of A. De Carolis, as well as A. Beardsley and L. Pissarro, which he knew through the magazine *Emporium*. In 1906 he exhibited woodcuts at the international exhibition in Milan. In 1908 he exhibited at the Quadriennale in Turin and in 1910, 1912 and 1914 at the Biennale in Venice. From 1911 to 1913 he worked on the magazine *L'Eroica* with a series of woodcuts. He illustrated the books *Canti di Faunus* and *Un tempio d'amore* by A. Beltramelli and children's stories by the same writer and by M. Moretti. Between 1924 and 1926 he founded and directed in Faenza the magazine *Xilografia*. From the Twenties he was particularly active in ceramics.
Postcards: p. in the series 'Espozione Emiliana di bianco e nero', 1912; publicity p. 'Inchiostri Gio Diletti, Brisighella'; publicity p. 'Acqua Minerale Meo', several p. in the series for the magazine *Il Plaustro*, which reproduced his illustrations; several woodcuts.
Bibl.: *Il Liberty a Bologna e nell'Emilia Romagna*, exhibition cat., Bologna 1977; Arrasich 1984.

Gaston NOURY
Elbeuf, Seine-Inférieure, 1866 – ?
Painter, illustrator, commercial artist, cartoonist, theatrical costumier.
He worked for several years in the physiological laboratory in Le Havre, making sketches and drawings for the albums *L'Acquarium du Havre* and *L'Estuaire de la Seine*. He illustrated some books on the natural sciences, eg. *La Nature* by Tissandier. In Paris he attended the courses of the flower painter Clément. He worked on the following newspapers: *La Chronique Parisienne*, *Saint-Nicolas*, *Gil Blas illustré*, *Journal amusant* (1889-90), *Les Hommes d'aujourd'hui*. Of his many posters, the one 'Pour les Pauvres de France et de Russie' (1892), also reproduced as a postcard,

and the one for the Salon des Cent are especially well known.
Postcards: 1 p. in the series 'Cinos', 1898, reproducing the poster 'Pour les Pauvres . . .', series of at least 10 . 'Les Chaussures', c. 1900; series of 12 p. 'Carte à jouer' (6 are about the *affaire Dreyfus*), 1901; 1 p. in the 'Collection des Cent' c. 1901; series of women's faces covered by veils; series 'Les Coffrets'.

Jenny Eugenia NYSTRÖM STOOPENDAAL
Kalmar, 13.6.1854 (or 1857 or 1867) – Stockholm, 17.1.1946
Painter, watercolourist, illustrator, graphic designer (calnedars, books).
From 1873 to 1881 she attended the Academy in Stockholm. She completed her studies in Munich and in Paris (1882-86), where she attended the Académie Julian. She became very popular in Sweden as a magazine illustrator *Ny illustrerad tidning* and *Svea* and of many books especially for children: *Barkamarensbok* (1882), *Svenska folksägner* (1882), *Urfolksagans rosengardar* (1889-90); *Franska sagor* (1903).
Postcards: in her rich production of p. which reaches several hundred designs, of particularly high quality are some series of scenes of Swedish life, in which she showed a personal reading of the work of Carl Larsson; the world of childhood is another subject which inspired p., she designed several greetings p.

O

Otto OBERMEIER
Munich, 23.7.1883 – Munich, 14.12.1958
Painter, commercial artist, graphic designer, applied arts designer.
He attended the Kunstgewerbeschule in Munich (M. Dasio, F. Widnmann).
Postcards: p. in the series 'Ausstellung München 1908'; publicity p. 'Drei König-Bier, Mathäserbräu München'.
Bibl.: Cat. Altonaer Museum, Hamburg 1970.

Willy Richard OERTEL
Langendreer, Westphalia, 4.11.1868 – ?
Watercolourist, commercial artist, graphic designer (books), illustrator.
He attended from 1886 to 1888 the Kunstgewerbeschule in Düsseldorf. He was a founder member of the Munich Cabaret 'die Elf Scharfrichter' (1901).
Postcards: p. in the series 10 of the 'Künstlerkarten', Stengel & Co, Dresden u. Berlin; several decorative p.
Bibl.: cat. Altonaer Museum, Hamburg 1970.

Edmond van OFFEL
Antwerp, 14.4.1871 – Gravenwezel, 5.9.1959
Illustrator, painter, poet, commercial artist, graphic designer (books, ex libris).
He studied at the academy in Antwerp. He wrote several volumes of poetry, which he also illustrated: *Bloei* (1896); *De Beproeving* (1899); *Evert Larock* (1901); *De getijden* (1910). He also illustrated the books: *Marioline* by D. de Vos (1899); *Rhijnsche legenden* by F. Mayer van den Bergh (1902); *De amman van Antwerpen* by P. de Mont (1903); *Zoo vertellen de Vlamingen* by P. de Mont and A. de Cock (1903); *Flick* by A. Callant (1905); *Versjes en liedges voor't jonge volkje* by H. van Tichelen (1906); *In dien tijd* by F. van Cuvck

(1908); *Op Wolksken* by D. Demers (1908); *Kruisbloemen* by C. Eeckels (1908); *Fiere Magriet van Leuven* by A. Dekkers (1910); *Formortinta Delsuno rakontita de li mem* by R. Vermandere (1910); *Natuurverklarende Sprookjes* by A. de Cock (1911-12); *De martelaars van Nicomedië* by A. Dekkers (1912); *Le clos-feuillu et son maître* by A. Hans (1912); *Bêtes et gens* by L. Scheltjens (1912); *Soldatentypen uit den grooten oorlog* by G. Raal (1914); *De ster met den Steert* by R. Vermandere (1914); *Leven en lijden van O. H. Jezus Christus* by J. Wiltlox (1914); *La Belle au bois dormant* by Ch. Perrault (1917).
Postcards: series of 4 p of the seasons: 1 p in the 'Byrrh' series, 1906.
Bibl.: Baudet 1978; Rostenne.

Eugène OGÉ
Paris, ? – ?
Designer, lithographer, commercial artist
He exhibited at the Salon des Artistes Français, where he received an honorary mention in 1901. He designed posters for the printer Ch. Verneau.
Postcards: p. in the series 'Les Affiches célèbres, Tuck, London; severe publicity p.
Bibl.: Baudet 1980.

Otto Josef OLBERTZ
Cologne, 12.11.81 – ?
Painter, commercial artist.
He attended the Academy in Munich (G. V. Hack, C. V. Marr). He worked in Leipzig and Munich.
Postcards: 'Gauklert-Tag 1907', Künstlerfestkarte, Druck H. Höhler, Munich.
Bibl.: cat. Altonaer Museum, Hamburg 1970.

Joseph Maria OLBRICH
Troppau (Opava), Western Silesia, 22.11.1867 – Düsseldorf, 8.8.1908.
Architect, commercial artist, graphic designer, illustrator, designer of fabrics, furniture, objects of daily use, of jewellery, of glass, of metalwork, ceramist.
He attended from 1889 to 1893 the academy in Vienna (C. V. Hasenauer). He was a member of the 'Siebener Club', established c. 1895. He was a founder member of the Viennese Secession for which he designed the headquarters (1897–98). In 1899 he moved to Darmstadt where he planned and organized the Künstlerkolonie of the Mathildenhöhe. He was a foremost Jugenstil architect in Austria and in Germany. He worked on the magazine *Ver Sacrum*. He took part in the exhibitions of the Viennese Secession.
Postcards: several in the first 5 series of the 'Wiener Künstler–Postkarten', called 'Artists' Correspondence', Philipp & Kramer, 1897, in collaboration with fellow members of the 'Siebener Club'; p. in the series 'Ver Sacrum', published for the 1st exhibition of the Viennese Secession, Verlag Gerlach & Schenk; Vienna, 1898, in collaboration with K. Moser; p. 'Das Haus der Secession', Kunstanstalt A. Berger, Vienna, c. 1898, in several colour versions; series for the Künstlerkolonie Ausstellung Darmstadt 1904, reproducing his designs for the houses of the colony and kiosks for selling postcards etc.; series of 6 p. for the Gartenbau Ausstellung, Darmstadt, 1905; p. for the Deutsche Künstausstellung, Cologne, 1906, 'Frauen Rosenhof'; p. for the Mannheimer Jubiläums–Ausstellung 1907, 'Damensalon' . . .
Bibl.: *Joseph M. Olbrich, 1867–1908, Das*

Werk des Architekten, cat. of the exhibition by various authors Darmstadt–Vienna–Berlin 1967; cat. Darmstadt 1976; *Joseph M. Olbrich 1867-1908*, cat. of the exhibition by various authors Mathildenhöhe Darmstadt 1983.

Filippo OMEGNA
Turin, 11.3.1881 – Montaldo di Mondovì, 1.9.1948.
Painter, decorator.
He was educated at the Accademia Albertina in Turin, where he was a student of F. Grosso. In 1902 he exhibited for the first time at the Promotrice di Belle Arti in Turin. In 1904 he won the 'Grand Prix' at the exhibition of painting in St. Louis. He was the professor of the nude and of the history of dress at the academy in Turin.
Postcards: publicity p. for the automobiles 'Padus' 1908; 'Esposizione di Belle Arti – 70 della Soc. Promotrice, Torino, via Zecca 25'.
Bibl.: Mordent 1982; Arrasich 1984.

Ricard OPISSO i SALA
Tarragona, 20.11.1880 – ?, 1966
Designer, illustrator, graphic designer (books, publicity and commercial graphics), commercial artist, caricaturist.
He was the son of the writer and journalist Alfred. In his youth he worked under Gaudì at the Sagrada Familia. As an illustrator and caricaturist he worked on the following magazines *Hispania, Hojas Selectas, Calendari del Cu-cut, Luz, Carba, Quatre Gats, Pèl & Ploma, Or y Grana, La Vanguardia, Xut, L'Esquella de la Torratxa*.
Postcards: publicity p. 'Farmacia Novellas', 1902, p. in the series for the artistic circle of Sant Lluc.
Bibl.: Trenc Ballester 1977.

Argio ORELL
Trieste, 17.9.1884 – Trieste, 10.1.1942
Commercial artist, painter, engraver.
He was a student of E. Scomparini at the Scuola Industriale in Trieste. In Munich he attended F. von Stuck's courses at the Academy and obtained an award reserved for foreign students in the second semester (1902-03). He returned to Trieste and began to show his paintings in the schollian shop and then he took part in the Permanente in 1906. He worked above all in graphic art and poster design.
Postcards: 'Covegno Studenti di Trieste, 1901'; 'Ricordo del Convegno Interregionale degli studenti, Trieste, 1906'; 'I Esposizione Provinciale Istriana, Capodistria 1910'; p. for the 'Lega Nazionale, Trieste', 1911.
Bibl.: Mordente 1982; Arrasich 1984.

Emil ORLIK
Prague, 21.7.1870 – Berlin, 28.9.1932
Painter, woodcut artist, etcher, commercial artist, illustrator, graphic designer (books, ex libris designer in applied arts, scenographer, theatrical costumier.
From 1889 to 1891 he attended the private school of H. Knirr in Munich; from 1891 to 1893 the Academy in Munich (W. V. Lindenschmit jr., J. L. Raab). In 1900-01 during a journey to Japan he learnt the techniques of colour woodcuts. From 1903-1904 he worked in Vienna, where he was part of the Secession and worked with the Wiener Werkstätte (plates with figures). From 1905 to 1935 he taught at the Kunstgewerbeschule in Berlin. He worked on *Jugend*.

Postcards: series of views of Amsterdam, c. 1896; c. with illustration of stories ('Hansel und Gretel', etc.), Verlag B. G. Teubner, Leipzig, c. 1910. He designed many single-copy p. which he sent to friends.
Bibl.: Lehrs 1898; cat. Altonaer Museum, Hamburg 1970; *Emil Orlik Malergrüsse an Max Lehrs* 1898-1930, edited by Adalbert Stiften Verein, Munich 1981.

Alfred OST
Zwijndrecht, 1884 – Antwerp (or Mechelen), 1945
Painter, designer, illustrator.
He attended the Academy of Fine Art in Antwerp. He illustrated the book *Malines jadis et aujourd'hui* (1908) by L. Godenne and worked for the political newspaper *Notenkraker*. He showed his work at exhibitions of painting in Brussels (1913) and Antwerp. A convinced pacifist, he was in Holland during the first world war.
Postcards: 'Sauve qui peut', 1907; series 'De Beiiaard', 1910; series 'Mechelen', 1911; series 'Oud Mechelen', Drukk. Van den Bossche, Mechelen, 1912; 'Boerenmin', 1912; 'Je t'aime', 1912; 'De Zoen', 1912; 'De Vlietjes', 1912; 'Au Faubourg', 1912; series of 6 p. 'Aux Bals Masqués de la Monnaie', Lith. J. Goffin Fils, Brussels, designed in 1913 but published for carnival in 1914; series of 30 p. 'La Dyle'; series 'Gedenkenis der Jubelfest van Hanswyck-Mechelen 988-1913', two series of 6 p. H. Conscience; 'De Belfortstrijd'; 'De Ommegang'; 'Der Reuzen'; series of philanthropic and patriotic p. for Holland; 'Carte de soutien d'oeuvres philanthropiques Belges'; series Stuis, Amsterdam.
Bibl.: Philippen 1977; Rostenne 1978, 1979; Holts 1983.

OST, pseudonym of Oskar PETERSEN
Marsnen, Livland, 24.4.1875 – ?
Painter, commercial artist, illustrator, writer.
He studied at the Academy in Munich. He worked on the satirical anticommunist newspaper *Rote Hand*. From 1924 he was working in Riga.
Postcards: different subjects but mainly winter sports.
Bibl.: Baudet 1980.

Wenzel OSWALD
Mies (Stríbro), Bohemia, 25.8.1885 – ?
Graphic designer, engraver, designer of glass and of jewellery.
He attended the Graphische Lehr-und Versuchsanstalt and from 1906 the Kunstgewerbeschule in Vienna (B. Löffler). Exhibitions: Kunstschau, Vienna 1908; Bugra, Leipzig 1914.
Postcards: 3 p. in the series of the Wiener Werkstätte; 2 greetings (nos. 146, 150), one 'Schiller in Karlsbad' (n. 213).
Bibl.: Baudet 1980; Hansen 1982.

P

Emilio PAGGIARO
Venice, 28.3.1859 – Venice, 1929
Painter.
He was educated at the Accademia de Belle Arti in Venice. He exhibited at the Biennale in Venice in 1899 and in 1920.
Postcards: 'I Esposizione Internazionale di cartoline postali illustrate, Venezia, 1899'; 'Carnevale di Treviso, 1899'; 'Anno Santo,

1900'; 'Lonigo – Fiera di Cavalli, 1904' 'Esposizione d'Arte Sacra Moderna, Venezia, 1908'; 'Ravenna – VI Centenario Dantesco, 1908'.
Bibl.: Bartoli-Mataloni 1979; Bobba 1979; Gaibazzi 1979; Mordente 1982; Arrasich 1984.

Alexander PAISCHEFF
Viipuri, 1.3.1894 – Helsinki, 15.9.1937
Painter, engraver.
He completed his studies at the art school in Viipuri (1908-12), then moved to Helsinki where he attended the Suomen Taideyhdistyksen piirustuskoulu (1912-14) and the Taideteollinen keskuskoulu (1912-15). He was known above all for his work as an engraver.
Postcards: several from the period 1910-20 with Finnish winter scenes.
Bibl.: Johanson – Termonen 1983.

PAL, pseudonym of Jean de PALEOLOGU
Bucharest, 29.8.1860 (or 1855) – ?
Commercial artist, illustrator, painter.
He attended the military Academy in Rumania and studied art in London, where he worked on magazines like *Strand Magazine*, *Vanity Fair* and *New York Herald*.
In 1893 he moved to Paris where he designed posters and worked on the magazines *La Plume*, *Le Rire*, *Cocorico*, *Le Froufrou*, *Sans-Gêne* and *La Vie en Rose*. He illustrated for editions Charpentier *Petits Poèmems-russes* (1893). In 1895 he took part in the collective exhibition in the gallery of the théâtre La Bodinière.
Postcards: 1p. in the series 'Cinos', reproducing the poster, 1898; 1p. in the series 'Affiches de Chemins de fer'.
Bibl.: Baudet 1980.

Giuseppe PALANTI
Milan, 30.7.1881 – Milan, 23.4.1946
Painter, commercial artist, scenographer and costumier, graphic designer (commercial and publicity graphics).
From 1895 he attended evening classes at the Scuola superiore d'Arte applicata all' Industria, where he got a diploma in 1901, and at the Scuola degli Artefici at the Accademia de Brera. From 1902 to 1914 he worked as a modeller and scenographer at the Scala. From the first year of the century, he worked as a commercial artist, above all for Ricordi for whom he designed several posters for operas. In 1905 he got a diploma from the school of painting at the Accademia di Brera. In 1907 he was nominated for a chair at the school of ornament at the Accademia de Brera and at the Scuola superiore di arte applicata all' industria. In 1910 he executed the decorations for the Italian pavilions at the exhibitions in Buenos Aires and Brussels.
Postcards: series of 16p. 'Pompei', publ. Ricordi, Milan 1905, reproducing watercolours; several in the series of the 'Cartoline ufficiali dell'Esposizione di Milano 1906', Officine Grafiche Pilade Rocco & C., Milan 1906 reproducing his watercolours of pavilions; 'Maratona italiana promossa dal Secolo di Milano', 1908; 'I Raid Aereo Milano-torino e ritorno', 1911; p. for the opera 'Isabeau', Ricordi, Milan 1912; reproducing the poster, 'Esposizione Nazional di Belle Arti dell'Accademia de Brera', 1912, reproducing the poster 'Comitato Nazionale Italiano Pro Palestina e Pro Lourdes'; publicity p. for 'Il Barbiere de Sivilglia'; several p. for the national war loan; '283 Compagnia Battaglione Pallanza', 1917; several regimental and war propaganda p.

Bibl.; *La Cartolina*, n. 4, 1982; Mordente 1982; Arrasich 1984.

Rodolfo PAOLETTI
Venice, 23.4.1866 – Milan, ?
Painter, illustrator, decorator.
He was educated at the Accademia di Belle Arti in Venice. He was intensely active as an illustrator in newspapers and magazines (particularly for *Natura é Arte*).
Postcards: '20 Settember 1870 – Roma intangibile – XXXI anniversario', design dated 1900; '2 novembre, Lith. Allievi Grasi, Milano 1900; 'Esposizione di Lodi-Concorsi internazionali di cartoline postali – 1901'; 'Esposizione enologica-gastronomica, Milan, 1901'; series of publicity p. for the magazine *Natura e Arte*; series publicizing 'Liquore Strega' with views of Rome; series publicizing 'Liquore Strega' with views of Benevento; series of views of Palermo; series of 'donnine'.
Bibl.: Bartoli-Mataloni 1979; Bobba 1979; Gaibazzi 1979; Mordente 1982; Arrasich 1984.

Ethel PARKINSON, pseudonym of Ethel CHAPMAN
Her biographical details are unknown.
Postcards: series for several publishers, especially C. W. Faulkner, London, with scenes (winter ones are typical) of couples, women, children, also in costume.
Bibl.: Holt 1980, 1983.

Bruno PAUL
Seifhennersdorf, Saxony, 19.1.1874 – Berlin, 17.8.1968
Architect, painter, commercial artist, illustrator, designer in the applied arts.
He attended from 1886 to 1894 the Academy in Dresden; from 1904 to 1907 the Academy in Munich (P. Höcker, W. v. Diez). From 1907 he taught at the Kunstgewerbeschule in Berlin. In 1897 he was a founder member of the Vereinigten Werkstätten für Dunst im handwerk. He worked for the magazines *Jugend* (from 1896), and *Simplicissimus*.
Postcards: p. in the first series of the 'Künstler-Poskarten' for *Jugend*, G. Hirth, Munich, 1898; p. in the series for *Simplicissimus*, c. 1900-1910; 'Kunst im Handwerk, München Ausstellung', 1901, reproducing the poster.
Bibl.: cat. Altonaer Museum, Hamburg 1970; Fildir 1983; Till 1983.

René-Louis PÉAN
Paris, 1.7.1875 – ?
Illustrator, commercial artist, lithographer, graphic designer (commercial graphics, song scores).
He was educated at the Ecole des Arts décoratifs in Paris. He made several paintings and pastels of Spanish scenes. He worked for the magazines *Supplément musical de l'Illustration* (1896-1900), *La Rampe* (1899), *Le Plaisir* (1906), *Le Sourire* (1920). He illustrated *Chanson d'Atelier* by Paul Delmet (1901). He was very active as a commercial artist, influenced above all by Jules Chéret.
Postcards: 1p. in the 'Collection des Cent', publ. Gréningaire, Paris, c. 1901; 1p. in the series 'Gala Henry Monnier', 1904; 1p. in the series 'Byrrh', 1906; p. in the series 'Affiches des Chemins de fer'; several reproducing posters; several publicity p.
Bibl.: Baudet 1978; Neudin 1983.

Dagobert PECHE
St. Michael im Lungau, Salzburg, 3.4.1887 –

Vienna, 16.4.1923
Architect, commercial artist, graphic designer (books), woodcut artist, designer of fabrics, tapestries, carpets, glass, stencils for wall decorations, frames for paintings and mirrors, metalwork, jewellery, enamels, furnishing, leather work, fashion, fashion accessories, toys, ceramist, scenographer and theatrical costumier.
He attended from 1906 to 1910 the Technische Hochschule (K. König, M. v. Ferstel, L. Simony) and from 1908 to 1911 the Academy in Vienna (F. Ohmann). He worked with the Wiener Werkstätte from 1915 in all departments, becoming one of its principal figures.
Postcards: 2p. with carnival costumes in the series of the Wiener Werkstätte (nos. 625, 626).
Bibl.: Mrazek 1977; Baudet 1980; Hansen 1982.

Andre PETRONI
Venosa, Potenza, 8.7.1863 – ?
Painter.
He finished his early artistic studies at the Istituto di Belle Arti in Naples. From 1884 to 1911 he took part in the exhibitions of the Promotrice 'Salvator Rosa' in Naples. In 1910 he exhibited in the Biennale in Venice.
Postcards: 'Esposizione d'igiene, Napoli, 1900'; 'I Cinquantenario della Insurrezione Lucana – Festeggiamenti a Potenza', 1910; p. for the V national loan, publ. Alfieri Lacroix, c. 1916; satirical p. on the first world war, 1915-18; publicity p. for the Neapolitan paper *Il Pungolo Parlamentare*.
Bibl.: Gaibazzi 1979; Mordente 1982; Arrasich 1984.

Valerie PETTER-ZEIS
Vienna, 23.9.1881 – Vienna 1.7.1963
Graphic designer, designer of tapestries, of wooden clock cases.
She studied at the private painting school Hohenberger and from 1904 at the Kunstgewerbeschule in Vienna (B. Löffler). Her works are published in the magazines *Muskete*, *Erdgeist*, *Die Fläche* (vol. II, 1909).
Exhibitions; Kunstschau, Vienna, 1908.
Postcards: 1 greeting sp. in the Wiener Werkstätte series (n. 153).
Bibl.: Dichand-Martischnig 1978; Baudet 1980; Hansen 1982.

Maria PRANKE
Pándorf, Hungary, 27.8.1891 – ?
Graphic designer.
She studied at the Kunstschule für Frauen und Mädchen and from 1910 to 1914 at the Kunstgewerbeschule in Vienna (K. Moser). She worked for the magazine *Erdgeist*.
Exhibitions: Kunstschau, Vienna, 1908.
Postcards: 6p. in the Wiener Werkstätte series all decorative (nos. 548-550, 567, 568, 803).
Bibl.: Hansen 1982.

James PRYDE
Edinburgh, 30.3.1869 – London, 24.2.1941
Commercial artist, painter, woodcut artist, graphic designer.
He attended the Royal Scottish Academy in Edinburgh and the Académie Julian in Paris (Bouguereau). He promoted the art of posters in Great Britain in collaboration with his brother-in-law W. Nicholson under the pseudonym 'The Beggarstaff Brothers', from 1894.
Postcards: see Beggarstaff Brothers.

Erwin PUCHINGER

Vienna, 31.7.1876 – Vienna 24.6.1944
Architect, painter, engraver, graphic designer (books).
He went to evening classes at the Graphischen Lehr und Versuchsanstalt (where from 1901 he taught and from 1892 to 1901 the Kunstgewerbeschule (H. Matsch) in Vienna.
Postcards: 'Ofizielle Postkarte, Internationale Jugdausstellung, Wien 1910'; 'International Post-Wertzeichen Ausstellung, Wien 1911, Secession'; 'Erste Internationale Jagdausstellung, Wien 1910' (at least 2p.).

Ivo PUHONNÝ
Baden-Baden, 19.7.1876 – ?
Painter, engraver, commercial artist, graphic designer (ex libris), illustrator, puppet designer.
He was the son of the landscape painter Victor. He attended the Kunstgewerbeschule in Vienna and the Academy in Karlsruhe (R. Poetzelberger). He went on study trips to Paris and Japan. He made wood cuts and lithographs for Verlag der Kunstdruckerei Künstlerbund-Karlsruhe. From 1913 to 1919 he was a member of the Deutsche Werkbund.
Postcards: series 'Gruss vom Bazar', c. 1899; series 'Gruss aus Paris', 'Restaurant Krokodil- . . . Baden-Baden', 1906.

R

Richard RANFT
Plainpalais, near Geneva, 18.7.1862 – ?, 1931
Painter, illustrator, engraver, commercial designer.
In Geneva he studied design with E. Sordet and A. Dumont and painting under the guidance of G. Courbet. Towards 1880 he moved to Paris, where he worked on several magazines and he made book illustrations for the following: *Mlle d'Orchair* (1892); *Scènes de courtisanes* by Lucian (1901); *L'illustre famille* (1913). He exhibited at the Salon of the Société Nationale des Beaux-Arts and of the Artistes Indépendants.
Postcards: 1 p. in the 'Collection des Cent', publ. Gréningaire, Paris, c. 1901.
Bibl.: Baudet 1978.

Armand RASSENFOSSE
Liège, 6.8.1862 - Liège 28.1.1934
Painter, engraver, illustrator, commercial artist, graphic designer (ex libris, books, publicity graphics).
He attended the Academy in Liège, where he was a student of A. Witte. A decisive event in his development was his meeting with F. Rops, who later exercised a profound influence on his graphic work. Together with Rops he developed a particular varnishing technique called 'Ropsenfosse'. He took part in the exhibition of the 'Société des Aquafortistes Belges' (1893, 1895), of the Parisian 'Salon des Cent' (February and November 1896) and in the 'Libre Esthétique'. With A. Donnay, E. Berchmans and M. Siville he founded the *Caprice revue*. Towards 1888 he began working as a commercial artist. Among the books he illustrated the most appreciated is the edition of *Les Fleurs du Mal* by Baudelaire (1899), commissioned by the Parisian Société des Bibliophiles. He also illustrated: *Almanach des poètes pour l'année 1897* (1896); *Le Rideau cramoisi* by Barbey d'Aurevilly; *La Femme et le Pantin* and *Au beau plafond* by Glesener.
Postcards: 1 p. in the 'Collection Job', series of

1914; several p. in limited editions using etching, p. reproducing paintings.
Bibl.: Wiener 1922-23; Rostenne 1979.

Maurice RÉALIER DUMAS
Paris 9.2.1860 – Chatou, Seine-et-Oise, 25.12.1928.
Painter, commercial artist, graphic designer (song scores).
He was a pupil of J. -L. Gérôme at the Ecole des Beaux-Arts in Paris. From 1886 he exhibited at the Salon of the Société des Artistes Français where he was often recognized; an honourable mention in 1886 and 1889, third-class medal in 1896. He won a bronze medal at the Exposition Universelle in Paris in 1900. He was the author of several posters for fashion-houses, for 'Champagne Jules Mumm', and for 'Madères Blandy'.
Postcards: 1 p. in the series 'Napoléon' designed for the magazine *Scribner's Magazine*.
Bibl.: Baudet 1980.

Georges REDON
Paris, 16.11.1869-?, 1943.
Cartoonist, commercial artist, lithographer, painter.
He exhibited at the Salon des Artistes Francais (where he received an honourable mention in 1904), at the Salon of the Société Nationale des Beaux-Arts, at the Salon d'Automne, and at the Salon des Humoristes.
Postcards: 1 p. in the series 'Cinos' 1898 (reproducing the poster 'Moulin de la Galette'), in the same series another two p. are attributed to him which reproduce the posters 'Souvenir du Moulin Rouge' and 'Souvenir d'une visite à Trianon'; 1 p. in the series 'Gala Henry Monnier', 1904; 1p. in the series 'Byrrh', 1906.
Bibl.: Weill 1977; Baudet 1980.

Fritz (Friedrich) REHM
Munich, 19.4.1871 – Lichtenfels, 5.10.1928.
Commercial artist, illustrator, graphic designer (ex libris).
He attended the Kunstgewerbeschule and the Academy in Munich. He was active as a publicity commercial artist.
Postcards: series of busts of women in medallions and friezes embossed in gold ('Wein', 'Märchen', 'Hexerei', 'Tanz', 'Liebe' etc.); publicity for 'Otto Perutz Trockenplatten-Fabrik München', A. Gierster Lith. Kunstanstalt, München, c. 1900.
Bibl.: Lebeck 1980; Drago 1981.

Ferdinand Freiherr von REZNICEK
Ober-Sievering, Vienna, 16.6.1868 – Munich, 11.5.1909.
Painter, commercial artist, illustrator.
He was a member of the Hagenbund in Vienna from 1902 to 1909. He was active in Munich working for the magazines *Jugend, Simplicissimus, Fliegenden Blätter. Album: Sic* (1900), *Unter vier Augen* etc.
Postcards: p. in the first 3 series of the 'Künstler-Postkarten' for *Jugend*, G. Hirth, Munich, 1898-99; several p. in the series for *Simplicissimus*, A. Langen, Munich, c. 1900-1910.
Bibl.: cat. Altonaer Museum, Hamburg 1970; Baudet 1980; Lebeck 1980; Drago 1981.

Louis Marie Joseph RIDEL
Vannes (Morbihan), 12.2.1866 - ?
Painter, illustrator, medallist.
He was a student of E. Delauney, G. Moreau

and A. P. M. de Richemont. He exhibited at the Salon of the Société des Artistes Français, where he received an honourable mention in 1896, a third-class medal in 1898 and second-class one in 1900. He exhibited at the Salon des Tuileries.
Postcards: 1p. in the series 'Byrrh', 1906.
Bibl.: Baudet 1978.

Paul RIETH
Pösznec, Thuringia, 16.6.1871 – Munich, 15.5.1925.
Painter, commercial artist, illustrator.
He attended the Academy in Munich (L. v. Löfftz) and from 1889 the one in Karlsruhe (K. Meyer). He worked on the magazine *Jugend* (1899-1904).
Postcards: 'Lyrisches Theater München'.
Bibl.: Till 1983.

Alexandre de RIQUER i YNGLADA
Calaf, Barcelona, 3.5.1856 – Palma in Mallorca, 13.11.1920.
Painter, interior decorator, illustrator, commercial artist, engraver, graphic designer (ex libris, books, lettering, song scores, commercial and publicity graphics, menus, programmes and dance carnets, birth and death announcements, Christmas notes and invitations), furniture designer, art critic, poet.
He began studying engineering, which he abandoned to enrol in the School of Fine Arts in Barcelona, where he was the student of T. Padró and of A. Caba. In 1879 he made a study trip to Italy, to Paris and London, where he later returned in 1894 to broaden his acquaintance with Pre-Raphaelite art which deeply influenced his work. In 1888 he won a second-class medal at the Exposition Universelle. He was active above all in the decorative and graphic arts, and he became one of its foremost Modernist exponents in the fields of ex libris, book design, posters and illustrations. His first production of ex libris was published in the volume *Ex libris d. A de R* (Barcelona 1903). He illustrated and designed the layout for *Los Estudiants de Tolosa* (1886). *La llegendeta lo Rossinyol* by F. Matheu (1887) and his own works *Quan jo era noy* (1897), *Crisantemes* (1889), *Anyoranses* (1902), *Aplech de Sonets* (1906) and *Poema del Bosch* (1910). In 1903 he was a founder member of the 'Societat Catalana de Bibliofils'. As a commercial artist his first poster appeared for the IV Exposición de Bellas Artes e Industrias Artisticas in Barcelona, for which he designed in the following year another poster, an important moment in the promotion of Catalan commercial art. In 1898 he won the second prize in the poster competition 'Anís del Mono'. He was artistic director of the magazines *Luz* (1897-98) and *Joventut* (1900-06). He worked on several Catalan magazines: *La Ilustració Catalana, La Ilustración Artistica, El Gato Negro, Hojas Selectas, La Ilustració Llevantina, Garba, Quatre Gats, Pèl & Ploma*. In 1893 he won the gold medal at the World Columbian Exhibition in the furniture section, in 1905 the first-class medal at the Exposición in Madrid and in 1907 the first-class medal at the Exposición de Bellas Artes e Industrias Artisticas in Barcelona.
Postcards: 1 p. in the series reproducing the eight sketches for the winning posters in the competition 'Anís del Mono-Vicente Bosch, Badalona', held in 1898; series of 4 p., the seasons, reproducing with variants decorative panels, c. 1901; first p. published by the Sociedad Cartofila Española in Barcelona re-

producing the design for the cover of the magazine *España Cartofila*, 1901; *Hispania Sociedad Cartafila Española*, second p. published by this society, Barcelona 1901; commemorative p. of the *Fiesta de la merced*, publ. L. Bartrina, Barcelona, 1902; commemorative p. of the exhibition organized in 1903 at the Barcelona Sociedad Cartofila Española; publicity c. for 'Anís Carabanchel', reproducing the poster; publicity p. for 'Orsola', reproduction of the poster; publicity p. 'Sol y Cia', reproducing the poster; publicity for Cançones Catalanes, reproducing the cover of the song score 'Sant Ramon', publ. Ll Bartrina, Barcelona; p. in the same series published by the artistic circle of Sant Lluc.
Bibl.: Trenc Ballester 1977; Baudet 1978; Fildier 1979.

Henri RIVIÈRE
Paris, 11.5.1864 – Paris, 1951.
Painter, engraver, lithographer, commercial artist, scenographer.
A student of E. Bin. In the last decade of the nineteenth century he became well known as designer of the sets at the shadow theatre founded by R. Salis in the cabaret 'Chat Noir'. Using shadows as a graphic technique he illustrated several musical poems by G. Fragerolle represented in this theatre; *la marche à l'Étoile* c. 1896; *Clairs de lune* (1897); *Le Juif Errant; L'Enfant prodigue; Héro et Léandre*. As a scenographer he also worked at the Théâtre Antoine, at the Théâtre Français, at the Opéra Comique and at the Vaudeville. He was an illustrator and engraver at the same time. He worked on the magazines *Revue illustrée*, *Le Courrier français* and *Le Chat Noir* and he illustrated the books *Farfadets* by Mélandri, *Voyages* by E. Goudeau and *Voyages* by A. Kempis. He made several woodcuts and lithographs, which show the dominant influence of Japanese prints, and the albums *Paysages bretons* (1894), *Ciels de Bretagne, Aspects de la nature* (1897), *La Seine, Trente-six vues de la Tour Eiffel* (1902), *Paysages parisiens, Le beau pays de Bretagne, Au vent de Noroît, Etudes de vagues et de voiliers*. He designed several posters for the theatre at the *Chat Noir*. From 1891 he was a member of the Société Nationale des Beaux-Arts.
Postcards: series of 15 p. 'La Marche à l'Etoile', reproducing the plates of the album, c. 1899.
Bibl.: *L'indicateur du philocartiste* (Milanó), I (1900, n. 1).

Georges ROCHEGROSSE
Versailles, 2.4.1859 (2.8.1859) – El Biar, Algeria, 1938
Painter, illustrator, lithographer, commercial artist.
He was a student of Boulanger, A. Dekodencq and J. Lefebvre. In 1882 he exhibited at the Salon of the Société des Artistes Français, where he won a third-class medal in 1882, a second-class one in 1883, and the Prix du Salon in 1888. He won a bronze medal at the Exposition Universelle in Paris 1899. He worked on the newspapers *La Vie parisienne* and *L'Illustration*. He illustrated the books: *L'Orestie* by Aeschylus (1889), *Herodias* (1892) and *Salammbô* (1900) by Flaubert, *Trois légendes d'or, d'argent et de cuivre* by J. Doucet (1901), *Akëdysséril* by Villiers de l'Isle-Adam (1905), *Satyricon* by Petronius (1909), *Les Fleurs du Mal* by Baudelaire (1910), *Les Egarements* by Demidoff, *Prin-*

cesses by T. Gautier, *L'Homme qui rit, Les Misérables* and *Hans d'Islande* by V. Hugo. He was the author of several posters, above all for opera.
Postcards: 1 p. in the series 'album Mariani', c. 1910; 2 p. in the 'Collection Job', 1911-14.

Carl RÖGIND
Randers, 16.7.1871 – Copenhagen, 19.11.1983
Cartoonist, illustrator.
He attended the Academy in Copenhagen, where he was a student of O. Bache. He worked as an illustrator on several magazines, not only Danish ones, including: *Familie-Journal, Dansk Familieblad, Puck, Nagels Lustige Welt*. He designed illustrations for children's books.
Postcards: several humorous p.

Auguste Jean-Baptiste ROUBILLE
Paris, 15.12.1872 - Paris, 1955.
Cartoonist, illustrator, commercial artist, graphic designer (commercial and publicity graphics, song scores), painter.
From 1897 he worked on magazines like *Le Courrier français, Le Rire, L'Assiette au Beurre, Fantasio, Cocorico, La Vie parisienne, Le Sourire, Cri de Paris, Le canard sauvage* and *Lustige Blätter*. He illustrated *Echo et Narcisse, Daphné* by P. Feuillatre (1911), *Le Noël de nos enfants* by F. Jammes and several books by Cl. Farrère, P. Loti and Colette. In 1900 he made the frieze for the *Maison du Rire* at the Exposition Universelle. He made a series of decorative panels for the Café d'Harcourt in Paris. He exhibited at the Salon des Humoristes (1907-12), at the Salon d'Automne, at the Salon des Indépendants and at the Union de l'Affiche française.
Postcards: 1 p. in the 'Collection des Cent', publ. Gréningaire, Paris, c. 1901; 1 p. in the series 'Cocorico', p. in the series 'Le Musée des Sires' and 'Le Musée des Souverains', publ. by the paper *Le Rire* reproducing designs used for its cover, 3 p. in the series 'Leur Côde'; 'Leur Discipline', 'Leur Justice' from the collection 'A bas la justice militaire', 1904; 1 p. in the series 'Pochette de la Paix', 1907; 1 p. in the series 'les Voeux de la France, Rire Rouge', 1914; 3 p. in the series 'Patriotisme et Colonisation', 'La Guerre et la Grève', 'Philosophie et Société' from the collection 'Les Temps Nouveaux'; p. in the series 'Les Affiches célèbres', publ. Tuck, London, several antimilitary p. made in a single copy by hand.
Bibl.: Baudet 1978, 1980.

Antonio RUBINO
Sanremo, 15.5.1880 – Bajardo, 1.7.1964
Illustrator, cartoonist, graphic designer (ex libris, calendars, musical scores).
In 1903 he got his degree in law in Turin. Initially self-taught, he exhibited his early work with the 'Amici del Arte' and at the Promotrice in Turin. In 1905 he illustrated L'Albatro by G. B. Colantuoni and he designed his first ex libris. From 1906 he worked on the magazines *Il Secolo XX, La Lettura, Il Giornalino della Domenica, Il Risorgimento Grafico* and *L'Arte decorativa moderna*. He designed the illustrations for Puccio's music publications. In 1908 he founded with S. Spaventi Filippi *Il Corriere dei Piccoli*. In 1909 he organized the 'Mostra omeopatica del cattivo gusto'. He illustrated the books: *Tesoro dorato e altre novelle* by H. C. Andersen (1911); *Madeo* by D. Dini (1912); *I tre talismani* by G. Gozzano (1913); *Storielle di Brachetta* by E.

Valori (1913); *La signorina Zesi* by A. Beltramelli (1913); *Rime piccoline* by Hedda (1914); *La primavera di Giorgio* by L. Capuana (1914); *Prima del concerto* by C. Antona Traversi and R. M. Pierazzi (1914); *Le tre noci* by D. Provenzal (1914); *La guerra* by C. Antona Traversi (1917). He was the author of books which he also illustrated. *Coretta e Core* (1909), *Versi e Disegni* (1911), *I balocchi di Titina* (1912), *In Flemmerlanda* (1913), *Viperetta* (1919), *Tic e Tac* (1919), *Fata Acquolina* (1919). In 1918 he was the chief editor and illustrator of the newspaper *La Tradotta*.
Postcards: publicity p. for the typewriter Underwood, 1907; 'Società escursionisti milanesi', 1907, numbered issue; 'Verrerie De Folembray, Milano', 1911; 'L'industria sportiva e del motore', 1914; 'Campo scuola militare di aviazione Cascina Malpensa', 1917; series of 12 p. 'Ricordo del Piave' ('Sul Piave piove . . .', 'Offensiva . . . a fondo', 'Ritorno dal lavoro . . .', 'L'offensiva della fame . . .', 'Il fante lavora a cottimo', 'Le fatiche d'Ercole', 'L'offensiva della sete . . .', 'Schiacciali! . . .', 'Tieni duro', 'Qua, qua!', 'Picchia sodo!', 'Offesi dall'offensiva'), publ. La Tradotta, 1918 c. showing an infantryman who crosses the Piave and crushes the Habsburg eagle, publ. Rizzoli, Milan, 1918; series of p. 'Addio per sempre addio . . .', 'Le campane di S. Giusto', 'Istria redenta', 'Trieste, sei mia', 'Piazza Pulita', 'Effetti fuori uso', 'E arrivato il castigamatti' publ. La Tradotta, 1918; 'Fuori i barbari', p. of the Leghorn patriotic propaganda committee, c. 1918; 'Austria Kaputt', a post free card, c. 1918, 'Va fuori d'Italia', a post free card, c. 1918; 'La classe del '99, fischia il vento l'aria e scura', a double card that could be opened, c. 1918; 'Sorelle dell'Acqua, Milano'.
Bibl.: Bartoli-Mataloni 1979; Gaibazzi 1979; F. Arrasich, 'Gli illustratori, Antonio Rubino', *La Cartolina*, 1 (1981, n. 2) pp. 21-23; Mordente 1982; Holt 1983; Arrasich 1984.

Santiago RUSIÑOL i PRATS
Barcelona, 25.2.1861 – Aranjuez, 13.6.1931
Painter, writer, playwright, illustrator, commercial artist, graphic designer (song scores).
He was a student of T. Moragas Torres. In 1885 he was in Paris, where he attended the Académie Gervex. From 1893 he was one of the leading spirits of the 'Festes Modernistes' of Sitges. With Ramon Casas, Miguel Utrillo and Pere Romeu he was one of the founders of the tavern-cabaret 'Quatre Gats'. In 1899 he had an exhibition in Paris in the 'Art Nouveau' room. He was recognized at the national exhibitions in Madrid in 1890, 1895, 1899, 1901, 1904, 1908, 1912 and 1929 and in the exhibitions in Barcelona in 1894, 1896, 1907 and 1911. He designed several posters which publicized his literary works, as an illustrator he worked on the magazines *L'Avenç, Luz, Quatre Gats, Pèl & Paloma*. His work is collected in the Cau Ferrat Museum in Sitges, opened in 1933 in his workshop.
Postcards: publicity p. for the popular song 'El Rossinyol', reproducing the cover of the score, publ. Il Bartrina, Barcelona; series of 5 p. 'Jardines de España', reproducing paintings, publ. Ll. Bartrina, c. 1903.
Bibl.: Trenc Ballester 1977.

Henry RYLAND
Biggleswade, Bedfordshire, 1856 – London, 23.11.1924
Painter, illustrator, glass window designer.
He studied in Paris with B. Constant, Boulan-

ger, J. Lefebvre, F. Cormon. The influence of the Pre-Raphaelites is clear in his work. He worked for *The English Illustrated Magazine*. His work was shown in all the principal English exhibitions.
Postcards: several series with women's heads and half torso, or women's heads, for several publishers including R. Tuck, London; M. Munk, Vienna etc.
Bibl.: Lebeck 1980; Drago 1981.

S

Enrico SACCHETTI
Rome, 28.2.1877 – Settignano, Florence, 1967
Illustrator, fashion designer, caricaturist, commercial artist.
He got his diploma at the Istituto Tecnico, he went to the painter Gelati's studio in Florence for a time, but he was mainly self-taught. He first started to work as an illustrator and caricaturist on the Milanese journals *Teatro illustrato* and *Verde Azzurro*. In 1905 he did the illustrations for *Le Roi Bombace* by F. T. Marinetti. From 1908 to 1911 he lived in Buenos Aires, where he worked as an illustrator for the newspaper *El Diario*. Later he was in France, where he stayed for three years and was mainly active as a fashion designer. At the outbreak of war he returned to Italy, where he worked as a war propaganda artist. He worked on the newspaper *La Tradotta*. Above all during the war years he was active designing postcards.
Postcards: series of caricatures of musicians, c. 1903; publicity p. for the paper *Verde Azzurro*, c. 1904 series of 6 p., fashion plates, Zenit ed. d'arte, F. Polenghi & Co., Turin 1916; series of 6 p., ladies hats through the ages, Zenit ed. d'arte Turin, Typ. Successori Pecco Turin, 1916; series of 6 p. 'The Hun', George Pulman & C., London 1916; caricatural p. of Franz Josef with the citation of Vamba, no publisher's name, c. 1916; 'Sottoscrivete! Si arrenderanno!', Stab. L. Salomone, Rome, 1916; series n. 11 of 6 p., fashion plates, publ. F. Polenghi, ed. d'arte Zenit, Torino, 1917; series n. 16, 'Lida Borelli', publ. F. Polenghi, ed. d'arte Zenit, Turin, 1917; series n. 19 of 6 p., women with dogs, publ. F. Polenghi, ed. d'arte Zenit, Turin, 1917; series n. 21 of 6 p., love in women's lives, publ. F. Polenghi, ed. d'arte Zenit, Turin, 1917; series n. 22 of 6 p., fashion of the day, publ. F. Polenghi, ed. d'arte Zenit, Turin, 1917; series of caricatures of soldiers of the Central Powers and their allies, 1917; series n. 23 of 6 p., sporting women, publ. F. Polenghi, ed. d'arte Zenit, Turin 1917 or 1918; series n. 24 of 6 p., dance in history, publ. F. Polenghi, ed. d'arte Zenit, Turin, 1917 or 1918; caricatural p. 'L'alleanza austro-germanica', publ. Opere Federate di Assistenza e Propaganda Nazionale, Rome, 1918.
Bibl.: Bartoli-Mataloni 1979; Gaibazzi 1979; Mordente 1982; Arrasich 1984.

Xavier SAGER
Austria, c. 1870 – United States, c. 1930
There are no biographical facts relating to this designer, who was active in France, and is known above all for his large production of postcards, which it is calculated reached 3,000 designs with a total issue of 3,000,000 examples. He usually signed his cards with a pseudonym (Léger, Salt Lake, etc.). The catalogues of his vast output are very approximate and are usually made according to the printing process-

es (Neudin 1980). He was the inventor of some caricatural genres (particularly of fashions and ladies hats) and had many imitators in Paris (Aris Mertzanoff, Charles Naillod, G. Mouton, Roberty, Robé, Vindier, A. Molynk).
Postcards: (a) monochrome p. in brown and black: letterpress without a screen: publicity p. (e.g. for brands of chocolate), c. 1900 and romantic scenes; halftone letterpress: political and fashionable events 1910-1914; women and leaves, 1910-14; (b) postcards in chromolithography or stencilled: c. Art Nouveau, c. 1902 erotic p., 1900-05; scenes of Parisian life, 1900-14; satire on fashion, 1900-14; dance, 1900-14; greetings, 1900-14; horses, 1900-14; science fiction; (c) postcards in colour in halftone letterpress: military scenes and women in uniform, 1910-25; Easter eggs, 1910-25. S. was also the designer of p. parodying those by R. Kirchner.
Bibl.: Kyrou 1966; Forissier 1976, 1978 (I, II); Jones-Ouelette 1977; Baudet 1978, 1980; Fildier 1979; Gaibazzi 1979; Neudin 1979, 1980; Zeyons 1979; Holt 1981, 1983.

Richard SCHAUPP
St. Gallen, 17.11.1871 – ?
Painter, illustrator, commercial designer, lithographer, decorator.
He studied at the Academy in Munich, where he was a student of K. Raupp, W. v. Lindenschmidt and W. v. Diez. Between 1894 and 1895 he stayed in Paris to finish his studies. He worked as an illustrator on several Swiss magazines and on *Jugend*. He designed posters, lithographs, and painted decorations for several buildings in Switzerland.
Postcards: p. in the series 'Gordon Bennet-Wettfliegen 30 Sept.-3 Okt., Zürich 1909', Graph., Anstalt J. E. Wolfensberger, Zurich; 'Die Wächter der Heimat pro patria' (postcard for the 1st August holiday 1910), no printer's name.

Rudolf SCHEFFLER
Zwickau, 5.12.1884 – ? Saxony
Painter, commercial artist.
He attended the Academy in Dresden (O. Guszmann, C. L. N. Bantzer, H. Prell). He made study trips in Great Britain, France, Holland, Italy.
Postcards: 'Gewerbe-u. Industri-Ausstellung. Zwickau i.S. 1906'.
Bibl.: cat. Altonaer Museum, Hamburg 1970.

Egon SCHIELE
Tulln, 12.6.1890 – Vienna, 31.10.1918
Painter, engraver, graphic designer.
He attended the Academy in Vienna from 1906 to 1909 (c. Griepenkerl). He was one of the leading figures of proto-expressionism.
Postcards: 3 p. in the series of the Wiener Werkstätte, reproducing his designs (nos. 288-290). Some other designs by him are also known for p. of the Wiener Werkstätte, but were never printed.
Bibl.: Mrazek 1977; Baudet 1978, 1980; Dichand-Martischnig 1978; Hansen 1982.

Erich SCHMAL
Vienna, 28.11.1886 – Vienna, 31.12.1964
Graphic designer, illustrator.
He attended Hohenberger's private painting school and the Graphische Lehr-und Versuchsanstalt, from 1905 to 1907 the Academy in Vienna; from 1908 the Kunstgewerbeschule (B. Löffler). He worked on the magazines *Erdgeist, Muskete, Simplicissimus*.

Postcards: 9 p. in the Wiener Werkstätte Series with views of Vienna (nos. 239, 277-282), with views of Karlsbad (n. 215), of fashion (n. 237).
Bibl.: Trost-Martischnig 1978; Baudet 1980; Lebeck 1980; Drago 1981; Hansen 1982.

Árpád SCHMIDHAMMER
Joachimsthal (Jachymov), Bohemia, 12.2.1857 – Munich, 11.5.1921
Painter, commercial artist, illustrator.
He was active in Munich in the period 1905-c. 1920. He worked on the magazines *Jugend* and *Fliegende Blätter*.
Postcards: in the series of the 'Künstler-Postkarten' for *Jugend*, G. Hirth, Munchen, 1898-99.
Bibl.: Baudet 1980.

Hélène SCHMITT
Her biographical details are unknown.
Postcards: 'Meisterwerke Muhammedanischer Kunst-Ausstellung, München 1910', F. Bruckmann, Munich.
Bibl.: Till 1983.

Léo SCHNUG
Strasbourg, 17.2.1878 – Strasbourg, 18.12.1933
Painter, watercolourist, etcher, commercial artist, illustrator, graphic designer (books).
He attended the Kunstgewerbeschule in Strasbourg. In 1897 he worked for Gerlach & Schenk in Vienna. In 1898 he was active in Vienna, with N. Gysis.
Postcards: 'Wiener Künstler-Postkarten', series XLV ('Neujahrs-Humor'), Philipp & Kramer, Vienna, 1899.
Bibl.: Baudet 1980; Neudin 1981.

Karl SCHULPIG
?, 25.5.1884 – Prettin, near Torgau, 19.11.1948
Painter, commercial artist, graphic designer (publicity graphics).
His biographical details are unknown. Around 1914 he had his own studio in Berlin.
Postcards: 'Die Bäder und der Krieg', J. C. König & Ebhardt, Hannover.

Carl SCHWALBACH
Mainz, 18.5.1885 – ?
Painter, commercial artist, illustrator.
He attended the Kunstschule and the Academy in Munich. He was active in Munich. He worked on the magazines *Meggendorfer Blätter, Jugend*. He was a notable illustrator.
Postcards: several p. with erotic subjects.
Bibl.: Baudet 1980.

Karl SCHWETZ
Kanitz, near Eibenschütz, Moravia, 4.7.1888 – Vienna, 21.3.1965
Graphic designer (books, commercial graphics), commercial artist, ceramist.
From 1904 to 1912 he attended the Kunstgewerbeschule in Vienna (W. Schulmeister, E. Mallina, A. V. Kenner, B. Löffler, M. Powolny). He worked with the Wiener Werkstätte, especially in applied graphics (the almanac of 1911, etc.). He also made posters, commercial and publicity graphics, book layout for different publishers. Exhibitions: Kunstschau, Vienna 1908, 1909; Bugra, Leipzig 1914.
Postcards: 58 c. p. of the Wiener Werkstätte series, all of views: 16 of Vienna (nos. 288, 292-295, 298, 299?, 302?, 433, 437, 491, 493, 536-540?), 15 of Karlsbad (nos. 206, 209, 211, 216-218, 220, 221, 225-228, 259, 260), 27 of

Austrian landscapes (nos. 208, 654-657, 665-674, 715-726); series of views of Vienna, Coblenz, etc., Kilophot, Vienna.
Bibl.: Dichand-Martischnig 1978; Trost-Martischnig 1978; Baudet 1980; Hansen 1982.

SEM, pseudonym of Serge GOURSAT
Perigueux, 23.11.1863 – Paris, 1934.
Caricaturist, illustrator, commercial artist.
He worked on the newspapers *Le Cri de Paris* and *Journal*. He was the author of several albums: *Album Sem* (1893): *Le vrai et le faux Chic* (1914); *Un Pékin sur le Front; Périgueux-Revue; Sem à la Mer; Monte Carlo; Le Nouveau Monde*. He was a member of the committee of the Salon des Humoristes.
Postcards: 1 p. in the 'Collection des Cent', publ. Gréningaire, Paris, c. 1901; 1 p. in the series 'Album Mariani', c. 1910; publicity p. 'Madame Cantharide'; publicity series 'Tournées Ch. Baret'; publicity 'Bénédictine Barnet'; several publicity caricatural p. for variety shows.
Bibl.: Weill 1977; Baudet 1978.

Augusto SEZANNE
Florence, 31.8.1856 – Venice, 6.5.1935.
Painter, architect, decorator, commercial artist, illustrator, graphic designer (stamps, scores).
He developed in the artistic circles in Bologna. He was professor of ornament at the Istituto di Belle Arti in Modena, and then at the Academy in Bologna (1882-93) and at the Istituto di Belle Arti in Venice (from 1893). In 1887 he published an illustrated poem in Paris *Acqua*, with an introduction by A. Daudet, 1880. From 1901 to 1932 he exhibited at the Biennali in Venice (in 1912 he had a room devoted to his work), for which he designed several posters. The Palazzini Majani in via Indipendenza in Bologna is one of his architectural works (1908).
Postcards: p. for the III (1899), V (1903), VII (1907), IX (1910), X (1912), XI (1914) and XII (1920) 'Esposizione Internazionale d'Arte della città di Venezia', reproducing the poster 'Veglione della cartolina, Venezia, 17.12.1900'; 'Esposizione Nazionale di Floricultura, Bologna 1900'; 'Rideva, rideva la gondola nera!' p. n. 11 of the series for Travaso delle Idee, c. 1910; 'Ne dubitare, ne temere', series for the weekly *Il Soldato*, 1915-18 (?).
Bibl.: Mordente 1982; *La Cartolina*, n. 9, 1983 e n. 10. 1983; Arrasich 1984.

Jutta SIKA
Linz, 17.9.1877 – Vienna, 2.1.1964.
Graphic designer, fashion designer, designer of glass, metalwork, decorative boxes, ceramist.
She attended the Graphische Lehr-und Versuchsanstalt, and from 1897 to 1902 the Kunstgewerbeschule in Vienna (K. Moser). From 1911 to 1933 she taught at the Gewerbliche Fortbildungschule in Vienna. She founded with others the 'Wiener Kunst im Hause'.
Exhibitions: Exposition Universelle, Paris 1900; Jahresausstellung der Kunstgewerbeschule, Vienna 1900; Kunstschau, Vienna 1908, 1909.
Postcards: 6 p. in the series of the Wiener Werkstätte: five with views of the Tyrol (nos. 632-636), one greetings p. (n. 760).
Bibl.: Baudet 1980; Hansen 1982.

Susi (Selma) SINGER-SCHINNERL
Vienna, 27.10.1891 – United States, 1965

Graphic designer, fabric designer, ceramist.
She studied at the Kinstschule für Frauen and Mädchen (T. Blan, A. Böhm, O. Friedrich). After her marriage she had her own pottery, the Grünbacher Kermik at Grünbach am Schneeberg.
Exhibitions: Kunstschau, Vienna, 1908.
Postcards: 12 p. in the series for the Wiener Werkstätte: 5 greetings (nos. 319, 320, 396, 734?, 804), 2 decorative (nos. 631, 733?), 5 fashion (nos. 754, 755, 757, 905, 906).
Bibl. Baudet 1978, 1980; Hansen 1982.

Jessie Willcox SMITH
Philadelphia, 1863 – New York, 4.5.1935.
Watercolourist, illustrator, graphic designer (publicity graphics).
She studied at Pennsylvania Academy of Fine Arts (with T. Eakins) and at the Drexel Institute (with H. Pyle). While still a young woman, she became one of the most appreciated artists in America because of her vast activity as an illustrator of motherly love and childhood. She illustrated many books: *Rhymes of Real Children* by Goodwin (1900), *Old Fashioned Girl* by Alcott (1902), *A Child's Garden of Verse* by Stevenson (1905), and the albums: *A Child's Book of old Verses*, publ. Duffield (1910), *The little Mother Goose*, publ. Dodd (1918). She worked on the magazines: *Ladies' Home Journal, Collier's, Harper's, Scribner's, The Century, Good Housekeeping Magazine* (she designed c. 200 covers for this magazine), *McClure's*.
Postcards: several in the series published by Reinthal & Newman, New York.
Bibl. Cope 1978; Holt 1983.

Adele (Adelaide Margareta) SÖDERBERG
Stockholm, 17.5.1880 – ivi, 3.3.1916.
Painter, designer, graphic designer.
She attended the academy in Stockholm from 1899 to 1904. She was valued as a landscape and marine painter, but she was well-known above all for her engravings.
Postcards: several greetings p. and scenes with children.

Hildur Andrea SÖDERBERG
Stockholm, 20.6.1895 – ?
Painter, illustrator, designer.
The sister of the painter Adelaide (Adele). From 1906 to 1911 she attended the art school in Stockholm. She was well known above all for her work as an illustrator of children's books.
Postcards: several greetings p. and scenes with children.

Serge de SOLOMKO
Dates of birth and death unknown.
Painter, illustrator.
He was of Russian origin. He worked on the magazine *Jugend*. He worked in Paris. He illustrated several books for French publishers, including Ferroud.
Postcards: several p. published in France, publ. I. Lapina with fantasy designs; p. in the series 'Les chansons de France de M. Boukay', c. 1915; other p. reproducing his paintings.
Bibl.: Baudet 1980; Bartoli-Mataloni, 1979.

Constantin SOMOV
St. Petersburg 1869 – ?, 1939.
Painter, graphic designer, commercial artist.
From 1888 to 1892 he attended the Academy in St. Petersburg (I. Répin), then he continued his studies in Paris. He was a member of the

group 'Mir Iskusstva'. He worked on *Mir Iskusstva, Zolotoe Runo, La Toison d'or, Jugend*.
Postcards: several decorative p. published in Russia.

Amy Millicent SOWERBY
?, 1878 – ?, 1967.
Illustrator, graphic designer.
She was the daughter of the designer and illustrator John G. Sowerby. Basically self-taught. She was particularly involved in illustrating children's book. She started designing postcards from 1905 for the publisher C. W. Faulkner in London. Some stylistic elements in her work which came close to Kate Greenaway's style led the publisher Misch & Co. to use titles like 'Greenaway Girls' or 'In Greenaway Times' for series by Sowerby. She worked on newspapers and magazines including *The Illustrated London News, The Pall Mall Magazine, The Tatler, The Windsor Magazine*.
Postcards: several series for different publishers, in particular C. W. Faulkner & Co., London (series 568, quotations from Shakespeare, etc.); Misch & Co., London; Hodder & Stoughton; Chatto & Windus (reproductions of illustrations of *Childhood*, 1907): Meissner & Buch, Leipzig; Humphrey Milford, London (at least 30 series in the period 1916-23); with fairies, flowers, stories, etc., as subjects); Reinthal & Newman, New York ('Weather', series 1911).
Bibl.: Cope 1978; Baudet 1980; Holt 1980, 1983.

Agnes SPEYER
Vienna, 23.12.1876 – ?
She studied from 1908 at the Kunstgewerbeschule in Vienna (K. Moser, F. Metzner).
Exhibitions: Kunstschau, Vienna 1908, 1909.
Postcards: a decorative p. in the Wiener Werkstätte series (n. 60).
Bibl.: Hansen, 1982.

Ferdinand SPIEGEL
Würzburg, 4.7.1879 – Würzburg, 1950.
Painter, commercial artist.
He studied in Munich with W. v. Diez. From 1916 he taught at the Academy in Berlin. He worked on *Jugend*.
Postcards: series of 10 p. 'Aus goldener Zeit', Druck H. Köhler, Munich; 'Bayerische Gewerbe Schau 1912 München', F. Bruckman, Munich, reproducing the poster.
Bibl.: cat. Altonaer Museum, Hamburg 1970; Till 1983.

Karel SPILLAR
Pilsen (Plzen) 21.11.1871 – Prague, 4.4.1939.
Painter, commercial artist, graphic designer.
He attended the School of Applied Arts in Prague (with prof Zeníska), where he was a lecturer from 1913. From 1902 to 1908 he was in Paris and in Normandy.
Postcards: 1 p. in the series 'Byrrh', Paris, 1906.
Bibl.: Baudet 1978.

Ferdinand STAEGER
Trebitsch (Trebí,) east Bohemia, 3.3.1880 – ?
Painter, etcher, illustrator, graphic designer (book design, ex libris).
He attended the School of Applied Arts in Prague (J. Schickanedra). He was a member of the Vienna Hagenbund from 1911 to 1912. In 1908 he settled in Munich, where he worked on the magazines *Meggendorfer Blätter* and *Ju-*

gend. He did important engravings and many book illustrations for Viennese and German publishers.
Postcards: p. in the series 'Künstler – Postkarten' for *Jugend*, c. 1910-14; several war propaganda p.

Hans C. STARCKE
His biographical details are unknown. He was active in Jena around 1900.
Postcards: several humorous p.

Alexandre Theophile STEINLEN
Lausanne, 10.11.1859 – Paris, 14.12.1923.
Engraver, illustrator, commercial artist, painter, sculptor, designer of fabrics, porcelain, graphic designer (song scores), scenographer and theatrical costumier.
He was the grandson of the painter and illustrator Christian Gottlieb. He attended the Faculty of Philosophy at the academy in Lausanne. Between 1879 and 1881 he worked as a fabric designer for the Mulhouse company while at the same time painting porcelain with designs taken from his grandfather's watercolours. In 1881 he moved to Paris, where he earned his living for a time designing fabrics. He was one of the artistic circle at the 'Chat Noir' cabaret and he worked from 1883 to 1895 on the paper with the same name. In 1885 in the foyer of the cabaret he executed the large mural painting 'L'Apothéose des chats'. From the 80s he was intensely active as an illustrator, working on the following magazines: *L'Album*, *La caricature*, *Chat Noir*, *Cocorico*, *Gil Blas illustré*, *Mirliton*, *Le Rire*, *L'Assiette au Beurre*, *Le Rêve Jugend*, *La Vie moderne*, *L'Echo de Paris*, and he could be characterized as a dedicated interpreter of the world of the urban poor and the disinherited. Under the pseudonym 'Petitpierre' he worked on the socialist newspaper *Le Chambard*. From 1893 he exhibited at the Salon des Indépendents. In 1901 he took French nationality. In 1905 he made some panels with views of Montmartre for the 'Taverne de Paris'. In 1911 he was one of the thirteen founders of the *Journal des Humoristes*, which had a short life. He exhibited regularly at the Salon des Humoristes. During the 1914-18 war he made a series of large formal lithographs which had as their subjects the Belgian and Serbian refugees during the German occupation. In 1918 on the front he made a series of drawings which were collected in an album *La guerre par Steinlen*. The abundant graphic work of Steinlen includes several posters, some dedicated to Yvette Guilbert and Aristide Bruant, for whom S. illustrated the scores and collections of the songs, *Dans la Rue* (1888) and *Sur la Rue* (1895). He was the author of the albums: *Dans la vie* (1901); *Contes Enfantins; Contes à Sarah; Les Chats*. He illustrated several books and collections of songs: *La Chanson de l'enfant* by J. Aicard (1884); *Entrée de Clowns* by Champsaur (1885); *Chasses d'automne* by A. Grassal (1886); *Roman incohérent* by Ch. Joliet (1887); *Prison Fin de Siècle* by Gegout and Malato (1891); *La Comédie Boulangiste* by M. Millot (1892); *Le Petit Poucet* by Perrault (1897); *Les Rondes de l'Enfance* (1897); *Jeannet et Colin* (1897); *Almanach du Bibliophile* (1898-1903); *Histoire du chien de Brisquet* by C. Nodier (1900); *Lulu* by Champsaur (1901; ill. with others); *L'affaire Crainquebille* (1901) and *Sur la tombe d'Emile Zola* (1902) by A. France; *Cinq Poèmes, les pauvres gens* by V. Hugo (1902); *Le Vagabond* by Maupassant

(1902); *La Maternelle* by L. Frapié (1908); *La chanson des Gueux* (1910) and *Dernières chansons* (1910) by J. Richepin; *Le nu aux Salons d'humoristes* by G. Normandy (1911; with others ill.); *Barabbas* by L. Descaves (1914); *Le Coeur populaire* by J. Rictus (1914); *Chanson rouges* by M. Boukay; *Femmes d'ami* and *Train de 8h-45* by G. Courteline; *Chansons de femmes* by P. Delmet; *L'Institutrice de province* by L. Frapié; *Les Gaietes Bourgeoises* by J. Moinaux; *Soliloques du pauvres e Cantilènes du Malheur* by J. Rictus; *L'hiver, Contes du Chat Noir* by R. Salis; *Les Gueules noires* by E. Morel. After the war he designed sets and costumes for the 'Ballets Russes' and 'Ballets Suedois'.
Postcards: 1 p. in the 'Collection des Cent', publ. Gréningaire, Paris, c. 1901; 1 p. in the series 'Cocorico'; 1 p. in the series 'Affiches Gerin', c. 1901, 1 p. in the series 'Leur Justice' from the collection 'A bas la Justice militaire', 1904; 1 p. in the series 'Pochette de la Paix', 1907; 1 p. in the series 'Album Mariani', c. 1910; 2 p. in the series 'La Guerre et la Grève' and 'Gravures de Berger' from the collection 'Les Temps Nouveaux'; 1 p. from the collection 'Journée du Secours National'; 1 p. in the series 'Les Chansons de France de M. Boukay', c. 1915; series of 10 p. with stencils 'Petites ouvrières', series of 10 p. 'Faubouriennes'; series of 10 p. 'U.A. Bruant'; series of 5 p. (?) 'Chanson du cabaret Bruant', some reproducing illustrations from the collection of songs *Dans la rue*; 'Pamphlet cartophile', 'La Maternelle', publicity for the book; series (?) 'Pauvres Gens'; series (?) 'Proletariat de l'amour'; series (?) 'La feuille'; p. for unilateral disarmament; p. for the Serbian cause, p. on the subject of families separated by war; series (?) 'Chanson des poilus'; 'Permission de la Victoire'.
Bibl.: Le Collectionneur Francais, n. 124, 1976; Weill 1977; Baudet 1978, 1980; Forissier 1978; Rostenne 1979; Holt 1981.

Aina STENBERG MASOLLE
Stockholm, 6.10.1885 – ?
Painter, watercolourist, designer, illustrator, graphic designer (books, calendars).
She studied at the technical school (1901-02) and at the Academy (1904-07) in Stockholm. She made study trips to London, Paris and L'Aja. Her paintings, particularly the watercolours, show the influence of C. Larsson. She was well known in Sweden as an illustrator of children's books. In 1911 she married the artist Erik Helmer Masolle.
Postcards: several greetings published by Forläg Eskil Holm, Stockholm.
Bibl.: Fildier 1980.

Eduard STIEFEL
Zurich, 5.4.1875 – ?
Engraver, illustrator, painter.
From 1898 to 1902 he studied in Munich with L. Herterich, P. Hahn and H. Zügel. From 1904 he lived in Zurich, where he was invited to teach graphics at the Kunstgewerbeschule. As a book illustrator he worked for Swiss and German publishers.
Postcards: 'Offizielle Festpostkarte Sechseläuten 18 april Zurich 1910', 'Lith. Anst. Gebr. Fretz, Zürich, 1910'; p. for the national holiday 1 August 1913.

Carl STRATHMANN
Düsseldorf, 11.9.1866 – Munich, 1939
Painter, commercial artist, illustrator, graphic

designer.
From 1882 to 1886 he attended the Academy in Dusseldorf (H. Crola, H. Lauenstein); from 1888 to 1889 the Kunstschule in Weimar (L. K. W. v. Kalchreuth). He worked on *Jugend* (from 1896) and *Fliegende Blätter*.
Postcards: several decorative p.
Bibl.: cat. Altonaer Museum, Hamburg 1970.

Georg A. STROEDEL
Reichenbback i. Vogtl., 24.12.1870 – ?
Painter, illustrator.
He attended the Academy in Dresden (F. Preller, H. Prell, C. L. N. Bantzer). He was active as an artist in Dresden.
Postcards: p. in the series 10 of the 'Künstlerkarte', Stengel & Co., Dresden u. Berlin.
Bibl.: cat. Altonaer Museum, Hamburg 1970.

Mario STROPPA, known also under the pseudonym MARIUS
Pandino, Cremona, 28.4.1880 – Cremona, 11.5.1964
Painter, illustrator, decorator, architect, commercial artist.
He attended the Academy at the Brera and then the Scuola superiore d'Arte Applicata at the Castello Sforzesco in Milan. In 1906 he won the first prize in the Milanese competition for the poster for the Simplon tunnel. In 1910 he exhibited a series of decorative panels of Italian cities at the Brussels exhibition. In 1911 he worked on the project for Corso d'Italia in Milan with the engineer Belloni. In 1912 he took part in the competition for the new station in Milan. In his work as a painter-decorator and as an illustrator the influence of the taste of the Vienna Secession is clear.
Postcards: publicity p. for the newspaper *Il Resto del carlino*, 1908; 'Fiera di Beneficienza di Porta Genova, Milano'.
Bibl.: Mordente 1982; Arrasich 1984.

Franz von STUCK
Tettenweis, Niederbayern, 23.2.1863 – Tetschen, 30.8.1928
Painter, etcher, illustrator, graphic designer, designer of furniture and objects of daily use.
From 1882 to 1884 he attended the Kunstgewerbeschule and then the Academy in Munich with W. v. Lindenschmit and L. v. Löfftz. He was a professor in Munich from 1895. He was one of the founder members of the Munich Secession in 1892. In 1898 he built the Villa Stuck in Munich. He worked on the magazines *Allotria, Fliegende Blätter* (1882-84), **Pan** (1896), *Jugend*.
Postcards: series on German women. Bibl.: cat. Altonaer Museum, Hamburg 1970.

Franz SÜSSER
His biographical details are unknown.
Postcards: several with views of Vienna, published Kilophot, Vienna.
Bibl.: Baudet 1980.

Árpád SZÉKELY
Marchendorff, Bohemia, 1861 – Budapest, 1914
Painter, engraver, illustrator.
His biographical details are unknown.
Postcards: 1 p. in the series 'Byrrh', Paris, 1906.
Bibl.: Baudet 1978.

T

Raffaele TAFURI

Salerno, 27.1.1857 – Venice, 1929 Painter.

He completed his early artistic studies in Naples, where he exhibited for the first time in 1880 at the 'Pro-motrice Salvator Rosa', where he continued to exhibit until 1896. Towards the end of the century he moved to Venice, where in 1895 he took part in the 1st Esposizione Internazionale d'Arte. He was often invited to exhibit at the Biennale in Venice (1905, 1907, 1909, 1910, 1914).

Postcards: 'Prima Esposizione Internazionale di cartoline postali illustrate a totale beneficio dell'Educatorio Rachitici Regina Margherita', Venice 1899, a postal letter, a limited issue of one thousand copies, of which there are two monochrome versions (one in green, the other in red); series of butterfly-women, 1899; series 'Tra Le farfalle', 1899; series of 16 p. 'Una tavolozza', 1899; series 'Le stagioni', 1899; series of a postcard-calendar, 1899; 'Culla di Jolanda Margherita', 1901 (it exists as a postcard and a postal letter); series of 25 p. 'Napoli illustrata'; series of 25 p. 'Venezia illustrata'; series of 12 p. 'Verona illustrata'; series of 6 p. numbered with views of Venice; series of 8(?) p. in black and white with views and Venetian costumes; series of 5p. 'Chioggia'; several Venetian perspectives with floral motifs and Liberty friezes; series of 6 p. 'Venezianine'; several greetings, also in a French edition; 'Pro Croce Rossa, sezione di Salerno'.

Bibl.: Maggioni 1899; Bartoli-Mataloni 1979; Bobba 1979; Gaibazzi 1979; Mordente 1982; Arrasich 1984.

Georg Willwelm TAPPERT

Berlin, 20.10.1880 – Berlin, 17.11.1957

Painter, commercial artist, illustrator, graphic designer.

From 1900 to 1903 he attended the Academy in Karlsruhe (L. Schmid-Reutte). In 1904 he was an assistant to P. Schultze-Naumburg in Saaleck. In 1906 he moved to Worpswede, where he established a Kunstschule. From 1910 he was in Berlin, where he was a founder member of the Neue Secession. He was part of the German expressionist movement.

Postcards: 'Neue Secession Berlin 1910 Ausstellung'; 'Karlsruhe-Künstlerfest', J. Schober, Karlsruhe, c. 1900.

Bibl.: cat. Altonaer Museum, Hamburg, 1970.

Margaret TARRANT (?), 1888 -?, 1959

Illustrator, graphic designer (calendars).

Her biographical details are unknown. She attended the Clapham School of Art and the Heatherley School of Fine Art in Westminster. In 1910 she began a long career as a book illustrator.

Postcards: several series with typical subjects of flower children for several publishers, like Faulkner & Co., London (series 923, 1909, etc.), Ward Lock; The Medici Society, London.

Bibl.: Cope 1978; Holt 1980, 1983.

Ignatius TASCHNER

Lohr a.M., 9.4.1871 – Mitterndorf, Bavaria, 25.11.1913

Painter, commercial artist, illustrator.

From 1889 to 1895 he attended the Academy in Munich (S. Eberle, J. Brade). From 1903 to 1905 he taught at the Academy in Breslau. He worked in Berlin and Dachau. He was a member of the Berlin Secession.

Postcards: 'Paul Brann's Marionettentheater Münchner Künstler', Druck H. Köhler, Munich.

Bibl.: cat. Altonaer Museum, Hamburg, 1970.

Aleardo TERZI

Palermo, 12.6.1870 – Castelletto Ticino, 11.7.1943

Painter, engraver, illustrator, commercial artist, fashion designer, graphic designer (publicity and commercial graphics, song scores books), designer of furniture, ceramics, interior designer.

He trained at the Academy of Fine Art in Palermo. In 1892 he moved to Rome, where he was invited to work on *La Tribuna Illustrata*. He did much work as an illustrator on the magazines *Novissima, La Lettura, Rapiditas, Ars et Labor, Roma, La Casa, L'Artista Moderno*. From 1898 he was working as a commercial artist first for the Officine Grafiche Ricordi, and then for Chappuis in Bologna. Between 1913 and 1915 he was one of the leading figures in the Roman Secession, where he exhibited his paintings. He designed the catalogue covers for the Secession and the installation of some of the rooms. From 1925 he directed the book design Institute in Urbino for five years.

Postcards: (a) Publicity p. and commemorative: series of 12 p. publicising the book *Piccola psicologia dell'Amore* by De Saint Merry, publ. E. Voghera, Roma, 1898; publicity for 'Vermouth Cinzano', 1899; 'Inaugurazione dell'Ospedale Umberto I – Lugo – 1900', publ. Gussoni, Milan; series of 6 p., 'Omaggio degli Editori Ricordi', publ. Ricordi, Milan, 1901; publicity for the magazine *Scena Illustrata*, 1901; 'Linda di Chamonix', Soc. Lith. Tipografica Lombarda, c. 1901; 'I. Pneumatici Pirelli s'impongono come i migliori'; publ. Ricordi, Milan, 1909; 'Roma 1911 – Esposizione Internazionale', publ. Chappuis, Bologna; series of 12 publicity p. for Cioccolato Talmone, publ. *Novissima*, sez. lavori di stampa, Rome; publicity 'Villa Igiea Grand Hotel – Palermo'; publicity 'Cognac Buton', publ. R. & C. Napoli; publicity 'Testolini-Verreries et meubles d'art, Venise'; 'The Artistic International Advertising Co.', Tricromia V. Turati, Milan; publicity for 'Spumante Gancia'; publicity 'Colorificio Italiano'; publicity series for the film 'Atlantide', publ. Prosdocimi, Rome; (b) Various: series on smoking, publ. A.G.M., c. 1904; series of 8 p., children printed for the Associazione Cardinal Ferrari, typ. Parini Vanoni, Milan; series 'Corpi Armati Pontifici', publ. Astro; (c) 'Donnine', period 1910-18: series n. 120 (pairs in a frame with quatrefoils), n. 360 (6 p., 'donnine'), n. 399 (6 p., 'donnine'), n. 440 (women in small frames), n. 459 (women with fans), n. 468 (6 p., women with dogs), n. 482 (foxtrot toilettes), n. 508 (women and animals), n. 509 ('Buon Natale' with dogs), n. 715 (6 c., female faces', publ. Dell'Anna e Gasperini, Milan; series without a publisher's name n. 262 (6 p., women with dogs), n. 287 (6 p., 'donnine'), n. 299 ('donnine'), n. 320 ('donnine'), n. 322 (6 p., 'donnine'), n. 323 ('donnine'), n. 419 (6p., 'Sognando'), n. 440 (6 p., 'donnine'); series probably printed by himself n. 186 (6 p., women in ovals), n. 187 (6 p., 'donnine'); n. 215 (6 p., women's faces'; (d) Patriotic and War; p. of propaganda for the national loan; no publisher's name; series of women in uniform ('Belgio', 'Inghilterra', 'Italia', ('Francia', ?); 'Trionfo della libertà', publ. Dell'Anna e Gasperini, Milan; 'Oh dolce patria! Ricordo del nob. Riccardo Muccioli, B. Aires', Tip. ed. romana.

Bibl.: Lebeck 1978; Fanelli 1981,° 1983; 'Gli illustratori. Aleardo Terzi', *La Cartolina*. II (1982, n. 7), pp. 23-26; Mordente 1982; Arrasich 1984.

Richard TESCHNER

Karlsbad, 22.3.1879 – Vienna, 4.7.1948

Painter, graphic designer (books, commercial graphics), designer of tapestry, furniture, metalwork, silversmithing, jewellery, ceramist.

He attended the Academy in Prague and from 1900 the Kunstgewerbeschule in Vienna. He worked with the Wiener Werkstätte in sculpture, he worked in embossed metal and made sports trophies, and children's books. Exhibitions: Kunstschau, Vienna, 1908.

Postcards: 7 p. in the series for the Wiener Werkstätte: two 'Gruss aus Mariazell' (nos. 318, 327), five with scenes showing children playing (nos. 334-338).

Bibl.: Baudet 1980; Hansen 1982.

Johan TESTEVUIDE, pseudonym of Jean SAUREL

Nîmes, 1873-Paris, 1922

Illustrator, caricaturist

He worked on the journals *Gil Bals illustré, Le Monde illustré, Le Rire, L'Assiette au Beurre, Le Sourire*. He was the author of the album *Quand, et quels malades doit-on envoyer à Bourbonne-les-Bains* (1901).

Postcards: 1 in the 'Collection des Cent', publ. Gréningaire, Paris, c. 1901.

Bibl.: Baudet 1978.

Carl Theodor THIEMANN

Karlsbad, 10.1.1881 – Dachau, 1966

Painter, xylographer, etcher.

From 1905 he attended the Academy in Prague (F. Thiele). In 1906 he settled in a studio in Libotz, near Prague with W. Klemm. From 1906 to 1907 he made study trips to Berlin, Dresden, Vienna and Lübeck. In 1908 he settled in Dachau. His activity in the field of colour woodcuts is particularly important.

Postcards: series of views of the Krupp factory reproducing the woodcuts designed by the artist for the centenary of the factory in Essen c. 1912.

Hans THOMA

Bernau, 2.10.1839 – Karlsruhe, 7.11.1924

Painter, engraver, graphic designer (ex libris).

He studied with Schirmer in Karlsruhe and then with Courbet in Paris (1898). He was president of the Künstlerbund in Frankfurt, then he was director of the museum and Academy in Karlsruhe (1899). He was an important figure in the revival of German painting at the end of the nineteenth century.

Postcards: several reproducing his graphic work.

Louis TITZ

Bruges, 24(or 21?).6.1859 – Brussels, 1932

Illustrator, engraver, watercolourist, scenographer, commercial artist, graphic designer (paper money, ex libris).

He trained at the Académie Royale des Beaux-Arts in Brussels, where he was later asked to teach. His early work shows the influence of Bossuet. In 1894 he got a mention at the international book fair in Paris. He was an illustrator for *La Belgique illustrée, Bruxelles à travers les âges, Anvers à travers les âges Salambò* by Flaubert, *Voyage sentimental* by

Sterne, *Le Carillonneur* by Rodenback, *Romeo et Juliette* by Shakespeare.
Postcards: series reproducing designs for ex libris; series of the alphabet.
Bibl.: Wiener 1922-23; Rostenne 1979.

Eveli TORENT
Badalona, 3.4.1876 – Barcelona, 4.10.1940.
Painter, designer, commercial artist, illustrator.
He got a degree in law, self-taught he devoted himself to painting. In 1896 he exhibited for the first time at the Sala Parés in Barcelona. He worked on the Catalan magazines: *Luz, El Gatu Negro, Blanco y Negro*. In 1901 he moved to Paris.
Postcards: publicity for 'Aceite Salat'; publicity for 'Licor Krüger'; several reproducing posters.
Bibl.: Trenc Ballester 1977.

Pere TORNÉ ESQUIUS
Barcelona, 1879 – Flavancourt, France, 1938
Painter, illustrator, graphic designer (books).
He was trained at the School of Fine Arts in Barcelona. In 1905 he moved to Paris, where he was active as a book and magazine illustrator. He worked on the Catalan magazine *Empori* and he was the author of the album *Els dolços indrets de Catalunya* (1911). He exhibited paintings in 1913 and 1916 at the Dalmau Gallery.
Postcards: series of 5 p. with female nudes and stylized floral elements, Imp. Tosella, Barcelona.

Henri de TOULOUSE-LAUTREC
Albi, 24.11.1864 – Malromé, Gironde, 9.9.1901
Painter, lithographer, commercial artist, illustrator, graphic designer (publicity graphics, song scores).
His contribution to postcards is very limited. Until now only two p. are known by him: one in the series 'Cinos' (1898) reproducing the poster 'Moulin Rouge – La Goulue' and another, signed with the pseudonym-anagram Treclau, in which a design for a song score by Aristide Bruant was re-used. Apart from the scores printed lithographically and listed in catalogues of the artist's graphic works, there are other unsigned works which may have been reproduced as postcards. Before 1914 there were postcards reproducing his paintings and designs.
Bibl.: Forissier 1976; Neudin 1977, 1981; Baudet 1978, 1980; Zeyons 1979.

Fernand TOUSSAINT
Brussels, 1873 – Brussels, 1955
Painter, commercial artist.
He trained at the Academy in Brussels, where he was a student of Portaels. He took part in the exhibitions of the artistic association 'Le Sillon'. In 1901 he exhibited at the Salon des Artistes Français and in 1910 at the Libre Esthétique in Brussels. Around 1895 he began working as a commercial artist (his first poster was probably the one for the group 'Le Sillon'). His posters were usually printed by the De Rycker lithographic company in Brussels.
Postcards: series of 12 p. depicting women from European capitals, publ. Dietrich & Cie., Brussels, c. 1899; commemorative p. of the 1905 Belgian festival, publ. De Rycker, Brussels; several depicting women.
Bibl.: Stoppani 1900; Bartoli-Mataloni 1979; Baudet 1980.

Hans TREIBER
Thalmässing, Franconia, 26.6.1869-?
Painter, commercial artist.
He was active in Munich from 1900 to c. 1910.
Postcards: '12 Deutsches Turnfest in Leipzig 12-16 Juli 1913', Kunstanstalt Rosch & Minter, Leipzig.

Josep TRIADÓ i MAYOL
Barcelona, 1870 – Barcelona, 1929
Painter, illustrator, commercial artist, graphic designer (books, ex libris, lettering, song scores, publicity and commercial graphics, programmes, invitations, menus), designer of ceramics and jewellery.
He attended the School of Fine Art in Barcelona where he got a grant to finish his studies in Madrid. With A. de Riquer, he was the main protagonist in the 'modernist' revival of book art and of ex libris in Catalonia. He designed many ex libris, which were collected in the *Primer Llibre d'Exlibris d'en Triadó* (1906) and in the later *Exlibris Triadó*. He was the artistic director of the *Revista ibérica de Exlibris*, of the *Revista Graphica* of the Institut Catalá de les les Arts del Llibre and of the *Anuari de les Arts Decoratives*. He illustrated the books *Sonets d'uns y altres* by J. Pin y Soler (1904) and *Dafnis y Cloe* by Longins 1908. He worked on the following Catalan magazines: *La Ilustración Artistica, Album Salon, El Gata Negro, Hispania, Hojas Selectas, Garba, Illustració Catalana, La Ilustració Llevantina*. As a painter and decorator he won prizes at national exhibitions in Madrid (1899, 1901) and at the Exhibition of Fine Art in Barcelona (1906). In 1902 he won the competition for the professor's chair in design at the School of Fine Art in Barcelona.
Postcards: series of 12 p. 'Lo zodiaco'; 1 p. in the series 'Papeles Roca para fumar'; 1 p. in the series for the magazine *Hispania*; 'Truró Park', Barcelona.
Bibl.: Trenc Ballester 1977.

Abel TRUCHET
Versailles, 29.12.1857 – Auxerre, 9.9.1918
Painter, engraver, cartoonist, commercial artist.
He was a student of J. Lefebvre and T. Robert-Fleury at the Académie Julian and of B. Constant. From 1891 he exhibited at the Salon de la Société des Artistes Français. He was the treasurer and founder member of the Société des Humoristes. From 1910 he joined the Société Nationale des Beaux-Arts. He was the author of several engravings which depict the world of the stage, the cabarets of Montmartre, and Parisian women. He worked on the magazine *La Caricature*.
Postcards: 1 p. in the series 'Cinos' reproducing a poster, 1898; 1 p. in the series 'Album Moriani', c. 1910.
Bibl.: Baudet 1980.

U

Otto UBBELOHDE
Marburg, 5.1.1867 – Gossfelden near Marburg, 8.5.1922
Painter, etcher, illustrator, graphic designer (ex libris).
He attended the Academy in Weimar; then from 1884 to 1890, the Academy in Munich (G. v. Hackl, W. v. Diez). From 1894 to 1895 he was a member of the Künstlerkolonie in Worpswede. From 1897 he settled in Gossfelden. He worked on the magazine *Jugend* from 1896.
Postcards: 'Hessische Bauern', Elwert's Buchhandlung, Marburg, c. 1897; p. for the vereins zur Hebung des Fremdenverkehrs in Lübeck; series with German landscapes 'Bildkarten aus Schwaben', A. Fischer Verlag, Tübingen; 'Margaretentag in Marburg 1911'.
Bibl.: Lehrs 1898; cat. Altonaer Museum Hamburg 1970.

Clarence F. UNDERWOOD
Jamestown, 1871 – ?, 1929
Painter, illustrator.
He was a student of B. Constant, J. P. Laurens, A. Bouguereau in Paris. He was active in New York.
Postcards: several series in the *glamour* genre, following the fashion set by C. D. Gibson, P. Boileau, H. C. Christy.

Antoni UTRILLO i VIADERA
Barcelona, 28.3.1867 – Barcelona, 8.10.1945
Commercial artist, lithographer, illustrator, painter, cartoonist, graphic designer (holiday programmes, commercial graphics).
He founded the lithographic firm A. Utrillo y Rialp, which was to become an important centre for the production of modernist Catalan posters. He was a member of the Institut Català de Llibre, he worked on several Catalan magazines: *La Barretina, El Neula, La Ilustració Catalana, Hispania, Hojas Selectas, Calendari del Cu-Cut, La Ilustració Llevantina*. From 1916 to 1926 he was Mayordom of the Deputació de Barcelona and of the Generalitat de Catalunya.
Postcards: series of 10 p. for the fashion house 'Figueras, Esteva y Sucesores de Hopjos', 1906; Series 'Carmen', c. 1902, series of Catalan holidays Lith. A. Utrillo & C. Barna; publicity 'Champagne Mercier', reproducing the poster; publicity series for Wertheim; p. in the series 'Hispania' reproducing the cover of the magazine; p. in the series of the Cercle de Sant Lluc; series on the beach resorts (S. Sebastián, Biarritz, etc.), Lith. A. Utrillo & C. Barna.
Bibl.: Trenc Ballester 1977; Neudin 1983.

V

Joan VALLHONRAT i SADURNI
Cornella de Llobregat, 1874 – Barcelona, 1937
Painter, commercial artist.
He was a student of A. Caba at the School of Fine Arts in Barcelona. He made a study trip to Paris during which he was mainly interested in French poster art and the work of Chéret. In 1902 he took part in the competition for the poster for Edward Roca's cigarette papers. From 1905 he taught design at the school in Lonja. In 1907 he won a prize in the poster competition sponsored by the *Circulo Artistico* in Barcelona and a third-class medal at the international art exhibition in Barcelona.
Postcards: series of 10 publicity – humorous p. for the Syphons of F. Clara y Cia, lith. Barral Huos, Barcelona, 1902 (he had entered the competition for publicity p. opened by this company). Bibl.: Trenc Ballester 1977.

Félix VALLOTTON
Lausanne, 28.12.1865 – Paris, 29.12.1925
Woodcut artist, lithographer, illustrator,

painter, commercial artist, graphic designer (publicity and commercial graphics), designer of fashion and clothes.

In 1882 he settled in Paris, where he attended from 1882 to 1885 the Académie Julian following J. J. Lefèbvre's and G. Boulanger's courses. From 1885 he exhibited at the Salon des Artistes Français and from 1891 at the Salon des Artistes Indépéndants. In 1893 he took part in the Nabis' exhibition. He exhibited also at the Salon della Rose-Croix and at the Libre Esthétique in Brussels (1894, 1895, 1902, 1908). He was one of the founder members of the Salon d'Automne. In 1893 he made a lithograph for *L'Estampe Originale* and he was invited to work on the paper *L'Escarmouche* published under the direction of Toulouse-Lautrec. He did much work as an illustrator for the magazines: *Le Courrier Français* (1894); *Le Rire* (1894-98), *Nib*, supplement of the *Revue Blanche* (1895); *Jugend* (1896); *Le Cri de Paris* (1897-1902); *Le Sifflet* (1898); *L'Assiette au Beurre* (1902); *Le Canard Sauvage* (1903); *Le Témoin* (1906); *La Grande Guerre par les artistes* (1914-15). His fashion designs were published in the magazine *La Mode pratique*. He illustrated the books: *Comment on forme une cuisinière* by D. Seignobos (1896); *Le livre des masques* (1896) and *Deuxieme livre des masques* (1898) by R. de Gourmont; *La maîtresse* by J. Renard (1896); *Der bunte Vogel von 1897* (calendar) by J. Bierbaum (1897); *Une belle journée* by Dolbeau (1898); *Rakkox der Billionär* by P. Scheerbart (1900); *Poil de carotte by J. Renard* (1903); *Die Schlangendame* by J. Bierbaum (1906); *Rassemblements* by O. Uzanne. As an art critic he worked from 1891 to 1895 on the *Gazette de Lausanne*. In 1907-8 he wrote the novel *La Vie meurtrière*, published posthumously in the *Mercure de France* (1927). In 1900 he took French nationality.

Postcards: 2 p. in the series 'Leur Côde and 'Leur Discipline' from the collection 'A bas la justice militaire', 1904; 1 p. in the series 'Byrrh', 1906, 1 p. in the series 'Pochette de la Paix', 1907; 1 p. in the series 'Gravures de Berger' from the collection 'Les Temps Nouveaux'.

Bibl.: Baudet 1978; Neudin 1980.

Louis VALTAT
Dieppe, Seine-Maritime, 8.8.1869 – Paris, 2.1.1952
Painter.

When he had finished his studies at Versailles, he attended the Académie Julian in Paris, where he met Bonnard, Vuillard, and Albert André. He attended for a short time the studio of G. Moreau. In 1895 he worked with Toulouse-Lautrec and A. André on the sets for the Indian play *Le Chariot de terre cuite*. In these years he enjoyed the company of the Nabi circle. From 1893 he exhibited at the Salon des Indépendants and from 1903 at the Salon d'Automne, where he was also present in 1905 ın the large room devoted to the Fauves. In 1952 the Salon d'Automne gave him an important retrospective exhibition.

Postcards: 6 p. in IV series (c.1899) and 1 p. in the VI series (1900) of 'Maîtres de la Carte Postale', publ. by the paper *La Critique*.

VAMBA, pseudonym of Luigi BERTELLI
Florence, 19.3.1860 – Florence, 27.11.1920
Caricaturist, publicist, illustrator.

He began his activities as a publicist and caricaturist for the Roman daily paper *Capitan*

Francassa, which he in part edited from 1884. In 1887 he left *Capitan Francassa* because of a political disagreement and he founded with E. A. Vasallo, E. Faelli, L. Lodi the daily paper *Don Chisciotte della Mancia*. From 1886 to 1890 he was on the editorial board of *Il Pupazzetto*, in which he published his political caricatures. As a caricaturist he also worked on *Carro di Tespi* (1889-1891), a weekly paper of theatrical criticism. In 1890 he founded in Florence the paper *L'O di Giotto*. As an illustrator he worked on the papers: *Domenica italiana* (1896-97), *Burchiello* (1897-98), *Il Giorno* (1899-1901), *Bruscolo* (1901-05). In 1906 he founded in Florence the *Giornalino della Domenica*, a weekly for the young which appeared from August 1906 to July 1911 and from March 1919 to December 1902. He was the author of the text and iilustrations of several children's books including *Giornalino di Gran Burrasco* (1912).

Postcards: several reproducing the covers of *Giornalino della Domenica*.

Bibl.: Arrasich 1984.

Eugène Charles Paul VAVASSEUR
Paris, 25.4.1863 – ?
Cartoonist, lithographer, commercial artist.

He was a student of A. Cabanel at the Ecole des Beaux-Arts in Paris. He made humorous drawings for the papers: *La Caricature*, *La Silhouette*, *L'Eclipse*, *La Gaudriole*, *Revue illustrée*. He designed the poster for the paper *Le Supplement*.

Postcards: 1 p. in the series 'Les affiches célèbres', R. Tuck.London; 1 p. in the series 'Byrrh', 1906; publicity p. 'Hammond machine à écriture visible'.

Bibl.: Baudet 1978; Neudin 1981; Arrasich 1984.

Carlos VÁZQUEZ i ÚBEDA
Ciudad Real, 1869 – Barcelona, 1944.
Painter, illustrator, commercial artist, graphic designer (commercial graphics).

He attended the San Fernando School of Fine Art and then he studied in Paris with L. Bonnat. In 1896 he settled in Barcelona. He won medals in the national exhibitions in Madrid in 1892, 1899, 1901, 1904 and 1910, and a first-class medal at the IV Exposición de Bellas Artes y Industrias Artisticas in Barcelona in 1898. He worked on the magazines *Album Salón*, *Pluma y Lápiz*, *Hispania*, *Quatre Gats*.

Postcards: 1 p. in the series for the magazine *Hispania*; publicity for 'Esteve & Cia' and for 'Dr Grau'.

Bibl.: Trenc Ballester 1977.

Anton VELIM
Vienna, 24.2.1892 – Vienna, 13.10.1954
He studied at the Graphische Lehr und Versuchsamstalt and the Academy in Vienna (A. Delug).

Postcards: 5 Christmas greetings p. in the Wiener Werkstätte series (nos. 874-878).

Bibl.: Dichand-Martischnig 1978; Baudet 1980; Hansen 1982.

Maurice Pillard VERNEUIL
St. Quentin, Aisne, 1869 – Chexbres, Switzerland 1942.
Graphic designer, illustrator, art critic, author of manuals on ornaments, commercial artist, painter.

A student of E. Grasset, he wrote the manuals: *L'animal dans la decoration* (1898); *Combinai-*

sons ornementales (c. 1900, in collaboration with G. Auriol and Mucha); *L'ornementation par le pochoir* (1901); *Etude de la Plante, son application aux industries d'art* (1908); *Etoffes japonaises tissées et brocheées* (1910); *Etudes de la mer* (1913). In 1904 he directed the publication of *Documents ornementaux*. He worked on the magazines for which he designed posters; *Art et Décoration* and *Le Monde Moderne*. He was the author of *Dictionnaire des symboles, emblèmes et attributs*.

Postcards: 1 p. in the 'Collection des Cent', publ. Gréningaire, Paris c. 1901.

Bibl.: Baudet 1978.

Pierre Eugène VIBERT
Carouge, Geneva 16.2.1875 – Carouge, 1.1.1937.
Painter, illustrator, commercial artist, engraver, graphic designer (lettering).

In 1893 he moved to Paris, where he exhibited for the first time some woodcuts at the Salon of the Société Nationale des Beaux-Arts in 1898. He worked on the magazines *La Plume, L'Image, L'Ermitage, Tendances Nouvelles*. He made illustrations mainly in woodcut for the books; *Paysages de l'Yveline* by P. Fort; *Serres chaudes* by M. Maeterlinck; *Mon village* by Ph. Monnier, *Blés mouvants* by E. Verhaeren; *Divertissements* by R. de Gourmont; *Jardin de Bérénice* by M. Barrè; *Contes de France et d'Italie* by H. de Regnier; *Coups d'oeil sur Paris* by C. Janin; *Le Centaure et La Bacchante* by Ch. de Guérin; *Sylvie* by G. de Nerval; *Idylles* by C. Gessner; *Le Nouveau Monde* by Villiers de l'Isle Adam (1913). He made a series of portraits (A. France, Stendhal, R. de Gourmont, Verhaeren and others) for the 'Collection des Maîtres du Livre'. In 1903 he joined the Salon d'Automne. In 1914 he was invited to teach at the Ecole des Beaux-Arts in Geneva.

Postcards: 1 p. in the first series of 'Maîtres de la Carte Postale', Paris, 1898; third series of 12 p. in woodcut for 'Maîtres de la Carte Postale' c. 189; 1 p. in the sixth series 'Maîtres de la Carte Postale', 1900; 1 p. in the series L'I.P.C.C.

Bibl.: Baudet 1980; Neudin 1980.

A. VIGNOLA
His dates of birth and death are unknown.
Commercial artist, illustrator.

He attended the artistic circle at the cabaret 'Chat Noir', for which he designed some posters. He illustrated the poem in music by G. Fragerolle Le Sphinx (c. 1896).

Postcards: series 'Le Sphinx', reproducing the plates in the album.

Aleardo VILLA
Milan, 12.2.1865 – Milan, 31.12.1906
Painter, commercial artist, graphic designer (commercial and publicity graphics, song scores).

He studied at the Academy at the Brera, where he was the student of G. Bertini and B. Giuliano. He first exhibited as a painter at the Mostra di Brera in 1891. He did much work as a commercial artist for Ricordi, which won international acclaim. In 1901 he won the first prize in the competition held in Buenos Aires for the poster for 'Cigarillos Parsi.'

Postcards; several publicity p. for Magazzini Mele in Naples, publ. Ricordi, Milan 1898-1905; series of 6 publicity p. 'Chocolat Talmone' publ. Ricordi, Milan 1900 (in coll. with F. Laskoff); (Milano-Teatro alla Scala – Stagione Carnevale Quaresima 1900-1901', 1900; 'Caffaro – primo giornale di Genova', publ. Ricordi, Milan 1900; 'Ricordo del Divino Veglione Dantesco', publ. F.lli Grassi, 1903; 'I concorso Nazionale' 'Pro Infanzia', 1904; publicity 'Oleoblitz', publ. Ricordi, Milan; series of 12 p. 'Giusepe Verdi e le sue opere', series for the opera 'Fedora'; series of 5 p. 'I cinque sensi'; 'Onore a Cronje, libertà Boera'; 'Avanti, garibaldini del mare'; series of 'donnine'.

Bibl.: Bartoli-Mataloni 1979; Bobba 1979; Gaibazzi 1979; *La Cartolina*, n. 4, 1982; Mordente 1982; Arrasich 1984.

Jacques VILLON, pseudonym of Gaston DUCHAMP Damville, 31.7.1875 – Puteaux, 9.7.1963.
Painter, engraver, commercial artist, illustrator.
He was the brother of the painters Marcel and Suzanne and of the sculptor Raymond. From the age of 16 he taught himself engraving. When he had finished his studies in law, he settled in Paris and enrolled at the Ecole des Beaux-Arts, where he attended Cormon's studio and an engraving studio. After taking the name of his favourite poet, Villon, he made humorous designs for the magazines 'L'Assiette au Beurre, Cocorico, Le Courrier français, Le Cri de Paris, Frou-Frou, Gil Blas, Le Gravroche, Au Quartier Latin, Le Rire, Le Sourire, La Vie en rose. He also made several posters for Parisian cabarets. From its foundation (1903) he was a member of the organizing committee of the Salon d'Automme, where he exhibited his own work. In 1912 he resigned from this position in protest against the opposition of some members of the committee to the admission of cubist painting. From 1911 he made a series of engravings for the publisher Clovis Sagot, in which he proposed a personal interpretation of cubism. He was among the founders of the group 'Section d'Or', which had its first exhibition in 1912 at the Galerie La Boétie. After a period (1922-30) of struggling with economic problems, he won international acclaim from the beginning of the Thirties, when through his brother's help he managed to hold some one-man shows in the United States. In 1949 he won the grand prix at the international exhibition of engraving in Lugano; in 1950 the Carnegie prize at the international exhibition in Pittsburgh; in 1956 the international prize for painting at the Biennale in Venice.
Postcards: 1 p. in the 'Collection des Cent', publ. Gréningaire, Paris, c. 1901; 7 p. in the series 'Gala Henry Monnier', 1904.
Bibl.: Weill 1977; Baudet 1978, 1980; Forissier 1978; Neudin 1979, 1980; Holt 1981; Mordente 1982.

André (Cornelis André) VLAANDEREN Amsterdam 1.9.1881 – Bruges, 5.8.1955
Painter decorator, lithographer, illustrator, graphic designer, (ex libris, books).
He attended the Quellinus School and then the Rijksakademie in Amsterdam (1898-99). From 1899 to 1905 he worked in the studio of the architect Ed. Cuypers. He taught at the Tekenschool voor Kunstambachten in Amsterdam. Towards 1929 he settled in Belgium.
Postcards: several greetings p. printed by Boekuil en Karveel uitgaven, Antwerpen.

Heinrich VOGELER
Bremen, 12.12.1872 – Kazakhstan, USSR,

14.6.1942.
Painter, etcher, commercial artist, graphic designer (ex libris, programmes etc.), illustrator, architect, designer of applied arts and objects of daily use.
From 1890 to 1893 he attended the Kunstakademie in Düsseldorf. He was a member of the Worpswede artistic colony, where in 1908, with his brother Franz, he founded the Worpsweder Werkstätte. In 1932 he decided to settle in the Soviet Union. He worked on the magazines *Jugend, Die Insel* etc.
Postcards: in the series of the 'Stollwercksche Chocolade', c. 1900; 'Jürgen Christian Findorff', c. 1902; p. in the series of the 'Kunstund Kunstge-werbehauses Worpswede', c. 1910; p. reproducing drawings of the first world war.
Bibl.: cat. Altonaer Museum, Hamburg 1970; *Graphik von Heinrich Vogeler*, cat. edited by e. Stüwe, Altonaer Museum Hamburg 1978; Lebeck 1980; Drago 1981; *Heinrich Vogeler, Kunstwerke, Gebrauchsgegenstände, Dokumente*', cat. of the exhibition, Staatliche Kunsthalle Berlin – Kunstverein Hamburg 1983.

W

Wilhelm WACHTEL
Lemberg (Lwów), 1875 – United States, 1942
Painter, lithographer, commercial artist, illustrator.
He studied at the Academy in Cracow and at the Academy in Munich. He was active for a long time in Vienna, and then in the United States. He was the author of several series of lithographic prints.
Postcards: series 'Typen aus Polen', H. Algenberg, Lwów, c. 1903; series with Jewish subjects, H. Altenberg, Lwów.
Bibl.: Neudin 1978.

Alice WANKE
Vienna, 11.4.1873 – Vienna, 1936
Commercial artist, graphic designer, illustrator.
She studied with Franz von Matsch and attended the Kunstgewerbeschule in Vienna. She was active in Vienna at the beginning of the century.
Postcards: series n. 452, M. Munk, Vienna; series n. 328, Théo Stoefer, Nürnberg; several unsigned series.
Bibl.: Holt 1983.

Albert WEISGERBER
St. Ingbert, near Saarbrüchen, 21.4.1878 – Formelles, near Ypres, 10.5.1915.
Painter, commercial artist, illustrator, graphic designer.
He attended the Kunstgewerbeschule from 1897 and from 1898 the Academy in Munich (G. v. Hackl, F. v. Stuck). from 1905 to 1906 he was in Paris. In 1913 he was a member of the group which founded the Neue Secession in Munich. He worked on *Jugend* from 1895.
Postcards: 'II Offizielle Ansichtskarte der bayerischen Jubiläums-Landesausstellung, Nürnberg 1906', Druck F. Schnell & Co., Nürnberg, reproducing the poster; publicity p. 'Der bunte Vogel, Künstler u. Studenten Kneipe'.
Bibl.: Weiss 1985 (II).

Emil Rudolf WEISS

Lahr, Baden, 12.10.1875 – Meersburg, Bodensee, 7.11.1942
Painter, commercial artist, graphic designer (books, lettering), illustrator.
He attended the Academy in Karlsruhe (L. V. Kalckreuth, H. Thoma), in Stuttgart and then the Académie Julian in Paris. From 1903 to 1906 he worked in Hagen for K. E. Osthaus and for the Folkwang Museum. From 1907 to 1933 he taught design in several schools in Berlin. He designed decoration and illustrations for several books including *Das schöne Mädchen von Pao* for Insel Verlag (1900), *Troilus und Cressida* by Shakespeare, the Poems of Sappho. He worked on the magazines *Pan* and *Die Insel*.
Postcards: p. in the series for the Karlsruhe Künstlerbund, c. 1898-1905.
Bibl.: cat. Altonaer Museum, Hamburg 1970.

Jacques WELY
?, c. 1873 – ?, c. 1910.
Caricaturist, illustrator, graphic designer (publicity graphics, song scores).
The artist was active at Montfort – l'Amaury (Seine-et-Oise). He designed the illustrations for the books *La maîtresse du Prince Jean* by Willy (1903) and *Âmes brétonnes* by C. Mauclair (1911). Postcards: series of 4 p. 'Marquis et Marquise', 1899; 3 p. in the 'Collection des Cent', publ. Gréningaire, Paris, c. 1901; 1 p. in the series 'Album Mariani', c. 1910; series 'Paris qui danse'.
Bibl.: Baudet 1980.

Brynolf WENNERBERG
Otterstad, Sweden, 12.8.1866 – Bad Aibling, Bavarias, 1950
Painter, commercial artist, graphic designer, illustrator.
From 1885 to 1886 he was a student at the School of Applied Arts in Stockholm, from 1887 to 1888 at P. S. Kroyer's school in Copenhagen and then at the Academies in Munich and Paris. In 1898 he settled in Munich. He worked on the magazines *Lustige Blätter, Meggendorfer Blätter* and *Simplicissimus* (1915).
Postcards: series of sporting ladies; several in the series for the magazine *Lustige Blätter*, c. 1910-14; several military propaganda p. in the series for *Simplicissimus*, A. Langen, Munich 1915.
Bibl.: cat. Altonaer Museum, Hamburg 1970.

Raimund WICHERA, Ritter von Brennerstein
Frankstadt, 18.8.1862 –?
Painter, graphic designer.
His biographical details are unknown. He attended the Academy in Vienna (H. Makart). Postcards: a wide production of genre p., greetings p., and p. with scenes in Biedermeier style, published by M. Munk, Vienna.

Hans Beatus WIELAND
Gallusberg, near Morschwyl, St. Gallen, 11.6.1867 – Kriens, 1945
Painter, illustrator, commercial artist, lithographer.
He studied at the Academy in Munich with N. Gysis, L. v. Löfftz, W. v. Lindenschmit from 1887 to 1892. He worked on the magazine *Jugend* from 1907 to 1918. He was a member of the Munich Secession and of the Deutsche Werkbund. In 1914 he returned to Switzerland.
Postcards: 2 series of 16 p. 'Sicilia', publ.

Ricordi, Milan 1902; p. for the national holiday, 1st August 1912, for the Red Cross, Graph. Anstalt J. E. Wolfensberger, Zurich.
Bibl.: *La Cartolina*, n. 4, 1982.

Manuel WIELANDT
Löwenstein, Württemberg, 20.12.1863 – Munich, 11.5.1922
Painter, watercolourist, engraver.
He studied at the Academies in Stockholm and in Munich (with G. Schönleber). From 1903 he worked in Munich. He made journeys to Malta and Italy, where he made several watercolours which were reproduced as postcards.
Postcards; series of 25 p. 'I Laghi Lombardi', publ. J. Velten Karlsruhe, c. 1898; series 'La Riviera', publ. J. Velten, Karlsruhe, c. 1899; series 'Venezia', publ. J. Velten, Karlsruhe, c. 1900; others of views of the French Riviera and German and Swiss places for the publishers Moser, Nister, Schmidt, Staub and Velten.
Bibl.: Joletta, 'I Laghi Lombardi', *Il Raccoglitore di cartoline illustrate*, I, n. 8, 5.11.1899; Stoppani 1900; Holt 1981; Arrisich 1984.

Adolf WIESNER
Prague, 31.3.1871 – Terezín (concentration camp), 18.9.1942.
Painter, illustrator.
He studied at the Academies in Prague (with M. Pirnér and V. Hynais) and in Munich (with O. Seitz)
He made study trips to Paris.
Postcards: several decorative and greetings p.

Hendrika WILLEBEEK LE MAIR
Rotterdam, 23.4.1889 – Den Haag, 15.3.1966.
Painter, watercolourist, illustrator.
She was a student of A. H. R. van Maasdijk and of D. G. Ezerman in Rotterdam (c. 1909-10) and of M. Boutet de Monve in Paris (1911). She was a painter of scenes of childhood and an illustrator of children's books.
Postcards: series of 12 p. 'Schumann's Children's Pieces', publ. Augener Ltd., London, and David McKay, Philadelphia, 1915; series 'Old Dutch Nursery Rhymes', publ. Augener Ltd., London, and David McKay, Philadelphia; series of 12 p. 'Little Songs of Long Ago', publ. Augener Ltd. London, and David McKay, Philadelphia; series 'Elves and Fairies', series publ. n. 76 of *The Enchanted Forest* by I. R. and G. Outwaited, publ. A. & C. Black Ltd. London.
Bibl.: Cope 1978; Holt 1981, 1983.

Adolphe Léon WILLETTE
Châlons-sur-Marne, 31.7.1857 – Paris, 4.2.1926
Caricaturist, illustrator, lithographer, commercial artist, painter, graphic designer (book, song scores), tapestry designer.
From 1875 to 1879 he attended the Ecole des Beaux-Arts in Paris, where he was a pupil of A. Cabanel. From 1881 he exhibited at the Salon of the Société des Artistes Français. After 1887 he progressively abandoned painting in favour of lithography and illustration. He was one of the artistic group at the cabaret 'Le Chat Noir', for which he designed a large panel 'Parce Domine', and he worked on the magazine of the same name. He made humorous designs and political satire for the papers: *Courrier Français*, *L'Echo de Paris*, *Le Figaro*, *L'Assiette au Beurre*, *Le Rire*, *Père-Peinard*, *Trois-Huit*, *Père Duchesne*, *Triboulet*. He founded the magazines *Pierrot*, *Le Pied de nez* and *La Vache enragée*, which had a short life. In 1910 he was among the founder members of

the newspaper *Les Humoristes*. He illustrated the books: *Farandole de Pierrots* by E. Vitta (1890) *Les Pierrots* and *Les Giboulés d'avril* by Melandri, *La Soeur de Pierrot* by A. Alexandre (1893). He was the author of the albums: *Pauvre Pierrot* (1887) the collection of designs published in *Le Chat Noir, Cent dessins de Willette* (1904), *Caricature* (1909). He designed windows and decorative panels for several Parisian theatres and cabarets ('Taverne de Paris', 'Auberge du clou', 'La Cigale', 'Le Bal Tabarin'), cartoons for Gobelin tapestries and for panels with scenes of Parisian life for the staff room at the Hôtel de Ville in Paris. In 1919 he published his autobiography *Feu Pierrot*. The graphic work of Willette, like that of Chéret, shows the influence of French eighteenth-century painting. His political satires often contained reactionary and anti-semitic messages (above all during the Dreyfus affair).
Postcards: 1 p. of a petition to Tzar Nicholas II, 1896; 1 p. in the series 'Cocorico'; 1 p. in the 'Collection des Cent', publ. Gréningaire, Paris c. 1901; 1 p. in the series 'Pochette de la Paix', 1907; 1 p. in the series 'Les Voeux de la France, Rire Rouge', 1914; 1 p. in the series 'Le Rire Rouge', 1915; 1 p. in the series 'Journées du Secours Nationale'; several of war propaganda, 'Pierrot d'après la poupée de A. Willette'.
Bibl.: Baudet 1978; Zeyons 1979; Neudin 1983.

Eduard Josef WIMMER-WISGRILL
Vienna, 2.4.1882 – Vienna 25.12.1961
Interior architect, graphic designer (commercial graphics), designer of fashion, of fashion accessories, of furniture, of fabrics, of carpets, of glass, of metal work, of leatherware, of objects of daily use, of installations and theatrical costumes.
He studied at the Handelsakademie and from 1901 to 1907 at the Kunstgewerbeschule in Vienna (A. Roller, J. Hoffmann, K. Moser). From 1912 he taught at the Kunstgewerbeschule. He worked with the Weiner Werkstätte and from 1912 he was the director of the fashion section. From 1923 to 1925 he lived in the United States and he taught at the Art Institute in Chicago. Exhibitions: Kunstschau, Vienna 1908, 1909.
Postcards: 10 p. of fashion in the series of the Wiener Werkstätte (nos. 861-870).
Bibl.: Baudet 1980; Hansen 1982; cat. Wien 1984.

Josef Rudolf WITZEL
Frankfurt a. M. 27.9.1867 – before 1925 Painter, commercial artist, illustrator.
He attended the Städelsches Institut in Frankfurt and in Karlsruhe. From 1890 he was active in Munich. He worked on the magazine *Jugend* (from 1896).
Postcards: several in the first three series of the Künstler-Postkarten for *Jugend*, G. Hirth, Munich, 1898-99; series of erotic pin-ups, c. 1912.
Bibl.: Lebeck 1980.

Heinrich Wilhelm WULFF
1870 –?
His biographical details are unknown.
Postcards: 2 in series I of the 'Künstlerpostlearten' for the Kunstdruckerei 'Künstlerbund in Karlsruhe, c. 1900.
Bibl.: cat. Altonaer Museum, Hamburg 1970.

Z

Carl ZANDER
Berlin, 26.5.1872 – ?
Painter, commercial artist, illustrator.
He attended the Academy in Berlin. From 1902 to 1911 he did much work in the field of book decoration for the publishers Fontane, Grote, Mittler, Schuster, Löffler. He was a member of the Verband Deutscher Illustratoren:
Postcards: series of the seasons, c. 1902.

Theodor ZASCHE jr.
Vienna, 18.10.1862 – Vienna, 15.11.1922
Painter, graphic designer, illustrator.
He was the son of the painter Josef. He attended the Kunstgewerbeschule in Vienna (F. Laufberger, J. v. Berger) He worked on the humorous Viennese papers (*Floh, Wiener Witzblatt, Wiener Luft*), the Berlin paper (*Lustige Blätter*) and the Munich paper (*Fliegende Blätter*).
Postcards: p. published by Gerlach & Schenk, Vienna, reproducing a variant of one of his illustrations for the volume *Radlerei*, by the same editor, 1897.
Bibl.: cat. Wien 1964.

Vittorio ZECCHIN
Murano, 21.5.1878 – Murano, ? – 1947
Painter, designer of windows, glass objects, furniture, ceramics, tapestries, embroideries, decorative panels, graphic designer (calendars, playing-cards).
From 1894 to 1901 he attended the Academy of Fine Art in Venice. From 1909 he exhibited at the Ca' Pesaro. In 1913, 1914 and 1915 he took part in the exhibitions of the Roman Secession. In 1914 he exhibited glass made in collaboration with the painter Teodoro Wolf Ferrari at the Venice Biennale, and he took part in the 'mostra dei Rifiutati' from the Biennale which was installed in the Excelsior Hotel on the Venice Lido. In 1916 he opened a workshop for the production of tapestries in the ex-convent in Murano. He exhibited decorative works at the Venice Biennali in 1922, 1924, 1926, 1928, 1930, 1932, 1934, 1936, 1938, at the exhibitions in Monza 1923 and in Paris 1925.
Postcards: at least 10 series of p. 'Smalti e murrine', reproducing cartoons for glass windows and drawings for murrines, c. 1918.
Bibl.: Bartoli-Mataloni 1979; Baudet 1980; Mordente 1982; Arrasich 1984.

Fritz ZERRITSCH jr.
Vienna, 28.8.1888 – ?
Painter, graphic designer.
He was the son of the painter Fritz. He attended from 1905 to 1910 the Academy in Vienna (C. Griepenkerl, A. Delug). In 1911 he made a study trip to Munich. In the same year he began to exhibit his work. From 1914 he was a member of the Künstlerhaus in Vienna and he took part in their exhibitions.
Postcards: 'Öst. Adria Austellung', Vienna 1913.

Fritz ZEYMER
Vienna, 7.12.1866 – Vienna, 3.3.1940
Graphic designer, designer of fabrics and furniture.
From 1902 to 1908 he studied at the Kunstgewerbeschule in Vienna (A. Roller, C. O. Czeschka, J. Hoffmann, F. Metzner). He worked with the Wiener Werkstätte in the applied graphics section designing illustrated

sheets, programmes, and scenic decorations for the 'Fledermaus' Cabaret'. Exhibitions: Kunstschau, Vienna 1908.

Postcards: c. 5 p. in the series of the Wiener Werkstätte: one for the Gertrude Barrison show at the cabaret 'Fledermaus' (n. 68), four greetings p. (nos. 144?, 303, 488?, 577?).

Bibl.: Dichand-Martischnig 1978; Hansen 1982; Schweiger 1982.

Ludwig von ZUMBUSCH
Munich, 17.7.1861 – Munich, 28.2.1927
Painter, commercial artist, illustrator.
He attended the Academies in Vienna, Munich (W. v. Lindenschmidt) and Paris. He was a member of the Hagenbund in Vienna from 1902 to 1912. He was a member of the Munich Secession. He worked on the magazine *Jugend*.

Postcards: several in series I – III of the 'Künstler-Postkarten' for *Jugend*, G. Hull 1898-99.

Bibl.: cat. Altonaer Museum, Hamburg 1970; Neudin 1979; Baudet 1980.

Hubert von ZWICKLE
Salzburg, 11.2.1875 – Golling, Salzburg, 15.3.1950
Graphic designer, illustrator, designer of furnishing elements, of exhibition installations, of jewellery.
He studied at the Staatsgewerbeschule and from 1892 at the Kunstgewerbeschule in Vienna (F. G. Matsch).

Postcards: 4 p. for the Kaiserjubiläum, 1908 in the Wiener Werkstätte Series (nos. 170, 174, 178, 182).

Bibl.: Baudet 1980; Hansen 1982.

Bibliography

Books, catalogues and articles

1894
Gleeson, White, 'Christmas Cards and their Chief Designers', The Studio, Winter Number, 1894, pp. 3-56.

1896
J. Grand-Carteret, *Vieux papiers. Vieilles images. Cartons d'un collectionneur*, A. Le Vasseur et Cie, Paris 1896.

1898
M. Lehrs, 'Künstlerpostkarten', *Pan*, IV (1898, n. 3), pp. 189-192.

1899
E. De Amicis, 'La poesia delle cartoline', *Il Raccoglitore di Cartoline illustrate*, I (1899, n. 7), p. 77. Deutsch, 'Jugend', *Il Raccoglitore di Cartoline illustrate*, I (1899, n. 6), p. 69.
A. Maggioni, 'La prima Esposizione Internazionale di cartoline postali illustrate a Venezia. Note e appunti', *Emporium*, vol. X (1899), pp. 310-332.
M. Serao, 'Cartoline illustrate', *Il Raccoglitore di Cartoline illustrate*, I (1899, n. 5), pp. 53-55.

1900
Catalogo Generale Prezzo Corrente Cartoline Postali Illustrate 1900, Stoppani F. lli, Milan 1900; anastatic copy, La Storia Postale, Filatelia di A.A. Piga, Genoa 1979.

1902
G. Gamma, 'Notizie storiche sulle origini e sullo sviluppo della cartolina postale illustrata', *La Cartolina Illustrata*, I (1902, n. 2), pp. 1-4.

1903
F. Carreras y Candi, *Las tarjetas postales in España*, Imp. de F. Altes, Barcelona.

1903
W. J. Scott, *All about Postcards*, Leeds 1903.

1903-04
J. Lubier, 'Die Steglitzer Werkstatt', *Deutsche Kunst und Dekoration*, Bd. XIII (1903-04), p. 63.

1904
A. Berthier, *La Carte Postale photographique et les procédés d'amateurs*, C. Mendel, Paris 1904.

1906
The Picture Postcard Annual & Directory, Rotherham 1906-1907[2].

1911
E. D. Bacon, *Catalogue of the Philatelic Library of the Earl of Crawford*, K. T., Philatelic Literature Society, London 1911.

1912
The Collectors' & Dealers Directory, Rotherham 1912. W. Hinzenberg, 'Russische Postkarten', *Mitteilungen d.V.f. Plakatfreunde*, 1912, pp. 22-27.

1920
R. Braungart, 'Künstlerische Ansichtsspostkarten', *Das Plakat*, 1920, n. 8, pp. 360-372.

1922-24
L. Wiener, 'La carte illustrée', *Le Musée du Livre*, I (1922-23), pp. 7-8, 14-16, 23-24, 30-32, 38-40, 43-48, 51-56, 61-64, II (1923-24), pp. 6-8, 14-16, 21-24.

1924
L. Renieu, *La carte postale illustrée considerée au point de vue des arts graphiques et des sujets représentés*, Brussels 1924.

1933
P. Eluard, 'Les Plus Belles Cartes Postales', *Minotaure*, 1933, n. 3-4, pp. 85-100.

1946
G. Guyonnet, *La carte postale illustrée, son histoire, sa valeur documentaire*, Chambre Syndicale Française de la Carte Postale Illustrée, s.1., s.d. (1946).

1953
A. Pinto, *La targeta postal*, Edit. del Nordeste, Barcelona 1953. J. J. Tharrats, *Christmas y Felicitaciones*, P.E.N., Barcelona 1953.

1954
G. Buday, *The History of the Christmas Card*, Rockliff, London 1954.

1957
J. R. Burdick (edited by), *Pioneer Postcards; the Story of Mailing Cards to 1898, with an Illustrated Checklist of Publishers and titles*, Nostalgia Press, New York 1957, 1964.

1960
H. Ankwicz von Kleehoven, 'Die Anfänge der Wiener Secession', *Alte und moderne Kunst*, V (1960, n. 6-7), pp. 6-10.

1961
H. Ankwicz von Kleehoven, 'Die Wiener Werkstätte, *Alte und moderne Kunst*, VI (1961, n. 42), pp. 20.

1962
F. E. Barba 'La collection de cartes postales à la Bibliothèque Nationale de Madrid', *Bulletin de l'Unesco à l'intention des bibliothèques*, vol. XVI (1962, n. 3), pp. 171-172.

1964
Wien um 1900, cat. of the exhibition, Vienna 1964.

1966
A. Kyrou, *L'Age d'or de la carte postale*, A. Balland, Paris 1966, 1968[2]; Terrain-Vague, Paris 1978[3].
F. Staff, *The Picture Postcard and its Origins*, Lutterworth Press, London 1966.

1967
Die Wiener Werkstätte, Modernes Kunsthandwerk von 1903-1932, cat. of the exhibition, Österr. Museum f. Angewandte Kunst, Vienna 1967.
G. Staad, *Verschrikkelijke, vermakelijke, verderflijke, Kunstminnelijke en soortgelijke*, Assen-Amsterdam-Rotterdam 1967.

1969
J. L. Lowe, *Bibliography of Postcard Literature*, Folson/Pa. 1969.

1970
F. Alderson, *The Comic Postcard in English Life*, David & Charles, Newton Abbot 1970.
Kunste und Postkarte cat. of the exhibition edited by G. Kaufmann and M. Mëinz, Altonaer Museum, Hamburg, 1970.

1971
R. Carline, *Pictures in the Post. The Story of the Picture Postcard*, London 1971.
M. R. Hewlett, *Picton's priced Postcard Catalogue and Hand-book*, London 1971 (there are later editions).

1972
I. & W. Bernhard, *Bildpostkartenkatalog/Picture Postcard Catalogue*, Germany 1870-1945, Hamburg 1972.

1973
A. Negri, *Le cartoline della nonna*, Florence 1973.

1974
J. M. Kaduck (edited by), *Rare and Expensive Postcards. A Price Guide*, Wallace Homestead Co., Des Moines/Iowa 1974. M. Klamkin, *Picture Postcards*, David & Charles, Newton Abbot 1974, 1976[2].

1975
B. Andrews, *A Directory of Postcards, Artists, Publishers and Trademarks*, Little Red Caboose, Irving/Texas 1975.
F. D. Lyons jr, The Artist Signed Postcard, L-W. Promotions, Gas City/Indiana 1975.
J. and G. Neudin (edited by), Neudin. *L'officiel international des cartes postales*, Paris 1975.
J. L. Lowe and B. Papell, *Detroit Publishing Company Collectors' Guide*, New York 1975.
W. Oullette, *Cartes postales fantastiques*, Henri Veyrier, Paris 1975; Eng. trans., Doubleday & Co, New York 1975, and Sphere Books, London 1976.
J. H. D. Smith, *IPM Catalogue of Picture Postcards*, London 1975 (there are also later editions).

1976
Bickhard and Bottinelli, *Die Post als Künstlermedium*, Kassel 1976.
S. S. Carver, *The American Postcard Guide to Tuck*, Carves Cards, Brooklyn/Massachusetts 1976.
A. Fildier (edited by), *Argus Fildier, Catalogue des cartes postales anciennes de collection*, Paris 1976.
B. Forissier, *La femme à la Belle Epoque*, Sodim, Brussels 1976.
B. Forissier, *25 ans d'actualités à travers la carte postale 1889-1914*, Les Editions de l'amateur, Paris 1976.
'La Collection des Cent, une collection inachevée' *Le Collectionneur Français*, 1976, n. 124, pp. 12-13.
G. & D. Miller, *Picture Postcards in the United States 1893-1918*, C. N. Potter, New York 1976.
G. Naudet, *L'Aéronautique à la Belle Epoque*, Sodim, Brussels 1976.
J. and G. Neudin (edited by), Neudin, *L'officiel international des cartes postales*, Paris 1976[2].

1976-77
Ein Dokument deutscher Kunst. Darmstadt 1901-1976, cat. of the exhibition, 5 vols., Darmstadt 1976-77.
K. Veit Riedel, 'Worpsweder Postkarten. Die Sammlung Kosenenann im Altonaer Museum', *Altonaer Museum in Hamburg Jahrbuch*, Bd. 14-15, 1976-77, pp. 99-122.

1977
'Ces dames de la Belle Époque en cartes postales', *Abc decor*, 1977, n. 156, pp. 35-41.
A. Fildier (edited by), *Argus Fildier, catalogue des cartes postales anciennes de collection*, Paris 1977[2].
T. and V. Holt, *Till the Boys Come Home, the Picture Postcards of the First World War*, MacDonald & Jane's, London 1977. *Kunst im Alltag. Plakate und Gebrauchsgraphik um 1900*, cat. of the exhibition Kunsthalle, Bremen 1977.
La carte postale illustrée, actes du Colloque de Chalon-sur-Saône, 6, 7, 8 mai 1977, Soc. des Amis du Musée Nicéphore Niépce, Chalon-sur-Saône 1977.
W. Mrazek, Künstlerpostkarten aus der Wiener Werkstätte, Verlag Galerie Welz, Salzburg 1977.
J. and G. Neudin, *Neudin. L'officiel international des cartes postales*, Paris 1977[3].
W. Ouellette-B. Jones, *Les Cartes Postales Érotiques*, Publ. Humanoïdes Associés, Paris 1977; Eng. trans., London s.d.
J. Philippen, *Histoire et charme de la carte postale illustrée*, Europa, Diest 1977.
M. and J.-P. Rostenne (edited by), *Cartes postales anciennes. Catalogue international*, Brussels 1977.
E. Trenc Ballester, *Las Artes Graficas a la Epoca Modernista en Barcelona*, Gremio de Industrias Graficas, Barcelona 1977.
A. Weill, *Art Nouveau Postcards*, Images Graphiques Inc., New York 1977; Thames & Hudson, London 1977; French trans., Publ. Henri Berger, Paris 1977; German trans, Gütersloh 1978.

G. Woeckl, 'Kunstpostkarten aus München und Wien. Ein Beitrag zur Geschichte der Gebrauchsgraphik der Jahrhundertwende', *Sammlerjournal*, 1977, n. 4-5.

1977-78
Glückwünsche auf Postkarten, cat. of the exhibition Altonaer Museum, Hamburg 1977-78.

1978
A. and F. Baudet, *L'Encyclopédie Internationale de la carte postale*, vol. I, S.N.R.A. publ, Paris 1978.
A. Byatt, *Picture Postcards and their Publishers*, publ. Golden Age Postcard Books, Malvern 1978.
D. and P. Cope, *Illustrators of Postcards from the Nursery*, East West Publications, London-The Hague 1978.
H. Dichand and M. Martischnig. *Jugendstilpostkarten*, Harenberg Kommunikation, Dortmund 1978.
W. Duval and V. Monahan, *Collecting Postcards in Colour 1894-1914*, Blanford Press, Poole, Dorset 1978.
A. Fildier (edited by), *Argus Fildier, Catalogue des cartes postales anciennes de collection*, Paris 1978[3].
B. Forrissier, *30 années d'elegance à travers la carte postale 1900-1930*, Les Editions de l'amateur, Paris 1978.
'Gala Henri Monnier', *Le Collectionneur Français*, 1978, féver.
A. Gontier, 'Les rapports entre la carte postale et l'affiche', *Trouvaille*, 1978, n. 10.
R. Lebeck, *Reklame-Postkarten*, Harenberg Kommunikation, Dortmund 1978.
G. and J. Neudin, 'Une production peu connue; les cartes postales viennoises du debut du XX', *La Gazette de l'Hôtel Drouot*, 1978, n. 4, pp. 20-22.
G. and J. Neudin (edited by), *Neudin. L'officiel international des cartes postales*, Paris 1978.
M. and J.-P. Rostenne (edited by), *Cartes postales anciennes. Catalogue international*, Brussels 1978[2].
S. Schnitzler (edited by), *Gedenke mein. Postkarten von Anno dunnemals*, Berlin 1978[2].
E. Trost and M. Martischnig, *Wiener Veduten. 47 Ansichtskarten der Wiener Werkstätte*, Molden Edition, Vienna-Munich-Zurich 1978.

1978-80
F. A. Fletcher and A. D. Brooks, *British Exhibitions and their Postcards. Part 1: 1900-1914; Part II: 1915-1979*, London 1978-80.

1979
F. Bartoli and I. Mataloni, *Cartoline d'epoca e gli illustratori italiani*, A. & B., Rome 1979.
C. Bobba, *Cartoline de collezione*, edizone in proprio, Asti-Torino 1979.
A. Fildier (edited by), *Argus fildier. Catalogue des cartes postales anciennes de collection*, Paris 1979.
B. Forissier, *Les belles années du cinema à travers la carte postale 1895-1935*, Paris 1979.
E. Gaibazzi, *Catalogo italiano delle cartoline d'epoca*, publ. F.A.R.A.P., Bologna 1979.
a. Gontier, 'Les rapports entre l'art et la carte postale', *Trouvaille*, 1979, n. 16.

R. Lebeck (edited by); *Angeber-Postkarten*, Harenberg Kommunikation, Dortmund 1979.
J. and G. Neudin (edited by), *Neudin, L'officiel international des cartes postales*, Paris 1979. Postkarten und Künstlerkarten. *Eine Kulturgeschichtliche Dokumentation*, cat. of the exhibition, Berlin s.d. (c. 1979).
M. and J.-P. Rostenne (edited by), *Cartes postales anciennes. Catalogue international*, Brussels 1979[3]. *Wiener Stilkunst um 1900, Zeichnungen und Aquarelle im Besitz des Historischen Museums der Stadt Wien*, cat of the exhibition, Historisches Museum der Stadt Wien, Vienna 1979.
S. Zeyons, *Le manuel de l'amateur. Les cartes postales*, Hachette, Paris 1979.

1980
A. and F. Baudet, *Nouvelle Encyclopédie illustrée de la carte postale internationale, vol. II*, Editions Joël Garcia – 'Trouvailles', Paris 1980.
P. Douliez, *Album Deutscher Volkslieder mit Postkarten von Paul Hey*, Stuttgart 1980.
E. J. Evans and J. Richards, *A social History of Britain in Postcards 1870-1930*, London 1980.
A. Fildier (edited by), *Argus Fildier, Catalogue des cartes postales anciennes de collection*, Paris 1980.
T. and V. Holt (edited by), *Stanley Gibbons Postcard Catalogue*, Stanley Gibbons, Colchester-London 1980.
R. Lebeck and M. Schutte, *Propagandapostkarten I*, Harenberg Kommunikation, Dortmund 1980.
R. Lebeck, *Jugendstil-Postkarten* II, Harenberg Kommunikation, Dortmund 1980.
J. and G. Neudin (edited by), *Neudin L'officiel international des cartes postales*, Paris 1980.

1980-81
Th. E. Range, *The Book of Postcard Collecting*, New York 1980.
L. Wittamer-De Camps (edited by), *La Belle Époque Masterworks by Combaz, Leo Jo and Livemont*, cat. of the exhibition, International Exhibitions Foundation, 1980-81.

1981
'Chiattone il tipografo illustratore', *La Cartolina*, I (1981, n. 3), pp. 23-25.
'Commemorative e pubblicitarie bolognesi', *La Cartolina*, I (1981, n. 3), pp. 19-22.
A. Drago, *Donne donne . . . Costume, sorrisi, allegorie e sogni proibiti nelle cartoline postali 1880-1940*, A. Mondadori, Milano 1981.
G. Fanelli, *Il disegno Liberty*, Laterza, Bari 1981, 1983[2]; Spanish trans., Editorial G. Gili, Barcelona 1982.
T. and V. Holt, *Stanley Gibbons Postcard Catalogue*, Stanley Gibbons, Colchester-London 1981[2].
'La galleria ferroviaria del Sempione', *La Cartolina*, I (1981, n. 3), p. 7.
R. Lebeck, *Das Zweirad. Postkarten aus alter Zeit*, Harenberg Kommunikation, Dortmund 1981.
V. Monahan, *An American Postcard Collector's Guide*, Dorset 1981.

H. Morgan, *Big Time: American Tall-Tale Postcards*, New York 1981.

L. Moriani, *Guerre in cartolina*, Edar, Arezzo 1981.

J. and G. Neudin (edited by), *Neudin, L'officiel international des cartes postalese*, Paris 1981.

'Targo Florio: prima era coppa . . .', *La Cartolina*, I (1981, n. 2), p. 7.

I. Vascotto, *Illustratori di caroline nati e attivi a Trieste*, Publ. Centro del Collezionismo di Muggia, 1981.

1982

F. Arrasich, 'Le cartoline in cartolina', *La Cartolina*, II (1982, n. 7), pp. 17-22.

A. Byatt, *Collecting Picture Postcards. An Introduction*, Malvern 1982.

'Edizioni Ricordi & Co.', *La Cartolina*, I (1982, n. 4), pp. 19-22.

'Emilia-Romagna', *La Cartolina*, supplemento speciale al n. 4 del 1982.

T. Hansen, *Die Postkarten der Wiener Werkstätte*, Verlag Schneider-Henn, Munich-Paris 1982.

B. Hillier, *Greetings from Christmas Past*, Herbert Press, London 1982.

R. Lebeck, *Auf- un Rückschläge. Aus den Kindertagen des Tennis*, Harenberg Kommunikation, Dortmund 1982.

M. Mordente, *Catalogo delle cartline illustrate italiane*, A & B, Rome 1982[2].

L. Myers, *The 1982 Postcard Collector's Handbook*, Boonveille/N.Y. 1982.

J. and G. Neudin (edited by) *Neudin, L'officiel international des cartes postales*, Paris 1982.

D. B. Ryan, *Picture Postcards in the United States, 1893-1918*, New York 1982.

W. J. Schweiger, *Wiener Werkstätte; Kunst und Handwerk 1903-1932*, Christian Brandstätter Verlag, Vienna 1982; Italian trans, Ed. Comunità, Milan 1983.

1983

'Biennale di Venezia', *La Cartolina*, III (1983, n. 9), pp. 12-14.

C. Bourgeois and M. Melot, *Les cartes postales. Nouveau guide du collectionneur*, Ed. Atlas, Paris 1983.

A. Dell'Aquila, 'Le grandi serie', *La Cartolina*, III (1983, n. 12), pp. 23-25.

S. Evangelisti and N. Zuccari, 'Prima Esposizione Marchigiana 1905', *La Cartolina*, II (1983, n. 8), pp. 5-7.

M. P. Ferraris, 'Attività grafica Ricordi, in *AA.VV., Musica, Musicisti, Editoria. 175 anni di Casa Ricordi 1808-1983*, Milan 1983, pp. 191-195.

T. and V. Holt (edited by), *Stanley Gibbons Postcard Catalogue*, Stnaley Gibbons, Colchester-London 1983[3].

E. Johanson and T. Termonen, *Suomalaista Postikorttitaidetta Osa I*, Kunstantaja, Lahti 1983.

D. Jajolo, *Su fratelli, su compagni. Cartoline delle lotte operaie 1896-1924. Archivio Franco Monteverde*, L'Arciere, Cuneo 1983.

J. & G. Neudin (edited by), *Neudin. L'officiel international des cartes postales*, Paris 1983.

L. Pertile, *Interi postali*, Milan 1983[3].

A. Ripert and C. Frère, *La carte postale. Son histoire, sa fonction sociale*, Lyon 1983.

E. Sturani, *Curarsi con le cartoline*, Minaldo Cutini Editore, Rome 1983.

W. Till, *Alte Postkarten* Battenberg Sammler-Kataloge, Munich, 1983.

'Una grande serie italiana', *La Cartolina*, III (1983, n. 10), pp. 20-22.

1984

F. Arrasich, Catalogo delle cartoline italiane, *La Cartolina*, Rome 1984.

M. Garnier, F. Lluch, *Post Card Illustrators: a Dictionary of Signatures and Monograms*, Paris 1984.

J. and G. Neudin (edited by), *Neudin. L'officiel international des cartes postales*, Paris 1984. *Wiener Mode und Modefotografie. Die Modeabteilung der Wiener Werstätte*, cat. of the exhibition, Österr. Museum f. angewandte Kunst, Vienna 1984.

W. Neuwirth, *Wiener Werkstätte. Avantgarde, Art Deco, Industrial Design*, publ. W. Neuwirth, Vienna 1984.

M. Pabst, *Wiener Grafik um 1900*, Verlag Silke Schreiber, Munich 1984.

1985

P. Weiss, 'Werbe-Postkarten. Von den Wundern der Elektrizität', *Graphik visuelles marketing*, XXXVIII (1985, n. 4), pp. 44-48.

P. Weiss, 'Werbe-Postkarten. 'München leuchtete'' auch in kleinem Format', *Graphik visuelles marketing*, XXXVIII (1985, n. 6), pp. 44-48.

Periodicals

BELGIUM
Courrier Philatélique Belge, Spa, I (1901) - ?

FRANCE
L'Amateur de la Carte Postale Illustrée, I (1899).
La Carte Postale Illustrée, Paris, 1899-1908.
Revue Illustrée da la Carte Postale, Nancy, 1900-1921.
I.C.C.P., Intermédiaire des Collectionneurs de Cartes Postales Illustrées et de Timbres Poste, Paris, I (1902) ?-?
Le Cartophile Illustrée, Paris, I (1904) - ?
Revue Cartophile Internationale, Paris, I (1904) - ?
Revue Française de la Carte Postale Artistique, Paris, I (1904)-?
La Diane. Revue litteraire de la carte postale artistique et du timbre-poste, Paris, 1908-1912.
Le Collectionneur Français, Paris, I (1965)-
Le Cartophile. Bulletin de cercle Français des collectionneurs de cartes postales, Paris, I (1966)-
Cartophilie & Affiches, Toulouse, I (1973)-
Le Cartopile vosgien. Bulletin de cercle des cartophiles vosgiens, Saint-Die, I (1978)-

GREAT BRITAIN
The Poster Collector, London, I (1899); in 1903 it changed names to *The Poster and Post Card Collector*, London, 1903-1904.

Postal Cards & Covers, Leeds, 1900-1901.
The Picture Postcard & Collectors' Chronicle, London, 1900-1907.
The Collector's Advertiser (then Magazine, then Journal), Rotherham, 1901-1907.
The Collectors' News, 1902-1903.
Picture Postcard Budget & Collector's Magazine, I (1904).
The Postcard Connoisseur for Postcard Collectors, 1904.
The Postcard Collectors Guide and News, 1958-1969.
Picture Postcard Collectors Gazette, 1974-1976, continued as *Postcard Collectors Gazette*, 1977-

ITALY
La Cartolina Postale illustrata, Milan (1898) - ?
Il Raccoglitore di Cartoline Illustrate, Milan, (1899) - ?
L'annunzio filatelico e filocartista, Florence, I (1900) - ?
Indicateur du philocartiste. Nouveau Journal de Kartophilie et variété pour collectionneurs, Milan, I (1900); in 1901 it changed titles to *La Rivista della Cartolina*.
La Cartolina del Progresso Fotografico, Modena, I (1901) - ?
Il Filocartista Italiano, Rome, I (1901) - ?

La Cartolina Illustrata, bollettino mensile delle case editrici di cartoline, Milan, I (1902)-?
La Cartolina Illustrata, rivista delle riviste, Turin, I (1902) - ?
Il Filocartista Siciliano, Caltanisetta, I (1902) - ?
Collezionismo Italiano. Enciclopedia delle raccolte curiose, Milan, I (1979), nn. 1-4.
La cartolina, Rome, I (1981)-

PORTUGAL
O philatelico Aveirense, Aveiro, I (1901) - ?

SPAIN
El Boletín de la tarjeta postal ilustrada, Barcelona, 1901-1904.
España Cartófila, Barcelona, 1901-1909.
La Unión Postal, Barcelona, 1906.

UNITED STATES
Atlas, Yonkers, I (1901) - ?
American Postcard Journal, Syracuse, N.Y.
Deltiology. A Journal for Postcards Collectors and Dealers, Newton Square, Pennsylvania.

Location of the Illustrations

Altonaer Museum, Hamburg: 214, 382, 386, 412. Biblioteca Comunale Forlì, Fondo Piancastelli: 565, 566, 580, 581, 597, 598. Biblioteca Reale, Stockholm: 484, 485, 495–497. Bibliothèque Fourney, Paris: 74. Collezione Bertarelli, Milan: 36, 80, 113, 116, 146, 147, 167, 179, 187, 435–441, 522, 530, 531, 551, 564, 573–575, 583, 599. Hablik Archiv, Itzehoe: 347. Musée des Arts Décoratifs, Paris: 12, 14, 32, 34, 122, 125, 131, 132, 136, 137, 155–157, 164, 166, 178, 198, 310, 311, 445–449, 471, 659, [Frontispiece].

Manfred Breitsprecher, Stuttgart: XXVI, XXXIV, XXXV, 9–11, 54, 340, 346, 376, 380, 381, 408, 409, 411, 421, 515, 655, 656. Pierre Brunet, Paris: 163, 199, 204, 213, 452. Chambre Cartophile de Belgique, Brussels: 53, 58, 59, 63–65, 67–73, 75–78, 365. 'Chichés du Passé', Marseille: 27, 29, 56, 81, 128, 139–145, 149, 152, 181, 189, 226–229, 232–234, 332–335, 339, 341, 466–469, 537. Antonio and Pia Dell'Aquila, Bari: 3, 109, 127, 148, 176, 177, 305, 306, 369, 389, 472, 473, 527–529, 589, 612, 613. Giovanni Fanelli: XII, XIII, XLII, 12, 15–17, 33, 62, 79, 83, 92, 101, 107, 175, 190, 193, 194, 216, 276, 297, 312, 357, 387, 416, 513, 514, 516, 567, 594, 595, 602, 649, 666, 667, 684, 688, 690, 692–708. 'Fil-tema', Florence: II, III, V, VI. Claudio Fini, Grassina: 316–318, 413, 532–534, 596, 601. Edmondo Gaibazzi, Parma: 433, 434, 562, 563, 571, 572, 579, 587, 603. Paolo Gigli, Faenza: 4, 151, 162, 174, 197, 225, 273, 274, 314, 422–424, 535, 538, 578, 590, 680–683. Ezio Godoli: 7, 8, 43, 60, 61, 66, 82, 84–91, 93–100, 102–106, 108, 111, 112, 123, 138, 168–173, 186, 188, 211, 212, 218–220, 223, 224, 244, 266, 284–288, 342, 350, 356, 360, 372, 390, 394, 401, 403–406, 415, 418, 426, 450, 451, 457, 461, 462, 478, 486–494, 498, 499, 517, 518, 523, 568, 570, 582, 585, 586, 591, 600, 604, 605, 631, 632, 668–676, 689, 691. André Gontier, Paris: 37–41, 50, 115, 119, 133–135, 180, 206, 307–309, 362, 391, 442, 456. Detlef Hilmer, Munich: 13, 18–26, 31, 51, 52, 110, 130, 195, 200, 203, 205, 207, 208–210, 221, 222, 231, 235, 242, 245–256, 258–261, 268–272, 275–282, 289–292, 294, 295, 298, 313, 343, 344, 351, 352, 355, 358, 359, 364, 368, 370, 373, 392, 395, 398, 400, 444, 459, 460, 475–477, 479–483, 520, 554, 555, 676, 677, 679. Landi, Siena: 302–304. Michel Lichiardopol, Toulouse: XXXVI–XLI, XLIII–XLVII, 114, 124, 184, 348, 349, 465. E. Michaelis, Cologne: 237, 239, 241, 354, 367, 371, 379, 384, 385. Paolo Riario, Florence: I, 42, 129, 153, 154, 161, 165, 185, 319–323, 363, 374, 375, 377, 378, 397, 399, 519, 521, 524–526, 546, 553, 556–561, 592, 593. A. Rollet, Paris: 117, 118, 120, 160. Pier Luigi Sonetti, Rome: 215, 226, 455, 544, 547, 548, 550, 552, 576, 588, 606–611, 685, 686. Henry Stolow, Munich: XI, 28, 35, 236, 238, 240, 243, 257, 262–265, 267, 283, 293, 296, 299–301, 313, 393, 396, 407, 410, 414, 420, 430, 432, 443. Teuvo Termonen, Espoo: 500–511. Paolo Vannini, Florence: 44–49, 57, 150, 217, 324–331, 336–338, 536, 549, 577, 584. Leandre Villaronga, Barcelona: XV, XXVII, 5, 6, 121, 126, 158, 159, 183, 191, 345, 353, 361, 366, 383, 454, 474, 539–543, 545, 569, 614–630, 633–648, 650–654, 657, 658, 660–665. Peter Weiss, Hamburg: 182, 427, 429.

Index

Index of Names

In addition to references in the introductory text (pages 9-87), the index includes the principal entries in the biographical section (pages 321-370). Appropriate city locations are given in brackets after the names of publishers, publishing companies, printing establishments and artistic associations. The numbers in italics refer to the numbered captions to the illustrations.

Index